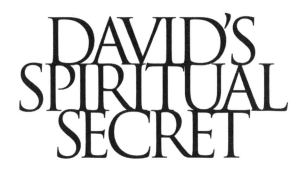

DAVID'S SPIRITUAL SECRET

A LIFE THAT SERVES GOD

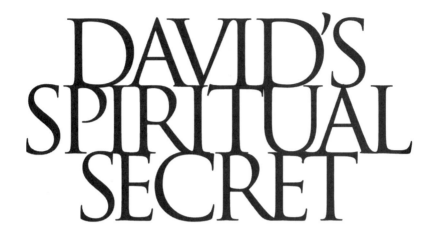

DAVID'S SPIRITUAL SECRET

A LIFE THAT SERVES GOD

DR. JOHN S. BARNETT

TULSA

To order a copy of this book write us at:
DTBM
5200 S. YALE SUITE 300
TULSA, OK 74135
or simply email us at:
books@dtbm.org

David's Spiritual Secret: A Life That Serves God | © 2009 by John S. Barnett

Published by Müllerhaus Publishing
5200 South Yale Ave. | Suite 501| Tulsa, OK 74135

Cover and Interior Design by
Müllerhaus Publishing Group | *mullerhaus.net*
ISBN 13: 978-0-9798345-4-7
ISBN 10: 0-9798345-4-6

First printing, 2009 | Printed in the United States of America
Library of Congress 2008943477
All Scripture quotations in this book, except those noted otherwise,
are from the New King James Version of the Bible.

9 8 7 6 5 4 3 2 1

DEDICATION

TO THE DAVIDS OF MY LIFE ...

Just as David and Jonathan shared such a deep, life-long, sacrificial friendship, I have been blessed by the immense, deep, sacrificial investments, and unwavering friendships of some dear partners in ministry.

I dedicate this book to the Lord's glory, and to the honor of these, who have been like a David to me:

- To the saints at Calvary Bible Church of Kalamazoo, who have received us with open arms and open hearts, as we give ourselves to them in prayer and the ministry of God's Word
- Dr. Hugh Clarke, who supported and encouraged me all the way through seminary
- Duke Weir, who has been the best, closest, and longest-term friend I've ever had
- Phil Smith, who has always said the Lord can do it and always helped it get done
- Randy Watson, who has stood with me through the deep waters and encouraged me
- Bob Nichols, who selflessly loves the lost with a heart of compassion and served with me in the ministry with unwavering loyalty

Thanks to each of you dear saints for investing in me so deeply; may God repay your kindness!

SPECIAL THANKS

BEHIND EVERY BOOK THAT IS published at Discover the Book Ministries (DTBM) is a veritable army of hardworking, behind-the-scenes experts. This whole team is watched over by our Director of Editing, Doreen Claggett. For almost ten years, Doreen has been shepherding the process of transforming my spoken words from the pulpit into printed words in these books. For *David's Spiritual Secret* she assembled another incredible team of volunteers and staff to work around her: Jack Babbitt, Dan Belcher, Marlene Bolton, Cindy Downing, Kellen Funk, Renee Gilligan, Gatra Miller, Phil Miller, Lincoln Mullen, Marcia Reeves, Phil Smith, Mark Turrell, and Karen Webb.

Not only are all fourteen gifted editors, but they also share a passion for the supremacy of Christ in all they do. Whether a stay-at-home mom or a globe-trotting international businessman, each editor has faithfully worked through these messages which were first delivered as sermons to the saints at Tulsa Bible Church in Tulsa, Oklahoma, starting in January of 2006.

We also thank Doug Miller and all the special talent working at Müllerhaus Publishing for taking our work at DTBM and packaging it for use as a book.

Thanks team! Without each of you, this tool would never have been sharpened and deployed for use by the Lord!

Introduction

WHY DID GOD DEVOTE so much of His Word to David's life? During the year 2006, that question prompted my intense, life-changing, thousand-hour Bible study of David's life. This book is a record of that journey in which I followed David through the Scriptures from his quiet boyhood among Bethlehem's hills to the citadel of David's Jerusalem, where he breathed his last.

Along the way in this study, I twice returned to the Holy Land to stand again on each of those physical locations where this spiritual work by God took place. Many of the key events in David's life happened in a relatively compact area. For example:

Elah was where David simply lived out what he was—a man absolutely convinced that God was all important. Therefore, David knew that not even Goliath was a problem the Lord couldn't handle (1 SAMUEL 17).

Nob was the place where David was first seen giving his treasures to God, which became a lifelong habit (1 SAMUEL 21).

Adullam was where David first looked up from his "Cave of Troubles" and saw the face of his gracious God shining down upon him (PSALM 142).

Jerusalem was where David worshiped and wept, sinned and repented (PSALMS 32, 38, 51), then continued to serve God to the very end. And there were many other similarly moving places.

Today, as I complete this book capturing only a small portion of David's life, I am looking out an airplane window as city after city, from Atlanta, Georgia, to South Bend, Indiana, drifts by below me. And I am freshly reminded that those cities represent millions of people going through life facing problems, troubles, and situations like I face, and the same ones David faced. The only difference is this: God showed David exactly how He wanted him to respond in each situation, and then included such insights in His Word. That is why this study began—and why God spent more time on David's life in Scripture than He did on any other person, except Jesus Himself.

When God wrote David's epitaph in Acts 13, He then revealed why David was used so greatly: David was a man "after God's heart" (v. 22) for he served God's purposes with all his being (v. 36)—in spite of weaknesses and failures. By the grace of God, and His empowerment, David thus loyally served God's purpose in his own generation—and so can we in ours. That was *David's Spiritual Secret: A Life That Serves God!*

NOTE: Study guide questions for each chapter follow at the back of the book, beginning on page 393.

The Secret of Eternal Rewards

1

1 Samuel 16–17; 2 Samuel 23–24; Acts 13:22, 36

"He [God] gave testimony and said, 'I have found David the son of Jesse, a man after My own heart, who will do all My will.'" —**Acts 13:22**

EVERYTHING SEEMS SO FLEETING THESE days.[1] News gets old in seconds, e-mails in hours, movies in days, electronic gadgets in weeks, cars in months, and buildings in years. Nothing seems enduring in our world.

More and more we live in a world that is temporary. Both the delete button on the e-mail screen and the trash can on digital cameras remind us that everything seems to be short-lived. Decay is prevalent everywhere. Even on the cosmic level all is headed toward what physicists call "heat death."

When we get to the end of everything, what is left? In other words, what will last forever? The Bible ends with the Book of Revelation. The last chapter is Revelation 22, and that chapter ends with only three things left in eternity that really matter: God, heaven, and one more element—servants worshiping and serving God (Revelation 22:3, 6, 9).

All that lasts in the universe are God and those who discipline themselves to serve Him. Since that is what His Word is about, we need to get a grip on who these servants of God are and how they serve.

One way the Lord identifies who is (and who isn't) His servant is through biographical portraits in the Scriptures. Until modern times, God's Word has been the single greatest source of biographical information known to man. In the Bible are records of more individuals from a wider scope of history than you'll find in almost any other single resource today.

The Life Most Noticed by God

Most of the nearly three thousand characters were only mentioned by name, but some were clearly examined and analyzed. Those deeply explained lives give us great reasons to pause and listen to what God had to say about them. After all, the lives of those singled out for biographies must be important because He took the time and effort to capture their portraits and deliver them to us in a "forever settled in heaven" Book—the Bible.

Of the many deeply explained lives in Scripture, one stands out above all the rest. God chose to write more about him than any other person in the entire history of the world, except Jesus Himself. Who is he? The answer is the young man of whom God gave testimony in Acts:[2]

> "And when He had removed him [King Saul], He raised up for them **David** as king, to whom also He gave testimony and said, I have found David the son of Jesse, a man after My own heart, who will do all My will " (ACTS 13:22).

What does someone look like who is "after God's own heart"? Put simply, the person is a servant in harmony with God—burdened with what burdens Him and wanting to obey all that matters to the Lord. In other words, the person will look like David, who was the Lord's servant all his days:

> "David had served God's purpose in his own generation"
> (ACTS 13:36 NIV).

The word "served" is the verb form (Greek *hupereteo*) of the word for an under-rower (Greek *huperetes*), a bottom-level galley slave. On Roman war ships there were two levels of rowing slaves. The ones on the lower deck were out of sight, and in the most dangerous place on the ship. An under-rower is a model of how to serve the Lord. Just as an under-rower was continually under the command of his ship's captain, so David was under his heavenly Captain's command; he consistently did whatever God asked him to do, willingly unseen and obscure, always wanting the Lord to get all the glory. For most believers today, this attitude represents a whole new way of looking at life.

David was "God's man"—a servant of the Lord for life—because his heart was *after* God, and *for* God: **David did what was right in the eyes of the LORD, and had not turned aside from anything that He commanded him all the days of his life, except in the matter of Uriah the Hittite** (1 KINGS 15:5).

Consequently, the Lord devoted more chapters (141+)[3] in His Word to the life of David than to any other person except Himself. That is a profound truth! We know more about David's words, thoughts, fears, strengths, and weaknesses than we do of anyone else who has ever lived, and we see all this from God's own perspective.

David is the most described man in the Bible for a reason: God has made him our prime Old Testament example of the life of God's servants because he so faithfully served God's purpose for his life. And that is what I like to call "David's Spiritual Secret."

What God's Servants Look Like

DAVID'S GREAT BIOGRAPHY, DIVINELY PENNED by the Author of All Things, God Himself, begins in 1 Samuel 13:14: *The LORD has sought for Himself a man after His own heart.* In 1 Samuel 16, using David's life as a model, He began to explain what a person's life looks like who is wholly committed to being His servant.

David's life was on God's mind. He was not the oldest, the strongest, or the one whom men considered as "most likely to succeed". *Samuel said to Jesse, "Are all the young men here?" Then he said, "There remains yet the youngest, and there he is, keeping the sheep." And Samuel said to Jesse, "Send and bring him. For we will not sit down till he comes here"* (1 SAMUEL 16:11).

As the youngest, David was neglected, unwanted, and left out. He was overlooked and even abused. Yet, in spite of all that potentially life-warping treatment, he just kept right on following the Lord he loved so much. What mattered most was that God had His hand upon him, and He delighted in using David's circumstances for His glory. God's choice of David, the younger over the elder, is another picture of the type of grace shown toward other saints like Abel, Isaac, Jacob, and Joseph.

David's life was disciplined. God loves to use diligent and hardworking people. When Samuel sent for him, he was right where he was supposed to be—watching the flocks: *So he sent and brought him in* (1 SAMUEL 16:12).

Have you ever wondered what David did during all those monotonous, endless hours with the dumb, fearful, and easily wandering sheep? Psalm 132:3–9 gives us a glimpse into how he lived:

- David sought God ahead of personal comforts (vv. 3–4);
- he made time for the Lord (v. 5);
- he was still a shepherd boy (v. 6);
- he longed for God (v. 7);
- he pondered the priority of personal purity (v. 9);
- he was strengthened by righteous living because the righteous are as bold as a lion—so he had quietness and assurance from God and his heart overflowed with joy (v. 9)!

David's life was available for God to use. He was clearly chosen by God: *Now he was ruddy, with bright eyes, and good-looking. And the* LORD *said, "Arise, anoint him; for this is the one!"* (1 SAMUEL 16:12).

Why did God choose David? He is always watching for loyal servants: *The eyes of the* LORD *run to and fro throughout the whole earth, to show Himself strong on behalf of those whose heart is loyal to Him* (2 CHRONICLES 16:9). David was on God's mind (1 SAMUEL 13:14); he was loyal (1 CHRONICLES 16:9); and, as the Lord later revealed, he was a man of integrity (PSALM 78:72):

He also chose David His servant, and took him from the sheepfolds … to shepherd Jacob His people, and Israel His inheritance. So he shepherded them according to the integrity of his heart, and guided them by the skillfulness of his hands (PSALM 78:70–72).

As David was shepherding sheep, God was schooling him for His divinely appointed destiny in history. What had it been like for David as a shepherd? Sheep vary little in their habits; they are basically helpless, dumb, and dirty. For example, they walk so often down the same path that it is soon a rutted canyon; they can't find food or clean themselves; and, as sheep walk around, they collect any and all filth with which they come in contact. Sheep can only be cared for by a patient person—like David.

David's character was wonderfully forged by God in the desert as he painstakingly watched those sheep. His life was trained by solitude, his will was shaped by obscurity and steeled by monotony; and His mind was trained by reality. When God trains His children on the inside, He always takes His time.

David became a patient man while he sat on the same hills where his grandfathers had sat, watched the same stars, and sought the same God. However, in David, God saw a man of integrity, a man of loyalty, a man whom He could trust and count upon.

David's life was empowered by the Lord. Just as He does for every believer who does anything worthwhile for God, the Spirit of the Lord anointed David: *Samuel took the horn of oil and anointed him in the midst of his brothers; and the Spirit of the LORD came upon David from that day forward* (1 SAMUEL 16:13).

Every time I read that verse my heart wells up with the cry of the hymn writer, Daniel Iverson:

Spirit of the living God, fall fresh on me;
Spirit of the living God, fall fresh on me.
Break me, melt me, mold me, fill me.
Spirit of the living God, fall fresh on me.[4]

Never forget that God is the One Who must empower His servants. Nothing done apart from Him will last, for only what is connected to the Lord can have any eternal value.

David's life was an example of godliness to others. His actions provided a powerful testimony to those who saw him, and they in turn willingly told others what they had seen: *One of the servants answered and said, "Look, I have seen a son of Jesse the Bethlehemite, who is skillful in playing, a mighty man of valor, a man of war, prudent in speech, and a handsome person; and the LORD is with him"* (1 SAMUEL 16:18).

Does that verse remind you of what we are all to be? Paul said we are to *be an example to the believers in word, in conduct, in love, in spirit, in faith, in purity* (1 TIMOTHY 4:12).

Because our lives are continually watched by others, we should often ask ourselves these questions about our current service for Christ: *What do people really see in my life? What do they remember about my actions? What is being reported to others? Are the reports pleasing or displeasing to the Lord?*

What type of "advertisement for God" have you been this week? Did your life present a good or a bad testimony?

David's life displayed true humility. He never sought the spotlight. Instead, whenever he had a job to do, he just humbly did it. He was consistent, faithful, dependable and, as a genuinely humble servant, unaware of himself. (A test of humility is whether or not one is unconcerned about who gets the credit for an achievement.)

Consider how David behaved after he had been anointed by Samuel as the next king. Did he run home and immediately hang up a "King David Lives Here!" sign? No, he simply went back to his obscure, humble, monotonous job with those helpless, dumb, and dirty sheep. So when Saul wanted David to play his harp for him, he *sent messengers to Jesse, and said, "Send me your son David, who is with the sheep"* (1 SAMUEL 16:19).

David never seemed to let accolades go to his head. He tended the sheep, and he worked as a courier for his father during the war by taking provisions to his brothers in the army. Then, after defeating Goliath, he was hired by the government (King Saul) and worked in its various departments. David provided entertainment by playing his harp; he served in the **military** by raiding and killing the enemy Philistines; and, as **a member of the cabinet**, he sat at Saul's table as his son-in-law and advised him on security and military issues.

David's life ministered to others. His love and passion for God comforted the souls of those around him. His spiritual influence even calmed demonized Saul: *Whenever the spirit from God was upon Saul... . David would take a harp and play it with his hand. Then **Saul would become refreshed and well**, and the distressing spirit would depart from him* (1 SAMUEL 16:23).

Our God of All Comfort wants His servants *to comfort those who are in any trouble, with the comfort with which we ourselves are comforted by God* (2 CORINTHIANS 1:4). He wants us to also be salt (preserving decay and adding flavor to life) and light (beacons of truth pointing a lost and dying world to Christ). By kindness and goodness our lost world can be impacted with Christ's love!

David honored God with his work. Because he was so responsible, he kept at any job assigned until it was finished. We see this trait when David *occasionally went and returned from Saul to feed his father's sheep at Bethlehem* (1 SAMUEL 17:15).

Can you imagine what a tragedy it would have been if David didn't finish things—like Psalm 23? If he was a procrastinator, perhaps he might have rationalized, "Oh, I'll get around to that someday." Had he never finished

Psalm 23 (and all the other incredible psalms he wrote), many generations to come would have been robbed of great blessings!

Nothing entrusted to him was too small to maintain, not even one little lamb:

> David said to Saul, "Your servant used to keep his father's sheep, and
> when a lion or a bear came and **took a lamb** out of the flock, I **went out
> after it** and struck it, and delivered the lamb from its mouth; and when
> it arose against me, I caught it by its beard, and struck and killed it"
> (1 SAMUEL 17:34–35).

As a shepherd, David risked his life for a lamb, his father, and his family because he took responsibility seriously. When do great men and women start to be great? Becoming great is just a continuation of making many little right choices. For Jesus said, "He who is **faithful in what is least is faithful also in much; and he who is unjust in what is least is unjust also in much**" (LUKE 16:10). Because current habits and character will only become more ingrained, you will never become something in the future that you are not becoming right now.

What has God entrusted to you? If you are an adult, you probably have a marriage, a family, a job, and a ministry. As a young person you may have these responsibilities: a smaller brother or sister, school duties, room, bike (or car), and perhaps a job outside your home. How are you doing with whatever God has put under your care? Are you responsible or careless? Are you self-absorbed or others-oriented? How do you think Jesus expects you to act?

David honored God with his habits. Have you been noticing David's habits? In this next verse, note the ways he acted disciplined, responsible, trustworthy, and obedient: **David rose early in the morning, left the sheep with a keeper, and took the things and went as Jesse had commanded him**. And he came to the camp as the army was going out to the fight and shouting for the battle (1 SAMUEL 17:20).

From what we've learned about David's habits so far, it's obvious that acting conscientiously was a way of life. Because habits grow, we must be careful which ones we allow to take root. Since every habit and action will have either a positive or negative consequence, we must avoid what is bad and foster what is good:

> Do not be deceived, God is not mocked; for **whatever a man sows, that
> he will also reap**. For he who sows to his flesh will of the flesh reap cor-

ruption, but he who sows to the Spirit will of the Spirit reap everlasting life. And let us not grow weary while doing good, for in due season we shall reap if we do not lose heart (GALATIANS 6:7–9).

Sin will pay us back with boredom, guilt, shame, loneliness, confusion, emptiness, loss of purpose, and loss of eternal rewards. Righteous actions, however, always produce eternal blessings.

David honored God with his life. Even in his youth, God-fearing David had a divine perspective. Therefore, when he arrived at the army's encampment with supplies for his brothers and discovered how intimidated the Israelite army was by Goliath, he immediately thought of one thing: *What can I do for the Lord?* Then David said to the men who were standing nearby:

> *"What shall be done for the man who kills this Philistine and takes away the reproach from Israel? For who is this uncircumcised Philistine, that he should defy the armies of the living God?"* (1 SAMUEL 17:26).

Eliab, David's oldest brother, was angry when he heard his youngest brother's comments to the men. In fact, he accused David of being prideful, insolent, and only wanting to *"come down to see the battle"* (1 SAMUEL 17:28). But because David had given his life totally over to the Lord, he stood his ground and stayed focused on the Lord's honor—even when no one would believe that a youth like him could be victorious over a seasoned warrior like Goliath.

David magnified God's hand in his life. When King Saul asked David to explain what qualified him for the job of facing Goliath, how did he respond? He magnified the Lord by telling the king that his greatest accomplishments came from the hand of God:

> *"Your servant has killed both lion and bear; and this uncircumcised Philistine will be like one of them, seeing he has defied the armies of the living God." Moreover David said, "The LORD, who delivered me from the paw of the lion and from the paw of the bear, He will deliver me from the hand of this Philistine." And Saul said to David, "Go, and the LORD be with you!"* (1 SAMUEL 17:36–37).

Do you also see the hand of God in your life? Are you excited about telling others what He is doing?

David honored God's Name with his mouth. Our world has marginalized God. The True and Living God, the Creator Who upholds all things by His mighty power, is slowly being erased from the public life. His truth is being minimalized, His Word is being neglected, and His people are being ignored. Yet, all He has ever asked of man is one thing: Magnify Me! David did that well. He continually stood up for the Lord's honor:

> David said to the Philistine, "You come to me with a sword, with a spear, and with a javelin. But I come to you **in the name of the LORD of hosts, the God of the armies of Israel, whom you have defied.** This day the LORD will deliver you into my hand, and I will strike you and take your head from you. And this day I will give the carcasses of the camp of the Philistines to the birds of the air and the wild beasts of the earth, **that all the earth may know that there is a God in Israel**" (1 SAMUEL 17:45–46).

Because David was so loyal to the Lord's Name, God showed Himself strong on his behalf by granting him a miraculous victory over Goliath!

David dedicated his treasures and trophies to the Lord. After he killed Goliath, he cut off his head as he'd vowed. Then *David took the Philistine's head and brought it to Jerusalem, and he put the Philistine's weapons in his own tent* (1 SAMUEL 17:54 NIV).

A few years later, where was the sword of Goliath carefully stowed away? Did David hang it on a wall in his room for all to see and to point to him as the greatest warrior? No, he had taken it to the tent of God, the place most associated with the Lord on earth. His treasure was on deposit with God:

> So the priest said, "**The sword of Goliath** the Philistine, whom you killed in the Valley of Elah, there it is, **wrapped in a cloth behind the ephod.** If you will take that, take it. For there is no other except that one here." And David said, "There is none like it; give it to me" (1 SAMUEL 21:9).

David took the sword of Goliath, the ultimate trophy of the day, but he didn't take it to show off how great he was. He happened to be fleeing for his life at the time, and since he had no weapon of his own, he chose to use Goliath's unique iron sword for protection.

David always measured life values from God's perspective. Throughout his life, any treasures or trophies received from his undefeated conquests seemed to have always been given back to the Lord as an honor to Him:

> *King David also dedicated these to the LORD*, along with the silver and gold that he had brought from all these nations—from Edom, from Moab, from the people of Ammon, from the Philistines, and from Amalek (1 CHRONICLES 18:11).

There is no limit to what God will do with a life that keeps being given back to Him!

David poured his life out as an irrecoverable offering to God. When the well from which he drank sweet water as a child was behind enemy lines, David was once heard longingly saying, *"Oh, that someone would give me a drink of the water from the well of Bethlehem, which is by the gate!"* (2 SAMUEL 23:15). In response, three of his greatest warriors who had come to him at the cave of Adullam fought through to the well of Bethlehem, drew water, fought their way back, and presented the water to David.

David amazed them, however, because *he would not drink it, but* **poured it out to the LORD**. *And he said, "Far be it from me, O LORD, that I should do this! Is this not the blood of the men who went in jeopardy of their lives?" Therefore he would not drink it. These things were done by the three mighty men* (2 SAMUEL 23:16–17).

David had poured out the water to the Lord as a drink offering; the ground absorbed every drop. He had irrecoverably given to the Lord what was most precious to him. Just like the treasures of his career, he poured out the water from the well because David believed that God deserved the best of his time, treasures, and talents. That is the life of a servant, and that is a life the Lord rewards.

David made costly sacrifices for God. The prophet Gad told King David that God expected a sacrificial offering on Mt. Moriah before He would remove the plague on Israel. *So David … went up as the LORD commanded* (2 SAMUEL 24:19). Although the owner of the threshing floor on Mt. Moriah offered to donate everything needed, David would not accept his gracious offer, saying:

*"No, but I will surely buy it from you for a price; **nor will I offer burnt offerings to the Lord my God with that which costs me nothing.**" So David bought the threshing floor and the oxen for fifty shekels of silver. And David built there an altar to the Lord, and offered burnt offerings and peace offerings. So the Lord heeded the prayers for the land, and the plague was withdrawn from Israel* (2 SAMUEL 24:24–25).

Now look at the end of David's life to see what he did with all his treasures:

*"Indeed **I have taken much trouble to prepare for the house of the Lord** one hundred thousand talents of gold and one million talents of silver, and bronze and iron beyond measure, for it is so abundant. I have prepared timber and stone also"* (1 CHRONICLES 22:14).

*"Now for the house of my God **I have prepared with all my might**: gold … , silver … , bronze … , iron … , wood … , onyx stones, stones to be set, glistening stones of various colors, all kinds of precious stones, and marble slabs in abundance. Moreover, **because I have set my affection on the house of my God**, I have given … **over and above** all that I have prepared for the holy house, **my own special treasure** of gold and silver"* (1 CHRONICLES 29:2–3).

It is no coincidence that these end-of-life treasures were used to later build God's house on the site of the threshing floor David had sacrificially purchased many years before.

Only One Life to Offer

AS THE TIME WAS NEARING for Solomon to take over the royal reins of Israel, David gave this spiritual exhortation to his son; it summarizes well what the life of a servant of God's should look like:

*"As for you, my son Solomon, **know the God of your father**, and **serve Him with a loyal heart and with a willing mind**; for the Lord searches all hearts and understands all the intent of the thoughts. If you seek Him, He will be found by you; but if you forsake Him, He will cast you off forever* (1 CHRONICLES 28:9).

You've probably heard the famous life motto the great missionary Charles Thomas Studd (1860–1931) lived and died by:

"Only one life, 'twill soon be past;
only what's done for Christ will last."

Few realize when he said those words. It was on his deathbed with his precious family gathered around him. He had already told each of his children that he wished he had something to give to them, but he had nothing left. Then he said, "I gave it all to Jesus long ago."[5]

This spiritual giant actually gave his children far more than anyone could imagine. His children had seen their father grow year by year in the Lord. They saw his personal devotion to the Word of God. They watched him being refined by constant health problems, recurring weakness, and bouts with intense pain. They had watched his tireless devotion to the Lord that carried their frail dad to the remotest and most dangerous spots on earth—all to share the glorious gospel of Christ. As a result of their father's great dedication to God, his children served the Lord to their last days!

When Avis B. Christiansen (1895–1985), the wife of the vice president of Moody Bible Institute, heard about those precious words spoken by C. T. Studd at his death, she began to ponder them. Six years later, in 1937, she wrote what is now a famous hymn, "Only One Life to Offer." Her reflections had turned into a prayer of devotion to the Lord Whom she, too, served with all her heart:

Only one life to offer—
Jesus, my Lord and King;
Only one tongue to praise Thee
And of Thy mercy sing;
Only one heart's devotion—
Savior, O may it be
Consecrated alone to Thy matchless glory,
Yielded fully to Thee.[6]

In closing, David was God's example of how someone who is "after God's heart" lives. And we, like David, should seek to be a servant in harmony with the Lord—burdened with what burdens Him and wanting to obey all that matters to Him. And just as He did in His servant David's life, God wants to use you for His glory through these areas:

- Your unchangeable features.
- Your disciplined life.
- Your available life.
- Your empowerment by the Holy Spirit.
- Your righteous actions.
- Your humility in service.
- Your ministry of comfort.
- Your diligent work.
- Your disciplined habits.
- Your giving of your life back to Him.
- Your remembrance of His hand in your life.
- Your honoring of His Name.
- Your dedication of personal treasures and trophies to Him.
- Your costly sacrifices for Him.

David was God-hearted: he had a heart to serve God's purpose for his life. Is that your deepest desire as well? Is your heart *for* God? Does He have your *whole* heart? For there is no limit to what God will do with a life that keeps being given back to Him!

2 | How Not to Waste Your Life Like Saul

1 Samuel 13–31

*"Rebellion is as the sin of witchcraft, and stubbornness is as iniquity and idolatry. Because you [Saul] have rejected the word of the Lord, He also has rejected you from being king." —*1 Samuel 15:23

THE LORD OF LIFE—THE Creator—God Himself, once said something very sobering.[7] He said that the day of our death is better than the day of our birth (ECCLESIASTES 7:1-2). Why would He tell us that? At the end, when the life is finished, the real person becomes known. That life with all its opportunities and obstacles, accomplishments and failures, is ready for its final review.

The chilling fact of God's Word is that after death God Himself performs an individual life analysis—an autopsy not of the cause of death, but of the purpose of life. That is why Paul's exhortations to us, the church, revolve around the constant theme of running the race of faith well. We must devotedly run all the way to the finish line for our life to survive the fires of the judgment seat and for us to hear Christ's *"Well done, good and faithful servant"* (MATTHEW 25:21, 23).

Facing the Consequences

THERE IS AN INESCAPABLE RECKONING day when every believer will receive the consequences of his or her choices made here on earth. Therefore, we need regular investment reviews to think about what we are really living for. As we will find shortly, had King Saul done that his life could have turned out far differently.

The *greatest* way to invest our lives, and live them well, is to serve God with our whole being—as David did. In contrast, the opposite is also true: the *greatest* waste of our life, and therefore the *worst* way to live, is to live for anything but serving the Lord—as King Saul did.

God's Word often teaches us by means of such contrasts, and the comparison of how David and Saul lived their lives is one of the sharpest and most solemn in the Bible.

Side by side in the Scriptures is the amazing record of how David loyally served God all his days and the equally amazing record of how Saul did *not* serve the Lord. This proximity of "how to serve" and "how *not* to serve" is thus very insightful.

One might call God's biographies of David's and Saul's lives "A Tale of Two Kings." These two men, who towered over their generations, each held the highest office on earth.

From their privileged positions, one was elevated to heavenly proportions and the other slipped hellishly down from the pinnacle where God had placed him as the first king of His people.

One started a royal line that shall never end; even to this day his name is spoken and sung with the joys of heaven. The other ended his miserable earthly life possibly apostate, hardened, and distant from God.

Yes, David and Saul were a striking contrast in so many ways, as is clear in the following examples of the stark differences between the two kings:

(See chart on the following pages.)

God picked David: *"Now therefore, thus shall you say to My servant David, 'Thus says the LORD of hosts: "I took you from the sheepfold, from following the sheep, to be ruler over My people, over Israel"'"* (2 SAMUEL 7:8).

The people picked Saul: *So they ran and brought him from there; and when he stood among the people, he was taller than any of the people from his shoulders upward. And Samuel said to all the people, "Do you see him whom the LORD has chosen, that there is no one like him among all the people?" So all the people shouted and said, "Long live the king!"* (1 SAMUEL 10:23–24).

David sought God's praises: *"And when He had removed him [King Saul], He raised up for them David as king, to whom also He gave testimony and said, 'I have found David the son of Jesse, a man after My own heart, who will do all My will'"* (ACTS 13:22).

Saul sought the people's praises: He did everything according to what the people thought, not God: *Now it had happened as they were coming home, when David was returning from the slaughter of the Philistine, that the women had come out of all the cities of Israel, singing and dancing, to meet King Saul, with tambourines, with joy, and with musical instruments. So the women sang as they danced, and said: "Saul has slain his thousands, and David his ten thousands." Then Saul was very angry, and the saying displeased him; and he said, "They have ascribed to David ten thousands, and to me they have ascribed only thousands. Now what more can he have but the kingdom?"* (1 SAMUEL 18:6–8).

David's kingdom was immortalized through Christ: *"Now therefore, let it please You to bless the house of Your servant, that it may continue before You forever; for You, O Lord GOD, have spoken it, and with Your blessing let the house of Your servant be blessed forever"* (2 SAMUEL 7:29).

Saul's kingdom was demonized at his own hands: *"For rebellion is as the sin of witchcraft, and stubbornness is as iniquity and idolatry. Because you have rejected the word of the LORD, He also has rejected you from being king"* (1 SAMUEL 15:23).

David was kind and giving: For example, *David said, "I will show kindness to Hanun the son of Nahash, because his father showed kindness to me." So David sent messengers to comfort him concerning his father. And David's servants came to Hanun in the land of the people of Ammon to comfort him* (1 CHRONICLES 19:2).

Saul was cruel and selfish: *Saul's anger was aroused against Jonathan, and he said to him, "You son of a perverse, rebellious woman!"* … *Then Saul cast a spear at him to kill him, by which Jonathan knew that it was determined by his father to kill David. So Jonathan arose from the table in fierce anger, and ate no food the second day of the month, for he was grieved for David, because his father had treated him shamefully* (1 SAMUEL 20:30, 33–34).

David was forgiving: He even forgave those who cursed him, threw rocks at him, and tried to kill him: *"And indeed, as your life was valued much this day in my eyes, so let my life be valued much in the eyes of the LORD, and let Him deliver me out of all tribulation"* (1 SAMUEL 26:24).

Saul was bitter: He never could let go of his bitterness during his entire life; he went to the grave as a dark-hearted, mysteriously haunted, bitter old man: *So Saul eyed David from that day forward* (1 SAMUEL 18:9).

David accused himself of sin: *David said to Nathan, "I have sinned against the LORD." And Nathan said to David, "The LORD also has put away your sin; you shall not die"* (2 SAMUEL 12:13).

Saul excused himself of sin: When sin was pointed out to him, Saul stepped back and accused someone else instead. He refused to take any responsibility for his sin. Saul even blamed the Israelites for his own rebellion: *"But the people took of the plunder, sheep and oxen, the best of the things which should have been utterly destroyed, to sacrifice to the LORD your God in Gilgal"* (1 SAMUEL 15:21).

David was full of boldness: *It came to pass that David attacked the Philistines, subdued them, and took Gath and its towns from the hand of the Philistines. Then he defeated Moab, and the Moabites became David's servants, and brought tribute* (1 CHRONICLES 18:1–2).

Saul was full of fear: He feared the Philistines greatly: *When Saul and all Israel heard these words of the Philistine, they were dismayed and greatly afraid* (1 SAMUEL 17:11).

David was at peace with God: *I will both lie down in peace, and sleep; for You alone, O LORD, make me dwell in safety* (PSALM 4:8).

Saul was at war with God: *But the Spirit of the LORD departed from Saul, and a distressing spirit* [a demon] *from the LORD troubled him* (1 SAMUEL 16:14).

Who we are spiritually is far more crucial than what we look like on the outside. King Saul was a prince of a man outwardly, but a demon of a man inwardly. He was a huge misfit because he refused to learn how to deal with sin God's way.

The Man Who Had It All

SAUL SEEMED TO HAVE EVERYTHING going for him. He was big, strong, blessed, gifted, chosen, empowered, and given every opportunity to serve the Lord, but he didn't. Saul failed because there were severe deficiencies in his character.

- God didn't need Saul's brain—He wanted his *character*.
- God didn't need Saul's brawn (huge, strong muscles)— He wanted his *integrity*.
- God didn't need Saul's wisdom, power, or wealth—He wanted his *obedience*.
- God didn't need Saul's ambitious confidence—He wanted his humble *dependence*.

If that were Saul's investment review, how might God summarize what his life was all about? What would his individual life analysis—God's autopsy of Saul's purpose for life—be like?

Throughout the Scriptures God summarized entire lives in a few words to commemorate their existence. Hebrews 11 is replete with monuments to those who spent their sojourn on earth pleasing the Lord. The significance of each life summary was twofold: 1) *God meant it*, and 2) *it was accurate*.

David's seventy years were distilled down to just nine words in English: *David had served God's purpose in his own generation* (ACTS 13:36 NIV). In contrast, God needed only one word to summarize Saul's life—**rejected**.

Because Saul rejected the Lord by disregarding His Word, God rejected Saul:[8]

[Samuel said to Saul,] *"Rebellion is as the sin of witchcraft, and stubbornness is as iniquity and idolatry. Because you have **rejected** the word of the LORD, He also has **rejected** you from being king.... I will not return with you, for you have **rejected** the word of the LORD, and the LORD has **rejected** you from being king over Israel"* (1 SAMUEL 15:23, 26).

*And Samuel went no more to see Saul until the day of his death. Nevertheless Samuel mourned for Saul, and **the LORD regretted that He had made Saul king over Israel*** (1 SAMUEL 15:35).

*The LORD said to Samuel, "How long will you mourn for Saul, seeing I have **rejected** him from reigning over Israel? Fill your horn with oil,* *and go; I am sending you to Jesse the Bethlehemite. For I have provided Myself a king among his sons"* (1 SAMUEL 16:1).

The word used for Saul's treatment of God, and the Lord's response, is a strong word (Hebrew *mawas* – Strong's #3988). It is used seventy-six times in the Old Testament and is most often translated "despise" (25), "refuse" (9), "reject" (19), "abhor" (4), "become loathsome" (depicting Job's boils and sores), and "melt away." In context, the word *mawas* is always bad whenever used to describe someone's response to God. For example, "despised" described Israel's murmuring in the wilderness just before He sent the plague to kill many of them; "despised" is also the word used for Israel's attitude toward worshiping God and thus the basis for His letting Israel be destroyed by her enemies and carried off into captivity.

By using selective, self-serving obedience in place of total and God-honoring obedience, Saul rejected God. His consequence for that terrible choice was that God rejected him as king—and chose David:

> Samuel said to Saul, *"You have done foolishly.* **You have not kept the commandment of the LORD your God,** *which He commanded you. For now the LORD would have established your kingdom over Israel forever. But now your kingdom shall not continue.* **The LORD has sought for Himself a man after His own heart,** *and the LORD has commanded him to be commander over His people, because you have not kept what the LORD commanded you"* (1 SAMUEL 13:13–14).

> *"And when He had removed him, He raised up for them David as king, to whom also He gave testimony and said, 'I have found David the son of Jesse, a man after My own heart, who will do all My will' "* (ACTS 13:22).

Although David was a God-hearted man, he wasn't perfect—just forgiven. At times he was impatient, depressed, distressed, fearful, hopeless, tempted, and even angry or wrathful. Yet, he didn't *like* being that way and didn't want to *stay* that way. As "God's man" David grieved over his sin because he valued what the Lord said. However, whatever God said didn't seem to matter to Saul.

Where did King Saul go wrong? How did his downfall begin?

What Wasted Lives Look Like

JUST AS THE SPIRIT OF God bears fruit, so does the flesh. When we don't obey God we are in rebellion against Him. There is no middle ground. The fruit of the flesh is easily spotted in ungodly attitudes and actions. King Saul, the man who *wasn't* after God's heart, would not walk in step with the Lord and so his flesh ruled his life.

Saul's pathway of rebellion is a caution to anyone who loves God, wants to serve Him, and seeks to follow the Lord. Here are some warning signs King Saul ignored and thereby wasted his life.

Saul neglected God's leadership. In 1 Samuel 13:1–7, Israel faced an entirely new type of adversary. But King Saul had ignored God's leadership so long he was unaware that the times since Joshua's conquest had produced a different and more ominous threat. Look at this fact file and you'll see why Saul so desperately needed God's help to defeat this newest enemy:

Fresh in from the Mediterranean islands, the sea peoples settled on the coasts, mixed with the ancient inhabitants, and became the Philistines.

- *The Philistines had a rich ethnic heritage.* They sailed from the Aegean world (Greece) and settled along the coast of Palestine from around 1400–1200 B.C., about the time of the Judges in Israel. The Philistines developed a sophisticated culture in a circle of five city states named in the Bible: Gath, Gaza, Ashkelon, Ashdod, and Ekron.

- *The Philistines had excellent logistics.* The five main Philistine city states were located near the Via Maris trade route, which went through the coastal plain or lowlands along the shores of the Mediterranean Sea of Israel. Thus, the Philistines dominated world trade and greatly influenced other nations.

- *The Philistines had massive industrial production.* These powerful businessmen had an elaborate olive pressing industry. At Ekron alone archaeologists have found the remains of about two hundred installations that could produce more than one thousand tons, or two million pounds, of olive oil! They were also famous for iron-making.

- *The Philistines had advanced military technology.* The excavations, graves, paintings, and etchings reveal that Philistine soldiers were quite tall, were clean-shaven, and wore breastplates and small kilts. The soldiers carried small shields and fought with straight swords and spears made of iron—all superior to their enemies' weapons.

- *The Philistines had sophisticated artistic skills.* These talented artisans were part of the centuries-old Greek culture. They continued to create intricate pottery with red and black geometric designs on white backgrounds.

- *The Philistines had an evil and dark religion.* Two words sum up the religious traditions of these sea peoples: sophisticated and immoral. The Philistines engineered and built carefully planned temples. These temples and their gods show up throughout the biblical record. There were Philistine temples in the south in Gaza and Ashdod, and in the north at Beth Shean. The Philistine gods also were the constant nemesis of the people of the Living and True God. Dagon, their main god, was thought to be the god of grain. The goddess Ashtoreth, believed to be his mistress, was associated with war and fertility. Baal-Zebul, thought to be Dagon's son, was worshiped at Ekron.[9]

Neglecting God's Leadership

As ISRAEL EMERGED FROM THE period of the judges and picked their first king, they had to battle these newcomers to the region whose weapons were far stronger than theirs. Israel's only hope was to rely upon their true source of power—the Lord God Almighty. The people chose Saul to lead them to victory, but his neglect of God's leadership led to failure because he underestimated their enemy's strength.

Underestimating our own enemy's strength can also be disastrous. We must never ignore God's leadership, for He has warned: *Be sober, be vigilant; because your adversary the devil walks about like a roaring lion, **seeking whom he may devour*** (1 PETER 5:8).

Saul was impatient with the Lord's timing. His impatience was an excuse to do his own thing instead of obeying God: *He waited seven days, according to the time set by Samuel. **But Samuel did not come** to Gilgal; and the people were scattered from him* (1 SAMUEL 13:8). Intolerance of the Lord's plan led to seeking man's approval rather than God's.

Saul neglected his primary responsibilities. By only taking care of his own needs, he was ignoring the responsibilities God had entrusted to him: *So it came about, on the day of battle, that **there was neither sword nor spear found in the hand of any of the people** who were with Saul and Jonathan. But they were found with Saul and Jonathan his son* (1 SAMUEL 13:22).

Saul made sure he had what was needed to defend himself, but not that those in his care were armed for battle. God views this practice very disapprovingly: *If anyone does not provide for his own, and especially for those of his household, he has denied the faith and is worse than an unbeliever* (1 TIMOTHY 5:8).

Saul was lazy and indifferent toward God. Because he got so out of touch with the battle raging around him and what mighty things the Lord could be doing, he missed it all: ***Saul was sitting** in the outskirts of Gibeah **under a pomegranate tree** which is in Migron. The people who were with him were about six hundred men. ... But the people did not know that Jonathan had gone* (1 SAMUEL 14:2–3). Saul's laziness and indifference made him oblivious to his own son's fate, the battle, and the victory God granted.

Saul used rash, angry words. His fleshly anger and pride led to saying and doing things that disabled, wounded, and harmed those around him: *And the men of Israel were distressed that day, for Saul had **placed the people under oath**, saying, "Cursed is the man who eats any food until evening, before I have taken vengeance on my enemies." So none of the people tasted food* (1 SAMUEL 14:24).

Saul spoke with no thought of the implications to his family or nation. Instead of his mouth being a fountain of blessing, it became a fountain of curses. But God says:

*Let every man be swift to hear, slow to speak, slow to wrath; for **the wrath of man does not produce the righteousness of God*** (JAMES 1:19–20).

*The tongue is a fire, a world of iniquity. ... **No man can tame the tongue. It is an unruly evil, full of deadly poison.** With it we bless our God and Father, and with it we curse men, who have been made in the similitude of God. Out of the same mouth proceed blessing and cursing. **My brethren, these things ought not to be so*** (JAMES 3:6, 8–10).

Saul's Pathway to Rejection

BY THE FIFTEENTH CHAPTER OF 1 Samuel, Saul was exhibiting specific signs of having rejected the Lord to serve himself. Now he faced a crossroads decision—to return to God's path or follow his own.

Saul had to choose whom he would serve. He knew full well what God wanted him to carry out, so he had to choose whether to obey the Lord or not.

*Samuel also said to Saul, "The LORD sent me to anoint you king over His people, over Israel. Now therefore, **heed the voice of the words of the LORD**. Thus says the LORD of hosts: 'I will punish Amalek for what he did to Israel, how he ambushed him on the way when he came up from Egypt. **Now go and attack Amalek, and utterly destroy all that they have, and do not spare them.** But kill both man and woman, infant and nursing child, ox and sheep, camel and donkey' "* (1 SAMUEL 15:1–4).

This was a turning point for Saul—like the crossroads decision Joshua asked the Israelites to make: *Choose for yourselves this day whom you will serve* (JOSHUA 24:15). Don't we likewise face the same choice every day of our lives? Hasn't God given clear directives to you and me as well? For example:

- Are you going out into the world to preach the gospel (MARK 16:15)?
- Are you consistently loving others as Christ has loved you (JOHN 15:12)?
- Are you daily presenting your body as a holy, living sacrifice to God (ROMANS 12:1)?
- Are you being transformed by the renewing of your mind through His Word (ROMANS 12:2)?

Saul played the pick-and-choose game. Rather than do all that God instructed, he only offered selective and partial obedience when he *took Agag king of the Amalekites alive* (1 SAMUEL 15:8). Yet, obedience is the clearest way to declare love for the Lord: *"He who has My commandments and **keeps them**, it is he who **loves Me**"* (JOHN 14:21).

Saul selfishly held on to the best of what God hated. Whatever Saul spared was kept for his own use: ***Saul and the people spared Agag** and the best of the sheep, the oxen, the fatlings, the lambs, and all that was good, and were **unwilling to utterly destroy them*** (1 SAMUEL 15:9).

That act of rebellion heralded the beginning of Saul's end—his final downfall and disgraceful death. God has clearly told us what He thinks of our loving what He hates: *Adulterers and adulteresses! Do you not know that friendship with the world is enmity with God? Whoever therefore wants to be a friend of the world makes himself an enemy of God* (JAMES 4:4).

Saul only gave God what he didn't want anyway: **Everything despised and worthless**, *that they utterly destroyed* (1 SAMUEL 15:9). What a contrast to David's conviction that the Lord deserves the first, the best, and the costliest of our time, treasures, and talents:

> *Jesus said to His disciples, "If anyone desires to come after Me, let him deny himself, and take up his cross, and follow Me. For whoever desires to save his life will lose it, but whoever loses his life for My sake will find it. For* **what profit is it to a man if he gains the whole world, and loses his own soul**? *Or what will a man give in exchange for his soul? For the Son of Man will come in the glory of His Father with His angels, and then He will reward each according to his works"* (MATTHEW 16:24–27).

Saul honored himself before others. Rather than glorifying the Lord, he reminded people of his own accomplishments: *When Samuel rose early in the morning to meet Saul, it was told Samuel, saying, "Saul went to Carmel, and indeed,* **he set up a monument for himself**" (1 SAMUEL 15:12).

Jesus' harshest criticisms were for proud religious leaders who did all their works to be seen by men. So He said, "**Whoever exalts himself will be humbled**, *and he who humbles himself will be exalted*" (MATTHEW 23:12).

Saul was deceptive about the true condition of his spiritual life. He made false claims about his dedication to God: *Samuel went to Saul, and Saul said to him, "Blessed are you of the LORD!* **I have performed the commandment of the LORD**" (1 SAMUEL 15:13).

Jesus honored honesty and condemned hypocrisy. For example, He rebuked the Pharisee who stood and prayed to impress others, but he praised the tax collector who *would not so much as raise his eyes to heaven, but beat his breast, saying, '***God, be merciful to me a sinner!**' *I tell you, this man went down to his house justified rather than the other"* (LUKE 18:13–14).

Saul blamed others for his failures. He defended himself by saying, *"They have brought them from the Amalekites; for **the people spared** the best of the sheep and the oxen"* (1 SAMUEL 15:15).

Saul only experienced God second-hand. He knew about the Lord from what others said about Him, but not from having first-hand and personal knowledge. Note that he didn't say *"my God"* in this verse. Instead, he said *"to sacrifice to the LORD **your** God"* (1 SAMUEL 15:15).

Saul developed an exaggerated view of his importance: *Samuel said, "When you were **little in your own eyes**, were you not head of the tribes of Israel? And did not the LORD anoint you king over Israel?"* (1 SAMUEL 15:17).

Saul did his own thing, not God's. Samuel reminded Saul of what God had explicitly told him to do: [Samuel said,] *"Now the LORD sent you on a mission, and said, 'Go, and **utterly destroy** the sinners, the Amalekites, and **fight against them** until they are consumed'"* (1 SAMUEL 15:18).

Saul argued with the righteous men God sent his way. Regardless of who God sent to point out how he was disobeying God, Saul defended himself. So he told Samuel:

> *"But I **have** obeyed the voice of the LORD, and gone on the mission on which the LORD sent me, and brought back Agag king of Amalek; I **have** utterly destroyed the Amalekites"* (1 SAMUEL 15:20).

> [Samuel said to Saul,] *"Rebellion is as the sin of witchcraft, and stubbornness is as iniquity and idolatry. Because you have **rejected** the word of the LORD, He also has **rejected** you from being king"* (1 SAMUEL 15:23).

Saul only half-repented. He made excuses for why he sinned: *Saul said to Samuel, "**I have sinned**, for I have transgressed the commandment of the LORD and your words, **because I feared the people and obeyed their voice**"* (1 SAMUEL 15:24).

Saul tried to "save face" when confronted with his sin. Instead of humble and contrite repentance, he merely offered confession: [Saul] *said,*

"I have sinned; yet honor me now, please, before the elders of my people and before Israel, and return with me, that I may worship the LORD your God" (1 SAMUEL 15:30).

That is admitting—not repenting. Here is a true confession: *David said to Nathan, "I have **sinned against the LORD**." And Nathan said to David, "The LORD also has put away your sin; you shall not die"* (2 SAMUEL 12:13). A person whose confession is genuine will also repent and can unashamedly sing of God's forgiveness, as David did in Psalm 51.

Saul doubted God's power. He forgot about the Lord's awesome omnipotence. He began to think that mere mortals (the Philistines) were greater than the Ancient of Days, so he and the Israelite army *were **dismayed and greatly afraid*** (1 SAMUEL 17:11). God said such people are *having a form of godliness but denying its power. And from such people turn away!* (2 TIMOTHY 3:5). David, however, trusted completely in God's power and won the victory over Goliath!

Saul was self-focused, not God-focused. He was so absorbed with his self-image that he began to constantly defend his reputation: *Saul was very angry, and the saying displeased him; and he said, "They have ascribed to David ten thousands, **and to me** they have ascribed only thousands"* (1 SAMUEL 18:8).

The more David the giant-killer won the hearts of Israel, the more King Saul became resentful. He measured his worth based on what others said about him. But that practice displeases God: *Not he who commends himself is approved, but whom the Lord commends* (2 CORINTHIANS 10:18).

Saul lived with constant insecurities. Believing he was the master of his own fate, he lived in constant fears and insecurities about his health, job, and future. Because he knew the throne of Israel rightfully belonged to David, Saul entrusted the care of his future security to himself and took it away from the Lord: *"Now what more can he have **but the kingdom?"*** (1 SAMUEL 18:8). Fear is always the realm of Satan:

> **God has not given us a spirit of fear**, *but of power and of love and of a sound mind* (2 TIMOTHY 1:7).

> *Do you not know that your body is the temple of the Holy Spirit who is in you, whom you have from God, and **you are not your own**? For you were bought at a price; therefore glorify God in your body and in your spirit, which are God's* (1 CORINTHIANS 6:19–20).

Saul let jealousy consume him. When God was blessing others, Saul looked upon them with suspicion and jealousy: *Saul eyed David from that day forward. ... Now Saul was afraid of David,* **because the LORD was with him,** *but had departed from Saul* (1 SAMUEL 18:9, 12).

Saul's lust drove him to keep others from having something he wanted for himself. This is the worst form of jealousy. Jealousy darkens our eyes to anything good about another. Consequently, David could never measure up to the king's expectations. Saul neither treasured nor sought God's blessing, favor, presence, or involvement in his life. He valued himself, neglected God, and feared David because the Lord was with him. What a tragic, misdirected life!

Saul's anger led to neglecting his family. He verbally tore down his wife and children when they didn't embrace his self-driven agenda to kill David: *Saul's anger was aroused against Jonathan, and he said to him,* **"You son of a perverse, rebellious woman!"** (1 SAMUEL 20:30). He did not nurture or care for his wife, and an undiscipled wife breeds many painful days.

Saul viewed everything from an earthly perspective. He looked at life as if it was just for the moment, living only for what he could grab and hold: *"For as long as the son of Jesse* [David] *lives on the earth, you* [Jonathan] *shall not be established,* **nor your kingdom.** *Now therefore, send and bring him to me, for he shall surely die"* (1 SAMUEL 20:31).

Saul wanted Jonathan to be the next king, not David. He wasn't able to see the eternal, the divine, and the spiritual dimension of life. He looked on his family, his future, and their success as only a physical pursuit, not a spiritual heritage. God was always left out of the equation for security, prosperity, and happiness.

Saul had no fear of the Lord. Because he could not physically see God, he had no fear of Him. There was no limit to Saul's actions because he saw no consequence in offending the Lord. Accordingly, he continued to pursue his obsession to hunt down God's anointed—David—to kill him. And he became so calloused he lost all respect and honor for God's servants: *The king said to the guards who stood about him,* **"Turn and kill the priests of the LORD, because their hand also is with David,** *and because they knew when he fled and did not tell it to me." But the servants of the king would not lift their hands to strike the priests of the LORD* (1 SAMUEL 22:17).

Saul supported the enemies of the Lord. He trusted in God's enemies and used them to advance his goals: *The king said to Doeg, "You turn and kill the priests!" So Doeg the Edomite turned and struck the priests, and killed on that day eighty-five men who wore a linen ephod* (1 SAMUEL 22:18).

If we love people, we hurt when they are hurt. We are loyal and reverent of the names of those we cherish. But Saul failed to cherish God enough to carry out His fierce wrath against the Amalekites. Instead, he used one of God's enemies (an Edomite) to kill the Lord's choice servants (the Levites).

The end of Saul was a catastrophe. He crashed against the rocks of his own disobedient life and sank into the dark waters of sin. His ignominious death was a disgrace to himself, to his family whom he failed to protect, to his country that he betrayed and brought to defeat, and to his God Whom he ignored and dishonored.

Saul's Tragic End

GOD SAID IT IS NOT how we start the race of faith that matters, but how we finish. David ran well all the way to the end. He could therefore triumphantly say, like Paul, *I have fought the good fight, I have finished the race, I have kept the faith* (2 TIMOTHY 4:7). In contrast, King Saul did not keep the faith; he fought "the bad fight" instead.

The last hours of his life were spent in the company of a witch, a demonic spiritist medium, trying to communicate with the dead (1 SAMUEL 28:3–8). Blinded by bitterness, driven by pride, and shackled by fear, he ate his last supper with that witch at Satan's side, dining on an ox roasted by fire like that which would soon roast his tormented soul.

The following summary of 1 Samuel 31 reveals how Saul ended his life— reaping God's final judgment for refusing to utterly destroy the Amalekites and all their possessions:

Three thousand years ago, after fiercely battling the Philistines all day on a windswept hill, enemy arrows gravely wounded King Saul. His sons and heirs to the throne already lay dead around him, night was falling, the enemy had retreated, and Saul was all alone.

The mightiest man of Israel, head and shoulders taller than anyone else, bit by bit dragged himself along to reach his sword that had fallen on the battlefield. When Saul had it at last, he pushed himself upon his weapon in an attempt to end his dreadful pain.

As the night passed and morning dawned, life still clung to him. Soon the sound of the victorious Philistine warriors echoed up the hillsides as they were coming back to abuse the wounded and strip the dead. Hanging there, impaled on his sword, King Saul, with life agonizingly clinging within his tortured body, looked around through the mists of death and desperately wanted to die. Before long, in the gray light of daybreak, a man appeared, scavenging whatever he could from the dead. Saul cried out, begging him to kill him; he obligingly struck down the King of Israel, and then took the crown off Saul's head. That man was an *Amalekite.*

What an ironic twist of fate! Saul died at the hand of an *Amalekite*—one of God's enemies whom he'd earlier refused to utterly destroy!

Saul had money, muscles, and charisma, but he didn't have integrity, humility, and a servant's heart. What was the final outcome of Saul's choice to serve himself instead of the Lord? When the life he'd lived was ready for its final review by God Himself, Saul reaped eternal disgrace.

Saul's death was a personal disgrace. While certain cultures view suicide in time of adversity as noble, God's people regard it as always dishonorable and wrong. Saul's decision to die by his own hand (1 SAMUEL 31:4) was the shameful way out.

Saul's death was a family disgrace. When Saul died, he took his whole household with him. The royal father and three sons, including the popular and noble Jonathan, were killed on the same battlefield (1 SAMUEL 31:6). Although the death of the king was tragic, the simultaneous loss of his heirs was disastrous.

Saul's death was a national disgrace. All his life Saul had defended Israel from enemy assault. Now he lay dead at the hands of his enemies (1 SAMUEL 31:7). His death now signaled a Philistine advance unequaled in Israel's history and unparalleled in scope.

Saul's death was an international disgrace. When the Philistines pinned his headless corpse to the wall of Beth Shan (1 SAMUEL 31:10), they made a strategic choice. Situated at the junction of the Jezreel and Jordan Valleys, Beth Shan controlled the crossroads of major highways. With Galilee and Damascus to the north, the Mediterranean to the west, and Jerusalem to the south, travelers from many nations passed through this prominent city. Here in this public place, Saul's fallen form was a silent witness to the triumph of the pagan powers. While thousands of residents whispered about it, tens of thousands of travelers trumpeted the news in every direction.

Saul's death was a spiritual disgrace. The greatest shame in Saul's death was that it was God's judgment. The end of his life was exploited as an opportunity for praise of pagan gods. The Scriptures tell us that his head was hung in Dagon's temple as a trophy of victory (1 CHRONICLES 10:10), and his armor was placed as a votive offering in the temple of the Ashtoreths. These five degrees of disgrace were the solemn epitaph of one who fulfilled the worst in his death because he failed to live up to the best in his life.[10]

The success or failure of a life really comes down to this: *Do you not know that to whom you present yourselves slaves to obey, you are that one's slaves whom you obey, whether of sin leading to death, or of obedience leading to righteousness? ... [Therefore,] present your members as slaves of righteousness for holiness* (ROMANS 6:16, 19).

Jesus clearly warned:

*"Lay up for yourselves treasures in heaven, where neither moth nor rust destroys and where thieves do not break in and steal. For **where your treasure is, there your heart will be also.** The lamp of the body is the eye. If therefore your eye is good, your whole body will be full of light. But if your eye is bad, your whole body will be full of darkness. If therefore the light that is in you is darkness, how great is that darkness! **No one can serve two masters**; for either he will hate the one and love the other, or else he will be loyal to the one and despise the other. You cannot serve God and mammon. Therefore I say to you, do not worry about your life, what you will eat or what you will drink; nor about your body, what you will put on. Is not life more than food and the body more than clothing?"* (MATTHEW 6:20–25).

What a grim testimony of neglected warning signs that led to shipwreck of a very promising life! Saul's failures should drive us to pray that these areas don't get solidified in our own lives or in the lives of those we love.

The story of David and Saul is one of the Bible's most amazing lessons of contrast. It is meant to be a sobering caution for all who claim to serve the Lord. Remember: this contrast was intentional. God purposefully showed the failure of King Saul and then flowed immediately into the integrity, humility, and obedience of David.

In contrast to Saul's wasted life of choosing to serve himself rather than God, look again at how David invested his life as a God-hearted servant:

- David was on God's mind.
- David was disciplined.
- David was available for God to use.
- David was empowered by the Lord.
- David was an example of godliness to others.
- David displayed true humility.
- David ministered comfort to others.
- David honored God with his work.
- David honored God with his habits.
- David honored God with his life.
- David magnified God's hand in his life.
- David honored God's Name with his mouth.
- David dedicated his treasures and trophies to the Lord.
- David poured out his life as an irrecoverable offering to God.
- David made costly sacrifices for God.

Remember: As it was with King Saul, God doesn't need our brains—He wants godly *character*. Nor does God need our brawn (huge, strong muscles)—He wants *integrity*. God certainly doesn't need our wisdom, power, or wealth—He wants faithful *obedience*. And finally, God doesn't need our ambitious confidence—He wants *humble dependence*.

Humble dependence is to pray like David prayed: *Search me, O God, and know my heart; try me, and know my anxieties; and see if there is any wicked way in me, and lead me in the way everlasting* (PSALM 139:23–24).

I encourage you to make the words of this timeless song your earnest prayer and heart's desire:

CLEANSE ME

Search me, O God, and know my heart today;
Try me, O Savior, know my thoughts I pray.
See if there be some wicked way in me;
Cleanse me from every sin, and set me free.

I praise Thee, Lord, for cleansing me from sin;
Fulfill Thy Word and make me pure within.
Fill me with fire, where once I burned with shame;
Grant my desire to magnify Thy name.

Lord, take my life, and make it wholly Thine;
Fill my poor heart with Thy great love divine.
Take all my will, my passion, self and pride;
I now surrender, Lord—in me abide.

—Edwin Orr (1912–1987)

The Power of Little Choices

3

Hebrews 12; 1 Samuel 15:3–16:1

"I greatly regret that I have set up Saul as king, for he has turned back from following Me, and has not performed My commandments."

—1 Samuel 15:11

L ITTLE CHOICES, MULTIPLIED BY THE passing of time—equals amazing potential! David and Saul both faced the Amalekites, a tribe of people that reflect the power of little choices. In 1 Samuel 15 God asked Saul to make the choice to obey Him completely. Saul only partially obeyed, and God cursed his life.

Have you ever wondered why God was so hard on Saul? To find the answer to that question, we must go back in our minds to 4,000 years ago and trace the far reaching consequences of a series of little choices made by one man.[11]

This man was rugged, handsome, hardworking, honest, athletic, strong—and proud.

From the perspective of those who lived around him he was a great guy, but from the One Who sees the heart, he was pitiful.

A spiritual scan would have revealed that he fed his flesh, gave in to his passions, and nursed his wounds until they festered into gangrenous abscesses oozing bitterness. That bitterness infected his entire life and he ended up becoming an enemy of God.

Who was he? Esau, the firstborn son of Isaac, the grandson of God's friend, Abraham. He was the natural heir to all the promised blessings of the God of the Universe and one who had everything that really mattered in life, except what mattered most.

Esau had everything but God. Yet, as Jesus once said, *"What profit is it to a man if he gains the whole world, and loses his own soul?"* (MATTHEW 16:26).

How did the life of this man who seemed to have it all (but God) turn out?

In Hebrews 12:15–17, God recorded the results of His autopsy on Esau's heart so that we could see the unseen and unchecked cancer that had been growing within. For greater insight, it's helpful to read those verses in these major Bible translations: [12]

- [Look] *carefully lest anyone **fall short of the grace of God**; lest any root of bitterness springing up cause trouble, and by this many become defiled; lest there be any **fornicator** or **profane person like Esau**, who for one morsel of food sold his birthright. For you know that afterward, when he wanted to inherit the blessing, **he was rejected, for he found no place for repentance**, though he sought it diligently with tears* (NKJV).

- *See to it that no one **misses the grace of God** and that no bitter root grows up to cause trouble and defile many. See that no one is **sexually immoral**, or is **godless like Esau**, who for a single meal sold his inheritance rights as the oldest son. Afterward, as you know, when he wanted to inherit this blessing, he was rejected. **He could bring about no change of mind**, though he sought the blessing with tears* (NIV).

- *See to it that no one **comes short of the grace of God**; that no root of bitterness springing up causes trouble, and by it many be defiled; that there be no **immoral or godless person like Esau**, who sold his own birthright for a single meal. For you know that even afterwards, when he desired to inherit the blessing, **he was rejected, for he found no place for repentance**, though he sought for it with tears* (NASB).

What a tragic end for someone with such a promising beginning! As the firstborn son of Isaac, Esau began with every imaginable opportunity and blessing; he lived with great earthly success and died surrounded by an abundance of everything but God in his life.

In Genesis 25:34 God recorded that Esau *despised his birthright.* As Isaac's firstborn son, all the rights of the family contained in the birthright were his: he was to be in contact with God; he was to be the priest of his family; and he was to be the man who had a covenant from God—the place of continuing a relationship with God like his grandfather Abraham and his father Isaac. But what did he do? He bartered that right, trading it for a momentary need. What Esau was really saying by that seemingly little choice at the time was this: "I'd rather have a bowl of soup than have a relationship with God."

Without the insight we get from Hebrews 12 we would not know all that had been going on within Esau's heart. He was not only immoral but he was also godless. He had no ethics or faith and no scruples or reverence. In other words, Esau had no regard for the good, the truthful, and the divine; he was totally worldly, totally secular, and totally profane. Yet, in spite of this, God allowed him to live a long life and have a large family with many descendants. (That is the goodness of the God Who Waits.)

Esau's Legacy of Sin—The Amalekites

ESAU'S GODLESS AND PROFANE FAMILY line went on to live in unbroken generations up to the time of Christ. This is the reason the writer of Hebrews warned Christians to be vigilant that "*no immoral or godless person like Esau*"[13] would contaminate Christ's body, His church.

Esau had many famous descendants described in the Bible, all of whom reflected the results of godless living in increasingly visible ways. Here are some who stand out the most:

- **Edom** and **Amalek** (nations by the time of Moses)
- **Agag** (in the time of Samuel and Saul)
- **Haman** (in the time of Esther and Mordecai)
- **King Herod the Great** (the most notable and infamous of all Esau's descendants—evil, godless, immoral, and murderous in the time of Christ)

For our purposes in this chapter, we need to focus on the descendant God wants us to know about in particular—Amalek, Esau's grandson: *Now Timna was the concubine of Eliphaz, Esau's son, and* **she bore Amalek** *to Eliphaz. These were the sons of Adah, Esau's wife* (GENESIS 36:12).

Amalek fathered the nation we know from the Scriptures as the Amalekites; they are behind the reason why God was so hard on Saul. For further details about what happened, let's move forward in our minds to the era of Exodus 17:8–16 and events that occurred 3,500 years ago.[14]

OVER FIVE HUNDRED YEARS AFTER ESAU … (1445 B.C.)

By this time the Amalekites, a nomadic race that inhabited the southern part of Canaan, had become perennial enemies of the Israelites. They were the fearful warriors whose intimidating presence was one of the reasons the Israelites disobeyed God and balked at entering the Promised Land at Kadesh-barnea (NUMBERS 13:29). Shortly after the Exodus, they viciously attacked Israel at Rephidim by ambushing them from behind, massacring the stragglers who were most weary (DEUTERONOMY 25:18). It was a cowardly attack by the most powerful and savage tribe in the whole region.

As we examine the famous battle when Aaron and Hur had to support Moses' arms (EXODUS 17:8–13) and the unusual way that the Lord instructed Moses in the battle and the aftermath, we see that something big was going on here. Look at the record of this famous battle:

> *Then Amalek came and fought against Israel at Rephidim. So Moses said to Joshua, "Choose men for us, and go out, fight against Amalek. Tomorrow I will station myself on the top of the hill with the staff of God in my hand." And Joshua did as Moses told him, and fought against Amalek; and Moses, Aaron, and Hur went up to the top of the hill. So it came about **when Moses held his hand up**, that **Israel prevailed**, and when he let his hand down, Amalek prevailed. But Moses' hands were heavy. Then they took a stone and put it under him, and he sat on it; and Aaron and Hur supported his hands, one on one side and one on the other. Thus his hands were steady until the sun set. So Joshua overwhelmed Amalek and his people with the edge of the sword* (EXODUS 17:8–13 NASB).

Because the Amalekites passionately loathed God and the Israelites, He supernaturally delivered Israel that day, and the Amalekites fled into hiding. Afterward, the Lord called Himself Yahweh-Nissi (The LORD Is My Banner) and promised that He would fight Amalek for generations to come:

Then the LORD said to Moses, "Write this in a book as a memorial, and recite it to Joshua, that I will utterly blot out the memory of Amalek from under heaven." And Moses built an altar, and named it The LORD is My Banner; and he said, "The LORD has sworn; **the LORD will have war against Amalek from generation to generation***" (EXODUS 17:14–16 NASB).*

What was going on here? God wanted to utterly destroy this nation and its ferocious, plundering, merciless culture of murder and wickedness. For sin left unchecked, like a deadly cancer, grows and grows. In Genesis Esau despised the blessing; he was proud and self-sufficient, profane and immoral. In a spiritual sense, Esau represents "the flesh," our old nature; his grandson Amalek is a biblical illustration of the lifelong battle each of us has with our flesh.

The truth from Exodus is that only God can give us the power to overcome life's unending struggles with "the flesh." We need to believe that truth and by faith seek His intervention in the battles of life. So then, there are three conclusions we can draw from Exodus 17:

1. God is going to get rid of Amalek ("the flesh"). In other words, God is going to get rid of the old nature.
2. The Lord will never compromise with the old nature. He will have war with Amalek ("the flesh") from generation to generation.
3. This constant conflict will go on for as long as we live. "The flesh" and the Spirit will always war against each other. Only the Holy Spirit can give us victory.[15]

The battle with Amalek was won by Moses with upraised hands. Joshua and the army could not win by physical means: they had to have God's intervention. If you read closely, you can see that the real battle was waged on the mountaintop. Moses was fighting and winning for as long as he sought the Lord through prayer, but when Moses' hands dropped the battle would turn against Israel. Without Moses and his upraised hands in prayer Israel would have been defeated.

The critical lesson is that only the Holy Spirit can defeat our flesh. We win daily battles with temptations by walking in the Spirit. When we go our own way, as King Saul did, we face Amalek (our flesh) and are defeated. As Paul said, the defeat of our flesh comes only through the victory Christ won for us on the cross. It is brought to us step-by-step, in the Spirit of God's power, as we walk believing that truth.

God's Word clearly warns that we cannot conquer our old nature by physical means such as asceticism, religious activity, or human effort. It can only be achieved through the power of the cross worked out in our life by the Holy Spirit. For there is always a war brewing between our flesh and the Spirit of God within us:

> *The flesh lusts against the Spirit, and the Spirit against the flesh; and these are contrary to one another, so that you do not the things that you wish* (GALATIANS 5:17).

Flesh can't defeat flesh. Resolves, promises, fighting and striving in our own power will only lead to further defeats. Victory is won by yielding to the power of the cross. What is the power of the cross? It is the defeat of death, sin, and Satan that Jesus accomplished once and for all when He died for us on Calvary.

Just as God commanded Israel to destroy their enemies completely, so He expects us to destroy ours through Christ.

- **Amalek was Israel's foe**: *"Remember what Amalek did to you along the way when you came out from Egypt, how he met you along the way and attacked among you all the stragglers at your rear when you were faint and weary; and he did not fear God. Therefore ... when the LORD your God has given you rest from all your surrounding enemies, in the land which the LORD your God gives you as an inheritance to possess, you shall blot out the memory of Amalek from under heaven; you must not forget"* (DEUTERONOMY 25:17–19 NASB).

- **The flesh is our foe**: *Consider the members of your earthly body as dead to immorality, impurity, passion, evil desire, and greed, which amounts to idolatry* (COLOSSIANS 3:5 NASB).

As John MacArthur points out, "The Amalekites make an apt illustration of the sin that remains in the believer's life. That sin—already utterly defeated—must be dealt with ruthlessly and hacked to pieces, or it will revive and continue to plunder and pillage our hearts and sap our spiritual strength. We cannot be merciful with Amalek or Agag, or they will turn and try to devour us. In fact, the remaining sin in us often becomes more fiercely determined after it has been overthrown by the gospel."[16]

One final truth we need to see is in Galatians:

*"I **have been** crucified with Christ; it is no longer I who live, but Christ lives in me; and the life which I now live in the flesh I live by faith in the Son of God, who **loved me** and **gave Himself for me**"* (GALATIANS 2:20).

*But God forbid that I should boast except in the cross of our Lord Jesus Christ, by whom the world **has been crucified** to me, and I to the world* (GALATIANS 6:14).

The battle is already won, the enemy defeated, and we just need to believe that truth and act upon it!

FIVE HUNDRED YEARS LATER—HACKING AGAG TO PIECES ... (1050 B.C.)

As we turn past another 500 years of sacred history we now come to Saul's time 3,000 years ago. The Amalekites' persistent hatred of God and violence against His people had to be judged. The stage had finally been set for God to carry out His vow to Moses that He would utterly destroy the Amalekites because of their vile sins.

How bad is sin? Sin is so bad it took God killing His own Son to pay the price of wrath sin deserved! That is an abstract thought until we see the price of sin in terms we can relate to.

When we see God's wrath upon sin it sometimes makes us uncomfortable, and it should. But in that discomfort we should respond in gratitude for Christ's gracious gift of redeeming love, atoning death, and endless life. To more fully appreciate what we have in Christ, we need to step back and consider an immutable truth God has consistently revealed about Himself: our Lord Jesus is always just, right, and blameless in all He does.[17]

Psalm 51:4 is just one example in Scripture where we can make a connection with the great wrath God has for sin and the high price that furious wrath demands. Look at how David responded to God when confronted with his sin:

*Against You, You only, have I sinned, and done this evil in Your sight— that You may be found just when You speak, and **blameless when You judge*** (PSALM 51:4).

When we see the Lord execute judgment, sometimes we pause and secretly wonder why He was so severe, as when God rejected Saul for disobeying this very clear command:

> " 'Now go and attack Amalek, and **utterly destroy all** that they have, and **do not spare them**. But kill both man and woman, infant and nursing child, ox and sheep, camel and donkey' " (1 SAMUEL 15:3).

First Samuel 15:3 clearly shows God's attitude about sin. Because He is also a God of wrath, that verse reveals what lies ahead for all who do not flee to the shadow of the cross. If we just look at verse 3 by itself, it seems harsh and out of place, but once we back up and see what else the Lord said about these people it becomes much clearer.

God was entirely blameless when he judged the Amalekites severely for their wickedness. As John MacArthur explains, "The Amalekites hated God, detested Israel, and seemed to delight in wicked and destructive acts. God's instructions to Saul, therefore, fulfilled the vow He swore to Moses. Saul was to wipe out the tribe forever. He and his armies were the instrument through which a righteous God would carry out His holy judgment on a sinister people."[18]

The High Price of Sin

ONE THING WE KNOW: THIS event in 1 Samuel 15:3 actually happened—God ordered it, recorded it, and wanted it to happen. After centuries of patience, the God Who Waits responded to the sin of the Amalekites, and that is why He ordered King Saul to utterly destroy them. Now look again at what Saul did:

> He also took Agag king of the Amalekites alive, and utterly destroyed all the people with the edge of the sword. But **Saul and the people spared Agag and the best** of the sheep, the oxen, the fatlings, the lambs, and all that was good, and were unwilling to utterly destroy them. But everything despised and worthless, that they utterly destroyed (1 SAMUEL 15:8–9).

Consider what J. Vernon McGee had to say about Saul's rebellion against God:

He thought, what a shame to destroy everything! So he saved Agag, who was the ruler of the Amalekites. Saul had no right to spare him any more than he had the right to spare the humblest peasant among these people. This nation was wholly given to evil, and the king, above all others, should have been destroyed and judged at this time. Neither had Saul the right to save from destruction the best of the cattle. It would appear that he made his attack for the purpose of obtaining booty and spoil, and God had forbidden that. The Israelites were bringing judgment upon the Amalekites for Almighty God in this particular case.[19]

To God, the Amalekites were like a toxic waste emitting dangerous spiritual radiation that would contaminate all that came into contact with them. When God gave them into Saul's hand he wasn't to spare even their livestock; everyone and everything was to be destroyed. Yet, they went through the things God hated and saved whatever they wanted most. They sorted the deadly contaminants and kept the prettiest, like in the second Gulf War when looters took the beautiful barrels from reactor sites in Iraq, ignoring the skull and cross bones painted in red on each one. Taking them home, they used the barrels to store drinking water, and within days were experiencing deadly radiation sickness.

Like radiation sickness, unchecked sin is deadly, as Saul tragically discovered:

[Saul] *said, "I have sinned; yet honor me now, please, before the elders of my people and before Israel, and return with me, that I may worship the* LORD *your God." So Samuel turned back after Saul, and Saul worshiped the* LORD. *Then Samuel said, "Bring Agag king of the Amalekites here to me." So Agag came to him cautiously. And Agag said, "Surely the bitterness of death is past." But Samuel said, "As your sword has made women childless, so shall your mother be childless among women." And* **Samuel hacked Agag in pieces before the LORD** *in Gilgal* (1 SAMUEL 15:30–33).

Writes McGee:

Agag came "delicately" unto Samuel because he knew he was in trouble. And Samuel killed Agag. Now that may be strong medicine for some folk today, but my friend, our God is a God of Judgment and He is going to judge wrong and evil. I am glad that God is going to judge. I don't know about you, but I thank God that no one is getting away with evil today. There may be those, even in high places, who think they are getting away with their sin, and dishonesty, and murder, and adultery, but they are not. God is going to judge them. No one is going to get away with sin, and we need to make that very clear today. So Samuel executed the judgment of God upon this vile, wicked ruler, Agag.[20]

Not even the first king of Israel could get away with sin. Saul was a self-serving man rather than a God-hearted servant, and his end was tragic. He disgraced himself, his family, his country, and the God he ignored. His life was an immense failure, and all because he neglected the Lord's warning signs that his life was headed for shipwreck.

God was thus very hard on Saul because he was unwilling to hate sin and obey the Lord by turning away from that which caused it. Saul grieved God's Spirit so much that He even confessed, *"I greatly regret that I have set up Saul as king, for he has turned back from following Me, and has not performed My commandments."* (1 SAMUEL 15:11).

Never underestimate how seriously God considers unchecked sin. Remember: Sin is *so bad* it took God killing His own Son to pay the price of wrath sin deserved! I want to underline in your heart and mind that any part of our old life that we spare will come back and rob us of God's blessing, fruitfulness, and rewards. In other words:

- Like Agag, any part of our flesh that we spare will come back with a vengeance and slay us.

- Like the Amalekites, our flesh will always come to strike us down when we are weakest—and then rob us of our crown.

When Samuel *hacked Agag in pieces before the LORD in Gilgal* (1 SAMUEL 15:33), he was God's man, His obedient instrument for that moment. Samuel's harsh action toward Agag is an example of how we must deal with our flesh to prepare for our own inescapable final day of reckoning.

The Final Day of Reckoning

DAVID AND SAUL'S LIVES FROM the Old Testament clearly contrast "how to serve God" versus "how *not* to serve God." There is no middle ground. Our *works*—what we did with our time, energy, resources, and bodies—will some-day reveal whether we were for Christ, or against Him.

With that in mind, I now want you to think about how the Apostle Paul and the other New Testament writers operated in the little things that fill ordinary life. To me, what is so fascinating is that they all seemed to keep track of life like a stock market day trader; every one of them knew their investment and sought a return on each day's works.

If you closely read the New Testament books Paul wrote, you will find this common thread: God is going to examine each of us individually for our works:

*Let each one examine **his own work**, and then he will have rejoicing in himself alone, and not in another* (GALATIANS 6:4).

*We are His workmanship, **created in Christ Jesus for good works**, which God prepared beforehand that we should walk in them* (EPHESIANS 2:10).

*Walk worthy of the Lord, fully pleasing Him, being **fruitful in every good work** and increasing in the knowledge of God* (COLOSSIANS 1:10).

*Let them do good, that they **be rich in good works**, ready to give, willing to share* (1 TIMOTHY 6:18).

*I want you to affirm constantly, that those who have believed in God should **be careful to maintain good works**. These things are good and profitable to men* (TITUS 3:8).

Peter also strongly urged the saints to be careful with what they did in their days and hours: *And if you call on the Father, who without partiality **judges according to each one's work**, conduct yourselves throughout the time of your stay here in fear* (1 PETER 1:17).

The New Testament writers were motivated by the idea of "the end of the race," or being faithful all the way to the finish line. Paul held a distinct conviction that life was a daily race with an end-of-life prize and that the only way to get the prize was to finish the race well. Look at what he wrote to Timothy:

*I have fought the good fight, **I have finished the race**, I have kept the faith. Finally, **there is laid up for me the crown of righteousness**, which the Lord, the righteous Judge, will give to me on that Day, and not to me only but also to all who have loved His appearing* (2 TIMOTHY 4:7–8).

The Apostle John was convinced we would either welcome Christ's coming or wither in shame before Him: *Abide in Him, that when He appears, we may have confidence and **not be ashamed before Him** at His coming* (1 JOHN 2:28).

John's recorded closing words of the Bible pointed to that truth: *"And behold, I am coming quickly, and My reward is with Me, to **give to every one according to his work**"* (REVELATION 22:12).

Since God is going to evaluate our service for Him by our works, what should we be doing?

> Not that I have already attained, or am already perfected; but **I press on, that I may lay hold of that for which Christ Jesus has also laid hold of me.** Brethren, I do not count myself to have apprehended; but one thing I do, forgetting those things which are behind and reaching forward to those things which are ahead, **I press toward the goal for the prize** of the upward call of God in Christ Jesus (PHILIPPIANS 3:12–14).

In 1 Corinthians 3:12–15, Paul expanded that idea by saying our daily works, deeds, and actions are transformed into either *"wood, hay, straw"* or *"gold, silver, precious stones"* (v. 12):

> **Each one's work** will become clear; for the Day will declare it, because it will be revealed by fire; and the fire will **test each one's work**, of what sort it is. If **anyone's work** which he has built on it endures, he will receive a reward. If **anyone's work** is burned, he will suffer loss; but he himself will be saved, yet so as through fire (vv. 13–15).

GOLD, SILVER, PRECIOUS STONES	WOOD, HAY, STUBBLE
Permanent	*Passing, temporary*
Beautiful	*Ordinary, even ugly*
Valuable	*Cheap*
Hard to obtain	*Easy to obtain*

More than to any other church, Paul spoke to the Corinthians about being careful to not lose their life's work. He seemed to imply that their often out-of-control lives threatened them with irrecoverable loss. Look again at verse 15: *If anyone's work is burned, **he will suffer loss**; but he himself will be saved, yet so as through fire.*

What does *"suffer loss"* mean to our lives as believers? The New Testament used this word several times. The clearest example of what it means is in Acts 27 where Paul was on the ship that went through a terrible storm before crashing on the rocks and being destroyed. In the midst of that traumatic event there is a very good picture of what it means to *"suffer loss."*

Life is similar to collecting the cargo in a ship; everything important is carried down and stowed in the hold. Keep that in mind as you read these verses from Acts 27:

> *Paul advised them, saying, "Men, I perceive that this voyage will end with **disaster and much loss**, not only of the cargo and ship, but also our lives" (vv. 9–10).*

> *But after long abstinence from food, then Paul stood in the midst of them and said, "Men, you should have listened to me, and not have sailed from Crete and **incurred this disaster and loss**" (v. 21).*

> *The rest, **some on boards** and **some on parts of the ship** … all escaped safely to land (v. 44).*

Paul warned that at the judgment seat of Christ some believers will see everything they lived for thrown overboard (burned up in the fire), so they will float to the shores of heaven *"on boards."* All that will be left of their life will be that they were barely saved (*"yet so as through fire"*). That describes so many lives in God's Word; they began the race with great achievement but failed at the end because they ignored God's rules. They did not lose their salvation, but they did lose their rewards. It happened to Lot (GENESIS 19), Samson (JUDGES 16), probably King Saul (1 SAMUEL 28; 31), and to Ananias and Sapphira (ACTS 5).

As Paul warned, loss of rewards can happen to anyone. He therefore wanted to avoid at all costs the disastrous loss that would come if he ignored God and His purpose for his life. Over and over he expressed this type of concern: *I discipline my body and bring it into subjection, lest, when I have preached to others, **I myself should become disqualified** (1 CORINTHIANS 9:27).*

The literal sense of the word *"disqualified"* is "tested and proved to be false or unacceptable." As one source notes:

- Borrowed from the athletic games, the word describes a contestant who, because of some infraction of the rules, is disqualified from winning the prize (1 COR. 9:27; CASTAWAY KJV).

- Another metaphor is possible: a "counterfeit faith" (2 TIM. 3:8, NRSV). This suggests a coin that has been tested, proven false, and disapproved as legal tender.[21]

The word "*disqualified*" also shows up in Hebrews 6 where it is translated as "*rejected*":

*For the earth which drinks in the rain that often comes upon it, and bears herbs useful for those by whom it is cultivated, receives blessing from God; but if it bears thorns and briers, it is **rejected** and near to being cursed, whose end is to be burned (vv. 7–8).*

"Rejected" is … the same word Paul used when writing to the Corinthian believers, "But I keep under my body, and bring it into subjection: lest that by any means, when I have preached to others, I myself should be a castaway" (1 COR. 9:27). "Castaway" is the same word … meaning "not approved." In effect, Paul is saying, "When I come into His presence I don't want to be disapproved. I don't want the Lord Jesus to say to me, 'You have failed. Your life should have been a testimony but it was not.' "[22]

God's Word contains sobering portraits of those who suffered loss. One of the greatest of these lessons in "how *not* to serve God" (and thus waste your life) is from Saul's life. He had a great start but a horrible ending. In God's race, the only ones who qualify for rewards are those who finish well; all the rest will "*suffer loss.*" They will have their life's work burned up before them, thrown overboard, and sunk in the depths of the sea—irrecoverably lost forever.

In essence, Paul was saying, "Don't load your ship with what God is going to throw overboard. Don't build with flammable materials if your house is going to go through a fire. In other words, don't *waste* your life."

If you want to avoid suffering loss, remember the ominous warning of Saul's life. He had the Spirit, knew God, and yet failed completely. His life stands today as an example of how *not* to live, how *not* to end, and how *not* to invest these precious days we have on earth!

If you have not begun to deal with ending habitual sin in your life, I pray you will heed this third stanza's message of "God's Final Call"—a song from a generation ago that was written about Esau and those like him:

If you reject God's final call of grace,
You'll have no chance your footsteps to retrace
All hope will then be gone, and doom you'll face:
O hear His call! O hear His call! [23]
    —John W. Peterson (1921–2006)

Christ's work on Calvary has forever given you the power and authority to *stop* anything that enslaves you and to *start* anything He asks you to do. Will you respond to Him in faith today? May God grant that you see, heed, and respond to His leading in your life!

4 | Our Sure Refuge in Loneliness

1 Samuel 16–18; Psalms 19 and 23

The LORD is my shepherd; I shall not want. … I will fear no evil; for You are with me. —**Psalm 23:1, 4**

LONELINESS HAS BEEN DESCRIBED AS the times in a believer's life when God takes something or allows someone to be removed from us—so that He can be closest to us.

Often loneliness shocks us when its shadow crosses our path. We think of it as always an enemy and never a friend—but not David. He saw loneliness for what it was: loneliness gave David the opportunity to flee to Christ as his Refuge. Consequently, he invested his life the greatest way possible by serving God's purpose in his generation (ACTS 13:36). For this reason, the Lord made David our prime Old Testament example of what the life of God's servants should look like.

Does it seem surprising, then, to hear that David, the man after God's heart, suffered with loneliness throughout his life? Although surrounded by a nation, an army, and his own family, he often felt lonely. In fact, most of his great psalms came from that reference point.[24]

Loneliness is no respecter of persons. From the greatest to the least of us, all experience the pain of loneliness at one time or another. And God has something to say about that—"It isn't good ..."

In the first recorded conversation with Adam, God spoke of this problem: "*It is **not good** that man should be alone*" (GENESIS 2:18a; emphasis added). He solved Adam's loneliness by making "*a helper suitable to him*" (18b). Eve was created to correspond to Adam's life, which is what God intended for all marriages—a complete correspondence, a completion, a gathering together in an unbreakable bond of two who become one.

Since God said it is not good to be alone, why do we often feel alone even when surrounded by people? After sin entered the world, Adam and Eve experienced the sting of the most dreadful form of loneliness—alienation from God (Genesis 3). We now live in a fallen world with the pre-Fall, non-sinful loneliness plus the horror of alienation from our Creator. The Lord wants to be close, to fully complete us, but we either won't let Him or else don't understand He is the solution to healing the gnawing void within us.

Because we are all fallen in Adam, we encounter loneliness in many forms. It may appear as desolation, unsatisfied longings, emptiness (like having a vacuum inside), or a sense of displacement after moving away from a cherished home and the comfortable and familiar.

The most acute form of loneliness, however, is probably the loss of someone precious to us through disagreement, distance, or death. The loss of a life partner especially, whether through death or divorce, can create a cavernous void that affects not only the partner left behind but also the children, family, and friends who likewise have an agonizing hole in their hearts.

But there is hope in all this! By rightly responding to God in our lonely times, He works in each situation for our good and His glory (ROMANS 8:28). One way the Lord teaches this truth is through biblical models whose character was forged in the furnace of loneliness:

- Joseph, as he trusted God in a lonely pit, palace, and prison, was being prepared for his future God-ordained role as second in command of the foreign world of Egypt.

- Moses, as he spent forty lonely years in the backside of the desert, was being humbled and readied for the monumental task of guiding God's people out of their Egyptian bondage.

- Daniel, lonely in far off Babylon, "made the most of the exile, successfully exalting God by his character and service. He quickly rose to the role of statesman … and served as a confidante of kings as well as a prophet of two world empires."[25]

- Paul, repeatedly thrown in lonely jail cells in distant Roman cities, gave a glorious testimony that in *all things we are more than conquerors through Him who loved us* (ROMANS 8:37)!

But more than anyone else in Scripture, David's life models the genuine hope we can find for our loneliness, hope which is in Christ—the loneliest Person to ever live on this planet.

Jesus is the perfect Refuge for the lonely. Think of it: He left the best, closest, and most intimate relationship in the universe—His oneness with the Father—and humbled Himself by taking on human form to seek and to save the lost. Yet, even His closest friends abandoned Him in His direst hour:[26]

Indeed the hour is coming … that **you will be scattered … and will leave Me alone.** *And yet I am not alone, because the Father is with Me* (JOHN 16:32).

To purchase our salvation, Jesus Christ had to endure the punishment sin deserves. On the cross, for an unknown period of time, He suffered the ultimate loneliness—alienation from God:

And about the ninth hour Jesus cried out with a loud voice, saying, "Eli, Eli, lama sabachthani?" that is, **"My God, My God, why have You forsaken Me?"** (MATTHEW 27:46).

As finite beings, we can never grasp the depth of the piercing aloneness that engulfed the infinite Son of God as He paid such an indescribably high price for our sin. But this we know: when overwhelmed with loneliness, we can find comfort in Christ because He is acquainted with our grief and sympathizes with our weaknesses. And Jesus invites us to *come boldly to the throne of grace, that we may obtain mercy and find grace to help in time of need* (see HEBREWS 4:14–16).

In periods of aloneness, David wonderfully found that comfort and closeness in the Good Shepherd. What was deepest within him when lonely was often reflected in psalms during different stages of his life: the growing years, the struggling years, the strong years, and the waning years. In this chapter, we will be focusing on truths David learned in his youth—his growing years.

Lessons from David's Youth

ACCORDING TO SOME RESEARCHERS, THE most intense loneliness is thought to be experienced by teenagers who feel neither young nor old. It's like they are in limbo between two worlds, but they can't seem to connect with either.

Because loneliness is something they don't expect, teens are commonly caught off guard and ill-prepared for its fierceness. To cope with the sting of feeling alone, they typically look for solace, approval, and acceptance from their peers. David's testimony from his teen years is especially powerful. His most well-known writings are often youthful expressions of the Lord's faithfulness, for David did not have an easy life in his growing years.

As the youngest of eight sons, from the earliest moment he was able to watch the sheep, this lowly job was dumped on him. Sometimes we tend to glorify David as a shepherd boy by envisioning him playing with his slingshot and having fun watching the sheep. But shepherding was a lonely job.

In 1 Samuel 16–18 David was overlooked, ignored, and disliked by his family. He was often left out of family gatherings and big feasts, unrecognized for achievements, and left alone much of the time. David keenly felt his family's rejection, but it drove him to meditate on the Lord's trustworthiness. God was always on David's mind, and he was on God's.

In 1 Samuel 16 the prophet Samuel invited Jesse and all his sons to sacrifice to the Lord, but only Jesse and David's older brothers went. When God made it clear none of the seven was His choice to be the next king, Samuel asked Jesse, "Are these all your boys?" "Oh, well, there's the youngest," said Jesse, "but he's not very important—he's out taking care of the sheep." When David was brought in, the Lord told Samuel, *"Arise, anoint him; for **this is the one!**"* (1 SAMUEL 16:12). David was anointed and *the Spirit of the LORD came upon David from that day forward* (1 SAMUEL 16:13). But afterward, he went back to tending sheep.

Most Bible scholars agree that Psalms 19 and 23 were written after David's anointing—when his heart overflowed as the Spirit of the Lord came upon him. Let's look at these psalms he wrote to testify of God's closeness during his youth.

Psalm 19—How David Overcame Loneliness

THERE ARE THREE BASIC LESSONS we can learn from the Psalm 19 period of David's youth:

1. When he was lonely David meditated upon God's character (PSALM 19:1–6):

> ¹ *The heavens declare the glory of God;*
>   *And the firmament shows His handiwork.*
> ² *Day unto day utters speech,*
>   *And night unto night reveals knowledge.*
> ³ *There is no speech nor language*
>   *Where their voice is not heard.*
> ⁴ *Their line has gone out through all the earth,*
>   *And their words to the end of the world.*
>   *In them He has set a tabernacle for the sun,*
> ⁵ *Which is like a bridegroom coming out of his chamber,*
>   *And rejoices like a strong man to run its race.*
> ⁶ *Its rising is from one end of heaven,*
>   *And its circuit to the other end;*
>   *And there is nothing hidden from its heat.*

David spent many lonely nights in the fields, woods, and hillsides of Judea. Rather than hating and fleeing those times, he meditated upon God and learned that *since the creation of the world His invisible attributes are clearly seen, being understood by the things that are made, even His eternal power and Godhead* (ROMANS 1:20). Likely, David's first recorded reflection was "*the heavens declare the glory of God*" (PSALM 19:1). Did you catch the truth practically screaming at us in that verse? David SAW GOD when he was alone!

He never gave in to self-pity and thinking like this: *Oh man, here I am growing up in Bethlehem … the world is passing me by … my family doesn't care about me … Woe is me! I'm alone—nobody loves me—and besides, these sheep stink!* Would you buy a song like that? Would you enjoy singing it or memorizing its words? No, the secret David shared is this: "The very fact the heavens declare the glory of God causes me to rise above my problems and see GOD!" With such a response, loneliness becomes a tool in the Lord's hands to draw us closer to Him!

2. When he was lonely David listened to God's Word (PSALM 19:7–11):

> 7 *The law of the LORD is perfect, converting the soul;*
>   *The testimony of the LORD is sure, making wise the simple;*
> 8 *The statutes of the LORD are right, rejoicing the heart;*
>   *The commandment of the LORD is pure, enlightening the eyes;*
> 9 *The fear of the LORD is clean, enduring forever;*
>   *The judgments of the LORD are true and righteous altogether.*
> 10 *More to be desired are they than gold,*
>   *Yea, than much fine gold;*
>   *Sweeter also than honey and the honeycomb.*
> 11 *Moreover by them Your servant is warned,*
>   *And in keeping them there is great reward.*

David wouldn't let loneliness totally shut him down. As he joyfully reflected upon God in the expanse of the heavens and His glory in the night skies, he replayed in his mind all he'd heard about the Lord at the tabernacle or when His Word was spoken elsewhere. The Scriptures so captivated David's heart that he hungered for every morsel. As a result, he truly listened to what God had to say as he meditated on the laws, testimonies, statutes, commandments, and the fear and judgments of the Lord.

3. When he was lonely David sought God's acceptance and approval (PSALM 19:12–14):

> 12 *Who can understand his errors?*
>   *Cleanse me from secret faults.*
> 13 *Keep back Your servant also from presumptuous sins;*
>   *Let them not have dominion over me.*
>   *Then I shall be blameless,*
>   *And I shall be innocent of great transgression.*
> 14 *Let the words of my mouth and the meditation of my heart*
>   *Be acceptable in Your sight,*
>   *O LORD, my strength and my Redeemer.*

Because David feared God's disapproval, he heeded His Word, not wanting to be guilty of even *"secret faults"*—unintentional sins (PSALM 19:13). David asked the Lord to empower him to be blameless in thoughts, words, and deeds. His Redeemer's acceptance and approval motivated David to make it through his lonely periods with right responses to God.

One of the prime characteristics of teenagers is their strong need for acceptance and approval from their peers. Since David was a teen at this point, he felt this need too. But he chose to let God meet it, so he broke with the crowd. Psalm 19:14 was a clear and beautiful cry from a teen who was after God's own heart!

So then, three ways we can overcome loneliness are: 1) meditate on God's character; 2) listen to His Word; and 3) seek the Lord's acceptance and approval above all others.

Psalm 23—How the Lord Was David's Shepherd

HOW DO WE KNOW DAVID wrote Psalm 23 in his youth? Because Psalm 132 testifies he discovered God when shepherding as a boy. That provides an incredible insight for what's going on here in his life. David took what he'd learned during his long dark nights and lonely days when he wrote Psalm 19 and applied those truths to Psalm 23.

If you can recite Psalm 23 fluently, its familiarity might cause a loss of blessing if you don't slow down as you read and ask yourself: *Have I REALLY experienced this psalm—or is it just a nice memory in my head and not my heart?* (There is a big difference between knowing about something and actually experiencing it.)

PSALM 23:1—THE SATISFYING SHEPHERD

- *The LORD is my shepherd* (Lord, when I'm lonely—**shepherd me**): As a shepherd, David knew sheep shouldn't be left alone; they need careful supervision to keep them from danger. So he said, "Lord, as one of Your sheep, don't leave me alone. I need Your shepherding to keep me out of trouble." Do you see how he applied his being alone with the sheep to his own need for a Shepherd? Jesus said, *"I am the good shepherd; and I know my sheep, and am known by My own"* (JOHN 10:14). When we're lonely, Christ cares: *He knows our frame; He remembers that we are dust* (PSALM 103:14). Our Good Shepherd knows our weaknesses! He came to give us life—not mere existence— but abundantly overflowing life (JOHN 10:10).

- *I shall not want* (Lord, when I'm lonely—**satisfy me**): David was saying, "When I'm alone, Lord, satisfy me as I can't satisfy myself!" The more we look for happiness apart from God, the more elusive it becomes. For example, some people think that money can buy happiness. It doesn't; it just buys more places to look for it. Only Christ can satisfy the deepest longings of our hearts. Jesus said, *"I am the bread of life. He who comes to me shall never hunger, and he who believes in Me shall never thirst"* (JOHN 6:35).

God warned that *in the last days perilous times will come ... for men will be ... lovers of pleasure rather than lovers of God* (2 TIMOTHY 3:1, 4–5). We see this all around us. Did you know research has even identified a part of our brains known as "the pleasure center"? An electrical impulse there produces an overwhelming euphoria similar to the situation in this study done on lab rats:

> In neurological studies the pleasure center was located in the hypothalamus of rats. An electrode was attached to each rat's brain. Three levers were then placed in front of them: one for food and water, one for pain, and one for an artificial pleasure. After training the rats to feed themselves, the lever that induced a sensation of pleasure was activated. This is one of the most shocking videos that every artificial pleasure-seeker should watch, whether it be alcohol, drugs, or immorality. On the video the "smiling" rats constantly pressed the pleasure lever to the neglect of all else. In the end, they starved to death; their last strength was spent dragging their wasted bodies to the lever for one last pull and jolt of pleasure.[27]

When humans repeatedly seek artificial pleasures, they experience a decreasing satisfaction. Yet, increasing the dose over and over can never bring fulfillment. David wisely said, "I'm learning this as a young person: *'I shall not want.'* Lord, when I'm all alone, only You can fully meet my need." Because God made us for Himself, we will be restless and unfulfilled until we let Him satisfy us. God alone offers the ultimate satisfying companionship.

PSALM 23:2—THE CALMING LEADER

- *He makes me to lie down in green pastures* (Lord, when I'm lonely —**calm me**): David cried out to the Good Shepherd, "As one of Your sheep, since I need to eat, rest, and digest food, make me rest." Restlessness—manifested in thought, conversation, and conduct—is the opposite of the ability to "*lie down in green pastures.*" This is usually a key indicator that someone is lost, having not become a sheep of Christ's flock.

We are a restless nation: everything seems to be going 24/7, 365 days a year, and it can't seem to be slowed down. For example, when a banker friend of mine introduced Internet banking to the small-town bank he ran, he expected only yuppies and thirty-plus jetsetters to access it. He was shocked when discovering that its primary users were older people who kept looking at their money day and night online. Restlessness compelled them to keep checking to make sure it was still there.

The only solution is to heed Jesus' invitation: "Come to Me when you're weary and I will give you rest, for I am the only One who can truly rest you."[28] That is primarily a salvation message, and if you've never received Christ as your personal Savior, His invitation is for you! But if you're already a child of God by faith, as you have received the Lord by resting in Him, so walk in Him. Say, "Lord, when I'm lonely, make me to 'lie down' and feel quietness within me!"

- *He leads me beside the still waters* (Lord, when I'm lonely—**lead me**): God wants us to *be still, and know that* [He is] *God* (PSALM 46:10). We can't hear His voice unless stillness reigns in our hearts. So teenaged David said, "Lord, I need You to lead me, to keep me still in my loneliness." *Jesus said, "I am the way, the truth, and the life"* (JOHN 14:6). If we follow Him, our peace will be "*like a river, and our righteousness like the waves of the sea*" (ISAIAH 48:18).

PSALM 23:3—THE RESTORING SANCTIFIER

- *He restores my soul* (Lord, when I'm lonely—**restore me**): David wanted God to mend the broken pieces of whatever made him lonely— perhaps a disagreement, being "out of sorts," feeling distant, losing the comfortable and familiar, or some other heartache. So David said, "Lord, I need restoration. I want to feel Your presence again, have Your peace, and be complete once more."

- *He leads me in the paths of righteousness for His name's sake* (Lord, when I'm lonely—**sanctify me**): Did you notice "*for His name's sake*"? David was saying, "Whatever I do, I want to do it in the Name of the Lord." That is sanctification—doing everything as set apart for the glory, Name, Person, and character of God. Many do terrible things in the name of loneliness; they don't understand God wants to use loneliness to lead us into righteousness for His Name's sake. So David said, "Lord, when I'm all alone, set me apart; help me see that You take something away to be closest to me. Make this a sacred time of coming close to You through the sweetest communion, companionship, and completion possible because You made me for Yourself, and want to sanctify me."

PSALM 23:4—THE PROTECTING GUIDE

- *Yea, though I walk through the valley of the shadow of death* (Lord, when I'm lonely—**walk close to me**): The *"valley of the shadow of death"* is not only a beautiful picture of going to the grave and into the presence of the Lord, but also a picture from the Middle East of a dangerous little canyon travelers had to pass through. On tours to Israel, I've guided people down different stretches of those ravines. We first walked on a small ledge for two miles before going down a gorge. As we went down that cliff there was a great drop-off on one side and a straight precipitous cliff going up another way. When shepherds led their flock, sheep had to closely follow behind them due to many dangers, including attackers. So David said, "When I'm all alone, it's a dangerous time, like in the Valley of the Shadow of Death. Lord, show me Your perfect path; I want to know Your presence and follow You as I walk."

- *I will fear no evil* (Lord, when I'm lonely—**protect me**): Like David, we need to often ask for protection when we're alone. In the 1980s, I was a corporate salesman for many years while I was in seminary. I lived in nice hotels on the road, and made a good wage. Because there are many things a person could do with that money, I remember always saying, "Lord, when I'm lonesome—protect me. I don't want to do anything dishonoring to You. I trust You, and will fear no evil."

- *For You are with me* (Lord, when I'm lonely—**remind me of Your presence**): David asked, "When I'm alone, keep my eyes on You by reminding me of Your presence!" Walking through *"the valley of the shadow of death"* can be fearsome if we don't keep our eyes on the Lord Who said, *"I will never leave you nor forsake you."* So we may boldly say: 'The LORD is my helper; I will not fear' " (HEBREWS 13:5–6).

- *Your rod and Your staff, they comfort me* (Lord, when I'm lonely—**console me**): The shepherd's club and crook are viewed as comforting instruments of protection and direction, respectively.[29] But this can also refer to the Lord's chastening and rebuke. In either case, David trusted God and looked to Him for needed comfort and reassurance in his alone times.

PSALM 23:5—THE SUPPLYING FRIEND

- *You prepare a table before me in the presence of my enemies* (Lord, when I'm lonely—**fill me with Your peace**): The metaphor here is that when an enemy is nearby, sheep can't eat because they are so consumed with fear their wool even falls off. As David thought about that he said, "In the presence of my enemies, the only way it would work to set a table before me is if You first calm me down." When we're feeling totally alone, sometimes we get desperate and cry out, "I just have to do *something* …" When feelings like that arise, if You ask Him, the Lord will graciously calm your heart. For Jesus said, *"Let not your heart be troubled"* (JOHN 14:6). When loneliness stalks, He is the Ultimate Calmer.

- *You anoint my head with oil* (Lord, when I'm lonely—**fill me with Your Spirit**): The metaphor of oil on the head was the anointing of the Spirit. David was saying, "Lord, when I'm all alone, empower me to go forward, to make right decisions, and to go Your way." God's power is vital to accomplish what we can't do normally—what we can't do humanly (JOHN 14:5).

- *My cup runs over* (Lord, when I'm lonely—**fill me to overflowing**): David knew the only cure for loneliness was the companionship of another Who understood what he was going through—the Lord. *Jesus said, "If anyone thirsts, let him come to Me and drink. He who believes in Me, as the Scripture has said, out of his heart will flow rivers of living water"* (JOHN 7:37–38). This is the joy that never runs out! God wants our lives to be full and overflowing as we minister to others. Daily life should not consist of "barely making it." David said, "Lord, when I'm lonely, make me overflow with joy, comfort, restfulness, and assurance. I want to go Your way, so I'm sanctifying my time for Your glory."

PSALM 23:6—THE ETERNAL PROVIDER

- *Surely goodness and mercy shall follow me all the days of my life*
  (Lord, when I'm lonely—**surround me**): I love this! Since the Lord was
  David's personal Shepherd, where was He? Right out in front! Sheep are
  never driven like a herd of cattle, they are led. The Good Shepherd was
  leading the way—and goodness and mercy were bringing up the rear.
  David was saying, "Lord, surround me with Your grace and blessing!"
  Christ's goodness and mercy always accompany us as He leads, for *of
  His fullness we have all received, and grace for grace* (JOHN 1:16).

- *And I will dwell in the house of the LORD forever* (Lord, when I'm
  lonely—**point me heavenward**): David asked the Lord, "Remind me
  that I'm not supposed to have a flower-strewn pathway all through life
  because this world is not my real home. I know You are preparing a
  place for me,[30] and when I'm lonely I have a pang, a longing, a desire
  to look heavenward even more!" God wants us to set our affections on
  things above, not on earth.[31] In times of aloneness, it is good to pray,
  "Lord, help me get my perspective heavenward!"

In closing, I exhort you to ask God to give you the same desires David had.
Tell Him you want to experience what David experienced—to echo each of
his affirmations and make them your own testimony. You may wish to also
make this your heart's prayer:

Dear Heavenly Father, when I'm lonely like David was in Psalm 23,
I need You to:

- shepherd me,
- satisfy me,
- calm me,
- lead me,
- restore me,
- sanctify me,
- walk close to me,
- protect me,
- remind me of Your presence,
- console me,
- fill me with Your peace,

- fill me with Your Spirit,
- fill me to overflowing,
- surround me, and
- point me heavenward!

I hereby consecrate myself to You, oh Lord, and ask for Your empowerment to be pleasing to You in my every thought, word, and deed! In Jesus' name I pray. Amen.

How to Stand Alone for God | 5

1 Samuel 17; Psalms 8, 132, 101

"This day the Lord will deliver you [Goliath] into my hand ... that all the earth may know that there is a God in Israel ... for the battle is the Lord's."

—1 Samuel 17:46–47

W HAT WOULD YOU LIKE TO have written on your tombstone?[32] After you've died, whenever people think of you, what do you want them to remember most about you?

If God sent down an order to the monument company to write out an inscription to commemorate your life, what wording would He send? Wouldn't you love for Him to write an epitaph like David's about you? Look again at the marker that captures his entire life in just nine words:[33]

When **David had served God's purpose in his own generation,**
he fell asleep; he was buried with his fathers and his body decayed
(Acts 13:36 NIV).

Acts 13:36 sums up what a servant is: David served God's purpose for his life. He was God-hearted, which meant he had a loyal heart to serve the Lord.

So when the life of the greatest recorded servant in the Bible ended, what was his legacy? (A legacy is what we leave behind to those we love.) What did David, God's servant, leave behind?

David's legacy was this: he was willing to stand alone for God's honor—regardless of the cost. And there were few more lonely spots in the history of the universe than the hillside of the Valley of Elah in the "no man's land" between the armies of Israel and of the Philistines.

Haven't we all wished we could have had a bird's-eye-view of David and Goliath's titanic confrontation? If a typical screenwriter of today were to try to recapture this battle for a Hollywood movie, it would most likely be centered on one theme: a "big bully" harasses the scared "underdogs" but then one of the "underdogs" stands up to the "big bully" and slays him. Thus "right" wins out over "might." However, that would be man's perspective and not God's.

To fully profit from the story of David and Goliath, we need to understand God's eyewitness to one of the greatest moments in biblical history. It was an account unseen by all but David—when God defeated Goliath—the most visible representation of all God is *not*.

In 1 Samuel 17, I believe we see the godliest characteristic of David's life. If you were ever to emulate a quality in a man's personality, this would be it!

David did something in that chapter most people don't catch because they focus on the main characters: David and Goliath. Hence the deeper truths of Scripture get obscured due to looking at the details and not the big picture—God's perspective.

David's Purpose—God's Glory

IT WASN'T THE PHILISTINES, IT wasn't the giant, and it wasn't the fear the Israelites felt. Nor was it the incompetence of the soldiers or the jealousy of David's brothers. It wasn't any of those things—and it certainly wasn't little stones, a sling, a small stream, or the Valley of Elah. That is not what the story of David and Goliath is about: it primarily concerns David's discovery of his entire purpose and motivation for life.

Let's go back in our minds to the crisp, cool air of a Middle Eastern morning 3,000 years ago to recapture the events that comprised this momentous occasion in David's life:

The Background: Two callused feet slipped quietly out from under the warmth of a wool fleece and deftly into the sandals left carefully beside the low wooden cot. In the twilight of early morning's predawn darkness, the possibly red-headed, teenaged-boy carefully crept out of the stone house on the outskirts of Bethlehem.

With the confidence of integrity and the joy of purity—young David was on his way to a moment never to fade from the pages of history.

Walking excitedly up and down the rocky paths in the hills of Judah, the young shepherd boy was headed to the Valley of Elah, a mere eight miles away. Arriving before breakfast, young David eagerly surveyed the eastern rim of the valley. Campfires and tents dotted the hillside as he looked at the army of God's people, Israel. With a heart filled with gratitude and wonder, David strode up to the first tent and asked if anyone knew where his brothers from Bethlehem were camping. The special provisions his dad had sent them needed to be delivered, but they were only a part of David's purpose in coming.

David longed to see the people who stood for his God. But even more, he so loved the God of Israel that he wanted to see Him at work. For David had sung of his God on his long vigils around the hills of Bethlehem caring for his father's sheep. In fact, in his favorite song from the hills where he sat day after day as a shepherd boy—he sang of the Lord Himself as being his Shepherd. And so, with that Psalm 23 heart, David came as "God's man" for this very climactic moment in history!

I've actually had the joyful privilege of standing in that valley and preaching on 1 Samuel 17.[34] The Valley of Elah is a broad plain, about a quarter mile wide, with a steep hill on both sides, and down the middle runs a very small stream. Up on one hill (like sheep grazing) were the massive armies of the Philistines; on the other side (like fearful little ants) was the Israelite army. Between the two enemies was sort of a battlefield upon which everyone had been focusing for forty days, morning and evening, as Goliath came forward and took his stand to taunt the terrified Israelites over and over again (1 SAMUEL 17:16).

At this point, the stage had been set for God to reveal the young shepherd's entire purpose and motivation for life. At his father's request, David, full of enthusiasm and anticipation, trotted up the hill to deliver supplies for his brothers.

The Big Picture: Suddenly, David's talk with his brothers abruptly ended as a loud voice brimming with evil rumbled up the hillsides of that valley. In the distance Goliath, God's enemy, encased in a pillar of armor, sprayed the venom of the ancient serpent from Eden across the faithless and frightened people of God.

Standing just above the height of a basketball rim, Goliath was a full three feet taller than Michael Jordan. He easily weighed over 400 pounds and was dressed in layers of shining armor of bronze that weighed in at another 150-plus pounds. Then at the end of an eight-foot-long pole was a metal spear point that weighed about 20 pounds. Goliath was equipped with the latest military weaponry and was a horrifying sight, so they all ran from him in great fear.

But young David had just heard for the first time this irreverent pagan reviling the God of Heaven—and he was shocked, grieved, and angered. Instantly, he wanted to stand for the honor of God at all costs. Unafraid, and with no concern for self, he embodied what God can do with all who think only of the Lord and not of themselves.

David also heard the men of Israel saying, *"Have you seen this man who has come up? Surely he has come up* **to defy Israel***"* (1 SAMUEL 17:25). He perceived that in essence they were saying, "Look at that guy! He's daring to defy us!" The idea that Goliath was simply defying Israel is sheer human wisdom.

David knew their human motivation for battling Goliath was self-serving: "If I can just defeat that giant, look at all I can get out of this—*'the man who kills him the king will enrich with* **great riches**, *will* **give him his daughter**, *and* **give his father's house exemption from taxes in Israel**' " (1 SAMUEL 17:25).

Now look at the divine perspective where David got to the heart of the matter: *David spoke to the men who stood by him, saying, "What shall be done for the man who kills this Philistine and takes away the reproach from Israel? For* **who is this uncircumcised Philistine, that he should defy the armies of the living God?***"* (1 SAMUEL 17:26).

Pay close attention to what David was saying because he was the *only person out of all Israel* who really understood what was happening. He was looking way beyond what was seen on the surface. David's view of this confrontation was from a divine perspective: Goliath wasn't taunting ISRAEL—but the LIVING GOD!

Did you catch that? As the cowering army of Israel stood on their hillside looking down at this ten-foot-high evil monster, they concluded, "He's defying Israel!" But this teenager courageously put them to shame when he said, "What's going to be done about this guy who is defying GOD?" David had hit the nail on the head, so to speak. In the entire battle arena, only he had been offended on God's behalf.

David's invincible motivation to honor the Lord clearly showed up in these verses:

> David said to the Philistine, "You come to me with a sword, with a spear, and with a javelin. But **I come to you in the name of the LORD of hosts**, the God of the armies of Israel, **whom you have defied**. This day the LORD will deliver you into my hand, and I will strike you and take your head from you. And this day I will give the carcasses of the camp of the Philistines to the birds of the air and the wild beasts of the earth, that **all the earth may know that there is a God in Israel**. Then all this assembly shall know that the LORD does not save with sword and spear; for **the battle is the LORD's**, and He will give you into our hands" (1 SAMUEL 17:45–47).

What a thrill it was to get to stand in that place and read those words! As I looked around, I could easily envision David as a short teenager looking up, up, up to the tip of Goliath's huge head! That would be like looking up at a basketball backboard as a little tyke when you can barely get the ball off the ground! So there's little David looking up ten feet in the air at the "hoop" (the huge Philistine who filled that space) and unflinchingly shouting: "You big bully! I don't care if you *have* taunted the Israelites—they've forgotten to Whom they belong, and where they are standing. If nobody else is concerned about God's Name—*I'll* be!"

Why do you think the Lord vindicated David so greatly that day? Nobody else really understood what was going on in the Valley of Elah—only that young shepherd boy who had arrived on the scene at the last moment. Thus he definitely had command of the situation when he strode down that valley, fearlessly looked up into that ominous giant's face, and boldly declared: "I want the whole world to know that Israel has a *Living and True God!*"

Without a doubt, the events of that day are indelibly sketched in our hearts and minds: the shepherd lad, a handful of stones, a homemade weapon, and GOD—who made an unbeatable army of One. When David defeated the giant he became an instant and enduring hero of all the ages. Why? Because David had begun thirsting to intimately know and serve God when he was still a young shepherd lad.

If we were to summarize David's entire purpose and motivation for life, it shows up here in 1 Samuel 17: *David was utterly concerned with God's honor, not his own.*

Lessons on Standing Alone for God

HERE ARE A FEW MORE insights into what made David the greatest servant of God in all history:

David could stand alone because he had God-consciousness. Most people observing David and Goliath saw only two people facing one another on the battlefield. But David saw *one more*—the Lord! He felt the presence of God, and that made all the difference! Just as he had sung on the lonely hillsides as a shepherd boy, David probably sang: *I will fear no evil; for You are with me* (PSALM 23:4)!

What David had thought, believed, and sung to the Lord was a reality in his life. God was as real to confident David as the fearsome giant Goliath was to the quaking Israelite army. David *knew* the battle was the *Lord's*!

David was enabled to stand alone because he had God-consciousness and saw that the Lord was with him, as did these other great Old Testament saints:

- Joseph saw God 800 years earlier when he faced Potiphar's wife and blurted out: "How can I do this evil in God's sight?" (see GENESIS 39:7–9).

- Moses saw God 400 years earlier when he chose *rather to suffer affliction with the people of God than to enjoy the passing pleasures of sin, esteeming the reproach of Christ greater riches than the treasures in Egypt … for he endured as seeing Him who is invisible.* (HEBREWS 11:25–27). In other words, Moses could *see* the God Who is invisible to those who are without faith.

- Joshua saw God at the crossing of the dried up Jordan River: [God dried up the waters] *that all the peoples of the earth may know the hand of the LORD, that it is mighty, that you may fear the LORD your God forever"* (JOSHUA 4:24).

- Solomon saw God at the temple as he prayed: *"When they sin against You (for there is no one who does not sin), and You become angry with them and deliver them to the enemy, and they take them captive to the land of the enemy, far or near; … when they return to You with all their heart and with all their soul in the land of their enemies who led them away captive, … forgive Your people … and grant them compassion … that all the peoples of the earth may know that the LORD is God; there is no other"* (1 KINGS 8:46, 48, 50, 60).

- Hezekiah saw God during the threat of Assyria: *"Now therefore, O LORD our God, I pray, save us from his hand, that all the kingdoms of the earth may know that You are the LORD God, You alone"* (2 KINGS 19:19).

Like all these saints who had God-consciousness, we need to recognize that the Lord is watching over us as well. Our lonely trials of life are not our problems alone—the battles are really *God's*. That kind of faith changes everything!

David could stand alone because he had perseverance. What is amazing about David is that, despite his youth, he stood alone for God in the face of these challenging obstacles:

- **David's oldest brother verbally abused him**: *Eliab's anger was aroused against David, and he said, "Why did you come down here? And with whom have you left those few sheep in the wilderness? I know your pride and the insolence of your heart, for you have come down to see the battle"* (1 SAMUEL 17:28). But David wouldn't be defeated by unfounded criticism.

- **King Saul tried to discourage David**: *Saul said to David, "You are not able to go against this Philistine to fight with him; for you are a youth, and he a man of war from his youth"* (1 SAMUEL 17:33). But David wouldn't be defeated by unfounded fears.

- **The giant Goliath cursed David**: He said, *"Am I a dog, that you come to me with sticks?" And the Philistine cursed David by his gods* (1 SAMUEL 17:43). But David would not let unfounded criticisms and fears deter him. Neither would he be defeated by an unholy, God-defying pagan! David went onward to victory!

In the face of his critics, even those of his own family, David chose to stand alone for God's honor. In the presence of his own king discouraging him, David continued to stand alone for God's honor. And, in the face of the very enemy of God who was calling down the devil's legions with his curses, David still stood his ground. But he was never *really* alone because God stood with him, beside him, and in front of him.

In the face of criticisms, fears, and abuse from others, are you able to stand alone for God's honor? Do you do what's right because you know you're not *really* alone? Like David in Psalm 23:1, you can say, *"I will fear no evil; for You are with me."*

David could stand alone because he had a divine perspective. Goliath represented more than a formidable military challenge—he embodied evil. His armor was described as having "scales" like the snake Satan embodied while tempting Adam and Eve. David recognized the true spiritual nature of Goliath's challenge and accepted it with the correct underlying perspective that *"all the earth may know that there is a God in Israel"* (1 SAMUEL 17:46).

Every time I read or hear that phrase, I love it! It shows up not only in verse 46 but also in Daniel and various other places in Israel's history. Why? God is constantly looking for loyal men and women through whom He can show Himself strong (2 CHRONICLES 16:9). The Lord seeks servants who are more concerned about His honor than their own—who are more concerned about His Name than theirs—who are more concerned about magnifying God in a world where He is belittled. And if God wasn't belittled in this situation with Goliath, then He will *never* be belittled.

These Israelites—representatives of the covenant, representatives of the redeemed, representatives of God's Name—were cowering in front of an uncircumcised pagan, an idol-worshiping nobody! These representatives of the Almighty God of the Universe let themselves become engrossed in what they might personally get out of killing Goliath. As a result, their focus switched to planning tactical strategies and they missed the whole heart of the matter: GOD was being derided. As His chosen people they had a responsibility to stand up for His honor, but only David heartily and willingly did so.

After David slew Goliath, the Spirit of the Lord came upon him and he penned a song of praise and worship. The most ancient Jewish Targums (paraphrases of the Hebrew Old Testament into Aramaic from the time of Ezra onward) specifically point to Psalm 8 as being about David and Goliath.

To the Chief Musician. On the instrument of Gath. A Psalm of David.

¹ *O Lord, our Lord,*
How excellent is Your name in all the earth,
Who have set Your glory above the heavens!

² *Out of the mouth of babes and nursing infants*
You have ordained strength,
Because of Your enemies,
That You may silence the enemy and the avenger.

³ *When I consider Your heavens, the work of Your fingers,*
The moon and the stars, which You have ordained,
⁴ *What is man that You are mindful of him,*
And the son of man that You visit him?
⁵ *For You have made him a little lower than the angels,*
And You have crowned him with glory and honor.

⁶ *You have made him to have dominion over the works of Your hands;*
You have put all things under his feet,
⁷ *All sheep and oxen—*
Even the beasts of the field,
⁸ *The birds of the air,*
And the fish of the sea
That pass through the paths of the seas.

⁹ *O Lord, our Lord,*
How excellent is Your name in all the earth!

The words in the manuscripts before Psalm 9 are actually the ending of Psalm 8. *Muthlabben* means "death of champion" and was paraphrased in the Targums referring to David's killing the "man of the space between the camps" in 1 Samuel 17:4. That "no man's land" between Israel's camp on one mountaintop and the Philistine camp on the other was dominated by Goliath, but conquered by David.

I encourage you to look at Psalm 8 as also being about Jesus Christ Who, when He came to save us, was made "*a little lower than the angels*" and crowned "*with glory and honor.*" David was a picture of Christ Who faced the enemy that held God's people captive in fear—and slew him. This reflects Hebrews 2:14–15 which says Jesus destroyed *him who had the power of death, that is, the devil.*

What a beautiful picture of Christ coming to destroy the works of Satan to set His children free! And much like Satan was defeated by Christ's coming to earth, David may have sung this psalm while in Saul's court to comfort him when the demons troubled him.

After the events of 1 Samuel 17 were over, David also wrote this next song—Psalm 132.

Psalm 132—Strength to Conquer Adversity

PSALM 132 IS TITLED "A Song of Ascents." The Targums say this psalm was David's spiritual secret of what made him a huge giant of faith. Psalm 132 explains youthful habits that fortified David to be able to conquer Goliath, withstand a life of hardship, and be so useful in serving God's purpose for his life. This quality also made him strong enough to live on the run while hiding out from King Saul, and then become a great king after God's heart.

When David started walking with the Lord as a young boy, choices he made impacted his entire life. Even little, incremental choices become big later in life[35]—like someone who commits to "one more push-up" daily and before long develops strong muscles.

Psalm 132 may have been written as a re-consecration to God after being anointed to be the next king, or later when he actually started his career as King David, remembered God's faithfulness in his youth, and once again affirmed his dedication to the Lord. Now let's look at some key truths from this psalm.

David put God ahead of comfort: *"Surely I will not go into the chamber of my house, or go up to the comfort of my bed; I will not give sleep to my eyes or slumber to my eyelids, until I find a place for the LORD"* (132:3–5). Half of the Bible scholars believe this was written specifically when David was thinking about his life, wanting to bring the Ark of the Covenant home. The Ark remained in Kiriath Jiram after the Philistines had captured it in Samuel's day, and then sent it back on a cart. Because the Ark stayed in that border town, David longed to make a place for it. Second Samuel 6 tells how King David had gotten over-excited and placed the Ark on a cart, as the Philistines had, but Uzzah put out his hand to keep it from falling and God killed him. David became angry with the Lord, and afraid of Him, so the Ark was left behind. Later, after David read how it was supposed to be handled, with great gladness he brought the Ark into Jerusalem the right way.

Time for God, which took precedence over David's own personal comfort, was his holy habit for life. That was the essence of what made David so special in God's heart. He vowed: "I won't go to bed or do what comforts my body until I spend time communing with the Lord." Such a simple habit—yet practiced by so few. Without consistent, disciplined time in God's Word we cannot grow spiritually and cultivate the mind of Christ.

David personally longed for God as a young shepherd boy: "*Behold, we heard of it in Ephrathah; we found it in the fields of the woods. Let us go into His tabernacle; let us worship at His footstool*" (132:6–7). During his long shepherding hours, he greatly looked forward to his family's pilgrimage up to the tabernacle to meet with God! Three times a year, every Israelite had to make that journey to bring a special sacrifice to worship the Lord. Although his family probably kept the Sabbath and the feasts, David was unique because he had a deep, personal longing for God. Do you? Or do you go to church because someone makes you? If you want to know the Lord intimately, ask Him to satisfy and complete you with a passion like David's to worship and serve Him. Reality in spiritual life only comes from an intense longing of our hearts for God.

David wanted to be clothed with righteousness: "*Let Your priests be clothed with righteousness*" (132:9a). David was looking back to when he was a young boy desiring to be clothed with that righteousness. Consecration was his choice; by how he lived, David wanted to go before God as a holy priest. Peter said that as living stones, we *are being built up a spiritual house, a holy priesthood, to offer up spiritual sacrifices acceptable to God through Jesus Christ* (1 PETER 4:5).

Would you like to shake things up and have an opportunity to share Christ? If you're asked, "What do you do?"—respond with, "I'm a priest." As the person looks at your collar to see if it's turned around, say, "No, I'm a real one. I'm a holy priest, part of the kingdom of holy priests. I offer up spiritual sacrifices to God through Jesus Christ, and I'm going to serve in His temple in heaven forever!"

David had a little foretaste of that. As God's holy priesthood, we are to spend our lives bringing Him offerings of worship and deeds of sacrificial service. Are you clothed with consecrated righteousness and living each day as a holy priest? If not, I encourage you to tell the Lord, "I no longer want to put my comforts first. I'm going to consecrate myself to have a sacred time with You—like a holy priest giving to God." Then, whenever you give at church, consciously offer the fragrant aroma of your adoration as you present your offering to Him.

David engaged in corporate worship: *"Let Your saints shout for joy"* (132:9b). Using the plural word *"saints"* is David's ultimate expression of his desire for corporate worship. He was saying, "I am excited about assembling at the tabernacle for the sacred festival and to worship God corporately!" Do you wholeheartedly engage in corporate worship? When you're in the Lord's house, does your spirit *"shout for joy"* over gathering together with other saints to worship the Lord? Or are you often distracted with incidents such as being upset they didn't sing your favorite song, or the pastor spoke too long, or the congregation was too loud (or not loud enough)—and so forth?

If we're not alert to Satan's schemes[36] we can slip into habitual criticisms and miss the blessings of corporate worship. David was a seeker of the Lord; he came into the congregation of saints with such zeal he wanted to *"shout for joy."* (He stated that again in verse 16.) We all get what we *really* want and David wanted to joyfully join his heart in worshiping the Lord God Almighty.

Now then, this next psalm captures David's resolves for personal conduct and consecration when he fled to the Lord as his Refuge from the sins of his youth.

Psalm 101—David's Pathway to a Godly Life

THIS PSALM MAY HAVE BEEN written as a resolve for David's young years, or later when he started his career as king and was testifying to God's past faithfulness and reaffirming his consecration to the Lord.

Here are some key truths from Psalm 101—David's pathway to a godly life through personal choices or resolves of holiness to God.

David sought personal integrity: *I will behave wisely in a perfect way. Oh, when will You come to me? I will walk within my house with a perfect heart* (101:2b). When a person acts the same way in public as in private, that is integrity. There's a great disconnect in our culture between public and private personas, but David wanted integrity to characterize his walk and behavior before God.

David made a personal pact of purity: *I will set nothing wicked before my eyes; I hate the work of those who fall away; it shall not cling to me* (101:3). He was saying, "Wickedness will never be a conscious, chosen part of my life. I will make a habit of scraping off anything displeasing to the Lord."

In my youth we had a horse barn. When it was my turn to clean out the barn, after finishing, because I loved my mother I'd always scrape off my boots and leave them outside. I didn't want to bring the odor of the barn into the house. Look at David's heart here: "The wickedness, the works of those who fall away, will not cling to me. When I come in from the 'barn of life' I will scrape off my boots so that nothing smelly clings to my life and displeases the Lord."

Since all of us gradually see wicked things, we should regularly heed Hebrews 9:14: *How much more shall the blood of Christ ... cleanse your conscience from dead works to serve the living God?*

Here's another applicable verse: *Let us draw near* [to God] *with a true heart in full assurance of faith, having our hearts sprinkled from an evil conscience* (HEBREWS 10:22).

David chose to limit his exposure to evil and things that would displease the Lord: *A perverse heart shall depart from me; I will not know wickedness* (101:4). He vowed: "I choose to limit my exposure to evil—things that displease the Lord. By no means will I allow myself to be intimately acquainted with wickedness." For me personally, I remember the time I chose to no longer listen to even conservative radio talk shows. When they continually talked and laughed about Monica Lewinsky, and everything going on with President Clinton, I decided it would be far more profitable for me to be as a child when it comes to iniquity. We are not to be experts in sin and smugly know every detail. We are to be sheltered from it.

David kept his eyes on the faithful: *My eyes shall be on the faithful of the land, that they may dwell with me; he who walks in a perfect way, he shall serve me* (101:6). Do you think David grew up in Bethlehem with a poster of Goliath on his wall? I don't think so. He emulated proper heroes. Do we have proper heroes today? Very few because, as Randy Alcorn (a great Christian author) says in his book on purity,[37] the American culture is getting immune to what is illicit and immoral. You need to limit your exposure to anything displeasing to the Lord; don't allow yourself to know iniquity. God will not have His eyes on those who do evil.

David had a lifelong plan to purge evil from around him: *Early I will destroy all the wicked of the land, that I may cut off all the evildoers from the city of the LORD* (101:8). David was talking about the Canaanite influence when the Israelites conquered the land. Archaeological digs discovered the Jews had put little idols in the gates of the city, and that would have required constant purging. In today's culture, rather than going out and smashing everything bad, I prefer to apply this verse by having a lifelong plan to purge evil from around me—getting rid of whatever is unacceptable in God's presence. Just as Paul told the Ephesians to burn anything to do with Satan, so we must rid our homes, cars, computers, lives, and minds of any pornographic or occultic books, videos, games, and music.

With the direction modern games are headed, most people won't even be afraid if they see a real demon. After all, they've been watching them for a long time as entertainment. Have you noticed that new releases try to exceed previous ones with even more hideous graphic images? It's no wonder young people aren't afraid of hell, demons, or future judgment. They are already into doom—playing it and thinking it—and those images are ever before them.

But David said, "I'm going to purge all evil from my life by having proper heroes, limiting my exposure to evil, and scraping off anything that doesn't please God." The issue is not what your church, youth leader, parents, or anyone else considers as evil. The higher standard—the True Standard—is whether what you allow pleases the Lord. That depends on whether you purpose to consistently choose God over personal comforts and pleasures.

If you've never made vows for personal conduct and consecration, don't long for God and don't want to be clothed with His righteousness, and don't love engaging in corporate worship, it could be you've compartmentalized your life. Perhaps you're not seeking a personal pact of purity, and have set evil things before your eyes. Everyone does, but is it a choice you regularly make? We see evil around us all the time. It's not possible to be in the world without getting defiled. But when you consciously seek it, God says it deadens your spiritual life. God's way is to be clothed with righteousness—Christ's. If you seek to learn these lessons, you will find them to be blessedly true! What psalms! What messages!

Truths God Can Use in Our Lives

IN ANY GIVEN SITUATION, IT is rare to find someone who will think: *What would God do in this instance? What would magnify His Name the most?* But if you *are* willing to stand alone in God's power, for His glory, this is what will happen:

God will use you to accomplish His purposes, even if you have seemingly little to offer. When you seek to accomplish the Lord's work, your motivation and faith in God is far more significant than your talent or resources. Even David, a man after God's heart, appeared to have little to offer as a young shepherd boy. Yet, he still acted as God's representative. David used his training and primitive tools to reveal Israel's God to the world of his day. He used a simple sling to throw a stone at a man who had the best military technology an advanced culture could offer, yet he triumphed when the Lord honored David's first stone throw. There's no limit to what can be accomplished through God's power!

God will use your particular gifts and talents to influence our culture for Him. David faithfully did whatever God had qualified and gifted him to do. Because he was motivated by righteousness, he made a powerful impact on his culture. To impact your own culture for Christ, rather than be concerned about your *ability*, focus on your *availability* to be used by the Lord as He sees fit. He has already given you all the gifts and talents necessary to accomplish His purpose for your life.[38] You don't have to try to be anything other than whom He created you to be.

God will work through you by using every resource to accomplish His purposes. This includes the tools and technology of your culture (its "iron"). The Israelites achieved a decisive victory over the Philistines when David killed Goliath. Unfortunately, the Philistines remained the superior culture for a long time afterward (1 Samuel 31). Only when the Israelites, under the reign of faithful King David, harnessed the Philistines' advanced iron technology and used it for God's purposes did they become a great influence and power. Today, Christians who hold a Bible-based value system and are able to shape and control the "iron" of their society will greatly impact their culture.[39]

What happened when David stood alone? Because of his divine perspective on life he did what others considered impossible, and God got the glory. David will forever be remembered as the servant who did all the Lord's will (1 KINGS 15:5) because he *served God's purpose for his life* (ACTS 13:36).

I encourage you to choose to be a lifelong servant of God, and that means deciding to stand alone for the Lord's honor.

- **You can stand alone for God by denying ungodliness.** When necessary, will you stand alone for God at work, at school, and at home? Whenever the conversation, entertainment, or activities begin to dishonor the Lord's Name, will you stand against it? God has called us to deny ungodliness in any form: *For the grace of God that brings salvation has appeared to all men, teaching us that, denying ungodliness* *and worldly lusts, we should live soberly, righteously, and godly in the present age, looking for the blessed hope and glorious appearing of our great God and Savior Jesus Christ* (TITUS 2:11–13).

- **You can stand alone for God by hungering for the Lord each day.**
  Will you stand alone for God by reading His Word when you travel or perhaps are away at school? Will you do so when at home by yourself? Will you also stand for God's honor by praying over your meals whether you are eating out or no one else is home at the time? Will you stand for God by memorizing His Word instead of watching TV? Our world believes that Jesus is unimportant and that *people* are the reason to live, not *God*. The only way to counter such a horrible lie is to show that you believe what Jesus said and therefore strive to live " *'by every word that proceeds from the mouth of God'* " (MATTHEW 4:4).

After Goliath, David had a lifetime of lonely situations where he had to stand alone for God. Through it all, he remained humble and disciplined, and he magnified God's hand in his life. In every trial he leaned upon God and demonstrated faith. When he was afraid, and felt all alone, he rose above it by trusting the Lord and triumphing through God's power!

Did David ever grow out of being God's servant? No, he stayed that way to the end. Having **a heart to stand alone** for God's honor is absolutely essential if you long to serve God's purpose for your life. If His honor is the highest priority, there's nothing you can't accomplish for Christ. That is why David is such a vivid example of how to serve the Lord.

I pray that you, too, will develop his all-consuming passion to stand up for God!

STAND UP, STAND UP FOR JESUS

Stand up, stand up for Jesus,
*   Ye soldiers of the cross;*
Lift high His royal banner,
*   It must not suffer loss.*
From vict'ry unto vict'ry
*   His army shall He lead,*
'Til every foe is conquered
*   And Christ is Lord indeed.*

Stand up, stand up for Jesus,
    The trumpet call obey;
Forth to the mighty conflict,
    In this His glorious day.
Ye that are men now serve Him
    Against unnumbered foes;
Let courage rise with danger
    And strength to strength oppose.

Stand up, stand up for Jesus,
    Stand in His strength alone;
The arm of flesh will fail you,
    Ye dare not trust your own.
Put on the gospel armor,
    Each piece put on with prayer;
Where duty calls, or danger
    Be never wanting there.

Stand up, stand up for Jesus,
    The strife will not be long;
This day the noise of battle,
    The next the victor's song.
To him that overcometh
    A crown of life shall be;
He with the King of glory
    Shall reign eternally.

—George Duffield, Jr. (1818–1888)

6 | Finding Strength in Hard Times

1 Samuel 19:11–18; 20:35–42; Psalms 59, 11, 64

To You, O my Strength, I will sing praises; for God is my defense, my God of mercy. —**Psalm 59:17**

CONFLICT CAN AFFLICT PEOPLE IN every stratum of society.[40] Even we who know and love the Lord experience that hollow aching from someone or something missing from our lives. But as God's children, we do not suffer without hope. For Jesus, Who *came to His own, and His own did not receive Him,*[41] empathizes with our painful loneliness. He was despised and rejected by humanity, yet as our sin-bearer on the cross Jesus willingly faced divine wrath and the ultimate loneliness—alienation from God—to destroy the works of Satan to set us free.

In his excellent book, *Growing Strong in the Seasons of Life,* Charles Swindoll has this to say about loneliness:

[Loneliness] is the most desolate word in all human language. It is capable of hurling the heaviest weights the heart can endure.

It plays no favorites, ignores all rules of courtesy, knows neither border nor barrier, yields no mercy, refuses all bargains, and holds the clock in utter contempt. It cannot be bribed; it will not be left behind.

Crowds only make it worse, activity simply drives it deeper. Silent and destructive as a flooding river in the night, it leaves its slimy banks, seeps into our dwelling, and rises to a crest of despair. Tears fall from our eyes as groans fall from our lips—but loneliness, that uninvited guest of the soul, arrives at dusk and stays for dinner.

There is simply no other anguish like the consuming anguish of loneliness. Ask the inmate in prison this evening … or the uniformed man thousands of miles at sea or in some bar tonight … or the divorcee in that apartment … or the one who just buried his or her life's companion … or the couple whose arms ache for the child recently taken … or even the single, career-minded person who prepares a meal for one and goes to bed early, *alone,* surrounded by the mute memory of yesterday's song and today's disappointment.[42]

Loneliness has many forms, but it has one purpose. Since God made us for Himself, He longs to satisfy and complete us by using our righteous responses in loneliness to draw us closer to Him. David has been made our prime Old Testament example of how to be such a God-hearted servant—even when our whole world feels like it's crashing in all around us and there's no escape!

David's Faithfulness in Lonely Times

ALTHOUGH IT'S BEEN 3,000 YEARS since David's time, his fervor for life and deep desire to please the Lord can still thrill our souls—if we do more than casually read the facts about his life as if they're about someone long ago and have no relevance for us today.

David's life was carved into the bedrock of God's Word for a wonderful purpose. Through his godly responses in trials, the Lord was giving Divine Truth to help us learn how to be overcomers in our own periods of loneliness. In fact, the Holy Spirit inspired David to write thirty-one psalms that captured how the Lord was his Refuge in his greatest challenges during these lonely stages of David's life: the growing years, the struggling years, the strong years, and the waning years of old age. Here's a chronological list of his biggest events and the songs he is believed to have penned in each:

DAVID SUFFERED INTENSE LONELINESS IN HIS GROWING YEARS—
- **He was overlooked, ignored, and disliked by his family** (1 Samuel 16–18). As a young shepherd boy David wrote **Psalms 19** and **23.**

After he slew Goliath, he wrote **Psalm 8**. **Psalm 132** explained youthful habits that had strengthened him for conquering such adversity. And in **Psalm 101** David revealed a list of resolves for his growing years—his pathway to a godly life.

DAVID SUFFERED INTENSE LONELINESS IN HIS STRUGGLING YEARS—

- **He endured family conflict and danger** (1 SAMUEL 19:11–18; 20:35–42). When King Saul wanted to kill him, David's wife became caught up in picking sides. In that time of feeling alone, David wrote **Psalm 59**. After Jonathan warned him to flee Saul's wrath, he felt even more lonely and wrote **Psalms 11** and **64**—how to overcome feelings of loneliness when suffering family problems and danger.

- **He lost his job and was separated from his family** (1 SAMUEL 21:1–9). As David fled to Ahimelech the priest, he wrote **Psalm 52**—how to overcome feelings of loneliness when experiencing a loss of work, home, and family.

- **He faced the unexpected twist of duress in a new location** (1 SAMUEL 21:10–12, 13–15). When David fled from Saul to the Philistine city of Gath and was captured, he wrote **Psalm 56**, which most likely was while he was in prison. After he feigned madness before the king and was sent away, he wrote **Psalm 34** reflecting his thoughts as he appeared before Achish—how to overcome feelings of loneliness and fear in a foreign situation.

- **He felt abandoned by God and then lived and worked with a troubled crowd** (1 SAMUEL 22:1–4). After David fled Gath, and before he arrived at the cave of Adullam in 1 Samuel 22:1, because he felt abandoned by everyone, including God, he wrote **Psalm 13**. He then penned **Psalm 40** depicting life in the pits and the pathway out. (**Psalm 70**, nearly identical to Psalm 40:13–17, is reflective of this time.)

  Upon entering the cave, he was joined by an incredibly difficult group of criminals and societal rejects. **Psalm 57** was a turning point in David's life because God refined his character through his cave troubles more than at any other time. **Psalm 142** then applied what he'd learned in Psalm 57—how to overcome feelings of loneliness and depression during troublesome times.

- **He had constant insecurities and huge responsibilities** (1 SAMUEL 22:5; 23:1–14). When hiding from Saul in the forest of Hereth with hundreds of men to care for, David's insecurities were compounded when they went to battle against the Philistines to rescue the city of Keilah. During this time period he wrote **Psalm 17**—how to overcome feelings of loneliness from having no sure place to live, no reliable source of income, and huge responsibilities.

- **He was betrayed by men he trusted** (1 SAMUEL 23:15–29; 1 SAMUEL 24). Not only did the men of Keilah, whom David had just rescued, want to deliver him over to Saul, but also the Ziphites as he went into hiding in the mountains of Ziph. During this time he wrote **Psalm 54**—how to overcome feelings of loneliness when betrayed by trusted friends. While living in the cave at En Gedi he then wrote **Psalms 35–36** to praise the Lord for being the avenger of His people.

- **He was wronged in a business deal** (1 SAMUEL 25). In the Wilderness of Paran, as he faced the danger of his anger toward Nabal *"the fool,"* David wrote **Psalm 53**—how to overcome feelings of loneliness when tempted to be bitter over being hurt in a business deal.

- **He suddenly lost his family, friends, and finances** (1 SAMUEL 30). Grieved and feeling endangered over the raid on his family and the city of Ziklag, David wrote **Psalms 16** and **39**—how to overcome feelings of loneliness when threatened with a great loss.

DAVID SUFFERED INTENSE LONELINESS IN HIS STRONG YEARS—
- **He was tempted and failed miserably** (2 SAMUEL 11:27–12:14). From the depths of conviction after his fall into sin with Bathsheba, David wrote **Psalms 38 and 32**—how to overcome feelings of loneliness when tempted and failing.

- **He was painfully chastised and then restored** (2 SAMUEL 12). As a result of the pain of chastisement leading to repentance and restoration, David sang of his faithful God in **Psalm 51**—how to overcome feelings of loneliness when going through chastisement and restoration.

- **He had to suffer the inevitable consequences of his sin** (2 SAMUEL 15:13–16:14). Though God forgives sins and forgets the iniquities, the consequences and losses can still be many, as David found out. One of his greatest heartaches was being deposed by a rebellious son, driven from his throne, banished from the city, and having to flee for his life. But David sang of his confidence in the Lord in **Psalms 3, 63, and 31**—how to overcome feelings of loneliness when attacked, slandered, and painfully abused.

DAVID SUFFERED INTENSE LONELINESS IN HIS WANING YEARS—
- **He had to come to terms with old age and impending death** (2 Samuel 22–23; 1 Kings 1–2). Despite the failures of the Bathsheba incident, David was truly a man after God's own heart. In the final days of his life, we see his humble obedience leading to joy as he used that time for God's glory. During this stage, David wrote **Psalms 71 and 18**—how to overcome feelings of loneliness when about to leave behind health, comforts, friends, family, and security. Psalm 18:46 gloriously summarized David's lifelong heart of praise to God: *The LORD lives! Blessed be my Rock! Let the God of my salvation be exalted.*

As a mere mortal man, David truly was so much like us. But, he learned to rise above the downward pull of his flesh and cling to the only One who could satisfy and complete him—Christ.

Loneliness in Family Conflicts and Danger

IN DAVID'S GROWING YEARS THE Lord was his Shepherd. Because a good shepherd stays with his sheep, he knew God was always with him. This was the ultimate cure for loneliness in his youth.

As a young adult, David then had to face the complex responsibilities of a job, family, and society. Everything he was inspired to write in Psalms 8, 132, and 101 that gave strength to stand alone for God and conquer adversity in his youth would now be needed more than ever!

The first big event of David's struggling years was the sudden and unexpected danger from his boss and father-in-law, King Saul, who wanted to murder him. After Saul tried to pin David to the wall with a spear, David ran away (1 SAMUEL 19:10), but Saul *sent messengers to David's house to watch him and to kill him in the morning. And Michal, David's wife, told him, saying, "If you do not save your life tonight, tomorrow you will be killed"* (1 SAMUEL 19:11).

Michal helped her husband escape through a window and deceived her father to provide time for David to get away safely. David then ran to Samuel to tell him what Saul had done to him (1 SAMUEL 19:12–18).

Can't you just feel David's heartbreaking loneliness to suddenly be thrust into this raging time of family conflict and danger? Yet, rather than let job and family pressures overcome him, he fled to the Lord and expressed his needs to Him. That is what David wrote about in Psalm 59—his pathway through loneliness to the One meant to be closest to us.

PSALM 59—THE PATHWAY THROUGH LONELINESS

To the Chief Musician. Set to "Do Not Destroy." A Michtam of David when Saul sent men, and they watched the house in order to kill him.

The above superscription is verse 1 in the Hebrew manuscript in the Bible carried by Jesus and the apostles.[43] Its wording is from 1 Samuel 19:11, which is the setting for Psalm 59. I recommend you note that reference at the top of Psalm 59 in your Bible. This method can change the way you look at the Psalms.

Because it is easy to find the book of Psalms in the middle of the Bible, most people simply open up to it and read, but rarely realize the meaning behind the psalm. What is the book of Psalms about? It is the record of the travail of the human soul; psalms express common emotions during hard times and how to find great relief in the Lord.

Psalm 59's Michtam (meditation) was set to the tune of "Do Not Destroy," and its title tells how David felt when he thought he'd be destroyed in his family conflict.

Family is an intensely precious part of life. For example, I once heard a news report about a Los Angeles man's devotion to his family as he was dying. While bleeding to death, he wrote bloody notes on a wall: **I love you honey. I love you kids.** Even though he soon fainted from blood loss, somehow he still managed to survive. Afterward, news cameras revealed the bloody notes he'd written to his family. When facing death, thinking about family and friends is normal, and David was no exception. But when thoughts of his family conflict and personal danger caused a tidal wave of sadness to crash over him, he turned to God to calm the storm within.

Psalm 59, which reflects David's lonely heart during this difficult time, is divided into three steps:[44]

STEP 1: DAVID TURNED TO GOD

¹ **Deliver me** from my enemies, O my God; **defend me** from those who rise up against me. ² **Deliver me** from the workers of iniquity, and **save me** from bloodthirsty men. ³ For look, they lie in wait for my life; the mighty gather against me, not for my transgression nor for my sin, O LORD. ⁴ They run and prepare themselves through no fault of mine. Awake to **help me**, and behold! ⁵ You therefore, O LORD God of hosts, the God of Israel, awake to punish all the nations; do not be merciful to any wicked transgressors. Selah

⁶ At evening they return, They growl like a dog, And go all around the city. ⁷ Indeed, they belch with their mouth; Swords are in their lips; for they say, "Who hears?" ⁸ But You, O LORD, shall laugh at them; You shall have all the nations in derision.

STEP 2: DAVID TRUSTED IN GOD

⁹ **I will wait for You**, O You his Strength; For God is my defense. ¹⁰ My God of mercy shall come to meet me; God shall let me see my desire on my enemies.

¹¹ Do not slay them, lest my people forget; Scatter them by Your power, and bring them down, O LORD our shield. ¹² For the sin of their mouth and the words of their lips, let them even be taken in their pride, and for the cursing and lying, which they speak. ¹³ Consume them in wrath, consume them that they may not be; and let them know that God rules in Jacob to the ends of the earth. Selah

¹⁴ And at evening they return, They growl like a dog, And go all around the city. ¹⁵ They wander up and down for food, and howl if they are not satisfied.

STEP 3: DAVID TRIUMPHED IN GOD

¹⁶ But I will sing of Your power; Yes, I will sing aloud of Your mercy in the morning; For You have been my defense and **refuge in the day of my trouble.** ¹⁷ To You, O my Strength, I will sing praises; For God is my defense, My God of mercy.

Whenever David fled to the Lord for refuge he triumphed through God's faithfulness. The good news is that Christ is our Refuge too—the safest spot in the universe!

DEFENSES AGAINST LONELINESS

Note the following truths David expressed in Psalm 59. As you read the list, ask yourself: *Are these personalized in my life?*

THE LORD IS:
- a defense (v. 9).
- mercy delivered (v. 10).
- a shield (v. 11).
- the ruler of all (v. 13).
- a defense and refuge in the day of trouble (v. 16).
- strength, defense, and mercy (v. 17).

Those are the facts. Now I want to challenge you to take the next step: learn to walk with the Lord beyond the facts. If you are like the average Christian, you are very academic in your devotional times. You have your devotions, find a truth, mark it, and close your Bible. But this fails to take the next step of going beyond the facts to *personalize what God has revealed to you through the Scriptures.*

This typical practice is rather like the challenge we men face when our daughters and wives go shopping. In general, women are browsers who love to "just look" at garage sales and in stores, but often they don't even try on or buy something. Amazing! In contrast, we men know what we want, go into a store and buy it, then leave. After all, why bother hanging around a store with a bunch of people "just looking" at all that stuff?

Most people "just look" during their Bible times; they never "try on" the Scriptures or "buy them." Instead, they just like to walk through and mark all the nice stuff: "Yes, He's a defense … merciful … a shield … ruler of all …" But then they close their Bibles, and put them away, and don't make the Scriptures really theirs.

Your Bible studies will be transformed if you "mine for gold" by digging for the hidden treasures in God's Word to apply them to your life. To "mine for gold" you must personalize the Scriptures. You must go to the checkout counter, buy them, put them in your bag, take them home, and use them. That is what Bible study is supposed to be—the final step if you want to be like God's servant David.

How can we apply God's Word to our life each day? Look at what David said in Psalm 59:9b: *"For God is ..."* What are the next words? *"my* defense." David didn't just say *"a* defense"; he personalized it by saying *"my defense."* He reached out and touched God by faith. This was David's habit since his youth. Think about the effect if he had written Psalm 23 like this: *The LORD is the shepherd; people shall not want. He makes people to lie down.* What was left out? The Lord is what? He is *my shepherd; I shall not want.*

I love to envision David singing Psalm 23 to the Lord out on the Judean hills during those long, lonely nights! *The LORD is MY Shepherd; I shall not want. He makes ME to lie down.* Do you see how intensely personal his relationship with the Lord was? It was not "third person"; it was not out there at arm's length; it wasn't hypothetical; it was experienced and highly personal. That is why David could talk about the Lord all his days, in every situation—he had a very intimate relationship with Him. Now I'm going to show you how to go through David's Psalm 59 list to personalize the verses and make them yours.

HOW TO PERSONALIZE PSALM 59

Verse 9—From your heart, say to the Lord, "Be **my** defense." Against what? You may add to this list, but for starters you could say, "Be my defense against loneliness, temptation, uncleanness, weariness, helplessness, ..."

Verse 10a—This verse means "Deliver mercy to **me.**" Do you know the difference between grace and mercy? Grace is getting what we don't deserve; mercy is not getting what we do deserve. David was saying, "Deliver mercy to me; remind me I'm not going to get what I deserve in this situation." Most of the time, we deserve to be in hell for what we've done against God. Therefore, the first way Satan tries to neutralize us is to make us doubt and deprecate our salvation. He doesn't want us to think about the greatness of our salvation— that God has forgiven ALL our sins. In Christ, no sin is unforgivable, and He will never remember our sins against us. So, like David, we can say, "Lord, deliver mercy to **me.** Remind me You're not going to give me what I deserve, but You've piled Your grace on me."

Verse 11—"Be **my** shield." Once I received a message about someone that made my heart sink, so I called my wife Bonnie and said, "This is the worst thing I've ever heard!" But she reminded me, "What are you studying this week about David? What does 1 Samuel 30:6 say? David encouraged himself in the Lord!" Whenever unplanned, unexpected situations strike, don't let the devil's fiery darts of discouragement and doubt cause you to question God's goodness. Remember: The Lord knows about your trials long before you do, and He's got everything under control.[45] So trust Him and say, "Be **my** shield from discouragement and doubt!"

Verse 13—"Rule over **my** life." Personalize this by saying to the Lord, "Take over my emotions, appetites, desires, fears, and anxieties." Do you know what anxiety is? Anxiety is when you meditate on your problems rather than on God's Word. The Lord wants you to meditate in His Word (not your problems, fears, and troubles) *"day and night"* (JOSHUA 1:8).

Verses 16–17—"Be **my** refuge in times of trouble." David understood how God wants us to respond to difficult conflicts. You can make this verse yours by saying, "Lord, be *my* refuge and strength today; show *me* Your mercy, and defend **me** from this painful loneliness!" Like God's servant David, you and I can triumph through the Lord's power. What a blessed Truth!

David was soon dealt another hard blow when his beloved friend, King Saul's son Jonathan, warned him that his father was indeed very intent on killing him. While hiding in a field, he saw Jonathan's pre-arranged signal to be used if David needed to flee immediately (1 SAMUEL 20:35–40). When the coast was clear, the two friends then spoke briefly:

> *David ... fell on his face to the ground, and bowed down three times. And they kissed one another; and **they wept together, but David more so.** Then Jonathan said to David, "Go in peace, since we have both sworn in the name of the LORD, saying, 'May the LORD be between you and me, and between your descendants and my descendants, forever.' "* So [David] *arose and departed* (1 SAMUEL 20:41–42).

Bowing three times before Jonathan was David's way of humbling himself before this prince of a man. The loss of his dear friend added to the loneliness and grief he felt, but as David meditated on his situation, he wrote Psalm 11 as a reflection on why he should not run away from dangers but instead flee to the Lord.

RUN TO GOD

This is another Truth David learned as he realized God was watching over him during his family conflicts and dangers, as captured in Psalm 11:

To the Chief Musician. A Psalm of David.

¹ *In the* LORD *I put my trust;*
    How can you say to my soul,
    "Flee as a bird to your mountain"?
² *For look! The wicked bend their bow,*
    They make ready their arrow on the string,
    That they may shoot secretly at the upright in heart.
³ *If the foundations are destroyed,*
    What can the righteous do?

⁴ *The* LORD *is in His holy temple,*
    The LORD's *throne is in heaven;*
    His eyes behold,
    His eyelids test the sons of men.
⁵ *The* LORD *tests the righteous,*
    But the wicked and the one who loves violence His soul hates.
⁶ *Upon the wicked He will rain coals;*
    Fire and brimstone and a burning wind
    Shall be the portion of their cup.

⁷ *For the* LORD *is righteous,*
    He loves righteousness;
    His countenance beholds the upright.

The following provides some insight into what was going on when David wrote Psalm 11:

The panic that launched this psalm was not David's, but that of his apparently well-meaning counselors. Their mood is panic, but David's is peace. In view of David's attitude, this psalm can be listed with the psalms of confidence (Pss. 4, 16, 23, 27, 62, 125, 131). Also, the solidarity of the theocratic king and the theocratic people is obvious, as indicated by the shifts back and forth between sing. and pl. phrasings. The developing verses and lines of this psalm reveal that, although two different "voices" were speaking to David in yet another context of personal and national crisis, he had made up his mind to trust only in the Lord.[46]

Psalm 11 is a neat song! As David was fleeing from King Saul, it's like he suddenly stopped and said, "Wait a minute! Why should I feel so lonely and frightened? In You, oh Lord, I choose to put my trust! You knew about this unexpected trial before I did, so I know You're watching over me and are in control of it."

It was no surprise to God when all this happened. The Lord was simply watching for David's reaction to being on Saul's "Most Wanted" list, and possibly never getting to see his wife and children again. As his struggling emotions gave way to faith, David correctly reasoned: "Since the Lord is righteous, He knows what He's doing, and whatever He does is right. So I am going to trust Him because He loves righteousness—and He wants the right response from me as He is watching."

A while ago I took my four youngest children to a local park. When the three "buddies" (sons) took off to persecute the turtles at the river by trying to capture them, their younger sister preferred to swing. So I told her, "Lizzie, you may go to the swing area, and Daddy will watch you." And then I sat down at a nearby picnic table where I could see her at all times—happily skipping, singing, and talking. But suddenly something happened to upset her (an unexpected bee? a creepy-looking bug?). She froze, and immediately turned around to see if my countenance was beholding her (11: 7)—she needed reassurance of my presence. When my daughter heard me say, "Lizzie," she looked right at me, and everything changed for her. She told me, "It's okay, Daddy. I wasn't really scared. I was just checking to see if you were still there." But her submissive demeanor conveyed to me: "Daddy, this situation falls under your wonderful, righteous plan. You're always watching me, and love it when I react righteously, so I want to respond to you correctly." When we are frightened, and feel all alone, the Lord wants us to realize we are safe in Christ because He is always watching, and is in control!

During this particular time of loneliness, David also wrote Psalm 64 which is about the poison of jealous, hateful, and hurtful tongues. If you've also suffered from verbal abuse and false accusations, I encourage you to read this psalm and personalize it. Especially note David's confidence and joy in verse 10: *The righteous shall be glad in the LORD, and trust in Him. And all the upright in heart shall glory.*

To the Chief Musician. A Psalm of David.

¹ *Hear my voice, O God, in my meditation;*
    Preserve my life from fear of the enemy.
² *Hide me from the secret plots of the wicked,*
    From the rebellion of the workers of iniquity,
³ *Who sharpen their tongue like a sword,*
    And bend their bows to shoot their arrows—bitter words,
⁴ *That they may shoot in secret at the blameless;*
    Suddenly they shoot at him and do not fear.

⁵ *They encourage themselves in an evil matter;*
    They talk of laying snares secretly;
    They say, "Who will see them?"
⁶ *They devise iniquities:*
    "We have perfected a shrewd scheme."
    Both the inward thought and the heart of man are deep.

⁷ *But God shall shoot at them with an arrow;*
    Suddenly they shall be wounded.
⁸ *So He will make them stumble over their own tongue;*
    All who see them shall flee away.
⁹ *All men shall fear,*
    And shall declare the work of God;
    For they shall wisely consider His doing.

¹⁰ *The righteous shall be glad in the* LORD, *and trust in Him.*
    And all the upright in heart shall glory.

Practical Ways to Overcome Loneliness

ALWAYS REMEMBER THAT YOU ARE never alone. Although your job, family, friends, or health may disappear, Jesus says, "I am NOT gone—and never will be." To overcome the pain of loneliness, **meditate on these truths about the Lord:**

- *"I am with you always, even to the end of the age"* (MATTHEW 28:20).
- *"My Presence will go with you, and I will give you rest"* (EXODUS 33:14).
- *"Call His name Immanuel,"* which is translated, *"God with us"* (MATTHEW 1:23).

Resist false guilt. Loneliness is not a sin, so don't become burdened with false guilt. However, wallowing in loneliness and letting self-pity build up is a sin. If you're tempted to succumb to that downward pull of the flesh, since the Lord said it is not good to be alone, remind Him of your need to be reassured of His presence.

Change the changeable. Some difficulties (long travels, work in distant places, military duty, or loss of a loved one) usually can't be changed. What can be changed is your attitude about your circumstances. Here is God's key to rising above your troubles: *Since ... you were raised with Christ, seek those things which are above* (COLOSSIANS 3:1; see also 1 THESSALONIANS 5:16–18).

When deadening loneliness starts to sink deeply into your soul, know that Jesus felt it. When you suffer feeling friendless, know that He is the *friend who sticks closer than a brother* (PROVERBS 18:24). When feeling forsaken, know what David knew: *Those who know Your name will put their trust in You; for You, LORD, have not forsaken those who seek You* (PSALM 9:10). So then, like God's servant David, trust that the Lord can make you glad in even sad and lonely times (PSALM 64:10)!

7 | How to Survive an Unexpected Job Loss

1 Samuel 21:1–9; Psalm 52

I will praise You forever, … I wait on Your name, for it is good.
—PSALM 52:9

CHRIST OUR REFUGE[47] IS THE place to go when life gets tough.[48] When we feel forsaken, all alone, and too weary to go on, Jesus wants us to flee to Him—the safest spot in the universe. For He says, *"Come to Me, all you who labor and are heavy laden, and I will give you rest"* (MATTHEW 11:28). Therefore, as soon as the river of loneliness starts to flood the banks of our lives, we need to flee to Jesus!

One person, more than any other in Scripture, shows us the hope we can find in Christ for our loneliness. More than anyone else in God's Word, David's life is laid down for us to examine from every angle. His discoveries about the Lord's faithfulness in the midst of acute loneliness were recorded in thirty-one psalms written during various life stages: his growing years, struggling years, strong years, and waning years of old age. David's life testimony thus captures loneliness in every facet.

Although most of us will never experience everything David went through in the most challenging events of his life, we've probably all felt the loneliness of youth. And some can identify with his pain of family conflict and danger while others can empathize with David's intense loneliness when he lost his job and was separated from his family.[49] The latter was the reason for David's greatest suffering: he not only lost his source of security, comfort, and income, but he also was separated from his heritage—his whole purpose for existence—the family to whom he had passed on his name.

Our world is increasingly noting the mental and emotional troubles that come hand in hand with losing a job. In some instances, constant financial strain from a breadwinner's prolonged unemployment can also lead to temporary or even permanent separation from family.

According to one of Germany's largest newspapers, fear of job loss has been labeled as that country's "new 'great depression.' " Rising unemployment has led to serious depression in their job force. This is true not only of workers who have lost their jobs but also of those who are afraid they are next to be laid off or fired. Here's the article:

GERMANY'S NEW "GREAT DEPRESSION"

Record numbers of Germans are suffering from depression and other mental illnesses … because of their fear of unemployment … . And the Germans not only are unemployed but the ones who are employed are afraid they're going to lose their jobs because … European Union people [are] moving in and immigrating into Germany and sucking up all the jobs and being willing to take half the wages … : According to the research, by a German health insurance firm, cases of depression among Berliners have risen by 70% since 1997. Up to 70% of Germans also say they are prepared to seek professional help for psychological problems. Mental health experts blamed the rise on Germany's faltering economy, which has seen unemployment rise to over 5m. German insurance firm DAK surveyed 2.6m employed Germans in an effort to discover the impact depression is having on modern working patterns.

Vicious circle. Workers in Germany's capital, regarded as one of Europe's most vibrant modern cities, emerged as an unhappy bunch more likely to miss work through depression than for any other reason. "In times of economic insecurity, young people in particular tend to develop psychological problems in response to professional and private obstacles," said DAK's Chief Executive Herbert Rebscher.

Nevertheless, most respondents said they would rather be depressed with a job than unemployed and happy. "How will someone ever get better," Burghard Klopp, a depression expert at Berlin's Charité hospital, told German broadcaster Deutsche Welle, "when they know their boss is just waiting to fire them?"[50]

That is a secular view of what it was probably like for David—the insecurity of the unknown—living in a topsy-turvy world where everything necessary to support his family and lifestyle was suddenly gone. From a spiritual standpoint, God planned to use David's loneliness not only to draw him closer to Himself but also bless generations to come through David's testimony of how his Good Shepherd was a safe Refuge in troubles.

David's Shock at His Job Loss

IF YOU HAVE EVER HAD to face sudden unemployment, you should be able to identify with how David felt as he was going through this very trying time.

David was always a hard worker. Because he had been continuously employed since his earliest youth, David never had time to think about unemployment. Either he was tending the sheep or acting as a courier to run provisions to his brothers at the front lines. After defeating Goliath, King Saul hired him to work in various departments of the government. Although David got to sit at Saul's table as his son-in-law, he had to earn his wife, Michal, by meeting a quota of killing 100 Philistines. However, as an "eager beaver" employee he went "the second mile" and killed 200 the next time.

Life sometimes throws us a curve. David lived by King Saul: he worked for him, ate with him, sang and played the harp for him, and married his daughter. All of his financial and family security was wrapped up in that job. Then suddenly everything drastically changed. Isn't that always what happens? Everything's just rolling along, we're up to our neck with an unbelievable workload, and then BOOM!—out of the blue we get notice our services are no longer needed. When Saul threw a spear at David to kill him,[51] that was the equivalent of today's "pink slip." (Getting fired was more direct and blunt 3,000 years ago.) Given that David had never felt the sting of a job loss, he was hard hit by the unexpected unemployment.

David's job loss was a big surprise to everyone but God. As David mulled over what had happened, he felt the immense pain of loneliness that usually accompanies the unanticipated loss of everything formerly relied upon. But God was in control, and He had allowed that unemployment for a refining purpose. So everything changed for David except what was most important—his growing relationship with God.

Here's a key point: habits you're forming now will determine your response to God when you're caught off guard by a new heartache. If you've made a habit of turning to God in all circumstances, it will be natural to flee to Christ as your Refuge the moment trouble strikes. Should you lose your job, or face a different trauma, everything will change except this: God—and His great love for you!

David reverted to his "default system." If you work with computers, you know that occasionally a malfunction causes a changed setting to revert back to its default, or original setting. When his unemployment malfunction occurred, David reverted back to his original settings, and that is reflected in Psalm 52.

In fact, Psalm 52:1 is a good example of what I call David's reflex action when, without even thinking about it, he declared: *The goodness of God endures continually.*

When I was a new pastor at Grace Community Church in Sun Valley, California, I remember coming home from a hard day's work and finding a bassinet in the middle of the walkway of our tiny, step-saver apartment. (That place was so small I could lie in bed to change Johnny's diaper and put it in the bathroom sink—and not even get up!) Anyhow, as I quietly crept in, trying to not wake the baby, I happened to brush against his bassinet. As soon as I bumped it, as soon as little Johnny's world got jostled, his arms jerked straight up. Well, I loved that response! So I passed by him at least once a day and kicked the bassinet just to see our precious baby's arms go up again (which probably affected him for life!).

Why would I do that? Because, when Johnny's world got shaken, I enjoyed seeing his response of wanting someone bigger and stronger and outside of him to come and rescue him—and that was ME. When I kicked his bed, he instinctively put his little arms up, and I got to cuddle him—to be his hero—his comforter. (Then Bonnie would say, "I was trying to put him to sleep, you know.")

Similarly, God often kicked David's "bassinet." He knew his arms would instinctively reach out for Him because that was His child's habit, His reflexive mode. Having trusted the Lord from his youth, David's abrupt and painful job loss quickly drove him to the God of All Comfort—and his relationship with his "Hero" grew even closer. We're going to see an example of that in

Psalm 52 shortly, but first I want to give you some background information to help you better understand this psalm.

DAVID'S BETRAYAL BY DOEG

> To the Chief Musician. A Contemplation of David when Doeg the Edomite went and told Saul, and said to him, "David has gone to the house of Ahimelech."

The superscription for this psalm is very interesting. At first glance, its wording doesn't seem to make sense. In fact, a comfortable, well-adjusted reader in America would probably just read it and keep going. No thought would be given to: *Who's Doeg the Edomite? He's from Edom? But this is Israel … Is he a good guy or a bad guy? Why on earth would that wording be at the front of Psalm 52?* A good study Bible may have a footnote that sheds light on the superscription, but if a person's Bible reading time is limited, a footnote is likely to be skipped.

To get the most out of the book of Psalms, remember that half the 150 psalms came from David's life experiences, and thirty-one were tagged with superscriptions like this one. No psalm just hung out there in a vacuum; each was tied to a particular event like the festivals, going up to the feast days, or the lengthening Hezekiah's life. Also, many psalms flowed out of the temple's worship director and all that was going on there.

Altogether, the Spirit of the Lord moved upon not only David but also more than six other men to write the Psalms: the sons of Korah wrote ten (PSALMS 42, 44–49, 84, 85, 87); Asaph penned twelve (PSALMS 50, 73–83); Moses contributed Psalm 90; and Solomon wrote Psalms 72 and 127. In addition, Psalms 88 and 89 were written by Heman and Ethan respectively. That leaves forty-eight anonymous songs, but Ezra probably authored some of them. I personally believe Psalm 119, the longest chapter in the Bible, is Ezra's testimony of the effects in his life from meditation on God and His Word.[52]

Now let's look at what was happening when David wrote Psalm 52—a reflection of events in 1 Samuel 21:1–9.[53] Look at the beginning of the first verse: *David came to Nob, to Ahimelech the priest.*

Why did David go to Nob? The answer is back in 1 Samuel 20:33: *Saul cast a spear at him to kill him, by which Jonathan knew that it was determined by his father to kill David.* After this attempt on his life, David fled to the priestly city of Nob (about a mile northeast of Jerusalem), which was quite a hike in those days.

Here's a short summary of 1 Samuel 21:1–8: When David arrived in Nob, Ahimelech was afraid of him and wanted to know what he was doing there. Fearing that the priest would tell Saul about his visit, David lied by claiming to be on a secret mission for the king. He then requested bread to eat, but nothing was available except consecrated bread, which is what the priest gave him. Having fled so quickly, David also needed a weapon and thus asked for any sword or spear on hand. Now look at verse 9 to see what was in Nob![54]

*So the priest said, "The **sword of Goliath** the Philistine, whom you killed in the Valley of Elah, there it is, wrapped in a cloth behind the ephod. If you will take that, take it. For there is no other except that one here." And David said, "There is none like it; give it to me."*

How did Goliath's sword get into the tent of God in the first place? Way back in Psalms 19, 23, and 132, David had decided that in everything he would turn to God with it. He never compartmentalized his life by including the Lord in some areas, but not in others. And that was true when he slew Goliath and got to keep the giant's sword—a very special trophy. (The Philistines, experts in iron, had made a one-of-a-kind sword for their most seasoned and honored warrior!)

So then, how did the sword get into the tent of God? David told the Lord, "I didn't defeat Goliath—You did. I don't deserve the credit for this—You do. This sword is like no other; I'm leaving it here in Nob in the tent of God because I want You to have all the credit." How can you go wrong with an attitude like that?

This Nob story is one of the greatest lessons in the Bible about how we should live our lives. Everyone who's been to the Holy Land on one of my tours has heard it. As a group we go to the top of the Mount of Olives to look off in the distance at the ruins of Nob, just outside of Jerusalem. As I relate what happened in 1 Samuel 21:1–9, I remind them that God also wants us to give all our trophies to Him because He alone deserves the credit and the glory for anything we accomplish. With such a heart to serve, there is no limit to what the Lord can do with, and in, and through us.

What happened after David got Goliath's sword from the priest? Because Doeg, King Saul's chief shepherd, had overheard David's conversation with Ahimelech and would certainly report that information to Saul, David was forced to stay on the run.

The Lord saw the big picture of His divine purpose in all that was happening, and He inspired in David to breathe-out (by the Holy Spirit) his testimony of what the Lord accomplished through this hard time—how to overcome feelings of loneliness when you're unexpectedly out of work, life has turned upside down, and all familiar routines and work patterns are gone. Psalm 52 captures this time in David's life.

> **Psalm 52:1**—*Why do you boast in evil, O mighty man? The goodness of God endures continually.*

We don't know the details of the conversation with Doeg, but he was a weasel of a guy who was both an informant and a murderer. In fact, at King Saul's enraged command, Doeg later slew the eighty-five priests from Nob because they knew David's whereabouts and did not tell the king (1 SAMUEL 22:18).[55]

It's uncertain whether Doeg is the one David was talking about in Psalm 52, but the most important point of the whole psalm is at the end of verse 1: *The goodness of God endures continually.* David was saying, "God's goodness endures through my job loss, my insecurities, my loss of comfort, and my loss of time with my family. Regardless of what is happening in my life, God is good!"

> **Psalm 52:2-4**—*Your tongue devises destruction, like a sharp razor, working deceitfully. You love evil more than good, lying rather than speaking righteousness. Selah[56] You love all devouring words, you deceitful tongue.*

This is a fact of life: at one time or another people will hurt us. When we're feeling the most desperate, it should come as no surprise if someone comes along and says things like:

- "You've lost your job? Oh well, they probably never needed you anyway."
- "Why don't you just deal with it and look in the help wanted ads?"
- "There must be a reason why you've been out of work so long. What's wrong with you?"
- "I thought you were jobless. Why are you spending money like that?"
- "What did you do to get fired?"

People can be mean and even take pleasure in hurting others. Whoever it was in verses 2-4, he had a sharp razor-like tongue and was deceitfully devouring David. (Sometimes this takes the form of a compliment that is actually a backhanded stab.) And David suffered through all that pain.

Psalm 52:5–7—*God shall likewise destroy you forever; He shall take you away, and pluck you out of your dwelling place, and uproot you from the land of the living. Selah The righteous also shall see and fear, and shall laugh at him, saying, "Here is the man who did not make God his strength, but trusted in the abundance of his riches, and strengthened himself in his wickedness."*

These verses reflect some imprecation; imprecatory prayers are when judgment is prayed down on someone, so we must be very careful about that form of prayer. (For example, never say, "God will destroy you," to friends who tease you when you're out of work.) The lesson David learned when unemployed and feeling insecure is in verse 7: *"Here is the man who did not make God his strength."* In this calamitous time, David was saying, "God, people can hurt me—those who do not make You their strength!"

What was David confessing? This is a case where the Truth is learned by the reverse. In other words, if the wicked didn't make God their strength, then David would. He thus said, "God is my strength. Trusting Him is how I'm making it through this lonely time. He is the reason I'm triumphing."

Psalm 52:8–9—*I am like a green olive tree in the house of God; I trust in the mercy of God forever and ever. I will praise You forever, because You have done it; and in the presence of Your saints I will wait on Your name, for it is good.*

Look at how David personalized verses 8–9: *I trust in the mercy of God. I will praise You forever.* A wonderful thing about Hebrew poetry is that it has a beautiful completion. At the end of verse 9 David came full circle by saying, *I will wait on Your name, for it is good.* How did he end verse 1? *The goodness of God endures forever.* How did he end verse 9? He pulled it all together by saying, "I will wait on Your name, Good Shepherd, Whom I've followed and trusted all my life, for Your name is good."

God rarely gives insights into the "why's" of suffering. Instead, He tells us the "what's"—what responses He wants from us. That is what we are responsible for, and not for why He's doing something. Righteous responses in tribulation are what He desires from us.

David Waited on the Lord

LOOK AGAIN AT PSALM 52:9: *I will praise You forever, because You have done it; and in the presence of Your saints **I will wait** on Your name, for it is good.* The Hebrew word translated *"wait"* is *hupomeno*, which is actually the Greek rendering of the Hebrew word *qavah* (Strong's #6960 – "hope that renews exhausted strength").[57] To better grasp its meaning, look at the most well-known verse in the Bible which uses this special word:

> *He gives power to the weak, and to those who have no might He increases strength. Even the youths shall faint and be weary, and the young men shall utterly fall, but those who **wait** on the LORD shall renew their strength; they shall mount up with wings like eagles, they shall run and not be weary, they shall walk and not faint* (ISAIAH 40:29–31).

This Hebrew verb for *"wait"* means "to twist and/or stretch." In the Old Testament world it was used of making rope by twisting and stretching many weak strands into a strong rope. In time, this concept of rope-making became a metaphor for waiting and receiving strength from God during weak times so we can endure the twisting and stretching of our lonely, painful trials. David was saying, "Lord, as You're twisting together all these unexpected events, I choose to cling to You, and wait for You, because You are good. And when You finish with all You want to accomplish in me through this trial, I'll be even stronger. Help me to never resist You by questioning why You're allowing these things. Because I love You, I want to do what You want me to do, and respond how You want me to respond."

Practically speaking, if you lose your job, by all means do everything necessary to find another one. Check the classifieds or employment agencies, get re-trained or acquire extra education to beef up your skills if needed, or relocate if that is what it takes to get back on your feet. But as you go out and "beat a path" to find a job, do so *confidently*, as David did in verse 9: *I will wait on Your name, for it is good.*

IS CHRIST YOUR REFUGE?

ASK YOURSELF: *Is Christ really MY Refuge? Is that MY chosen reality or just a fact I've heard?* Remember this: God will kick your bassinet just to see what you will do. In your loneliness He wants to be your "Hero"—your Comforter as you instinctively reach out to Him, trust Him, and triumph through Him. Put simply, loneliness is a tool to glorify God.

- Are you feeling the loneliness of being overlooked, ignored, and disliked by your family? Jesus says, *"I am always with you!"*
- Are you feeling the loneliness of facing family conflict and danger? Jesus says, *"I am always with you!"*
- Are you feeling the loneliness of job loss and family separation? Jesus says, *"I am always with you!"*
- Are you feeling the loneliness of moving to a new location under duress? Jesus says, *"I am always with you!"*
- Are you feeling the loneliness of living and working with a tough crowd? Jesus says, *"I am always with you!"*
- Are you feeling the loneliness of unemployment and an unsettled home life? Jesus says, *"I am always with you!"*
- Are you feeling the loneliness of betrayal by friends? Jesus says, *"I am always with you!"*
- Are you feeling the loneliness of being wronged in a business deal? Jesus says, *"I am always with you!"*
- Are you feeling the loneliness of the sudden loss of family, friends, and finances? Jesus says, *"I am always with you!"*
- Are you feeling the loneliness of temptation and failure? Jesus says, *"I am always with you!"*
- Are you feeling the loneliness of chastisement and restoration? Jesus says, *"I am always with you!"*
- Are you feeling the loneliness of old age? Jesus says, *"I am always with you!"*

If you trust God enough to take His help as He weaves His Word into your weaknesses, you will find, like the Apostle Paul, that God's grace is sufficient, and His strength is made perfect in weakness (2 CORINTHIANS 12:9). Trusting God with his job loss was what gave David the "waiting hope" to make him stronger to overcome the next wave of life's unending, lonely struggles. In God's hands, righteous responses when you're feeling all alone will actually become a blessing as He twists and stretches you into the "waiting hope" that will draw you ever closer to Him!

8 | How to Survive Life's Unexpected Twists

1 Samuel 21:10–15; Psalms 56 and 34

Whenever I am afraid, I will trust in You.—PSALM 56:3

L IFE IS FULL OF UNEXPECTED twists—those sudden changes we never see coming.[58] Unanticipated changes often lead to loneliness, one of the most powerful human emotions. If you live long enough you will lose your spouse, your job, your best friend, or your health. None of these are expected, they just happen. When they do, things no longer feel the same, and an intense feeling of aloneness can creep in. For the believer, as soon as that ache appears it's time to remember Christ, like David did. Everything is usually different in change except for one thing—the relationship Christ has with us. He is always close, always available, and always there to encourage, comfort, and strengthen.

When life takes those unexpected twists, especially traumatic ones where we have no human support base, it's incredibly difficult. Most of us can cope with the unforeseen if we have someone to lean upon, but loneliness becomes intensified when we must go through agonizing changes all alone.

Because David experienced nearly every form of loneliness known to man, he understood the pain of going through unexpected changes without a human support base. After his family's rejection of him in youth, for many years he struggled through family conflict and danger; job loss and insecurity; duress from relocating; feeling abandoned by God, then living and working with a tough crowd; constant insecurities and huge responsibilities; betrayal by friends; being wronged in a business deal; and losing his family, friends, and finances.

In unguarded moments during David's strong or peak years, he was tempted and failed miserably by committing adultery and murder. Until God restored him, David experienced humiliation and a heartbreaking aloneness while being chastised by the Lord Whom he loved so much. Finally, in his waning years, he had to come to grips with old age and all that it entails. Yet, in no life change was he ever truly alone. Because he always fled to Christ for refuge, David could still triumphantly declare, "God, You are good!"

Nothing was too big or too small for David to bring to God. And both his deepest distresses and precious victories were captured in the form of songs containing testimonies of how the Lord continually strengthened and cared for David in constant troubles, countless dangers, and relentless stresses. And that is exactly what David was experiencing in one of his gravest hours as he fled from Saul and was captured by the Philistines.

When the Unexpected Becomes Overwhelming

JUST BECAUSE WE LOVE AND serve the Lord doesn't mean we will miss the storms and skids of life. When the unexpected becomes overwhelming, and we feel as if we can't go on any longer, what can we do? We can remember that through divinely inspired psalms David has shared the spiritual secret of how to serve God's purpose in our own unending struggles.

What David learned about God's way to conquer the terrors in Gath was recorded in Psalms 56 and 34—how to overcome loneliness when in a foreign situation. Psalm 56 is believed to have been written in the midst of his captivity and Psalm 34 after he had escaped from Gath.

THE SETTING FOR PSALM 56—DAVID FLEES TO GATH

> *Then David arose and fled that day from before Saul, and went to Achish the king of Gath. And the servants of Achish said to him, "Is this not David the king of the land? Did they not sing of him to one another in dances, saying: 'Saul has slain his thousands, and David his ten thousands'?" Now David took these words to heart, and was very much afraid of Achish the king of Gath* (1 SAMUEL 21:10–12).[59]

After King Saul gave David his "pink slip" by throwing a spear at him to kill him, David fled to the priestly city of Nob.[60] Alone, frightened, and on the run, he got bread from Ahimelech plus a very special sword he'd given to the Lord a long time before—the sword of Goliath.

As he continued to run for his life, David ended up in the Philistine city of Gath—not by choice, but under duress. He was soon captured, and the intense loneliness he was suffering caused Psalm 56 to literally pour out of him by the inspiration of God. If you carefully consider this psalm's superscription, which is like a map to David's life, you'll find it quite insightful:

> To the Chief Musician. Set to "The Silent Dove in Distant Lands." A Michtam of
> David when the Philistines captured him in Gath.

"Michtam" is a Hebrew word for cutting or engraving; it means "something that penetrates." J. Vernon McGee explains, "It speaks of that which is substantial, or enduring, or fixed."[61] So David was saying, "This is something that went really deep into my life, and I'll never forget it!" The Michtam's "captured" doesn't just mean "came across him"; it actually means "caught him, imprisoned him"—David was a captive in Gath.

Most Bible commentators believe Psalm 56 was actually written while David was imprisoned.[62] The title of the song—"The Silent Dove in Distant Lands"—is reminiscent of Psalm 55:6 when David said, *"Oh, that I had wings like a dove! I would fly away and be at rest."* That provides a valuable insight into what David was feeling during this dangerous time. He longed to escape from the pain of his troubles!

In times of desperation, it's normal to wish we were anywhere else other than in the midst of a traumatic event. But David couldn't fly away from the foreign situation he was in. He was in a place where his troubles had arrested him. That is why the song was set to the tune of a dove in a distant land—his wings had been clipped; he couldn't fly away because he had been "captured."

What could be better than having wings like a dove in a circumstance like this? Having the God Who *made* the dove—the God Who could give David wings! For David was convinced it was better to have the Lord *with* him than to merely escape his problems.

Real victory is not escaping all our problems; real victory is not evading every difficult situation we can possibly evade. The greatest triumph comes from glorifying God as we go through each difficult trial *with* Him. That is what David did; he sought the Lord. And as we shall shortly see in Psalm 56, he cried out to Him four times in three verses (vv. 4, 10, 11). David cried out to Elohim—the Creator of the dove and everything else—because he had confidence that God cared for him!

Nothing is too small for God's care. After one of the greatest Bible teachers of all time had finished his preaching service, a woman once asked this question of him: "Dr. Morgan, how small can a need of mine be before it is too small for me to bring to God?" Being very British, and highly proper, he replied, "Madam, is anything in the universe not *small* to God?"[63]

If we truly meditate on the Lord God Almighty's awesomeness, we'll realize that in comparison to His glory and honor and power,[64] everything in our life is infinitesimal. Whether it's something like terminal cancer, or a lost cat, in the spectrum of life—from death to the seemingly insignificant—it's all "small stuff" to the Lord. And yet He lovingly says to you and me, "I don't want to be out of touch with any part of your life. I am not distant, detached, or unacquainted with your suffering. Both the big and small things in your life are important to Me. So cast all your care upon Me, for I truly care for you!"[65] The Lord loves to be needed, sought after, and asked to help. What a God!

If you've ever gone to a place with a struggle in your heart, you'll understand what David was feeling as he penned Psalm 56:

> ¹ *Be merciful to me, O God, for man would swallow me up;*
>   *Fighting all day he oppresses me.*
> ² *My enemies would hound me all day,*
>   *For there are many who fight against me, O Most High.*

David was all alone—feeling desperate. He was in a foreign situation with no family, no friends, and no other human support base during this unexpected twist in his life.[66] What type of fear would make someone run away from home and into the hometown of the very person you killed in public, before thousands of witnesses? That's right, this is Gath, the hometown of the best known fighter of the Philistine nation—Goliath. For David to walk into the city where his picture was on a thousand "Most Wanted" posters means that he was utterly desperate:

> ³ *Whenever I am afraid,*
>   *I will trust in You.*

⁴ In God (I will praise His word),
In God I have put my trust;
I will not fear.
What can flesh do to me?

David was afraid—he knew he'd made a huge mistake. He had just fled the priestly city of Nob and now here he was, all alone, walking into Gath with the accent of a Hebrew from Judea and carrying the one-of-a-kind sword that had been held by Gath's champion, Goliath! He probably figured that with Goliath's sword on his shoulder he could handle anything—all he had to do was wait it out until things cooled down back home. But David had no idea what he was walking into! So the Philistines quickly spotted him, caught him, and imprisoned him.

By the way, what can flesh do to us? Flesh can do a lot: flesh can kill, destroy, deride, bully, scoff at us, and so forth. What David was really saying is that humans can't do anything to us that God isn't superintending and in control of. He therefore appealed to the Lord to rescue him:

⁵ All day they twist my words;
All their thoughts are against me for evil.
⁶ They gather together,
They hide, they mark my steps,
When they lie in wait for my life.
⁷ Shall they escape by iniquity?
In anger cast down the peoples, O God!

In the midst of all the evil assailing him, David cried out, "You're the One Who is in control, O God!"

⁸ You number my wanderings;
Put my tears into Your bottle;
Are they not in Your book?

The *"tears into Your bottle"* phrase speaks loudly of God's promise to never leave us, never forget us, and never be indifferent to the cares of any of His children. Nothing is too small for God! Not even the tears we shed. The Lord is so compassionate that He keeps track of all our wanderings—and all our tears! Wow! Don't you find His compassion *amazing*?

⁹ *When I cry out to You,*
  Then my enemies will turn back;
  This I know, because God is for me.

That was David's triumphant reality. He said, "It doesn't matter if everybody else is against me because God is *for* me!"

¹⁰ *In God (I will praise His word),*
  In the LORD (I will praise His word),
¹¹ *In God I have put my trust;*
  I will not be afraid.
  What can man do to me?

¹² *Vows made to You are binding upon me, O God;*
  I will render praises to You,
¹³ *For You have delivered my soul from death.*
  Have You not kept my feet from falling,
  That I may walk before God
  In the light of the living?

What a testimony! Psalm 56 was very popular. In fact, it was quoted by the writer of Hebrews 13:6 (PSALM 56:4, 11); by Paul in Romans 8:31 (PSALM 56:9); and most of all by Jesus Himself when He said, *"I am the light of the world. He who follows Me shall not walk in darkness, but have the light of life"* (JOHN 8:12).

Real life is only lived in Christ; real light comes only by the sunshine of His face; real peace is only in His presence—and that is what David found!

DAVID'S RESOLVES IN PSALM 56

How did David survive the intense loneliness of this horribly foreign place? In Psalm 56 he made no less than nine resolves—choices while facing the "distant land" of a lonely new place of struggle. Here they are:[67]

1. *Whenever I am afraid,* **I will trust in You** (v. 3). Being all alone and afraid makes for a very volatile situation. David was saying, "In the midst of my loneliness, when I feel fear coming on—that cold wave of terror that floods my soul—I choose to trust in You, oh God!"

2. *In God (**I will praise His word**)* (v. 4a). How much of God's Word did David have? He had the Books of Moses: Genesis, Exodus, Leviticus, Numbers, and Deuteronomy.[68] While some may consider the first five books of the Bible as boring, they were David's passion—the very words of the God of the Universe speaking to him! Thus he chose to completely trust such a powerful God—no matter what.

3. *In God **I have put my trust*** (v. 4b). David was saying, "Lord, I made a huge miscalculation in coming to Gath, and I shouldn't have carried Goliath's sword with me. But I've been caught off guard and desperately need Your help because I don't know what they're planning to do to me. However, I do know this: I choose to put my trust in You!"

4. *I will not fear. What can flesh do to me?* (v. 4c). Jesus said to not fear those who can merely destroy our bodies, but to fear the One Who can cast both our bodies and souls into hell.[69] Martin Luther put it this way: Fear the Lord and you won't have to fear anybody else. So David said, "I choose to fear You, oh Lord. No one else is as awesome!"

5. *When I cry out to You, then my enemies will turn back; this **I know**, because **God is for me*** (v. 9). When a person applies for a job, a scholarship, an appointment to a military academy, or any other position, it's common to look for someone "on the inside" with enough clout to pave the way. But David already knew the One "on the inside" Who was for him—GOD. Can you find anyone higher or more powerful than the Lord?

   A wise person once said this: God plus one equals a majority. In other words, *if God is for us, who can be against us?* (ROMANS 8:31). You never have to feel alone, even if the majority in your situation is against you: GOD plus YOU equals an unbeatable MAJORITY.

6. *In God (**I will praise His word**)* (v. 10a). Rather than letting fear defeat him as the Philistines ranted and raved around him, bragging that they caught the Goliath-killer, David chose to focus on praising God for his Word and a safe refuge.

7. *In the LORD (**I will praise His word**)* (v. 10b). What Word was David holding onto while he was in prison? He was probably recalling

1 Samuel 16 when God anointed him to be the next king. He therefore said to God, "No matter how it looks right now, I know I'm going to get out of this because You said I'm going to be the king someday. That has to mean You will rescue me in this terrible situation!" So in faith, choosing to trust the Lord, he praised God's Word because he knew he could count on it.

8. *In God **I have put my trust*** (v. 11a). This is a renewal of the same choice he made in verse 4.

9. ***I will not be afraid.*** *What can man do to me?* (v. 11b). This is a renewed choice to keep his eyes on God rather than his circumstances!

The great nineteenth-century British explorer, David Livingstone, drew great comfort from David's courage in Psalm 56. When Livingstone reached the edge of the dark continent of Africa, he could see the smoke of a thousand villages. After pitching his tent, scouts from those savage tribes found him and began to dance and make dreadful, fiendish sounds around his tent. On January 14, 1856 he wrote in his journal: "I fear for my life and safety; I think I should flee under the cover of darkness and abandon my desire to take the Gospel to the heart of Africa." Fear is always the realm of Satan! Had Livingstone abandoned his calling it would have been a tremendous coup for the dark side in the battle of the heavenlies! As God would have it, he remembered Christ's words: *"Lo, I am with you always"* (MATTHEW 28:20). And that encouraged him to claim Psalm 56:3—*"Whenever I am afraid, I will trust in you."* Livingstone continued on to become one of the greatest missionaries of all time!

The Apostle Paul had this to say about not giving into fear:

> **Be anxious for nothing**, *but in everything by prayer and supplication, with thanksgiving, let your requests be made known to God; and the peace of God, which surpasses all understanding, will guard your hearts and minds through Christ Jesus* (PHILIPPIANS 4:6).

The literal construction of that is a beautiful imperative which says this: Nothing will I be anxious about; I will worry about nothing; I will pray about everything. That is the tremendous lesson David learned while imprisoned in Gath. Now then, how did he get out of the mess he was in?

THE SETTING FOR PSALM 34—DAVID ESCAPES FROM GATH

So he changed his behavior before them, pretended madness in their hands, scratched on the doors of the gate, and let his saliva fall down on his beard. Then Achish said to his servants, "Look, you see the man is insane. Why have you brought him to me? Have I need of madmen, that you have brought this fellow to play the madman in my presence? Shall this fellow come into my house?" (1 SAMUEL 21:13–15).

David had bottomed out emotionally; he was unable to go on because of complete fear, loneliness, and danger. Out of desperation, he deceived Achish by acting like he was crazy (letting saliva dribble down his beard was a great offense in the East).

Because God was superintending all that was happening to David, however, He caused Achish to send him away. For *the king's heart is in the hand of the LORD, like the rivers of water; He turns it wherever He wishes* (PROVERBS 21:1).

Remember this about David: not everything he did was right—but the inspired lessons God gave us through his example are always right. What really counted was not what happened to David's short-term, but the long-term direction of his heart.

Even the Apostle Paul could identify with the intensity of David's struggles as the unexpected twists of life threatened to overwhelm him:

For we do not want you to be ignorant, brethren, of our trouble which came to us in Asia: that we were burdened beyond measure, above strength, so that we despaired even of life (2 CORINTHIANS 1:8).

But we have this treasure in earthen vessels, that the excellence of the power may be of God and not of us. ⁸ We are hard-pressed on every side, yet not crushed; we are perplexed, but not in despair; ⁹ persecuted, but not forsaken; struck down, but not destroyed— ¹⁰ always carrying about in the body the dying of the Lord Jesus, that the life of Jesus also may be manifested in our body (2 CORINTHIANS 4:7–10).

Both David and Paul found a place where they could always flee for safety and security; the Lord was their Refuge, and He is ours as well. Christ is the safest spot in the universe—the place to go when life gets tough.

Let's now turn our attention to Psalm 34, written after David escaped from Gath and was on the run to the cave of Adullam. The details of 1 Samuel 21:13–15 are the backdrop for this psalm—especially when comparing the record in Psalm 34:13 with that passage.[70] This song expresses how David had felt in the courts of the great warlord of the Philistines. Even though he had acted out of fear before Achish, he realized that God was watching and understood how much he needed deliverance.

A Psalm of David when he pretended madness before Abimelech, who drove him away, and he departed.[71]

Psalm 34:1-2—David delighted in the Lord: *I will bless the LORD at all times; His praise shall continually be in my mouth. ² My soul shall make its boast in the LORD; the humble shall hear of it and be glad.*

This was not prideful boasting on David's part because the Lord was the object of his boasting. God says, *"He who glories, let him glory in the LORD"* (1 CORINTHIANS 1:31).

Psalm 34:3—David gave glory to God: *Oh, magnify the LORD with me, and let us exalt His name together.*

How can we exalt the Lord together? We do so by acknowledging that He is watching over us just as He did with David.

Psalm 34:4-5—David sought God in fearful times: *I sought the LORD, and He heard me, and delivered me from all my fears.⁵ They looked to Him and were radiant, and their faces were not ashamed.*

David consistently sought God in his troubles. And when he asked something of the Lord, he waited expectantly for His answer. Waiting on God is like an echo: you can't hear an echo unless you wait around to listen for it—and that is how prayer is. God always answers our prayers: He may answer with a silent "Wait"; He may answer with "No"; or He may answer with "Yes." But we can be confident that if we ask anything according to His will, He hears us, and will grant our petitions. (See 1 JOHN 5:14.) So David said, "When I sought the Lord, He heard and answered me. Because He's continually watching over me, I'm so grateful that I want to magnify Him!"

David still had to go through all that this unexpected twist entailed, but he went through it *with* God, Who delivered him out of it all. There's nothing sinful about fearing. As a parent, if one of your children becomes afraid of something and runs to you for reassurance, throwing his little arms around you, what do you do? You hold on tight and comfort him. That is what this is all about—being comforted by God as He delivers us out of our fears.

David was saying, "God, because You're watching me, I want to be radiant in my distressful time—to magnify You by acknowledging Who's really in control of all this!"

Psalm 34:6–7—David had a proper view of himself during tough times: *This poor man cried out, and the LORD heard him, and saved him out of all his troubles. 7 The angel of the LORD encamps all around those who fear Him, and delivers them.*

The Lord said, *"Blessed are the poor in spirit"* (MATTHEW 5:3). That is the same idea here; David had a proper view of himself. When this *"poor man cried out,"* the Lord heard and saved him! Do you see how he keeps putting the emphasis on magnifying the Lord? David was saying, "I know You see me, and I want everyone to know that You have saved me out of my troubles." Where was he always putting the focus? He took the focus off of himself, his fears, and his troubles, and looked up to exalt the Lord!

Dwelling on our problems, rather than the One in control Who can deliver us, leads to defeat. The opposite is also true: the Lord will not come to our rescue if we act like the Laodiceans and say we *"have need of nothing."*[72] For example, when Jacob wanted God's blessing in Genesis 32, he first had to be broken by the Lord. The Lord will never bless the flesh—the proud who are confident in their own abilities, plans, and schemes.

To get what he wanted, Jacob tried to use God just as he had his brother Esau, his father Isaac, and his father-in-law Laban. But God will not be used. He will not bless the schemes of the proud and their confidence in their abilities. God will break them instead. And that is what He did to Jacob. He crippled him until all he could do was hold on to God. Like David, Jacob had to come to a point where he humbly cried out to God.

If in humility we approach God in our need, He will strengthen us, for the Angel of the Lord encamps around those who fear Him to rescue them. Isn't that beautiful? David was saying, "Oh Lord, I want to magnify You because You're encamping around me to rescue me!" Sometimes God's form of rescue might be to take us *out* of a situation; sometimes He will deliver us *through* the situation; and sometimes He lets the situation grind us to a pulp to remove our self-sufficiency. But one way or another, He *will* deliver us out of our troubles. Isn't this marvelous?

There is no limit to what the Lord can do with a needy person who has cried out to Him. For God has promised: *Humble yourselves in the sight of the Lord, and He will lift you up* (JAMES 4:10)!

Psalm 34:8—David personally experienced God: *Oh, taste and see that the LORD is good; blessed is the man who trusts in Him!*

David said, "Lord, because You are watching, I'm going to tell people that they should taste and see that You are good. I've experienced that and want them to also." Since God is always watching us, when we need a refuge, a Refuge can be found!

Psalm 34:9-14—David practiced the presence of God:

Oh, fear the LORD, you His saints! There is no want to those who fear Him. [10] *The young lions lack and suffer hunger; but those who seek the LORD shall not lack any good thing.* [11] *Come, you children, listen to me; I will teach you the fear of the LORD.* [12] *Who is the man who desires life, and loves many days, that he may see good?* [13] *Keep your tongue from evil, and your lips from speaking deceit.* [14] *Depart from evil and do good; seek peace and pursue it.*

David practiced the presence of God—acknowledging Him is to fear Him. His changed behavior follows this principle: if we believe right, we will behave right.

Are you getting the picture that David wants us to grasp that God is always watching over us and thus we ought to seek Him? The Lord wants to be part of our lives, to be involved, to impact things for us. Consider this illustration: A Goodyear blimp flies overhead with its TV cameras to capture important moments—like runners racing in a marathon, or a runner carrying the torch to light the fire that signals the start of the Olympic Games. Such runners know that people worldwide are watching because of that camera. Similarly, God is watching over us all the time, in tune with us, wanting us to look up and acknowledge His presence. So He says, "Seek Me and you'll not lack any good thing! I'm watching over you to offer My grace like the waves of the sea and My peace like a river."

Psalm 34:15–21—David knew he was in touch with God during the dangerous times:

The eyes of the LORD are on the righteous, and His ears are open to their cry. ¹⁶ The face of the LORD is against those who do evil, to cut off the remembrance of them from the earth. ¹⁷ The righteous cry out, and the LORD hears, and delivers them out of all their troubles. ¹⁸ The LORD is near to those who have a broken heart, and saves such as have a contrite spirit. ¹⁹ Many are the afflictions of the righteous, but the LORD delivers him out of them all. ²⁰ He guards all his bones; not one of them is broken. ²¹ Evil shall slay the wicked, and those who hate the righteous shall be condemned.

In verse 15 David once again magnified the Lord by acknowledging His ever-present watch care. Sometimes we may act like Elisha's terrified servant whose focus was on the enemy troops around Dothan instead of God (2 KINGS 6). But then Elisha prayed, "Lord, open his eyes so he can see the real picture!" And then the servant could actually see the glorious armies of the Lord encamped all around them! That is what David was seeing when he said, *The eyes of the LORD are toward the righteous.* So he again rejoiced because he was in touch with the living God!

Not only does God watch over us, but He also listens to us. David testified that *His ears are open to [our] cry.* As Romans 8:31 says, *If God is for us, who can be against us?* That is why the Lord said, *"Vengeance is Mine, I will repay"* (ROMANS 12:19). We should never follow the world's motto: Don't get mad—get even! We should never try to get even, or go after anyone, or protract the agony in any way. God will recompense—God will vindicate. For His face is against evildoers to the extent that He will *cut off the remembrance of them from the earth* (PSALM 34:16).

Do you see how David was cycling through this? He continually brought up the fact that God is watching, and directly involved to give us every possible opportunity to understand that because He is a God who hears, He will also deliver us out of all our troubles! What a comfort!

If you want to truly magnify the Lord, and bring honor to Him, then acknowledge that He is near, that He is your unseen companion, that He wants to be your acknowledged partner in every single thing you do. For the *LORD is near to those who have a broken heart, and saves such as have a contrite spirit. Many are the afflictions of the righteous, but the LORD delivers him out of them all* (PSALM 34:18–19).

Psalm 34:22—David made the Lord his ultimate refuge in hard times:
The LORD redeems the soul of His servants, and <u>none of those who trust in Him</u>
<u>*shall be condemned.*</u>

This whole Psalm was a vivid testimony that through this great time of distress God was very much a part of everything David did. Out of this terrifying time of fleeing to Gath and acting crazy before a Philistine warlord, David acknowledged: "I will magnify the Lord because He is my Refuge—the only safe place to be." He could have been overcome with fear, grief, and despair during this traumatic event, but God upheld him.

To whom do you turn when lonely? Because David's life was carved into the bedrock of God's Word, we know he habitually turned to the Lord in his lonely trials. But what happens if a person doesn't have the Lord to turn to?

A classic example of being all alone without the Lord is found in the life of William Cowper who was orphaned at age six. He was from a grand British family; his grand uncle was the prime minister of Britain in its greatest hour. Because his family was well off, William was sent off to a boarding school. However, being a small, young, and weak boy, he was mercilessly hounded and preyed upon by older boys. Bullied to the point of depression, he grew up in the shadows of life.

Having not had a personal relationship with the Lord in his youth, as David did, William attempted to hang himself. He failed, and then lost his mind over the guilt of thinking he had committed the unpardonable sin. Consequently, he ended up spending many years in an insane asylum.

But in 1764, at age 33, our merciful God drew William to Christ for salvation. Soon afterward he was taken in by John Newton and they became best friends. Even though William struggled with crippling depression until he died, it never stopped him from writing hymns. He became one of the most well-known hymn writers of the nineteenth century. Here is his best known hymn:

THERE IS A FOUNTAIN FILLED WITH BLOOD

There is a fountain filled with blood
Drawn from Emmanuel's veins;
And sinners, plunged beneath that flood,
Lose all their guilty stains.
The dying thief rejoiced to see
That fountain in his day;

And there may I, though vile as he,
Wash all my sins away.

Dear dying Lamb,
Thy precious blood
Shall never lose its power,
'Til all the ransomed Church of God
Be saved, to sin no more.

And since, by faith, I saw the stream
Thy flowing wounds supply,
Redeeming love has been my theme,
And shall be 'til I die. Amen.
　　—William Cowper (1731–1800)

David chose to trust God's promises and be led in triumph! And that rather echoes this New Testament verse:

Now thanks be to God who always **leads us in triumph in Christ,** *and through us diffuses the fragrance of His knowledge in every place* (2 CORINTHIANS 2:14).

If you are currently experiencing an unexpected and painful twist in your life, are you seeking God's help to be a fragrance for Christ by how you handle it? Can others see that you are turning to God rather than giving in to despair? Does God view you as being led in triumph or sinking in self-pity? You may not be able to change most of your circumstances, but you can change your attitude in them.

Remember: Life is full of unexpected twists—those sudden changes you never see coming. But when you are desperate, God is not. When you are alone, God is there. When you are troubled, God is a very present Refuge and help for you to flee into His loving and waiting arms!

How to Overcome Feelings of Being Abandoned by God

9

Psalm 13

How long, O LORD? Will you forget me forever? —**Psalm 13:1**

FOR QUITE SOME TIME EVERYTHING had been going well for David as the hero giant-killer, the worship leader for the king, the king's chief warrior, a member of the king's cabinet, and the king's son-in-law. But then everything unexpectedly fell apart![73]

David had to flee for his life; his wife stayed behind with her father, King Saul; his parents were sent to Moab; his job, his standing, and his home were all lost; and when he fled to Gath he was captured by the Philistines. Consequently, David lost any remaining sense of personal safety and started to feel frantic.

As a believer, regardless of the extent of our spiritual maturity, it's possible to reach a point so low we actually feel that everyone—even God—has abandoned us. That was David's desperate condition when he wrote Psalm 13.

Psalm 13 reveals that Christ can't be our Refuge if we don't hear His invitation to flee to Him, or remember He's there. Sometimes we have to hit bottom, go through dark waters, or face incredible convulsions in our lives to really see Him even though He's been there all the time.

The Life Most Noticed by God

I LEARNED THAT LESSON WELL at 27,000 feet while flying home from a Shepherds Conference in Los Angeles. Through that harrowing experience I gained an unforgettable insight.

Having heard the preflight safety lecture dozens of times, I started to read and ignored it, never thinking about anything other than what I needed to do before landing in Tulsa, Oklahoma.

At first, the flight seemed uneventful. An empty seat beside me became my desk, and as the world slowly drifted by outside my window, I worked. After a bit, clouds began to darken the sky, so I turned on the light and kept studying. An announcement to fasten seatbelts appeared ordinary, not at all uncommon.

Suddenly, the plane did its first roller coaster move; it quickly dropped and then immediately went straight up like an elevator. When a very hard jolt knocked open a few overhead compartments and belongings fell out, I heard scattered cries of fear.

From that moment on this unexpected twist captured my rapt attention and all I thought about was this: *Who, exactly, is up front flying this plane? How much experience do they have? How skilled are they in thunderstorm management?*

What tremendous lesson did I learn on that flight? That it's perfectly normal to not pay much attention to stuff in general as long as our lives are going along smoothly!

Who even thinks about the pilot until the weather gets rough? But when the plane jolts, jumps, rocks, and swerves—that is ALL we can think about. And then we want to know: *Who is steering this careening machine?* The pilot instantly becomes very important because our safety is in his hands!

The same is true in life. The fewer the bumps, the more likely the Pilot will be ignored. The smoother the ride, the more likely the One Who holds our safety in His hands will be forgotten.

But let the rough family times, the roller coaster ride of our emotions, the crash of our finances, or the plummet of our health come—THEN the Pilot captures our rapt attention.

God was about to capture David's full attention after Psalm 34's terrible situation in Gath where he acted crazy before Achish the king and was fleeing to the wilderness to live in the cave of Adullam. This launched David's "cave times" period, which would soon prove to be one of his deepest trials.

Psalm 13 appears to reveal what was happening to David *after* he fled Gath but *before* he arrived at the cave, which is 1 Samuel 22:1. As he ran for his life, he felt abandoned by everyone—including God.

Many Feel Abandoned

As a pastor, biblical counselor, and a follower of Christ for over forty years, I am convinced feelings of abandonment are very common among believers.

What are some causes of such cave times? Here are just a few to help us identify with being in David's shoes:

- Cave times may start through a lengthy illness when strength never comes, future plans fade, and so does hope. As a result, we start feeling like God has let us down because He's abandoned us by not helping us get well.

- Cave times often begin with an unanticipated job loss and subsequent tangled, growing, and seemingly hopeless financial needs.

- Cave times commonly occur in prolonged marriage and family difficulties. Wayward children can cause immeasurable pain to believing parents. Other heartrending examples are having an alcoholic or abusive spouse and unsaved family members.

- Cave times can occur through a demanding and unreasonable boss, a grueling and monotonous work schedule, or a jealous, spiteful, and injurious co-worker.

Cave times usually make us feel depressed and all alone. Because others no longer seem as supportive or as friendly, an abandoned feeling leads into the downward spiral of thinking: *No one cares for me!* Like David, we may then conclude: *God has also abandoned me!*

After reading every commentary I have on the Psalms and the life of David, especially the time surrounding Psalm 13, I was amazed to find that there's little said or written in Christian literature about helping believers who feel abandoned by God. Even D. Martyn Lloyd Jones's classic, *Spiritual Depression: Its Causes and Cure,* doesn't cover this topic.[74]

Why do you suppose this is? I think it is because we have been taught that Christians are not to experience such things, that we are only to have "life more abundantly" or to "live victoriously." James Boice explains:

The dying French atheist Voltaire ... said, "I am abandoned by God and man." We are not surprised to hear an unbeliever say that. But if any of us should admit to such feelings, many of our friends would look askance at us, shake their heads, and wonder whether we are Christians. Isn't that true? Isn't that the chief reason why you do not talk to other Christians about this or about many other problems?"[75]

Thankfully, David talked about his painful loneliness. Aren't you glad he didn't cover up his struggles or hide his bad feelings? David didn't mind being thought of as weak, failing, or troubled; he simply cried out to the Lord all the more.

Remember: This was David the psalmist, the one who wrote almost half of the 150 psalms; this was David the spiritual giant, the only one who believed God to defeat Israel's chief nemesis, Goliath; this was David, the king God chose—the man after His own heart—who unashamedly bared his dark struggles of the soul for all to see.

Now let's look at how David survived his deepest, darkest hour of loneliness which took place in that little junction of time between 1 Samuel 21:15 and 22:1, the setting of Psalm 13.[76]

To the Chief Musician. A Psalm of David.

[1] *How long, O LORD? Will You forget me forever?*
  How long will You hide Your face from me?
[2] *How long shall I take counsel in my soul,*
  Having sorrow in my heart daily?
  How long will my enemy be exalted over me?

[3] *Consider and hear me, O LORD my God;*
  Enlighten my eyes,
  Lest I sleep the sleep of death;
[4] *Lest my enemy say,*
  "I have prevailed against him";
  Lest those who trouble me rejoice when I am moved.

[5] *But I have trusted in Your mercy;*
  My heart shall rejoice in Your salvation.
[6] *I will sing to the LORD,*
  Because He has dealt bountifully with me.

In the first two verses David expressed the depths of his soul in four cries of anguish. Each cry reflects something from his background, and is a figure of speech called *erotesis*—asking questions without waiting for or even expecting an answer. This is often a sign of deep emotional stress.

His four cries also represented a second form of speech called *anaphora*—when the same word is repeated at the beginning of successive sentences. David cried in anguish as he asked God four times: "How long?" He never paused because he was overcome with sorrow and grief.

The opening words in Psalm 13:1–2 reveal four deeply wounded areas of David's life. By repeating himself he showed how profound this feeling ran. His confessions sometimes strike a chord in our own hearts:[77]

MY LIFE FEELS LIKE AN ENDLESS STRUGGLE:

How long, O LORD? Will You forget me forever? (13:1a).

Everyone had left David: he was being hunted by his own family (father-in-law); his own people (like Doeg the Edomite in Saul's army); his covenant people of God; and threatened by enemies as he entered a bleak, desert region. With every fiber of his being, David felt dejected and abandoned.

One commentator writes, "Well must David have understood what this was, when, hunted by Saul, he knew not where to betake himself, at one time seeking refuge among the Moabites, at another in the wilderness of Ziph; now an outlaw hiding himself in the cave of Adullam, and anon a captain in the service of the King of the Philistines; and amid all his projects haunted by the mournful conviction, 'I shall now one day perish by the hand of Saul.' " [78]

David was saying: "I just can't go on!" Perhaps you've also reached a point in your marriage, family, work, or school where you feel like saying, "I just can't go on!" If so, remember this: David was feeling those feelings with you as he wrote how he felt, and yet he testified to the Lord's faithfulness in all his constant struggles.

MY LIFE SEEMS TO HAVE LOST GOD'S BLESSING:

How long will You hide Your face from me? (13:1b).

In Psalm 34 he looked back on how he had felt before Achish: "Even though I'm with my enemy and feel desperate, You're still blessing me." But somewhere between fleeing Gath and arriving at the cave of Adullam, David started to grieve over having acted on his own before the king and he lost the sense of the Lord's blessing. So he cried out in anguish, "Not only is my life an endless struggle, but Your apparent blessing has also disappeared!"

Sometimes we don't sense that God is there, but He is; sometimes we don't think He is blessing us, but He is; sometimes we don't think He is watching over us, but He is. But in David's distress he lost sight of God's presence and blessing.

Reality and perception both deeply influence our lives. For example, if you perceive someone doesn't like you, it doesn't matter whether they do or not because your perception changes how you relate to that person. When David perceived a lack of the apparent blessing of God, he said, "Nothing is like it used to be. Every part of my life is troubled and is suffering from a lack of Your blessing!" Now relate how David felt to what it might be like in your own life:

- **My family doesn't seem blessed anymore.** Examples:
  Reality: The early joys of newly wedded life have faded as personality differences have stressed the relationship.
  Perception: God has ceased to bless our marriage because we don't feel like we did in those early days.

  Reality: Those quiet, smiling children are growing into selfish, rebellious teens. The joy of home life has been replaced with the tension of confrontation, correction, and sorrow.
  Perception: God has ceased to bless our family.

- **My work doesn't seem blessed anymore.** Example:
  Reality: The early days of idealism, creativity, and boundless energy that led to growth and success in my career have been replaced with constant obstacles and personal stagnation.
  Perception: God has ceased to bless my work.

- **My ministry doesn't seem blessed anymore.** Example:

  Reality: The spring in my step is gone; my feet feel like lead as I cross the parking lot to teach Sunday school (or serve in AWANA, the youth ministry, the choir, the orchestra, or join in with my group). The joy and sense of purpose are gone.

  Perception: God has ceased to bless my ministry.

- **My spiritual life doesn't seem blessed anymore.** Example:

  Reality: God's Word seems stale; my singing is lifeless; coming to worship is drudgery; my sins feel unforgiven; my past is coming back to haunt me; I feel stained, distant, and as if no one, not even God, cares about my soul!

  Perception: God has ceased to bless me spiritually.

David was saying: "I no longer perceive Your blessing in my home, my work, or my life!"

MY MIND SEEMS SO TROUBLED:

How long shall I take counsel in my soul, having sorrow in my heart daily? (13:2a).

Kiel and Delitzsch, the great German Hebraists, point out that the construction of David's words reflects that he had dark feelings and uncontrolled emotions. He loved the Lord, but the stress of being hunted by Saul, captured by the Philistines, and on the run again had drained him of all peace and joy.

David's experience of being swept away by his emotions is common. He couldn't calmly reflect on God's faithful hand in the past; nor could he feel the comfort of trusting the future to Him. He had ruminated so long on disaster after disaster that he was feeding on the dark thoughts of hopelessness. He couldn't stop it— almost like his thoughts were snowballing, going down faster and faster.

To go through an emotional upheaval like this, you don't have to be running from the Philistines or have a personal adversary who's trying to kill you. There are often several causes for the feelings David confessed, and we can see these same feelings in the lives of others in Scripture. Here are some common causes:

- *Emotional Temperament.* David's temperament was probably the type most prone to discouragement. When I was still in seminary, I asked John MacArthur to compare the way he preached with how another well-known pastor taught. He looked at me with a big smile and said, "No matter what happens to me, I look at life with a continuous attitude—very straight and stable, sort of like a flat line on a monitor. But my friend is up and down—like a roller coaster, or an up and down jagged line. He has his highs and his lows, and that is why we preach differently."

  Did you know that both the "flat line" and the "up and down" people represent personality types? Can you tell which best describes David? If you read the Psalms much, it's easy to conclude he was an "up and down" type. For he had an unbelievable spiritual capacity to soar in the heavenlies with his beloved God and yet he also struggled with temperamental feelings prone to discouragement.

  In his monumental book, *Spiritual Depression: Its Causes and Cure,* Lloyd Jones writes in the opening pages: "**foremost** among all causes of spiritual depression is **temperament**" (emphasis added).[79] There is no such thing as a good or bad temperament. But "flat line" people often think that "up and down" people are out of control; and the "up and down" people view "flat line" people as not caring about anything because they have no feelings. The truth of the matter is that God designed us all as beautiful, spiritual snowflakes; no two people are exactly alike. Because we are all wired differently, some, like David, are more prone to discouragement. That is not just an emotional temperament; it is a common cause for what we find in Scripture for these feelings David confessed.

- *Physical Weakness.* A plunge into disquieting thoughts and emotions can be caused by physical factors—illness, for example. Charles Haddon Spurgeon, one of the greatest evangelical leaders of the last century, suffered from severe bouts of depression. Why would such a spiritual giant, such an incredible expositor, such an extraordinary writer and pastor have severe bouts of paralyzing depression? The main reason is that he suffered from gout, marked by painful inflammation of the joints and an excess of uric acid in the blood. It was common in the last century due to people's eating habits and lack of fresh air and exercise, and this drained Spurgeon's energies. Times of extreme fatigue and physical weakness are an open door for the devil or the flesh to try to push any of us down.[80]

- *Let down.* Another weak and vulnerable time is after great events. Following the feeding of the 5,000 and preaching campaigns, Jesus retreated from the crowds because He needed extra time alone with God to refresh and renew His life. Jesus said, "Father, I want to always please You by doing Your will." Not because He was lacking anything, but to set an example that He could not exist apart from retreating to be strengthened and renewed by His Father. The same holds true for us as well.

  Elijah is another example. When he came down from the mountaintop after having fearlessly stood against a nation, a king and his entire army, and an army of false priests of Baal, he felt so low he was ready to die. But God led him to a quiet place, fed him, rested him, and then personally met with him. (See 1 KINGS 18–19.) James tells us that *Elijah was a man with a nature like ours* (JAMES 5:17). So since Jesus, Elijah, and David all needed to exercise care to protect themselves during vulnerable periods, so do we.

David was saying: "I can't stop these feelings of dejection and abandonment!" If this is a pattern in your life, watch out for let-downs that can lead to an emotional roller coaster ride of rampant feelings of discouragement and abandonment. Learn to head off these pitfalls through a personal retreat in the Word and prayer. It is a good idea to also ask your spouse and/or close friend to hold you accountable when you are succeeding. Because let-downs often follow high moments, your accountability partner should remind you: "Be careful; this could be a vulnerable time for you. You need to constantly be putting *on the whole armor of God, that you may be able to stand against the wiles of the devil* (EPHESIANS 6:11)."

MY LIFE SEEMS TO HAVE LOST GOD'S VICTORY:

How long will my enemy be exalted over me? (13:2b).

David said, "It's no use. Saul is going to win. He has all the troops, resources, and time he needs. He will end up destroying me!" Do you realize what was really happening here? David was actually saying, "God, didn't You promise me I was going to be the next king someday? Isn't that what your Word says? Isn't that what Your prophet Samuel said when he anointed me with Your oil? And didn't he say I would sit on the throne? But God, my enemy's going to triumph over me! If it's not the Philistines, Saul's going to get me! But I thought Your Word said ..." When David got to that point he was right where Satan wanted him. What did Satan do to Eve in the Garden of Eden? He tricked her into doubting God's Word, God's goodness, and God's plan. Satan planted these seeds of doubt: "Has God said that? Did He *really*?"

- Most likely, you don't have literal human enemies (at least not serious ones). But if you are a Christian, you do have one great spiritual enemy who is worse than any human enemy you can imagine—the devil, whom Peter compared to *a roaring lion, seeking whom he may devour* (1 PETER 5:8).

  How does Satan devour us? He has no literal teeth, as do actual roaring lions. But his "teeth" are far more dangerous! The devil sows seeds of doubt to get us to question God's promises, faithfulness, goodness, and timing. The devil wants to trick us into this type thinking: "Lord, are You even paying attention to me? After all, look at my age and yet I have no worthwhile career, life partner, or children. I don't even have enough savings and I'm nearing the end of my working time. What's wrong with Your timing?"

  That is exactly how David felt, so Satan thought he had won the upper hand when David said, "It's no use. Saul's going to win! God's promises aren't true after all!" The devil wants to devour each of us. His tactics, however, differ; they are not all the same for every person.

- Lloyd-Jones says of this foe: "The devil [is] the adversary of our souls. He can use our temperaments and our physical condition. He so deals with us that we allow our temperament to control and govern us, instead of keeping temperament where it should be kept. There is no end to the ways the devil produces spiritual depression. We must always bear him in mind." [81]

David was saying: "I am constantly defeated!" If the devil wants to get you down, he lets your emotions run your life. But what is supposed to be running our lives? The Apostle Paul said, *Walk in the Spirit, and you shall not fulfill the lust of the flesh* [our emotions, or temperament] (GALATIANS 5:16). God commands us to be *bringing every thought into captivity to the obedience of Christ* (2 CORINTHIANS 10:5). That was David's greatest need as he voiced his four cries of anguish: "Lord, I'm doubting Your promises; my mind is so troubled; I'm just endlessly in struggles; and I no longer have Your blessing!"

How did David find the doorway of hope when he felt so hopeless? How did he find God's presence in his perceived abandonment? How did David survive this terrible time? *He decided he would not live in the pits!*

David's turning point was prayer. To rise above the downward pull of his emotions, all he had to do was to look up and talk to the Lord—the One he thought had abandoned him!

In my own life, there have been times when dealing with everybody else's problems, problems in the family, and personal problems, something occurs like a car breaking down or the house needing repair, and suddenly it all feels overwhelming. When that happens, I tend to quietly retreat to my desk, but my sweet Bonnie always finds me—just looking down, not doing anything. So she asks, "Honey, what's wrong?" If I reply "Nothing's wrong" and fail to look up at her, she knows instantly that I'm looking down at my problems, meditating on them.

Anxiety is nothing more than meditating on problems rather than the One Who holds the solution. But God clearly commands us to meditate on His Word instead:

> *"This Book of the Law shall not depart from your mouth, but you shall* **meditate in it day and night**, *that you may observe to do according to all that is written in it. For then you will make your way prosperous, and* **then you will have good success**. *Have I not commanded you? Be strong and of good courage; do not be afraid, nor be dismayed, for the* LORD *your God is with you wherever you go"* (JOSHUA 1:8–9).

When everything seems overwhelming to me, how does my wonderful Bonnie minister to my pain? It's really very simple: she just puts her hand under my chin and says, "Honey, look up at me!" If I keep my eyes down she says, "No, I want to *see* your eyes." If you have children, when you're talking to them, you've probably said, "Look at me." If they keep looking down rather than looking you in the eyes, that is acting like a child, isn't it? That is what we often do with the Lord, just as David did. When he finally heard God say, "Look at Me!"—and looked up to Him—he got the lift in his soul that gave him the power to break free from his uncontrolled emotions. Because the turning point was his prayer, we could put these words of the poet into David's mouth:

When all things seem against us,
　To drive us to despair,
We know one gate is open
　One ear will hear our prayer.[82]

Whose ear is that? The One David addressed in this next verse: *Consider and **hear me**, O LORD my God; **enlighten my eyes**, lest I sleep the sleep of death* (PSALM 13:3).

When David asked for three things, that was exactly what God wanted to hear, and why all the turbulence hit his life. Do you remember what I said about being at 27,000 feet when the plane did its roller coaster moves, the luggage fell out, and screams were heard? That immediately caused us all to think about the pilot's reliability!

God never wants us to ruminate in feelings of abandonment, hopelessness, dejection, and despair. He wants us to think of Him as our Pilot by asking ourselves: *Who's really flying the plane of my life? I'm certainly not qualified!* That is what David said when he looked up to the Lord and asked these three things—and God answered him:

1. **Look at me:** <u>*Consider*</u> *and hear me, O LORD my God; enlighten my eyes, lest I sleep the sleep of death* (13:3a). David felt as if God had turned His back on him, so he asked the Lord to turn around and look at him. Actually, God was looking at David all the time—just as Bonnie looked at me when I felt so overwhelmed. And when she lifted up my chin and said, "Look at me"—I beheld her gentle eyes of love and smile of comfort!

   David's perception was that the Lord left him, but in reality he was the one who looked away from the Lord. David's wrong perception of God led him into an emotional roller coaster ride until the Lord said, "Look at Me!" When God lifted David's face to look at Him, he beheld the Lord's gentle eyes of love and smile of comfort—and knew He'd heard his cries!

2. **Answer me:** *Consider and <u>hear me</u>, O LORD my God; enlighten my eyes, lest I sleep the sleep of death* (13:3b). David felt like God had stopped talking to him. This Hebrew word literally means "answer." David was asking the Lord to let Him hear His voice again, just as he had in the old days; he wanted God to *answer* him. Applying that to today, this is when

we should take God's Word and say, "Open Your Word to my heart again. Let me cling to Your Truth. Help my unbelief!"

3. **Restore me:** *Consider and hear me, O LORD my God; enlighten my eyes, lest I sleep the sleep of death* (13:3c). David was saying, "Lift up my chin, Lord, so I can see You! Say something to me, and when You do, it will enlighten me. It will bring light into the darkness of my soul."

David's proneness to discouragement and dejection was actually what made him so powerful; his being so emotive is what enables us to feel what he felt. However, "up and down" temperaments who can feel so powerfully can also feel great darkness. For that reason, it's not surprising that David felt he was going to die and never be king. In his alarm he appealed to God to do what He promised: "You promised to never leave me—I need Your presence again. You told me You loved me to the uttermost—I need Your power again. You said You would comfort me—I need Your peace again. Restore me by enlightening me!"

Now look at Psalm 13:4–6—

^{4} *Lest my enemy say, "I have prevailed against him"; lest those who trouble me rejoice when I am moved.* ^{5} *But I have trusted in Your mercy; my heart shall rejoice in Your salvation.* ^{6} **I will sing to the LORD,** *because He has dealt bountifully with me.*

I love how Psalm 13 ends—David is *singing* to the Lord! In my mind's eye, I can easily envision this hunched-over man weeping and wailing and crying out, "How long? How long? How long? How long?" But suddenly he stops, lifts up his chin, looks up toward heaven, and says, "Lord, consider me; answer me; enlighten me!" And in that spiritual moment God gives David the presence, power, and awareness he needed so that what started out as cries of anguished abandonment now turn into him singing praises to the Lord!

WALKING OUT OF THE CAVE

Wouldn't it have been great to witness David walking to the cave singing from some of the psalms he'd been inspired to write as he fled from Saul to Nob, to Gath, and now on his way to the cave of Adullam? As his emotions calmed down, having been reassured that God hadn't abandoned him, he remembered His faithfulness and may have sung verses like these:

The LORD is my shepherd; ... I will fear no evil; for You are with me (PSALM 23:1, 4).

To You, O my Strength, I will sing praises; for God is my defense, my God of mercy (PSALM 59:17).

In the LORD I put my trust; how can you say to my soul, "Flee as a bird to your mountain?" (PSALM 11:1).

The righteous shall be glad in the LORD, and trust in Him (PSALM 64:10).

I will wait on Your name, for it is good (PSALM 52:9).

Whenever I am afraid, I will trust in You (PSALM 56:3).

Oh, taste and see that the LORD is good; blessed is the man who trusts in Him! (PSALM 34:8).

I will sing to the LORD, because He has dealt bountifully with me (PSALM 13:6).

Did you know that many praise songs we sing today are actually David's words? That is what God offers us also when we feel abandoned!

If you find yourself feeling that the Lord has abandoned you, think on this: *To be abandoned means that once you were not.* You can't say your spouse abandoned you if you never had a spouse; you can't say your friends abandoned you if you didn't have any friends. So when David said the God he loved, knew, and walked with had abandoned him—that meant he once had a God Who loved, knew, and walked with him. Think of the implications:

> For the true child of God there is always some awareness of this truth, regardless of how deep his or her depression may be. We may be depressed even to the point of feeling utterly abandoned. But the fact that we feel abandoned itself means that we really know God is there. To be abandoned you need somebody to be abandoned by. Because we are Christians and have been taught by God in Scripture, we know that God still loves us and will be faithful to us, regardless of our feelings.[83]

In conclusion, the devil wants to make you doubt God's goodness, plan, timing, and Word. But if you let doubt take over your emotions, your temperament is running the show—piloting your plane. You'll quickly head into a nose-dive and roller coaster rides. In that case, you need to examine your thinking: *Who, exactly, is up front flying this careening machine of my life?* Then look up and say, "Lord, don't let my temperament, my emotions, my doubts, or my feelings usurp Your rightful place as the Pilot of my life. For You I want to look at; You I want to listen to; You I want to rescue me!"

David found hope in his dark hour because troubles and temptations always pushed him toward the Lord. The greater the turbulence in his life, the more he entrusted himself to the One piloting his plane. Even when he felt all alone, he discovered that his Pilot was still there flying him safely through the storms. Dark times merely surfaced the reality deep down in David's soul: God was his choice, his habit, and his desire, because he supremely loved the Lord! Do you share his passion?

10 | How to Get Out of the Pits of Life

Psalms 40, 70, 113

I waited patiently for the LORD; and He inclined to me, and heard my cry. —**Psalm 40:1**

DISASTROUS EVENTS LIKE THE FOLLOWING are unforgettably imprinted upon our memories as an example of what it's like to be living life in the pits:

> NEWS BULLETIN ... **August 29, 2005** ... Hurricane Katrina makes landfall in New Orleans ... Severe loss of life and property ... Millions of lives disrupted ... Tens of thousands lost everything ... Homeless thousands out of touch with friends and family ... Food and water scarce ... Multiplied thousands jobless ... Refugees fleeing the flood and devastation overwhelmed by an uncertain future ... .[84]

The fear, pain, and hopelessness reflected in the faces of the crowds waiting to be rescued in the aftermath of Hurricane Katrina was a collective picture of what some individuals face every day. Yet, what we witnessed as hundreds of thousands faced devastation together is what David faced alone.

Where was David when he wrote Psalm 40? He was remembering life at the bottom—life in the pits:

- David had lost everything.
- David was homeless.
- David was out of touch with his family and friends and did not know who had survived and who hadn't.
- David had no sure supply of food or water.
- David had to find an escape route to flee the dangers he faced.
- David's life and emotions were flooded by a hurricane of troubles.

Learn to Flee to Christ

RATHER THAN SINK INTO UTTER despair in the pits, David fled to the Lord and found the pathway back up after hitting bottom. Psalm 40 represents "the truth that muddy times may be the experience even of the greatest saints and slimy pits the lot even of kings and preachers."[85]

Believers in Christ aren't protected from bottoming out in the unexpected traumatic twists in life; they just have a way back up. In fact, most of God's greatest servants have spent significant time in what we could call "life in the pits."

That truth is aptly illustrated in the life of a famous Christian author who was highly acquainted with suffering: he lost his first wife to death, had handicapped children, and faced constant hardships and losses as he sat in a lonely prison cell for a third of his adult life. Who was he? John Bunyan.

Like David in Psalm 40, Bunyan fled to the Lord for strength to overcome his unending struggles. As a result, he, too, produced a long-lasting legacy of praise to the Lord. His testimonies about God's faithfulness in hard times became songs, hymns, and well-known books.

BEDFORD JAIL BLUES

Amidst the stench and filth of a seventeenth-century English prison called the Bedford Jail, God produced great things through Bunyan's sufferings. Although he authored sixty books, the most renowned is *Pilgrim's Progress*. Begun as a story to entertain his children on their visits to his jail cell, it has become one of the most eminent and enduring works of Christian fiction.

Bunyan wrote most of *Pilgrim's Progress* on the brown paper covers his wife used as stoppers on the milk jugs she brought to him while he was in jail a second time.[86] First published in 1678, the book sold more than 100,000 copies in its first year in print and remains a Christian best-seller to this day.[87]

Bunyan describes his salvation and the hard pathway of life in this world as a believer. Perhaps better than anyone, he expressed the quest for God that marks the Christian life. *Pilgrim's Progress* is the allegorical story of a man who, in a dream, meets a man named Evangelist who asks the despondent hero why he is crying. His answer is poignant:

> Sir, I perceive by the Book in my hand, that I am condemned to die, and after that to come to Judgment; and I find that I am not willing to do the first, nor able to do the second.

The hero suffers from two problems. He is unwilling to die. He is also unable to stand before God. This is not the inability to appear at judgment—that is inevitable—but to *survive* the judgment of God. He verbalizes his fear by saying:

> I fear that this Burden that is upon my back, will sink me lower than the grave.

The place "lower than the grave" is the abyss of hell. Like a fishing line with a small piece of lead attached at the end to make it sink to the depth of the lake, so the person weighted down by a massive burden of sin will sink into the depths of hell.

Christian, the hero of Bunyan's story, flees from the wrath to come, and sets his face toward the shining Light and the Wicket Gate to seek an inheritance that is incorruptible, undefiled, and which fades not away. That is his salvation experience.

His course toward glory is marked by obstacles, however. Friends named Obstinate and Pliable mock him and try to dissuade him from his mission. He encounters the Slough of Despond early in his pilgrimage and falls into it. A man named Help rescues him from his plight and says:

> This miry slough is such a place as cannot be mended: It is the descent whither the scum and filth that attends Conviction for Sin doth continually run, and therefore it is called the slough of Despond; for still as the Sinner is awakened about his lost condition, there ariseth in his soul many fears and doubts, and discouraging apprehensions, which all of them get together, and settle in this place: And this is the reason of the badness of this place.

What Christian has never visited the Slough of Despond? Who has never tried to avoid it altogether? Our souls have all been assailed by doubts, fears, and discouragements. It is not by accident that the most frequent admonition from the lips of Jesus in the New Testament is the exhortation to "Fear not."[88]

DAVID'S DESCENT INTO THE PITS

What led to David's descent into living life in the pits—the miry "Slough of Despond"? It all started when he allowed his mind and emotions to rule over his spirit:

- **Excited**. Can you imagine how you would feel if you were a military hero who had actually saved an entire army and liberated a nation from military occupation? That describes David's life as a teenager. His confrontation with Goliath sent shock waves throughout the entire region. The Philistine army had held Israel in mortal fear by fielding the ultimate weapon—a ten-foot-tall "Terminator" who could kill any challenger with dread fear just by his sheer size. David's swift victory stunned and confused the enemy army and led to a resounding victory. *But exciting times can fade so fast.*

- **Popular**. Can you imagine what it would be like to be the best known musician for an entire nation? That describes David's late teenaged years. He played for the royal events in King Saul's palace. He was known, heard, seen, and sought after as a brilliant musician and lyricist. He could write, he could play, and he could sing. No one else in the entire country could compare to him. *But popularity can fade so fast.*

- **Secure**. Can you imagine what it would be like to be an undefeated warrior? There is no record of David ever suffering a military defeat. Although he faced much larger armies, much fiercer foes, and much greater danger than anyone else in his day, he returned victorious again and again. Soon he was credited as having killed ten times as many enemy soldiers as even the king himself. *But security can fade so fast.*

- **Happy**. Can you imagine being married to the best-known and most beautiful woman in the country? That was David's wife, Michal, the king's daughter. When you add his being the best-known musician and the best-known soldier, it sounds like everything was going well for David. He was on top of the world—he had it all! *But happiness can fade so fast.*

- **Wham**. Can you imagine how devastated David must have felt when the king suddenly got angry at him, his job was terminated, all future plans were cancelled, his family left, and his home was abandoned? Life got so hard that David had what we would describe as a complete emotional and mental breakdown when he acted crazy before Achish, King of Gath. *Everything in David's life changed so fast!*

When David wasn't running from Saul, he was fleeing his own countrymen, the Philistines, and everything in between. And when you add his sense of failure for having acted on his own before Achish, this led to his dark days in Psalm 13 where he recorded having hit bottom and living in the pits of despondency after he fled from Gath. Emotionally, physically, and spiritually exhausted, David felt dejected, depressed, and discouraged— all alone, unwanted, and abandoned even by the Lord. So if anyone could rightfully wallow in the pit of despair due to all the worst circumstances, David sure could.

The Way Out

THE APOSTLE PAUL'S TESTIMONY FROM New Testament times gives us more insights into what life can be like living in the pits of hard circumstances:

> *For I think that God has displayed us, the apostles, last, as men condemned to death; for we have been made a spectacle to the world, both to angels and to men. We are fools for Christ's sake, but you are wise in Christ! We are weak, but you are strong! You are distinguished, but we are dishonored! To the present hour we both hunger and thirst, and we are poorly clothed, and beaten, and homeless. And we labor, working with our own hands. Being reviled, we bless; being persecuted, we endure; being defamed, we entreat. We have been made as the filth of the world, the offscouring of all things until now* (1 CORINTHIANS 4:9–13; see also 2 CORINTHIANS 6:4–10; 11:24–28).

Did Paul stay in the pit of those circumstances? No, because God reminded Him that his strength was to come from the Lord, and not his own efforts.[89]

*And He said to me, "**My grace is sufficient for you, for My strength is made perfect in weakness.**" Therefore most gladly I will rather boast in my infirmities, that the power of Christ may rest upon me. Therefore I take pleasure in infirmities, in reproaches, in needs, in persecutions, in distresses, for Christ's sake. **For when I am weak, then I am strong** (2 CORINTHIANS 12:9–10).*

Paul embraced Christ's gracious offer—as David did when he wouldn't let his circumstances defeat him and confessed: *Blessed is that man who makes the* LORD *his trust* (PSALM 40:4).

We don't get to choose our hard times, and we normally can't change most of our circumstances, but we can choose how we respond. At the end of Psalm 13, David literally saw the Light as he looked up and realized God was there, and he sang to Him. However, that didn't instantly change everything. Coming to God, or even coming back to God, doesn't immediately solve all our problems, but it does give us the pathway and solution we need.

Most of us don't know very much about the dark side of life. We avoid it, flee from sin, and try to stay happy, busy, and care free. But David was willing to talk about what many of us have felt and some of us fear. Thus, he bared his soul for the entire world to see. With his amazing confession comes the pathway he followed in Psalm 40 to escape the pit of despair he felt before he arrived at the cave of Adullam, which is recorded in 1 Samuel 22:1. Although David didn't know it at the time, God was preparing him for yet another unexpected event—having to babysit 400 malcontents in the cave!

David's Pathway Out of the Pits

How DID DAVID GET RESCUED from living life in the pits? If you are living in the pits right now, or know someone who is, learn from these six steps—the Lord's divine gift to us from His Word!

FIRST STEP: REMEMBER GOD'S WORK IN YOUR LIFE.

I waited patiently for the LORD; *and **He inclined to me**, and **heard my cry**. He also **brought me up** out of a horrible pit, out of the miry clay, and **set my feet upon a rock**, and **established my steps**. He has **put a new song in my mouth**—Praise to our God; many will see it and fear, and will trust in the* LORD (PSALM 40:1–3).

In verses 1–3, as David remembered God's work in his life, he noted various ways the Lord had directed His grace toward him. If you are a born-again child of God, you should also take time to reflect upon the ways the Lord's grace has been bestowed on you—especially your salvation experience.

If you are presently in the dark side of life, know that the loving and merciful God of the Second Chance who rescued this man from the dark pit of sin is the same God Who can rescue you from living life in the pits:

Who am I? My godly mother died when I was a young child. Reared by a sea-captain father, taken to sea at age eleven, I soon forgot the Scriptures she had taught me.

Several years later, I was pressed into the British navy and became a midshipman. By then I had earned the reputation of being able to curse for two hours straight without repeating a word. Restless and wild, I tried to desert, was caught, stripped, whipped severely, and degraded to the ranks. I eventually ran away to Africa, but only so "I might sin my fill." And I did.

Debauched and distant from God, I fell into the hands of a Portuguese slave trader. For months the chief woman of the trader's harem treated me like an animal, beating me and forcing me to grovel in the dirt for my food.

Reduced to a mangy cur of a man, I finally escaped and made my way to the shores of Africa. Picked up by a passing ship I earned the position of first mate because I was a skilled navigator. But while the captain was ashore one day, I broke out the ship's rum and got the entire crew drunk. When the captain came back, he was so furious he hit me, knocking me overboard.

I would have drowned were it not for a sailor who pulled me back on board by spearing my thigh with a boat hood. The wound was so large that it left a scar big enough to put my fist in. Some weeks later, when the ship neared the coast of Scotland, it sailed into a storm and almost sank. For days I manned the pumps below deck in what seemed a hopeless nightmare.

It was then that I desperately called out to God. He answered my helpless cry, and I emerged from the hold of that ship to later become the
chaplain of England's Parliament and even to preach before the king. I
am the vile blasphemer whom many would subsequently refer to as the
second founder of the Church of England. And it was I who wrote:

Amazing grace! how sweet the sound,
That saved a wretch like me!
I once was lost, but now am found,
Was blind, but now I see.

These were the lyrics born out of my wayward, free-versed life. And
to my ears, there is no sweeter sound than grace in all the world. Who
am I? John Newton.[90]

Newton's remaining stanzas of "Amazing Grace" speak of the marvelous
grace Christ gives to each of His children of faith:

'Twas grace that taught my heart to fear,
And grace my fears relieved.
How precious did that grace appear
The hour I first believed.

The Lord has promised good to me,
His Word my hope secures;
He will my Shield and Portion be,
As long as life endures.

Through many dangers, toils and snares,
I have already come;
'Tis grace hath brought me safe thus far,
And grace will lead me home.
                    —John Newton (1725–1807)

When was the last time you cried to the Lord and He responded? How
many times has He rescued in the past? Have you thanked Him for His faithfulness? Have you thanked Him for His love? Have you lavished praise on
Jesus Christ for His saving grace? As you remember God's wonderful work in

your life, ask the Lord to bring someone to mind whom He wants you to tell about all He's done!

SECOND STEP: REAFFIRM YOUR TRUST IN GOD.

Blessed is that man who makes the LORD his trust, *and does not respect the proud, nor such as turn aside to lies. Many, O LORD my God, are Your wonderful works which You have done; and Your thoughts toward us cannot be recounted to You in order; if I would declare and speak of them, they are more than can be numbered* (PSALM 40:4–5).

David refused to let his disheartening circumstances defeat him. That is what he confessed in verse 4 by *verbally* saying he was trusting God. Sometimes we need to break the spiritual silence in our heart by *talking to God—telling Him* what we know is true. We may also need to *preach the gospel* to ourselves! Thus, David reaffirmed his trust in God. Have you done that lately?

The following lyrics, written by Charitie Lees Bancroft in 1863, are a great sermon to preach to your soul. I hope you will repeat these words to the Lord as you remember His work in your life:

BEFORE THE THRONE OF GOD ABOVE

Before the throne of God above
I have a strong and perfect plea.
A great high Priest whose Name is Love
Who ever lives and pleads for me.

My name is graven on His hands,
My name is written on His heart.
I know that while in Heaven He stands
No tongue can bid me thence depart.

When Satan tempts me to despair
And tells me of the guilt within,
Upward I look and see Him there
Who made an end of all my sin.

Because the sinless Savior died
My sinful soul is counted free.
For God the just is satisfied
To look on Him and pardon me.
Behold Him there the risen Lamb,
My perfect spotless righteousness,
The great unchangeable I AM,
King of glory and of grace,

One in Himself I cannot die.
My soul is purchased by His blood,
My life is hid with Christ on high,
With Christ my Savior and my God!
    —Charitie L. Bancroft (1841–1923)

THIRD STEP: RENEW YOUR SUBMISSION TO GOD.

Sacrifice and offering You did not desire; <u>my ears You have opened</u>.
Burnt offering and sin offering You did not require. *Then I said,*
"Behold, I come; *in the scroll of the book it is written of me. I delight* **to**
do Your will, *O my God, and Your law is within my heart"*
(PSALM 40:6–8).

These verses are Christ's marching orders for us—the key to understanding Psalm 40. And when you consider how Christ and the apostles used this psalm, you have something very powerful!

Until the New Testament was written, the power in these verses was not clear to the reader. Who was David talking about in verses 6–8? About himself or Someone to come—Someone greater than David? We find the answer in Hebrews 10:5–9:

Therefore, when He came into the world, He said: **"Sacrifice and offer-**
ing You did not desire, *but a body You have prepared for Me.* **In burnt**
offerings and sacrifices for sin You had no pleasure. *Then I said,*
'Behold, I have come—*in the volume of the book it is written of Me*—**to**
do Your will, *O God.' " Previously saying, "Sacrifice and offering, burnt*
offerings, and offerings for sin You did not desire, nor had pleasure in
them" (which are offered according to the law), then He said, **"Behold,**

I have come to do Your will, O God." He takes away the first that He may establish the second.

The writer of Hebrews was explaining that Psalm 40 contained a promise of Christ in the Old Testament—and that is exactly what Jesus came to do. God's will was Christ's plan; it was Christ's marching orders which He gladly followed.

What was Jesus' repeatedly stated goal throughout His earthly life? Look at what He said in the Gospel by John:

- *Jesus said to them, "My food is **to do the will of Him who sent Me**, and to finish His work"* (JOHN 4:34).

- *"I can of Myself do nothing. As I hear, I judge; and My judgment is righteous, because **I do not seek My own will but the will of the Father who sent Me**"* (JOHN 5:30).

- *"For I have come down from heaven, **not to do My own will, but the will of Him who sent Me**"* (JOHN 6:38).

- *"And He who sent Me is with Me. The Father has not left Me alone, for **I always do those things that please Him**"* (JOHN 8:29).

In the Garden of Gethsemane, here are Christ's last words of prayer that prepared Him for the cross: *He knelt down and prayed, saying, "Father, if it is Your will, take this cup away from Me; nevertheless **not My will, but Yours, be done**"* (LUKE 22:41–42).

Now back to Psalm 40:6 and the phrase *"my ears You have opened."* In Hebrew this is literally "ears" or "two ears You have dug for me." David was picturing his desire to reflect Christ's coming obedience and dedication. Psalm 40 is a messianic Psalm (a look ahead through David's life at the coming Christ). He was told by the Spirit of God that this would be Christ's desire, so David chose to embrace it as well—even in the deepest pits of discouragement, depression, despair, and loneliness.

No matter what sin tripped him up, what emotion pushed him down, what dark thought pierced him through, or what temptation to quit surrounded him, David declared, "I want to do Your will, oh God. I dedicate myself as Your lifelong servant!"

If you are in the pits right now, nothing can keep you there if you desire to do God's will with all your heart. Inviting the Lord to open your ears is the key to submission with God, and it involves two steps: (1) clear out any hindrances that are in the way, and (2) submit to the permanent marking of ownership.

First, the Hebrew word for "ears" or "two ears You have dug for me" literally means "to dig out." Notice two other times this word is used:

1. " 'My father made me swear, saying, "Behold, I am dying; in **my grave which I dug for myself in the land of Canaan**, there you shall bury me." Now therefore, please let me go up and bury my father, and I will come back' " (GENESIS 50:5).

   Like the grave: A grave was where they laid what was dearest to them on earth. In other words, "You dug things out of my life so there was room for You to fill me. Through excruciating times, You are making room in my life to deposit something special."

2. "**The well** the leaders sank, **dug** by the nation's nobles, by the lawgiver, with their staves." And from the wilderness they went to Mattanah (NUMBERS 21:18).

   Like the well: "You took everything out of my life in these lonely times, painful as it was, so that I could hear Your voice clearly and let your water flow into my life."

Both are pictures of clearing things out of the way so that the water can flow into the well and make room for something in the grave. So David was saying, "You 'dug my ears.' You are tunneling a well of water to refresh me; You are making room to bury into my life Your greatest treasures." This is like Newton's "T'was grace that taught my heart to fear, and grace my fears relieved" What a beautiful way to look at hard times!

But that is not all that David shared from this time in the pits. There is another exciting picture of what submission to God means.

The second way David used this word was to look back at an ancient Mosaic ritual. When slaves had worked their term of service, and it was time to be freed, they were released to start out on their own. But slaves who loved their master and their work could request a lifetime of servitude. This fascinating ritual is explained in Exodus 21:1–6:

*"Now these are the judgments which you shall set before them: If you buy a Hebrew servant, he shall serve six years; and in the seventh he shall go out free and pay nothing. If he comes in by himself, he shall go out by himself; if he comes in married, then his wife shall go out with him. If his master has given him a wife, and she has borne him sons or daughters, the wife and her children shall be her master's, and he shall go out by himself. But if the servant plainly says, 'I love my master, my wife, and my children; I will not go out free,' then his master shall **bring him to the judges**. He shall also bring him to the door, or to the doorpost, and his master shall **pierce his ear** with an awl; and he shall **serve him forever**."*

Note that such a sacrifice was public, painful, and permanent. On this side of the cross, Romans 12 reveals that God longs for the same commitment from each of His children—the desire to become His bondslaves—His servants for life:

Present [aorist infinitive—"remain in the state of"] *your bodies a living sacrifice, holy, acceptable to God, which is your reasonable service. And **do not be conformed** [present imperative—"do not allow yourself to get squashed"] **to this world**, but be transformed by the renewing of your mind, that you may prove what is that good and acceptable and perfect will of God* (ROMANS 12:1–2).

If this is your desire, you should declare that commitment *publicly*: "I want to serve the Lord all my days!" Then you need to make some *painful* choices to limit your flesh, discipline your life, and invest in the world-to-come instead of merely this world. When you give yourself completely to the Lord, it is a *permanent* service which lasts forever:

*I have been crucified with Christ; **it is no longer I who live, but Christ lives in me**; and the life which I now live in the flesh I live by faith in the Son of God, who loved me and gave Himself for me* (GALATIANS 2:20).

FOURTH STEP: REPEAT TRUTHS ABOUT GOD.

*I have proclaimed the good news of **righteousness** in the great assembly; indeed, I do not restrain my lips, O LORD, You Yourself know. I have not hidden **Your righteousness** within my heart; I have declared **Your*** *faithfulness and **Your salvation**; I have not concealed **Your loving kindness** and **Your truth** from the great assembly. Do not withhold **Your tender mercies** from me, O LORD; let **Your lovingkindness** and **Your truth** continually preserve me. For innumerable evils have surrounded me; my iniquities have overtaken me, so that I am not able to look up; they are more than the hairs of my head; therefore my heart fails me (PSALM 40:9–12).*

As David looked back over his life of loneliness, desperation, sorrow, and fear, he saw one truth most clearly: God is righteous. The key New Testament book on righteousness is Romans where God's righteousness and our need of it is mentioned sixty-six times.

Paul declared in Romans that God is righteous in these key areas that matter for eternity:

Chapters 1–2—God is righteous in declaring us as hopeless in our **sin**.
Chapters 3–5, 9–11—God is righteous in providing for our **salvation**.
Chapters 6–8—God is righteous in demanding our **sanctification**.
Chapters 12–16—God is righteous in bestowing gifts for our **service**.

God's Word recorded that David's entire life testified to God's righteousness. God was righteous in *David's perilous years* when he was a fugitive; God was righteous in *David's prosperous years* when he was victorious in every battle and sat upon the throne of Israel; God was righteous in *David's punitive years* when he sinned and was chastened by the Lord; and God was righteous in *David's peaceful years* when he gathered treasures to build the temple!

FIFTH STEP: REJOICE IN GOD IN THE PITS OF LIFE.

*Be pleased, O LORD, to deliver me; O LORD, **make haste to help me!** Let them be ashamed and brought to mutual confusion who seek to destroy my life; let them be driven backward and brought to dishonor who wish me evil. Let them be confounded because of their shame, who say to me, "Aha, aha!" **Let all those who seek You rejoice and be glad in You; let such as love Your salvation say continually, "The LORD be magnified!"** But I am poor and needy; yet the LORD thinks upon me. You are my help and my deliverer; do not delay, O my God (PSALM 40:13–17).*

When we choose to obey and flee to the Lord like David, we will find the place he could always reach for safety and security in any situation. Just as the Lord was his Refuge, so the Lord is our Refuge also. Christ is the safest spot in the universe—the only sure place to go when life gets tough! Because He is our pathway out of the pits, we can rejoice anytime and anywhere.

Psalm 70, which is reflective as David looked back on this time and shared the Lord, is nearly identical to Psalm 40:13–17. Compare the similarities (a couple of them are highlighted for you):

> *Make haste, O God, to deliver me!* **Make haste to help me**, *O* LORD! *Let them be ashamed and confounded who seek my life; let them be turned back and confused who desire my hurt. Let them be turned back because of their shame, who say, "Aha, aha!"* **Let all those who seek You rejoice and be glad in You; and let those who love Your salvation say continually, "Let God be magnified!"** *But I am poor and needy; make haste to me, O God! You are my help and my deliverer; O* LORD, *do not delay* (PSALM 70:1–5).

Life was so bad at this time that David cried out for help from God four times: "Make haste! Come now! Hasten to me! Don't wait!" It's like he was saying, "Lord, I am sinking and am going to perish! Unless you help me quickly, I am not going to make it in this job, this marriage, this family, this sickness, this disaster!"

The bottom line in life is this: *Whom do you want to please?* There are only two possible choices at the deepest level. Either we please God or we in one way or another are seeking to please ourselves. David consistently wanted to please God, and this began way back in his youth when he wrote: *Let the words of my mouth and the meditation of my heart be acceptable in Your sight, O* LORD, *my strength and my Redeemer* (PSALM 19:14).

Early in life, David broke with the crowd; he stopped getting and seeking approval from his peers and went straight to the top. He wanted God and God alone to be his goal—and that was still his desire in this seemingly unending trial.

One way or another we all get what we really want. Without a doubt, David wanted God! Do you? Down deep in your heart of hearts are you searching for ways to give God more of your life? David was, and did, and he became forever settled in heaven as a man after God's own heart.

The primary message of Psalms 40 and 70 is summarized in one of Paul's most repeated exhortations:

Be anxious for nothing, but in everything by prayer and supplication, with thanksgiving, let your requests be made known to God; and the peace of God, which surpasses all understanding, will guard your hearts and minds through Christ Jesus (PHILIPPIANS 4:6–7).

Those verses can be condensed in the form of two imperatives: **Worry about nothing; pray about everything!**

David rejoiced in God.
Troubles—yes; pessimism—no!
Poor and needy—always!
As David did, you, too, can rejoice in the Lord always!

SIXTH STEP: PRAY AND PRAISE IN THE PITS.

The last step in the pathway out of the pits is to pray and praise. In fact, if we back up through what we have seen so far, it all makes so much sense. When we pray we can praise; when we praise we can repeat truth about God; when we repeat truth about God we can renew our submission to God; when we renew our submission to God we can reaffirm our trust in Him; and when we reaffirm our trust in Him we can remember His work in our life. Then back again to prayer and praise as God's final pathway out of the pits!

What can God do with our hard, lonely, dark, and fearful times? If we give ourselves over to Him during such periods, He can use them for our good and His glory. By the power of the Holy Spirit we can follow: *Rejoice always, pray without ceasing, in everything give thanks; for this is the will of God in Christ Jesus for you* (1 THESSALONIANS 5:16–18).

Does that apply in the twenty-first century as well? After all, the Psalms are 3,000 years old, so do they still work? To find out, let's look at a testimonial from Paul, the writer of half the New Testament.

Psalm 40 is a song David wrote and sang to the Lord as he faced the lowest point of his life. Now look at how Paul dealt with one of his low points: *At midnight Paul and Silas were **praying and singing hymns** [Greek humneo] to God, and the prisoners were listening to them* (ACTS 16:25).

Many words were pulled out of the Greek language into English. For example, *humneo* even sounds like "hymns." Paul and Silas were singing hymns to God. (Amazingly, the prisoners were listening to them.)

It is fascinating that we can know what they were singing because *humneo* doesn't just mean randomly singing. It is the same word used at the Last

Supper with Jesus Christ: *And when they had sung a **hymn** [humneo], they went out* (MATTHEW 26:30). Translating Hebrew events in the Greek language always meant that they were singing from the Psalms.

Psalms 113–118 and 136 were the hymns (*humneo*) Jews sang at special events. They did not have the New Testament at this point. The book of Acts is a very early part of the canon of the New Testament. Most of the Gospels came later, and Paul's Epistles followed. So they didn't have Colossians 3:16's *"psalms and hymns and spiritual songs."* Therefore, they sang from the Old Testament.

PRAISING GOD THROUGH THE PAIN

Psalm 113 shows how to praise the Lord even through family, social, physical, emotional, mental, or financial pain. Think about Paul being bent over and bleeding in a dark, stinky prison with no ventilation, no sanitary facilities, and no pest removal service to kill all the vermin—but he still sang these words to the Lord:

> *Praise the LORD! Praise, O servants of the LORD, praise the name of the LORD! Blessed be the name of the LORD from this time forth and forevermore!* (PSALM 113:1–2).

Like David, Paul was saying, "I intend to praise the Lord—right now and always!" God wants to see this same spirit in us as well. You can learn to do this by first praising the Lord when you are *not* in pain. If you consistently praise Him while things are going well, that habit will enable you to eventually praise Him in all circumstances.

Pray and praise systematically: *From the rising of the sun to its going down* (PSALM 113:3A). Don't compartmentalize your life by thinking that prayer and praise is for Sundays only. God should never be just sporadically praised; He deserves our prayers and praises every day!

Pray and praise reverently: *the LORD's name is to be praised* (PSALM 113:3B). Praise is not about what you and I are going through, what we feel right now, or what we hope is going to happen. Praise is something changeless, such as God's Name, His Word, His character, and His Christ. Focus on His immutable character, which He does not change. Our circumstances—life's "ups and downs"—will come and go, but God will always be the same.

Pray and praise confidently: *The LORD is high above all nations, His glory above the heavens. Who is like the LORD our God, who dwells on high?* (PSALM 113:4–5). How can you sing if you're in the pits right now?

- Trust that your sovereign God is in control. He is higher than anyone or anything that may be causing you to suffer at the moment.

- Believe that your omnipotent God is able to rescue you out of your pit. If you are kept in the pit, it is only because you need to be there for awhile as part of His perfect plan for your life.

- Adore the Lord as majestic, awesome, and beyond comprehension! He wants you to know about Him, and that may be why He's allowing you to go through your painful situation.

If life consisted of all that was perfect and good, we would have no time for God. That is why He sends suffering and hard times to draw us close to Him, the One Who is higher than us!

Pray and praise humbly: *Who humbles Himself to behold the things that are in the heavens and in the earth?* (PSALM 113:6). God is in touch with us; He bows down His ear to hear, and opens His eyes to behold what is happening in our lives. He wants to get our attention, and that is what Paul was singing about in prison.

Picture Paul down there bleeding in the stocks, with bugs crawling everywhere, saying, "God is in control; God knows all things; He owns all things; He can set me free in an instant if He wants to!" What do you think went through the prisoners' minds as they listened? Most of them probably thought Paul was crazy. But, you know what? *Suddenly there was a great earthquake, so that the foundations of the prison were shaken; and immediately all the doors were opened and everyone's chains were loosed* (ACTS 16:26). As a result, the frightened keeper of the prison and all his family were saved and baptized (ACTS 16:31–33)! And that same God is able to rescue you out or your own prison of circumstances!

Pray and praise meditatively: *He raises the poor out of the dust, and lifts the needy out of the ash heap, that He may seat him with princes—with the princes of His people. He grants the barren woman a home, like a joyful mother of children. Praise the LORD!* (PSALM 113:7–9).

What was Paul meditating upon in his prison cell? He was pondering the compassion of our great God. You see, there aren't many things as strong as a woman's desire to have children when she is barren. Such a woman will usually go to any length and expense if there is even a slight possibility of bearing a child.

In the Hebrew economy, there was no higher or greater desire than to have children. Back then, a woman's worth was in raising godly children. (If the Lord does not give physical children to a woman, He wants to fulfill her through having spiritual children.)

Regardless of what your deepest needs might be, you serve a great, majestic, compassionate, and awesome God Who stays in touch with your life and wants to satisfy those needs.

PRAYER AND PRAISE GETS US THROUGH THE PITS

Prayer and praise not only gets *us* through the pits, but also those we pray for who are likewise suffering. Look again at the conclusion of Psalm 40:

> Let all those who seek You rejoice and be glad in You; **let such as love Your salvation say continually, "The LORD be magnified!"** But I am poor and needy; yet the LORD thinks upon me. You are my help and my deliverer; do not delay, O my God (vv. 16–17).

At the end of Psalm 40, we find God's ultimate goal for us. Real victory is not evading or escaping the majority of troubles that head our way—real victory is responding in a way that exalts God through whatever He chooses to do with us in the pits of life.

Though we may be desperate at times, God is not. He knows what is coming before it ever starts, and He is already managing every detail to cause it to work for our good. Therefore, in Psalm 40:4 David trusted God and prayed for others who were seeking Him: *Blessed is that man who makes the LORD his trust.*

What does that say to us? When we are alone and struggling, it is the perfect time to pray for those who are going through similar trials. Here is a simple plan for how to intercede for others:

- Are you sick? Pray for those who are sick because you know what they are going through.
- Are you abused by co-workers, family members, or classmates? Pray for those who are suffering from the same hurts.

- Are you in a dead-end job? Pray for hope for those facing the daily struggle of how to survive in the days ahead.
- Are you successful and tempted to be selfish? Pray for those you know who are experiencing prosperity; ask God to keep them from selfishness and pride.

Start a Personal Barrier to the Pits

IN CLOSING, HERE ARE A few practical steps to overcome loneliness in the pits of life:

Don't be surprised by troubles. Remember who was going through all this: David, the man after God's own heart. David, the one Jesus was named after ("Son of David"), had a difficult life! But so did Moses, Elijah, Paul, Peter, and so on. Scripture's greatest saints all seem to have had a hard life, so why be surprised when you're called upon to suffer at times?

Live with mysteries. You won't always know why God is allowing painful circumstances. In fact, Jesus told His disciples, those closest to Him: "*What I am doing you do not understand now, but you will know after this*" (JOHN 13:7). Because of who Christ is, however, you can trust Him to do all things well (MARK 7:37)!

Accept your situation. What is unchangeable must be accepted and lived through by God's grace. The Lord wants you to echo what Paul said: *I can do all things through Christ who strengthens me* (PHILIPPIANS 4:13).

David's whole time in the pits was intended by God to prepare him well for the throne. And what a great king he was! This reminds me of a profound lesson from God's creation where the mother eagle shows her love for her offspring by destroying their nest. Without this rude and painful start in their lives, they would be too comfortable to ever learn to soar. She knows her young will protest loudly, but the destruction of the nest must continue until it is too painful to sit on all those sharp sticks—and the young take flight.

In much the same way, the Lord allows irritants in our lives to cause us to *mount up with wings like eagles, … run and not be weary, … walk and not faint* (ISAIAH 40:31)—so that we may soar in the heavenlies with our God!

11 | Living Life Successfully in a Cave of Troubles

1 Samuel 22:1-4; Psalm 57

Be merciful to me, O God, be merciful to me! For my soul trusts in You; and in the shadow of Your wings I will make my refuge, until these calamities have passed by. —**Psalm 57:1**

HAVE YOU EVER FELT LIKE you were living in a cave of troubles—troubles that just wouldn't go away?[91] That is exactly how the homeless refugees felt after they fled from the flooding and devastation of 2005's Hurricane Katrina and were herded into the New Orleans Superdome!

As news about conditions in the Superdome began to leak out, the images boggled our senses. Think of 20,000 bodies packed into that dark, cavernous space day after day! So many people in such a small space for such a long time equaled a sickening stench of odor, multiple bathroom backups, garbage sitting around too long, dirty water, and unrefrigerated food. When you add intensive heat and humidity into this mix, the resultant horrible fog was too hard to adequately describe!

Now go back in your mind to 3,000 years ago and another group of refugees. Think of 400 tough men living in the same cave under harrowing conditions—and then mix in time, heat, plus the fact they were all under great duress and in danger from Saul who was hunting David—and you have the sights and smells of 1 Samuel 22:1-4.

After David fled from Gath and arrived in the cave of Adullam, he not only had to cope with his own problems but also those of hundreds of distressed men who had multiple troubles that just wouldn't go away. But living and working with these men in the "Cave of Troubles" was the Lord's perfect plan to teach David lessons he could only learn in the School of Affliction. You see, these lessons were all necessary to well prepare David to serve God's purposes as the next king of Israel.

When God puts us in a place of constant troubles, and we respond properly, He will use those hard times to give us some of the greatest blessings and growth in our lives. For example, look at how these now famous people of the past faced their trials with a positive attitude and triumphed:

- Cripple him, and you have a Sir Walter Scott.
- Lock him in a prison cell, and you have a John Bunyan.
- Bury him in the snows of Valley Forge, and you have a George Washington.
- Raise him in abject poverty, and you have an Abraham Lincoln.
- Strike him down with infantile paralysis, and he becomes Franklin Roosevelt.
- Burn him so severely that the doctors say he'll never walk again, and you have a Glenn Cunningham who set the world's one-mile record in 1934.
- Deafen him, and you have a Ludwig van Beethoven.
- Have him or her born black in a society filled with racial discrimination, and you have a Booker T. Washington, and a George Washington Carver.
- Call him a slow learner, and write him off as uneducable, and you have an Albert Einstein.[92]

Now look at how David was learning to respond to God properly in his loneliness in hard times:

- Have him grow up as an overlooked and neglected last child, and you have *David the shepherd boy.*
- Have him accused by his brothers and slighted by his countrymen, and you have *David the giant-killer.*
- Have him on the run for his life, hiding in a cave surrounded by hundreds of emotional cripples, and you have *David the sweet Psalmist of Israel.*

Living in the "Cave of Troubles" was going to be an incredible crash course in "How to Conquer Afflictions God's Way." This would prove to be the turning point in David's life—the time when his character was refined more than in any other period!

David Entered a Cave of Troubles

IF YOU THINK ABOUT THE cave of Adullam in light of the many descriptions of the Superdome after Hurricane Katrina, you can better sense the emotional and physical furnace of adversity David had entered.[93]

> *David therefore departed from there* [Gath] *and escaped to the cave of Adullam. So when his brothers and all his father's house heard it, they went down there to him. And **everyone who was in distress, everyone who was in debt**, and **everyone who was discontented** gathered to him. So he became captain over them. And there were about four hundred men with him. Then David went from there to Mizpah of Moab; and he said to the king of Moab, "Please let my father and mother come here with you, till I know what God will do for me." So he brought them before the king of Moab, and they dwelt with him all the time that David was in the stronghold* (1 SAMUEL 22:1–4).

Adullam is a cave in the region between Hebron and Philistia (Gaza). It is located in the canyon formerly called Rephaim, which means "the Valley of Giants." This is where Joshua, Caleb, and the other ten spies passed through as they spied out Canaan (the ten were "scared to death" of the giants).

The cave became David's headquarters, but living conditions were so gross that he appealed to the Moabite king to let his parents live in Moab until things settled down in his life.[94] The original group of around 400 distraught refugees gradually expanded as a growing number continued to come for comfort and to follow David. By 1 Samuel 23:13, about 600 had joined him.

J. Vernon McGee had this to say about these desperate people:

> The men who came to him were, first of all, those who were in distress. Saul was in power, and David was rejected and out yonder in the caves. Saul persecuted and oppressed many of his subjects and these men who were in distress wanted deliverance and relief. They heard of David and went out to him. Many a man came into the camp of David in desperation and said, "I have been hounded like you have

been hounded. I have been hated as you have been hated, and I have come to join up with you."[95]

Now let's expand upon what David faced as he learned to live God's way in the midst of hundreds of troubled people. Three types of men came to him for help:

1. **Men in distress came to David.** The words David used to describe the condition of these deeply stressed men reveal just how much they were suffering. The first word for those in *"distress"* (Hebrew *matsowq* – Strong's #4689) means "squished and trapped and unable to escape." Here is an expansion on what that word means from other parts of the Old Testament:

- *"Distressed"* is used for being "at the end of your rope," feeling that "death is knocking at your door," and "no hope or help is possible" (DEUTERONOMY 28:53–57).

- *"Distressed"* is also a condition of deep sadness that can happen to even very strong believers like Ezra: *Trouble and **anguish** have overtaken me, yet Your commandments are my delights* (PSALM 119:143).

- *"Distressed,"* in ordinary use, stands for an unusually hopeless condition when people do things they would never do at any other time, but are willing to do because they are in such distress, such as when Jeremiah said, *"I will not make mention of Him, nor speak anymore in His name." But His word was in my heart like a burning fire shut up in my bones; I was weary of holding it back, and I could not* (JEREMIAH 20:9.)

Satan tries to persuade God's children to permanently despair, feel abandoned, and eventually give up. But David discovered that his soul would be kept safely in the arms of the Lord when he fled to Him for refuge:

For we do not have a High Priest who cannot sympathize with our weaknesses, but was in all points tempted as we are, yet without sin. Let us therefore come boldly to the throne of grace, that we may obtain mercy and find grace to help in time of need (HEBREWS 4:15–16).

2. Men in debt came to David. The word for those in "debt" (Hebrew *nasha* – Strong's #5378) means "money lent at usury." It describes those who are hopelessly in debt. In Saul's day, many men in debt were in danger of being sold into slavery. But before they could be taken away, they ran off and joined up with David; that is the context of 1 Samuel 22:1–2. David could accept these indebted men, and encourage them, but as far as we know he never paid any of their debts.

Americans are also confronted with indebtedness; we are surrounded by the pressures our debt-driven society heaps upon us. Competition, rivalry, discontentment, pride, and greed all combine to make Americans work long hours and multiple jobs, and yet still not have all they want. As a nation we are flooded with overwhelming debt—worse than New Orleans was with water after Hurricane Katrina. The toll of the mental, physical, and emotional pressures and stresses is mounting daily.

3. Men who were discontented came to David. The word for *"discontented"* (Hebrew *mar* – Strong's #4751) means "bitter." It is actually the word for "bitterness of the soul." All who came to David had some poison of bitterness ravaging their soul, and so they were discontented with life. They had wanted to make an honest living but saw the injustice of Saul's reign, saw the way things were going, and one day simply dropped their tools, left it all, and joined up with David.

Today, many millions of bitterly discontented people—not only in our land but also around the world—wake up daily longing for change. They feel hopelessly unable to have and do what they yearn for. Consequently, they spend their days wanting to be somewhere else, to do something else, or to have something else. Day after day, they are living with growing discontentment and desperation as they watch time quickly pass them by.

David—one who had himself just come out of living life in the pits—was called by God to live and work with this crowd of cantankerous, needy men who had invaded his life. And they were with him morning, noon, and night. He couldn't escape them! This was a perfect recipe for a relapse into despair and a subsequent return to the pits. It would have been much easier to merely walk away from the whole situation, but that was not the Lord's plan for him. David needed to learn that life is hard, pain is real, suffering is unavoidable, and weariness with life is normal.

How did God teach David to conquer his problems and at the same time minister to the needs of these desperate men? The Holy Spirit came upon him to write down the secret to overcoming afflictions while not letting your own life and emotions be dragged down by others who are also suffering. As you read Psalm 57, note the emotional condition of everyone who joined up with David and how he responded. This was a crucial psalm for his spiritual nurture and development, just as it is for us.

To the Chief Musician. Set to "Do Not Destroy." A Michtam of David when he fled from Saul into the cave.

¹ *Be merciful to me, O God, be merciful to me!*
>   *For my soul trusts in You;*
>   *And in the shadow of Your wings I will make my refuge,*
>   *Until these calamities have passed by.*

² *I will cry out to God Most High,*
>   *To God who performs all things for me.*
³ *He shall send from heaven and save me;*
>   *He reproaches the one who would swallow me up. Selah*
>   *God shall send forth His mercy and His truth.*

⁴ *My soul is among lions;*
>   *I lie among the sons of men*
>   *Who are set on fire,*
>   *Whose teeth are spears and arrows,*
>   *And their tongue a sharp sword.*
⁵ *Be exalted, O God, above the heavens;*
>   *Let Your glory be above all the earth.*

⁶ *They have prepared a net for my steps;*
>   *My soul is bowed down;*
>   *They have dug a pit before me;*
>   *Into the midst of it they themselves have fallen. Selah*

⁷ *My heart is steadfast, O God, my heart is steadfast;*
>   *I will sing and give praise.*

⁸ *Awake, my glory!*
Awake, lute and harp!
I will awaken the dawn.

⁹ *I will praise You, O LORD, among the peoples;*
I will sing to You among the nations.
¹⁰ *For Your mercy reaches unto the heavens,*
And Your truth unto the clouds.

¹¹ *Be exalted, O God, above the heavens;*
Let Your glory be above all the earth.

GETTING STABILIZED

According to J. Vernon McGee:

This psalm brings us to another delightful cluster of psalms (56–60) known as the michtam psalms. What does *michtam* mean? It speaks of that which is substantial, or enduring, or fixed. *Michtam* literally means "engraven" or "permanent." This word pictures that which is unmoveable, steadfast, stable and enduring. In Psalm 57:7 when David says, "My heart is fixed," that is a *michtam.*[96]

Here is the full verse in the KJV: *My heart is fixed, O God, my heart is fixed: I will sing and give praise.* David's heart, now steadfast, led him to confidently say:

- "I'm not going back to trying to rescue myself like I did in Gath where I miserably failed" (PSALM 34).
- "I'm not going back to refusing to look at You and feeling abandoned—as I suffered during those long dark days" (PSALM 13).
- "I'm not going back to wallowing in the mud of my sin and despair—living in the pits of life" (PSALMS 40 AND 70).
- "My heart is fixed—because I am holding on to You, I can now also minister to others when surrounded by troubles" (PSALM 57:7).

The word translated "fixed" (Hebrew *kuwn* – Strong's #3559) is a perfect picture of what the Lord wants to accomplish in us through our "Cave of Troubles."

A heart to minister while engulfed in hard times is a heart that is "fixed." Fixed on what? Look at the other times this Hebrew word *kuwn* is used:

A heart to minister is ...

a heart prepared to seek God's Word: *Ezra had <u>prepared his heart to seek the Law of the Lord</u>, and to do it, and to teach statutes and ordinances in Israel* (Ezra 7:10).

a life ordered by God's Word: *The <u>steps</u> of a good man are <u>ordered by the Lord</u>, and He delights in his way* (Psalm 37:23).

a way established by God's Word: *He also brought me up out of a horrible pit, out of the miry clay, and set my feet upon a rock, and <u>established my steps</u>* (Psalm 40:2).

a spirit renewed by God's Word: *Create in me a clean heart, O God, and <u>renew a steadfast spirit within me</u>* (Psalm 51:10).

emotions anchored by God's Word: *He will not be afraid of evil tidings; <u>His heart is steadfast, trusting in the Lord</u>* (Psalm 112:7).

a walk directed by God's Word: *<u>Direct my steps by Your word</u>, and let no iniquity have dominion over me* (Psalm 119:133).

a mind guarded by God's Word: *Commit your works to the Lord, and <u>your thoughts will be established</u>* (Proverbs 16:3).

a heart guided by God's Word: *A man's heart plans his way, but <u>the Lord directs his steps</u>* (Proverbs 16:9).

Having a heart to minister in the lonely cave times of our lives is the key to living triumphantly! Look again at all that God offers us in such times: a heart prepared; a life ordered; a way established; a spirit renewed; emotions anchored; a walk directed; a mind guarded; and a heart guided. Isn't *that* worth whatever it takes to get it?

GETTING BACK ON THE ROAD OF LIFE

Here are four more lessons David learned while living in the midst of tough, troubled people. Each parallels the unexpected twist of having a car break down—which is sort of like "the last straw" when so many other things seem to be going wrong.

1. **When troubles came—David pulled over and called for help from the Lord:**

*Be merciful to me, O God, be merciful to me! For my soul trusts in You; and in the shadow of Your wings I will make my refuge, **until these calamities have passed by**. I will cry out to God Most High, to God who performs all things for me. He shall send from heaven and save me; He reproaches the one who would swallow me up. **God shall send forth His mercy and His truth*** (PSALM 57:1–3).

In his earlier life he was in great distress. In his cave time, David was just coming off a weak period, which is when depression often hits. His problems in 1 Samuel 24 were the backdrop as he searched for strength in Psalm 57, which he found in God Himself. DAVID'S HOPE WAS IN THE LORD.

2. **David had to "wait" on the "Tow Truck":**

*Have mercy on me, **O God**. I cry out to **God Most High,** to **God**, who fulfills his purpose for me. … **God** sends his love and his faithfulness. … Be exalted, **O God**, above the heavens. … My heart is steadfast, **O God**. … I will praise you, **O Lord**. … Be exalted, **O God*** (PSALM 57:1–3, 5, 7, 9, 11 NIV).

David was saying that God, and God alone, is enough. He knew, trusted, and rested in the God Who Is Enough! DAVID'S STRENGTH CAME FROM THE LORD.

3. **As David sat in the "waiting room" he grew in faith:**

*Have **mercy** on me, O God, have **mercy** on me, for in you my soul takes refuge. I will take refuge in the shadow of your wings until the disaster has passed. …. Be exalted, O God, above the heavens; let your*

*glory be over all the earth. … My heart is **steadfast**, O God, my heart is **steadfast**; I will **sing** and **make music**. … Be exalted, O God, above the heavens; let your glory be over all the earth*
(PSALM 57:1, 5, 7, 11 NIV).

For emphasis, note how David doubled three aspects of God's nature: God is gracious, God is steadfast, and God is praiseworthy. With this truth to hold onto, he got his focus off his troubles—his own little cave world—and focused on the Lord instead. DAVID'S DISCOVERIES WERE ABOUT THE LORD.

4. David "drove off" from the breakdown of hard times and was deeply blessed:

*I am in the midst of lions; I lie among ravenous beasts—men whose teeth are spears and arrows, whose tongues are sharp swords. Be exalted, O God, above the heavens; let your glory be over all the earth. … For great is your love, reaching to the heavens; **your faithfulness reaches to the skies**. Be exalted, O God, above the heavens; let your glory be over all the earth* (PSALM 57:4–5, 10–11 NIV).

First Peter 5:8 tells us that Satan *walks about like a roaring lion, seeking whom he may devour.* (By the way, he has a lot of little lions helping him!) David finally understood that perspective and this insight lifted him above the storm of Saul's murderous pursuit, above the din of hundreds of needy and desperate men—and into the peaceful calm around the throne of God! No longer giving in to self-pity or gloom, he now clung to the Lord. DAVID'S FOCUS WAS ON THE LORD.

When we are at our depths—God is inviting us to His heights!

As Paul has reminded us in the New Testament:

*Therefore, having been justified by faith, we have peace with God through our Lord Jesus Christ, through whom also we have access by faith into this grace in which we stand, and rejoice in hope of the glory of God. And not only that, but we also **glory in tribulations**, knowing that **tribulation produces perseverance**; and perseverance, **character**;*

and character, **hope.** *Now hope does not disappoint, because the love of God has been poured out in our hearts by the Holy Spirit who was given to us* (ROMANS 5:1–5).

In the midst of all his tribulation, David didn't relapse into despair and a return to the pits. He had finally learned what we need to learn: life in a cave of troubles is not merely something physical—like "The air conditioning doesn't work!" or "Gas costs are sky high!" or "Oh, no! Now the car has broken down!" No, David came to grips with the fact there is another dimension that the world in general doesn't see: living in a cave of troubles is an ongoing spiritual battle.

Cave Times Are Spiritual Battles

THINK ABOUT THIS: Who is *really* calling the shots in this world? Does it surprise you to know that it is the god of this world—the devil? Perhaps you're wondering: *I thought GOD is sovereign and almighty.* Yes, God Almighty does ultimately rule, but He allows Satan to run rampantly with evil throughout our world.

Satan and his hordes of evil spirits are looking for opportunities to have a place in our lives, yet few rarely think about that. The Apostle Paul therefore warned us to not *give place to the devil* (EPHESIANS 4:27). In Ephesians 6:10–13 he then gave an additional exhortation:

> *Be strong in the Lord and in the power of His might. Put on the whole armor of God, that you may be able to stand against the wiles of the devil. For we do not wrestle against flesh and blood, but against principalities, against powers, against the rulers of the darkness of this age, against spiritual hosts of wickedness in the heavenly places. Therefore, take up the whole armor of God, that you may be able to withstand in the evil day.*

What is so amazing is that Paul was writing this to the most spiritual church in the New Testament. If you read his two prayers in chapters one and three of Ephesians, you will see that he is talking about the stratospheric lives of saints who seemed to always be on a spiritual retreat because of their deep love for the Lord. Yet, Paul still felt it necessary to warn them to not leave any door open for the devil to gain a foothold in their lives.

Even David was aware of the truth described in these verses:

*But even if our gospel is veiled, it is veiled to those who are perishing, whose minds **the god of this age** has blinded, who do not believe, lest the light of the gospel of the glory of Christ, who is the image of God, should shine on them* (2 CORINTHIANS 4:3–4).

When David started acting in his own strength instead of God's, Satan gained a foothold in his life to drag him down into living in the pits of bad habits, sins, and negative emotions. By the time David finished Psalms 40 and 70, God had opened his eyes to understand that it wasn't the type sword he carried or his expertise in warfare that delivered him—it was the Lord. So David realized that the battle wasn't about Saul, Doeg the Edomite who caused him so much trouble, or all the other little weasels in life. It was all about the Lord getting him through each spiritual battle.

Satan is *"the god of this age"* who blinds lost people's minds; he is also the *"roaring lion"* who constantly seeks to devour believers in Christ. So when we *"give place to the devil,"* even though he can't come in to possess us, he can squeeze in things like the sense of despair that crippled David; the feelings of abandonment that paralyzed David; and lust-filled hints of little delicacies like that which later destroyed David with Bathsheba.

The Bible is very clear that we are sealed by the Holy Spirit, but it is equally clear in Ephesians 4:27 that if we don't stay alert to the wiles of the devil, we can leave a place for him to squeeze into our lives.

Consider this illustration: Our family had a beehive that we processed every July. When it was time to get the honey from the bees, I put on my "Winnie the Pooh" type outfit and then the bees swarmed all over me as I stole their honey comb. Afterward, my wife Bonnie and I would cut it, spin it, and then put the honey in jars. But no matter how hard we tried to spotlessly clean the outsides of the jars, inevitably a tiny bit of honey would seep out of them after they were placed on the shelves. What did that attract? Ants! And then the battle began!

So I got out the insecticide spray to kill the ants, which sometimes required repeat entomological conflicts throughout the month of August—in spite of additional cleanings in an effort to not leave even a miniscule place to attract them. The battle usually went like this: ants appeared in only one place at first, so I'd kill them, but suddenly a new group would find a different jar seeping honey, and so on it went. It took a lot of work to win the battle of the ants—and that is what spiritual warfare is like!

Even though Satan and his demons can't inhabit Christians, he certainly can hamper us through frustration, discouragement, and depression. First John 5:18 clearly shows how big this problem is: *We know that whoever is born of God does not sin; but he who has been born of God keeps himself, and the wicked one does not touch him.*

This verse tells us the bottom line on the devil. As believers we are no longer characterized by being slaves to sin—we've been set free! The truth of 1 John is that those who believe never stop believing because in Christ they are no longer slaves to Satan. All who have been born of God are no longer as they were. They are a new creation, with a new heart, and a new spirit as the new covenant gives us, and so *he who has been born of God keeps himself, and the wicked one does not touch him.*

When we yield our members as instruments of unrighteousness, we temporarily act like an unbeliever and that is why we may feel unsaved because of a distant, cold feeling from disobeying the Lord. But when that happens, God wants us to flee to Him and confess, repent, and be cleansed (1 JOHN 1:9).

Satan is the wicked one, the one seeking to devour us, but we are the ones who are supposed to keep ourselves from leaving a place for the devil to come and bring coldness, doubt, despair, darkness, and feelings of abandonment and rampant lust into our lives.

SATAN CAUSES PROBLEMS AND DIFFICULTIES

Satan is the one who causes our problems and difficulties in the world. The only way the world around us can escape this terminal distress is to flee Satan's rule in their lives and come to Christ. Turning to Christ, or repenting, is the pathway out of the distress the sin pit causes.

For the believer, the way to remain free of the pits of life is to not leave a place for the devil to squeeze in. When David truly grasped this truth, he conquered his cave world and then showed his distressed, indebted, and discontented cavemates how to be liberated from all their troubles.

When we came to Christ for salvation, we likewise came distressed in sin, in debt to God with an un-payable debt, and discontented. The greatest thing we know—and therefore the greatest thing Satan wants us to forget—is that we're FORGIVEN. We get to come before God, to bow before Him, and to whom much has been forgiven the same loves much. And so we know we are loved by the Lord because He's forgiven us! Listen to what this person wrote:

Not far from New York, in a cemetery lone,
Close guarding its grave, stands a simple headstone,
And all the inscription is one word alone—Forgiven.

No sculptor's fine art hath embellish'd its form,
But constantly there, through the calm and the storm,
It beareth this word from a poor fallen worm—Forgiven.

It shows not the date of the silent one's birth,
Reveals not his frailties, nor lies of his worth,
But speaks out the tale from his few feet of earth—Forgiven.

The death is unmention'd, the name is untold,
Beneath lies the body, corrupted and cold,
Above rests his spirit, at home in the fold—Forgiven.

And when from the heavens the Lord shall descend,
This stranger shall rise and in glory ascend,
Well-known and befriended, to sing without end—Forgiven.
      —Author Unknown

Each of those hundreds of men under duress in the cave of Adullam needed to experience the same thing we did when we came to Christ, and the same thing distressed people around us who are at the end of their rope, feeling like life isn't worth living, need to experience: FORGIVENESS of SINS! True born-again Christians are the only ones who can dispense that liberating secret of how to be reconciled to God. We have been left here for a purpose— to be dispensers of this free reconciliation!

When David dispensed the liberating secret of reconciliation to God, his cavemates became his mighty men who led his army to victory for forty years. And, having completed his crash course in "How to Conquer Afflictions God's Way," David went on to experience his most fruitful years. He had an unbroken string of spiritual and material triumphs where he rose to the highest levels of leadership, worship, and heritage. What an incredible outcome of his "Cave of Troubles"!

Where are you today? Still distressed, in debt, and discontent? Or have you come to the One who died for you, offers to save you, and gives life that is real and abundant?

12 | The Certainty of God's Consequence Engine

Galatians 6:7–9; Psalm 57

My heart is fixed, O God, my heart is fixed: I will sing and give praise.
—Psalm 57:7 KJV

ALL OF US OPERATE UNDER some very powerful but often unseen laws—the laws of the physical universe.[97] The laws of gravity, chemistry, and physics are inflexible, unstoppable, and very unforgiving; and we must all bow before them.

But what we seldom consider are the other laws—the laws that govern the spiritual world around us. In the pits of despair, David learned about those laws that say there are unavoidable consequences for our choices.

When David decided to solve his problems with the Philistines in his own strength rather than seek God's help, something happened. As he was fleeing to the cave of Adullam, he felt totally abandoned by God—a consequence of his disobedience in the spiritual world. He was saddened, troubled, fretful, anxious, depressed, and finally despairing.

But David wanted positive consequences; he hated the negative ones of living in the pits. So when he analyzed all that had happened, he realized the Lord had allowed his suffering as a consequence of his disobedient choices.

In Psalm 57:7 David declared: *My heart is fixed, O God, my heart is fixed: I will sing and give praise* (KJV). Because his heart was now fixed ("steadfast" in NKJV), he told the Lord that he would not slip back into the pits of despair by trying to overcome situations in his own way and strength. Instead, he said, "I'm going to trust in You and seek Your help, Your strength, and Your guidance to live my life for Your glory!" That is the center of this incredible Psalm—a turning point in his life—where David learned how to minister in a place where troubles surrounded him and yet not be dragged down by those around him.

By Psalm 57 David had learned this important law of the spiritual universe: *there is an unavoidable consequence for every act.* As sure as the laws of nature are, so are the laws of the spiritual world. Galatians 6:7–9 is a great passage to help us understand this concept:

> *Do not be deceived, God is not mocked; for **whatever a man sows, that he will also reap**. For he who sows to his flesh will of the flesh reap corruption, but he who sows to the Spirit will of the Spirit reap everlasting life. And let us not grow weary while doing good, for in due season we shall reap if we do not lose heart.*

The Laws of the Spiritual World

WE NEED TO SEE GOD reflected in the world around us and then consider the implications of what His Word teaches us. Ray Stedman (1917–1992), a giant among Bible expositors of a generation ago, wrote:

> All of us have had some sample, some contact, some encounter with the power of nature—we are awed by the mighty thundering of a storm that breaks upon our heads suddenly, or by the power of breakers dashing upon the shore. ... God is a God of power, and that power indicates to us a force behind nature. Nature is alive with power. We are told that everything is in motion—the atoms that constitute this pulpit are constantly in motion. And behind the motion is the pulsating force of energy. Nature is one great mass of energy.
>
> But, more than that, all of us have experienced some knowledge of the sovereignty of God in nature. We don't play around with the laws of nature. Have you noticed that? When we discover a natural law, we are careful to observe it because, oftentimes, our very lives are at stake. You don't go fooling around with the law of gravity. You don't get on

top of a 15-story building and shove your hands in your pockets and nonchalantly stroll over the ledge to show people how superior you are to the law of gravity. You won't break the law of gravity—you'll just illustrate it. They'll just scoop you off the pavement!

We don't play around with the laws of electricity. When a wire is charged with 10,000 volts, we know that it will operate according to a strict and precise law, and we are careful to observe that law because one little mistake is enough to cause us to forfeit our life.[98]

Just as God sovereignly directs the laws of nature at work in the physical realm, so He directs the even more important laws at work in the spiritual realm. And those laws tell us that God is just, loving, and merciful, and that is what Paul was talking about in Galatians 6:7–9.

GOD REWARDS GOOD AND PUNISHES EVIL

God always rewards good and eventually punishes all evil. Although He may not immediately punish evil, no detail, no matter how minute, escapes His attention. For that reason He tells us to not be deceived, or lulled into complacency, thinking He's overlooking something wrong, evil, or disobedient.

Most lost people and many immature believers speculate that because God is good, He grants some type of general amnesty to humanity by adding up good deeds, subtracting the bad, and then throwing in extra mercy so that just about everybody can make it to heaven.

Nothing could be further from Christ's Word in the Bible. Every human choice and every action has consequences, whether good or ill. We are all affected by our own choices as well as those of others. This reality of consequences and God's laws that govern the physical and spiritual universe I like to call the "consequence engine." It is at work around us all the time. The more you understand this, the more you will understand why things happen as they do personally as well as throughout the world.

That is why David's life is so fascinating as we read about him in the Scriptures and clearly see God's laws at work in and around his choices. Whatever David did, God responded either positively or negatively. For instance, as a shepherd boy David looked up at the sky and penned a psalm about the heavens declaring the glory of God—the Good Shepherd. That choice led to a wonderful positive consequence of his later becoming Israel's worship leader who wrote almost half the book of Psalms!

When David chose to rely on pride in his own abilities and strength at Gath, it led to his downfall. On his way to the cave of Adullam, he suffered the negative consequence of feeling abandoned even by God and thus a despondent David plunged into life in the pits. That is when he wrote Psalms 34, 13, 40, and 70 as he poured his heart out to God and sought the Lord's pathway out of the mess he was in. After David entered the cave, Psalm 57 tells us he then made a choice that had good consequences—his heart became "fixed" on God!

Later on in life, however, David's choice to stay home from the war against the Ammonites gave place to the devil's enticement of lust-filled little delicacies that destroyed David with Bathsheba and led to some heartbreaking, lifelong negative consequences.

The Psalms were written to show us both the positive and negative consequences in the life of David—a man after God's own heart! Because God and His laws are unchanging, the more we understand this inspired record of God's dealings with David, we can better choose our own course. The bottom line is this: Every choice you and I have made, or will make, has either a positive or negative consequence, and we will reap what we have sown.

God's consequence engine applies to everyone—believers as well as unbelievers. Consequences abound all around us. For example:

- Driving over the speed limit can get a speeding ticket, but staying within the limits is not only safer but also gives peace of mind because of not worrying if there's a police car just around the bend.
- Driving under the influence or fighting an alcohol or drug addiction can have severe consequences, but non-substance abusers don't have the legal (or medical) problems.
- Not paying the rent can cause a renter to lose his residence, but faithfully paying on time may merit a discount or make the difference in getting approved to be a new resident.
- Not showing up for work on time can get one fired, but hard workers are normally rewarded with pay increases and promotions.
- Disobedience to a drill sergeant in military basic training can prove painfully costly, but obedience with a good attitude usually earns a promotion in due time.

Sensible people who are law-abiding and moral cause less trouble for themselves compared to those who are not. This present life goes more smoothly for those who see the intrinsic order in the world and follow it as best they can—even if their motives are self-serving and they do not know God.

Always remember that God takes note of everything going on; nothing escapes His notice, especially a person's motives:

> *Judge nothing before the appointed time; wait till the Lord comes. He will bring to light what is hidden in darkness and **will expose the motives of men's hearts**. At that time each will receive his praise from God* (1 CORINTHIANS 4:5 NIV).

It is not possible for us to accurately know why people do things, but God does, and He says, "I will reward and punish each one according to their motivation."

The Negative Consequence Engine

THE VAST MAJORITY OF PAGANS (unbelievers) are not interested in knowing the true God—they are actually His enemies. This general animosity toward Him is the main reason behind the invention of earth's many religions. That is the heartbeat of where "religion" originated. But God gives all people everywhere enough knowledge of His existence and attributes so that they are without excuse (ROMANS 1:18–21).

When it comes to sharing the gospel, we never know who will respond to Christ's invitation, but we need to do so anyhow. For example, once Bonnie and I went to a restaurant where a man drove in beside our car and waved. When I waved back, he kept waving. So Bonnie said, "He wants to talk to you." "But honey, I haven't seen you for two days and I want to talk to you instead," I replied. However, she again said, "I think he *really* wants to talk to you." When I rolled my window down, he announced, "Your car is scratched!" "I know—but thanks," I said, and started to roll my window up. He waved again and shouted, "I fix scratch!" I wasn't interested so I told him, "It's an old car with 200,000 miles on it, and I don't want to pay to fix the scratch." But he insisted, "I fix scratch; I come where you work." I then gave in and said, "Okay, great."

He came over to our church and fixed the scratch and, of course, I had to pay him. But do you know what happened? I got the privilege of sharing the gospel with him! How did the Lord lead in all this? First, He had somebody wave at me; then He had Bonnie tell me to roll my car window down; and then He broke down my resistance to having the scratch fixed. Why? Because God had brought someone to receive the tract I had already prayerfully packed in my wallet!

REJECTING GOD

Although that particular man was very receptive to the gospel, when someone rejects Jesus, the silent, invisible wrath of God rests upon him or her. There will be a gradually increasing emptiness in the lives of those who refuse God's grace and mercy (JOHN 3:36). In Ecclesiastes, Solomon states clearly that enjoyment in life is a gift from God—*given only to those who please Him*—and not obtainable any other way:

> *Nothing is better for a man than that he should eat and drink, and that his soul should enjoy good in his labor. This also, I saw, was from the hand of God* (ECCLESIASTES 2:24).

The consequence engines of life, inexorable and unavoidable though they may be, do not usually bring instant consequences in response to a person's actions. An old proverb says, "The mills of God's justice grind slow, but they grind exceeding fine."

The wages of sin—death—is an unavoidable consequence for the pagan (ROMANS 6:23). But sin also pays lost people back with boredom, guilt, shame, loneliness, confusion, emptiness, and loss of purpose. And in the end, not only do they face physical death itself, but also final separation from God because they never laid hold of the saving life of Christ.

Paul, Peter, John, and Jesus all clearly state that some forms of life-style behavior even exclude a person from entry into the kingdom of God altogether, thus revealing that many who *say* they are Christians never were in the first place (MATTHEW 7:21–29)! A list of these moral absolutes in the universe is found in 1 Corinthians 6:9–11 and Ephesians 5:1–6. Those are the inexorable laws of God.

The record books of life are being kept up daily by recording angels who miss no details. God's judgment is totally fair and just. Punishment is appropriately proportional, following the great principle outlined in Romans 2. God weighs the motives of the heart as well as behavior, and takes into account the individual's actual knowledge of God—whether he or she has received the grace of Jesus Christ which is able to forgive and cleanse sin.

What happens to nonbelievers when they die? Nonbelievers do not cease to exist; nor do they pass into limbo or purgatory. After death they end up intact and conscious at the last judgment described in Revelation 20:12–13:

*I saw the dead, small and great, standing before God, and books were opened. And another book was opened, which is the Book of Life. **And the dead were judged according to their works, by the things which were written in the books.** The sea gave up the dead who were in it, and Death and Hades delivered up the dead who were in them. And they were judged, each one according to his works.*

BELIEVERS BEWARE

The negative consequence engine also operates for believers. Negative consequences in time and eternity occur when believers in Jesus Christ act in their own natural energy and strength. A number of New Testament passages highlight this. We all know that the lost are going to go to eternal destruction, but we forget the negative consequences for what we as believers do. Many just comfortably sit under God's "umbrella of grace" and forget that grace only covers the forgiveness of sins. It does not remove the consequences of our sins. Look at Galatians 5:19–21:

*Now the **works of the flesh** are evident, which are: adultery, fornication, uncleanness, lewdness, idolatry, sorcery, hatred, contentions, jealousies, outbursts of wrath, selfish ambitions, dissensions, heresies, envy, murders, drunkenness, revelries, and the like; of which I tell you beforehand, just as I also told you in time past, that those who practice such things will not inherit the kingdom of God.*

"*Adultery, fornication*" is the most frequently listed sin in the New Testament. Why? Because our flesh wants to gratify itself, and if it can get loose, it will do so! "*Uncleanness*" refers to thinking about it, and wanting it, but "lewdness" is acting it out. "*Idolatry*" involves elevating anything above God; "*sorcery*" is the same word for drug use. Except for "*murders, drunkenness, revelries, and the like,*" the others—"*jealousies, outbursts of wrath, selfish ambitions, dissensions*"—are some works of the flesh that even many Christians tolerate or practice.

When believers fail to see the negative consequences of bad choices right away, they are often persuaded to make bigger and more foolish mistakes. And if God's judgments are long delayed, many of them think the Lord never judges at all.

As Christians we are not judged for our sins, but we are thoroughly evaluated for all our choices in life—just like everyone else. You see, God was talking to both believers and unbelievers in Galatians 6:7–9. Believers are told to not be deceived, and instead sow to the spirit. In contrast, lost people can't sow to the spirit; they can only sow to the flesh.

One of the features of the negative consequence engine at work is that we do not get to choose the consequences of our sins—God does. For instance, I grew up watching my parents help newly saved men from our local rescue mission get a fresh start. I'll always remember what my dad said: "God saved their soul but He doesn't give them a new stomach or liver!" Many of those radiant new converts went on to have years of terrible health problems—negative consequences of poor choices earlier in their lives.

CONSEQUENCES TO AVOID

What possible negative consequences can there be for those who are in Christ? Here are just a few:

1. We have lost opportunities for service if we aren't alert to God's leadings. Had I continued to ignore the man waving at me who wanted to fix the scratch on my car, I would have lost the opportunity to share the gospel of Jesus Christ with him.

2. We have a greater propensity to make the same bad choice the next time we're tempted after having yielded to a particular sin. For example, every time a believer rationalizes to find an excuse for not attending church, it becomes easier and easier to forsake the gathering together of God's people. An increased vulnerability to temptation applies to anything in life.

3. We run the risk of an early death. I've often thought that sometimes believers don't go to communion services because they know the Bible says if you partake with unconfessed, unrepentant sins, God will judge you and bring weakness and sickness into your life—and may ultimately take you home to heaven in an untimely death.

Remember that God's consequence engine is regulated by the law of sowing and reaping. He has never revoked, altered, or amended this great truth. The consequence engines connected with sowing and reaping run with 100 percent reliability century after century in every generation: *Whatever a man sows, that he will also reap* (GALATIANS 6:7).

Although we often forget about it, both halves of this verse impact all of us. In reality, most people find that they are still reaping the unpleasant long-term consequences of past bad choices. And yet, at the same time, as forgiven sinners we are probably also sowing to the Spirit for a future positive harvest.

That was happening to David in Psalms 13, 34, 40, and 70. His bad choices in Gath led to guilt and shame, numbing loneliness, profound confusion, emptiness, and a complete loss of purpose. But by Psalm 57:7 in the cave of Adullam his heart had become fixed on God!

The negative consequence engine for the Christian should never be thought of as punishment for sins because Jesus has already been fully punished for the believer's sins—all of them. Negative consequences of bad choices are not the same as punishment for sin. Neither are they to be confused with God's corrective discipline of his wayward sons and daughters (HEBREWS 12:6–17).

Remember: *He who **sows to his flesh** will of the flesh reap corruption, but he who **sows to the Spirit** will of the Spirit reap everlasting life* (GALATIANS 6:8).

The Positive Consequence Engine

LIKE NEGATIVE CONSEQUENCES, THE EFFECTS of the positive consequence engine at work in our lives do not usually show up immediately; they are long term. (This can be frustrating for those who crave instant gratification and expect daily rewards.) The big payoff for followers of Christ is in the next life rather than the here and now, as Jesus reminds us in His Sermon on the Mount:

> *"Do not lay up for yourselves treasures on earth, where moth and rust destroy and where thieves break in and steal; but **lay up for yourselves treasures in heaven**, where neither moth nor rust destroys and where thieves do not break in and steal. For where your treasure is, there your heart will be also"* (MATTHEW 6:19–21).

Much of a positive consequence is also internal. Positive consequences of knowing God include wonderful inner qualities of wholeness, fulfillment, and contentment. As we yield in obedience to the Lord, over time we become all we ever dreamed of being as whole men and women. For God will produce in and through us the fruit of the Spirit which *is love, joy, peace, longsuffering, kindness, goodness, faithfulness, gentleness, self-control* (GALATIANS 5:22–23).

We only have two choices in life—pleasing God or pleasing self. As Paul explained in Romans 6, we are all servants (slaves) to one of two masters—whichever one we choose to serve:

> *Do you not know that to whom you present yourselves slaves to obey, you are that one's slaves whom you obey, whether of sin leading to death, or of obedience leading to righteousness? But God be thanked that though you were slaves of sin, yet you obeyed from the heart that form of doctrine to which you were delivered. And having been set free from sin, you became slaves of righteousness. I speak in human terms because of the weakness of your flesh. For just as you presented your members as slaves of uncleanness, and of lawlessness leading to more lawlessness, so now present your members as slaves of righteousness for holiness. For when you were slaves of sin, you were free in regard to righteousness. What fruit did you have then in the things of which you are now ashamed? For the end of those things is death. But now having been set free from sin, and having become slaves of God, you have your fruit to holiness, and the end, everlasting life. For the wages of sin is death, but the gift of God is eternal life in Christ Jesus our Lord* (ROMANS 6:16–23).

We also only have two building materials in life—what will last and what will not. The positive choices we make that are energized by the grace of God and His Spirit produce lasting building materials. That is another New Testament description of the positive consequence engine at work in the Christian. What we do (build) will either endure or we will suffer loss. Look at 1 Corinthians 3:10–15:

> *According to the grace of God which was given to me, as a wise master builder I have laid the foundation, and another builds on it. But let each one take heed how he builds on it. For no other foundation can anyone lay than that which is laid, which is Jesus Christ. Now if anyone builds on this foundation with gold, silver, precious stones, wood, hay, straw, each one's work will become clear; for the Day will declare it, because it will be revealed by fire; and the fire will test each one's work, of what sort it is. **If anyone's work which he has built on it endures, he will receive a reward.** If anyone's work is burned, he will suffer loss; but he himself will be saved, yet so as through fire.*

*We must all appear before the judgment seat of Christ, that **each one** **may receive the things done in the body, according to what he has** **done, whether good or bad.** Knowing, therefore, the terror of the Lord, we persuade men; but we are well known to God, and I also trust are well known in your consciences* (2 CORINTHIANS 5:10–11).

The positive consequences in life are empowered by God's Spirit. What really counts in life—actions that lead to positive consequences—are the works Jesus does in and through us when we make ourselves available to God. The basic rule of Christian life is this: Nothing coming from me, but everything coming from Him!

UNLEASHING GOD

It is by trusting and acting upon what the Lord has promised that we unloose the power of God working in us so that His consequence engine runs in our favor. That was the reason for David's Psalm 57:7 declaration: his heart was fixed on God; his will was yielded; his life was offered as a sacrificial offering; he became a God-hearted servant. Jesus is more than willing to live through us whenever we give Him permission. Someone has said, "There is no limit to what God will do through any individual, if that person doesn't care who gets the credit."

When a person comes to know the Lord through salvation, bad habits that everyone agrees are socially undesirable are usually abandoned—getting drunk, living in a sexually immoral life style, being dishonest in business, lying, stealing, cheating, and so on. But what is harder to recognize and deal with regarding the flesh is its "good" side. We see that vividly in the tragic example of King Saul's not dealing with the "good" side of his flesh and consequently losing his throne in 1 Samuel 15.

In God's sight, there is nothing at all in us, in our natural lives, that is able to please Him. We must die to self and be replaced by Christ living in and through us:

*Jesus said to His disciples, "If anyone desires to come after Me, **let him** **deny himself, and take up his cross, and follow Me.** For whoever desires to save his life will lose it, but whoever loses his life for My sake will find it. For what profit is it to a man if he gains the whole world, and loses his own soul? Or what will a man give in exchange for his soul? For the Son of Man will come in the glory of His Father with His angels, and then He will reward each according to his works"* (MATTHEW 16:24–27).

*I through the law died to the law that I might live to God. I have been crucified with Christ; it is no longer I who live, but Christ lives in me; and **the life which I now live in the flesh I live by faith in the Son of God**, who loved me and gave Himself for me. I do not set aside the grace of God; for if righteousness comes through the law, then Christ died in vain* (GALATIANS 2:19–21).

Identifying the flesh in our lives is a life-long task because our flesh will do anything it takes to avoid being put to death. That is why Paul described the Christian life as *agonizomai*. What word in English sounds like that? Agony. In other words, he was saying that the Christian life is a long, hard spiritual battle. In fact, if you're not struggling, you are probably not making a lot of good choices. The more good choices you make, the more your life will become spiritually embattled because it's an agonizing thing to bring the flesh under the domination of the Spirit of God.

We cannot readily recognize the flesh in ourselves apart from our daily obedience to Jesus plus our ongoing feeding on the Word of God. Hebrews offers key insights into our daily walk in the Spirit:

*He who has entered His rest has himself also ceased from his works as God did from His. Let us therefore **be diligent to enter that rest**, lest anyone fall according to the same example of disobedience. For the word of God is living and powerful, and sharper than any two-edged sword, piercing even to the division of soul and spirit, and of joints and marrow, **and is a discerner of the thoughts and intents of the heart**. And there is no creature hidden from His sight, but all things are naked and open to the eyes of Him to whom we must give account* (HEBREWS 4:10–13).

GOD'S PATHWAY

In closing, you need to thoughtfully and deliberately respond to the truth of God's Word in this chapter. And I know of no clearer pathway to killing self-ishness and encouraging consecration than adopting the same life purpose that Thomas Chisholm (1866–1960) embraced in "Living for Jesus." His lyrics express the marching orders of one who read these Scriptures and said, "Lord, how do I harness my life?" Chisholm did it the same way David did in Psalm 57:7 when he declared, "My heart is fixed on You!" The only difference was in his wording:

O Jesus, Lord and Savior, I give myself to Thee,
For Thou, in Thy atonement, didst give Thyself for me.
I own no other Master, my heart shall be Thy throne.
My life I give, henceforth to live, O Christ, for Thee alone.[99]

I exhort you to affirm his flesh-crucifying, life-consecrating words. Say them to the Lord because there is a positive consequence to what you express to Him. Decide today that you want to sow to the Spirit by denying and crucifying your flesh—and then make every day a day of living for Jesus!

Life in the Minor Key: Is Depression Sin?

13

Psalm 142

Bring my soul out of prison, that I may praise Your name; the righteous shall surround me, for You shall deal bountifully with me. —**Psalm 142:7**

Most of the Bible is in the major key—saints fearlessly witnessing, churches valiantly serving against all odds—and what a joy those sections are to our souls.[100] But side by side with all that is the minor key. God's Word contains true glimpses into the weaknesses and frailties that God understands and shows us in the lives of some of His greatest saints. These are men and women who were sad, discouraged, and depressed—yet the Lord did not correct them and tell them they were in sin. He just encouraged these great saints and helped them go on.

Life in the minor key—is it always sin that makes us depressed? Is it always a sin to be depressed?

No, it is not, is the answer from God's Word.

In our highly stressed twenty-first century, more and more Christians are living a caveman sort of existence. For many, life amounts to a vicious swirl of getting up, working hard at a job, at school, or in the home, and then dropping into bed exhausted at the end of each day. As they fall further and further behind in their efforts to get ahead, life more and more feels like an endless pursuit of nothingness.

Such daily struggles are a far cry from the expectations of those who heard this type promise before they became a Christian: "Just get saved and everything will be great from then on!" But that is not always true, is it? Even saved people can go through cave times like David experienced: family conflicts; losing a job; losing a home; moving to a new location under duress; working with a tough crowd; being betrayed by friends; being wronged in a business deal; suffering the sudden loss of a family member, friend, or finances, and so forth.

Trials like that are not foreign to most of us. And, if we're honest, we'll admit that sometimes it is difficult to praise the Lord when we are going through a period of unending troubles. Feeling lonely and abandoned, as David often felt, may even lead to a struggle with overwhelming depression.

A Shared Struggle

WHAT DID MOSES, ELIJAH, HEZEKIAH, Job, Ezra, Jeremiah, Jonah, and Paul all share in common with David as well as with us today? They were all Spirit-filled servants of the Lord who struggled with negative emotions. In light of this, we must be careful to never say that anxiety, depression, discouragement, and other negative emotions are in themselves sinful because we see these same emotions in some of God's greatest servants. Even Jesus experienced negative emotions:

> In Christ we see **anger** that is not sin, **deep emotional distress**, **grief**, and **anguish**—all of which were perfectly displayed. In the Garden of Gethsemane, he "began to be **very distressed and troubled**. And He said to them, 'My soul is **deeply grieved** to the point of death'" (MARK 14:33–34). Jesus, in coming to earth, took upon himself the form of a human with all its frailties, yet he did not sin [emphasis added].

> The key is not to call each occurrence of a negative emotion sin— the key is to not stay there. That is what David explains to us. "The Christian who remains in sadness and depression really breaks a commandment: in some direction or other he mistrusts God—His power, providence, forgiveness."[101]

Webster's definition of "depression" gives us a fascinating insight into ways this negative emotion can also affect believers:

1. a state of feeling sad; a disorder marked especially by sadness, inactivity, difficulty in thinking and concentration, a significant increase or decrease in appetite and time spent sleeping, feelings of dejection and hopelessness, and sometimes suicidal tendencies
2. A reduction in activity, amount, quality, or force; a lowering of vitality or functional activity

Each of the following servants of the Lord suffered from crippling and sometimes even paralyzing depression:[102]

- **Moses:** *"I am not able to bear all these people alone, because the burden is too heavy for me. If You treat me like this, please kill me here and now—if I have found favor in Your sight—and do not let me see my wretchedness!"* (NUMBERS 11:14–15). Moses was confessing that he could not humanly do what had to be done. But this state of mind was actually a blessing because when he felt squashed and depressed by his work, he came to an end of self-reliance and learned to trust the Lord more fully.

- **Elijah:** He stood alone against an entire nation, an entire army. He also stood alone against the most heinous and wicked of all the corrupt religious people of the day, including Jezebel, whose name is synonymous with sin, the occult, and wickedness. But after all that life in the major key, after his greatest time of victory Elijah slid into depression:

  > But he himself went a day's journey into the wilderness, and came and sat down under a broom tree. And he **prayed that he might die**, and said, "It is enough! Now, LORD, **take my life!**" (1 KINGS 19:4).

  This despondency followed having 850 angry prophets of Baal destroyed on Mount Carmel and then outrunning a chariot! This took supernatural courage, strength, and faith. But when he heard the rumor that Jezebel wanted to kill him, he became dejected. In spite of his great victories,

Elijah wasn't perfect; when wearied and drained emotionally, he was subject to being overcome by complete discouragement. However, God didn't rebuke him for that negative emotion; He first dealt with the physical causes of Elijah's depression before teaching the spiritual lesson he needed to learn.

- **Hezekiah:** When facing a terminal illness, *he turned his face toward the wall, and prayed to the LORD, saying, "Remember now, O LORD, I pray, how I have walked before You in truth and with a loyal heart, and have done what was good in Your sight." And Hezekiah wept bitterly* (2 KINGS 20:2–3). Turning his face to the wall was an act of desperation, but God didn't say his bitter weeping was wrong. Instead, He responded to Hezekiah's prayer with patience and gentleness and added fifteen years to his life.

- **Job:** *"Why did I not die at birth? Why did I not perish when I came from the womb?"* (JOB 3:11). Job felt like he couldn't go on any longer! So he poured out his woes to the Lord: *"I cannot eat for sighing; my groans pour out like water. … My life flies by—day after hopeless day. … I hate my life. … For God has ground me down, and taken away my family. … But I search in vain. I seek him here; I seek him there, and cannot find him. … My heart is broken. Depression haunts my days. My weary nights are filled with pain. … I cry to you, O God, but you don't answer me"* (JOB 3:23–24; 7:6, 16; 16:7; 23:8; 30:16–17, 20 TLB).

  In his depression over losing his property and children, the Bible said that *Job did not sin nor charge God with wrong* (JOB 1:22). As he suffered through trial after trial, feeling abandoned by even God, Job was never rebuked for having negative feelings. However, the Lord did reprove his three friends for accusing him of sin and for failing to speak what was right about God, as Job had (JOB 42:7–8).

- **Ezra:** His was a stellar personality! Tradition records that he memorized the entire Old Testament, wrote one chapter,[103] and another ten chapters were about him. But look at his testimony in Psalm 119:25: *My soul clings to the dust; revive me according to Your word.* Note that he didn't say, "In my wicked sinfulness I'm clinging to the dust." No, he simply said, "That's how life is!"

If you study Psalm 119 closely, it is filled with what I believe are Ezra's constant struggles with both people and his emotions. He also made a wonderful prayer request—*"revive me"*—because he knew the Lord was his only hope and source of strength to get through his struggles.

- **Jeremiah:** Look at his painful declaration: *"See, O LORD, that **I am in distress; my soul is troubled; my heart is overturned within me,** for I have been very rebellious. Outside the sword bereaves, at home it is like death* (LAMENTATIONS 1:20). What was he talking about? Jeremiah didn't like what he saw happening to Jerusalem! He was rather like a CNN on-the-spot news correspondent watching Nebuchadnezzar destroy the city and butcher the people. Thus, as he wrote about the smoke rising and the carcasses being piled up, he cried out to the Lord, "I don't like what's going on!" Being *"rebellious"* didn't mean that Jeremiah was fighting against the Lord; he was just struggling greatly with acceptance of what the Lord was allowing in Jerusalem. In his heartbreak, he was freely expressing that grief to God.

- **Jonah:** This incredibly empowered prophet of the Lord, whom the Lord rescued from death in the midst of the sea, probably saw the single greatest evangelistic impact that anyone has ever had—Nineveh's hundreds of thousands of people who all turned to the Lord and repented. But after that amazing ministry, he crashed emotionally: *And it happened, when the sun arose, that God prepared a vehement east wind; and the sun beat on Jonah's head, so that he grew faint. Then he wished death for himself, and said, "**It is better for me to die than to live**"* (JONAH 4:8).

- **Paul:** His comments on troubled times are insightful: *When we came into Macedonia our flesh **had no rest,** but we were **afflicted** on every side: **conflicts** without, **fears** within* (2 CORINTHIANS 7:5 NASB). What was Paul going through here? He was depressed. Was that a sin? No, it was a common result of his having *"had no rest."* He was in the most Roman of the Roman Empire, just coming from Asia Minor where the pagan idolatry and emperor worship was very strong. Like David, Paul was constantly pursued, so he eventually became weary and fearful for his life. But, as he wrote Timothy, he understood that fear is always the realm of Satan: *God has not given us a spirit of fear, but of power and of love and of a sound mind* (2 TIMOTHY 1:7). Although Satan buffeted a vulnerable

Paul with conflicts and fears until depression set in, he refused to remain in that state.

How did this mature saint, who had mastered much of the Old Testament and wrote books for the New Testament, find comfort in his distress? Through the ministry of another believer! He testified: *God, who **comforts the depressed,** comforted us **by the coming of Titus**"* (2 CORINTHIANS 7:6 NASB). By this, we can conclude that the Lord is grieved if we find fault with a brother or sister in Christ who is feeling "down." The God of All Comfort wants us to be *encouragers* of His suffering children—not discouragers!

In later centuries, have God's servants fared any better than these from the Bible? Let's look at three of the world's best known saints:

- **Martin Luther** (1483–1546): In perhaps his deepest depression, this Reformer wrote one of Christendom's greatest hymns—"A Mighty Fortress Is Our God." Like other great saints, he recognized the spiritual warfare involved in his struggles. In 1527 he wrote: "For more than a week I was close to the gates of death and hell. I trembled in all my members. Christ was wholly lost." In his journal he said that at this point he picked up his ink well and threw it at the devil! Satan was so vivid to him that he not only felt his presence in the room but could also see him. If you go to Lutherstadt in Wittenberg, the ink's black stain is still visible on the wall of Luther's study.

  Here is Luther's testimony of the great discoveries he made about God while he described himself as being in melancholy, heaviness, depression, dejection of spirit—downcast, sad, and downhearted:

  A mighty fortress is our God, a bulwark never failing;
  Our helper He, amid the flood of mortal ills prevailing:
  For still our ancient foe doth seek to work us woe;
  His craft and power are great, and, armed with cruel hate,
  On earth is not his equal.
  Did we in our own strength confide our striving would be losing;
  Were not the right Man on our side, the Man of God's own choosing:
  Dost ask who that may be? Christ Jesus, it is He;
  Lord Sabaoth is His Name, from age to age the same,
  And He must win the battle.

And though this world, with devils filled, should threaten to undo us,
We will not fear, for God hath willed His truth to triumph through us:
The Prince of Darkness grim, we tremble not for him;
His rage we can endure, for lo, his doom is sure,
One little word shall fell him.

That word above all earthly powers, no thanks to them, abideth;
The Spirit and the gifts are ours through Him Who with us sideth:
Let goods and kindred go, this mortal life also;
The body they may kill: God's truth abideth still,
His kingdom is forever.

For nineteen years after Luther wrote that hymn he still battled with persistent melancholy, discouragement, and depression. But his hope was always in the Lord. He shared his struggles with negative emotions so that believers could come beside him and encourage him. That is what his life was—a testimony—not hidden in a cloistered cell of anguish, but a saint sharing with other saints his need for their compassion and help.

In what we call the Reformation, Martin Luther translated the whole Bible into the language of the people and, by God's grace, single-handedly turned the tide of Romanism's darkness to shed light on the Scriptures. His faithfulness to God, no matter what, led to restoring the heart of salvation—justification by faith—which down through the centuries produced the true church's adherence to Scripture!

- **Charles Haddon Spurgeon** (1834–1892): This famous preacher lit the fires of the nineteenth-century revival movement. His poor health caused Spurgeon to struggle so severely with depression that he was forced to be absent from his pulpit for two to three months a year. In 1866, at the age of thirty-two, he told his congregation of his struggle: "I am the subject of depressions of spirit so fearful that I hope none of you ever get to such extremes of wretchedness as I go to."

   Spurgeon's marvelous ministry in London made him perhaps the greatest preacher England ever produced. Having a unique photographic mind, he knew the Bible inside and out plus the contents of all 25,000 volumes in his library. I've been in his church and seen his library, which has been enshrined. And this God-hearted servant left a legacy of inspired writings that still blesses us today!

- **Dr. John Henry Jowett** (1864–1923): After Spurgeon, he was the next great man of God who was also called in his day "The Greatest Preacher in the English-Speaking World." He pastored leading churches, preached to huge congregations, and wrote books that were bestsellers. In a message he confessed:

> "You seem to imagine that I have no ups and downs, but just a level and lofty stretch of spiritual attainment with unbroken joy and equanimity. By no means! I am often perfectly wretched and everything appears most murky."

If you've likewise felt "murky," you can empathize with God's stellar luminaries who led the way in doctrine and preaching after refinement periods that prompted struggles with negative emotions. The "Who's Who of Ministry" is chock-full of such testimonies.

As we look back on history, many of these saints, like Spurgeon, suffered because their physical conditions led to depression. One Christian medical doctor who has spent his lifetime helping people shares this example:

> Consider this thought experiment. Give me the most saintly person you know. If I were to administer certain medications of the right dosage, such as thyroid hormone, or insulin, I could virtually guarantee that I could make this saint anxious with at least one of these agents. Would such chemically induced anxiety be explained as a spiritual sin? What if the person's own body had an abnormal amount of thyroid hormone or insulin and produced nervousness?[104]

Though willful sin should never be condoned, we ought to accept that a number of saints suffer from emotional symptoms not related to unconfessed sin. And some godly believers—especially those with an "up and down" type temperament like David's—will always struggle with periods of feeling "down" because, by nature, they tend to live in the minor key.

So then, it's possible to feel horrible and be in great emotional anguish and yet be obedient to the Lord. David, God's sweet psalmist, often testified to that very truth in his inspired writings. So let's go back in our minds to 3,000 years ago and the harsh conditions of the cave of Adullam to see what else God was teaching David in his "Cave of Troubles."

David's Testimony on How to Overcome Depression

AT THIS POINT, DAVID WAS at the depth of loneliness. He had been on the run for years and was now hiding in a desolate cave in the midst of a crowd of malcontents—feeling very much alone. He had two choices: 1) stay in the cave of loneliness and descend into self-pity and sin, or 2) look up to God and use this time alone to grow in the Lord.

David—a man so prone to doubt, discouragement, and depression—chose to look up to God for strength to overcome his battles with negative emotions. Psalm 142 reveals what kept him from being sidelined and paralyzed by depression in the cave of Adullam.

A Contemplation of David. A Prayer when he was in the cave.

¹ *I cry out to the LORD with my voice;*
With my voice to the LORD I make my supplication.
² *I pour out my complaint before Him;*
I declare before Him my trouble.

³ *When my spirit was overwhelmed within me,*
Then You knew my path.
In the way in which I walk
They have secretly set a snare for me.
⁴ *Look on my right hand and see,*
For there is no one who acknowledges me;
Refuge has failed me;
No one cares for my soul.

⁵ *I cried out to You, O LORD:*
I said, "You are my refuge,
My portion in the land of the living.
⁶ *Attend to my cry,*
For I am brought very low;
Deliver me from my persecutors,
For they are stronger than I.
⁷ *Bring my soul out of prison,*
That I may praise Your name;
The righteous shall surround me,
For You shall deal bountifully with me."

David learned a very valuable lesson: **lonely (depression) times are wonderful opportunities to grow in the Lord**. Depression is like a warning light on a car's dashboard that indicates a problem such as: low tire pressure, oil needs changing, car overheating, or low fuel. In other words, a warning light provides an opportunity to either do something about the problem or be sidelined on the road somewhere. Just as those indicator warnings can be a blessing, so depression can be a blessing by alerting us to something we need to do to grow in Christ through our difficulties.

When we feel imprisoned by circumstances and emotions, such loneliness can lead to great discoveries about God. In fact, that really summarizes David's whole life—a heart continually fleeing to Christ for refuge and always finding satisfaction through discovering more wonderful things about the Lord!

Psalm 142 Overview

THE FOLLOWING OVERVIEW OF THESE dark days in David's life is yet another example of how God faithfully met his needs:

CAVE TIMES ARE USUALLY ACCOMPANIED BY GREAT DISTRESS.
Psalm 142:3–4 is an encapsulation of the depth of David's loneliness and deep distress in his "Cave of Troubles":

> When **my spirit was overwhelmed within me**, then You knew my path. In the way in which I walk they have secretly set a snare for me. Look on my right hand and see, for there is no one who acknowledges me; refuge has failed me; **no one cares for my soul.**

These verses are filled with symptoms of depression commonly associated with hard times. Note how David described his negative emotions and then how a wounded soul of today might word similar feelings:

- David felt **overwhelmed in spirit** (v. 3a): "The roof is caving in!"; "Everything's going wrong at once!"; "This always happens to me!"; "Oh no, not now!"; "Just what I need—more bad news!"

- David thought his adversaries had **hidden a trap** for him (v. 3b): "They're all out to get me!"; "I've been railroaded"; "I've been framed!"; "They're not playing fair!"

- David feared there was **no escape** from his babysitting job (v. 4b): "I'm on a one-way trip to nowhere with my job"; "I'm too old for that great position"; "I don't have enough qualifications to do the job I want"; "I don't have the time or the money to re-train"; "My life is an unending mess—there's no way out!"

- David felt that **no one acknowledged or cared** for him (vv. 4a, 4c): "No one called ..."; "I'm just a nobody"; "Poor me ..."; "I have no friends left"; "I'm all alone ..."; "Nobody loves me!"

Have you ever let such deadening thoughts as these cross your mind? They will bring gloom as fast as a storm front in a summer thunderstorm. At this point, David could either descend into self-pity by dwelling on his problems or he could flee to the One he knew truly cared for him. The latter is where faith comes in—and that is what David chose to exercise.

Only God had the power to completely heal his wounded heart—and that is precisely why the Lord allowed David's cave times in the first place. Loneliness, which takes many forms, has but one purpose: God longs to satisfy and complete us by using our righteous responses in loneliness to draw us closer to Him.

If any of the above typical symptoms of depression ring true in your own life, these practical steps can help you break free:

1. **Deal with sin**. Be sure there is no unconfessed or unforsaken sin that can give the devil a place in your life. (EPHESIANS 4:27)
2. **Share your burdens**. Clearly tell the Lord all your fears, all your struggles, all your pains—for He knows that your frame is but dust. (PSALM 103)
3. **Abandon self-pity**. Constant self-sorrow is a one-way ticket to loneliness. Self-pity denies we have a responsibility to deal with our emotions and thus frustrates any cure. As Jesus said, taking up your cross and following after Him requires denying self interests. (LUKE 9:23)

CAVE TIMES CAN REAP GREAT DISCOVERIES ABOUT GOD.

*I cried out to You, O LORD: I said, "You are **my** refuge, **my** portion in the land of the living" (PSALM 142:5).*

After David voiced the depths of his despair, he rallied in verse 5 by answering his negative emotions with truths about God: "No one cares for me? YOU care for me, O God! No way to escape? YOU are my way of escape!" David didn't get out of the cave right away, but he did discover that the Lord was with him IN the cave! (God didn't immediately deliver the three Hebrews from the fiery furnace—He came *into* the furnace to walk alongside of them.)

*Attend to **my** cry, for I am brought very low; deliver me from my persecutors, for they are stronger than I. **Bring my soul out of prison**, that I may praise Your name; the righteous shall surround me, for You shall deal bountifully with me* (PSALM 142:6–7).

David was saying, "Lord, I'm choosing to flee to You for refuge! Although You won't remove these malcontents who are such a problem for me, I'm trusting you to undo the shackles my soul feels so I can freely praise Your name!" When you and I don't feel we can praise the Lord, we must choose to go in the right direction by saying, "Lord, bring my soul out of prison so that I, too, may praise Your name!" Then we must go where the righteous are (shepherds are supposed to go after the sheep, but sheep are to stay and bountifully minister to one another).

CAVE TIMES OPEN WAYS TO KNOW GOD MORE INTIMATELY.

If you are suffering depression from life's unending struggles, here's how you can personalize Psalm 142:5–7 to be an overcomer like David:

Depression means it's time to flee to the Lord your Refuge. Say to the Lord, "When I'm depressed I learn that You alone are my true REFUGE (v. 5a)—anytime and anywhere. I choose to believe Your promise and turn to You as my Refuge right now." The first step to recovery is to flee to the Lord when you're feeling distressed.

Note what David said back in verse 1: *I **cry out** to the LORD **with my voice**; with my voice to the LORD I make my supplication.* He cried out *loud*. Sometimes you have to voice a plea aloud for your own benefit: "Lord, help me!" Preach to yourself often by audibly saying what you believe about Christ being your true Refuge. Then speak like-comfort to others who are suffering rather than just sit at home and pray for them. This means that sometimes God will direct you to go pray with someone—not just point the person to certain Scriptures. You and I should minister in this way to our hurting brothers and sisters in Christ because, like Paul, they may desperately need to *hear* a comforting voice!

Depression means it's time to feed on the Lord your Portion. Say to the Lord, "When I'm depressed I learn that You alone are my true PORTION (v. 5b)—just as You, the Great Physician, prescribed in Your Word! I choose to believe Your promise to be all I'll ever need in this hard time."

A parent feeding a baby or toddler off an adult's plate will first chop up the food or mash it to suit the little one's eating readiness. In the same manner, the Lord is the One Who prepares His "just right" portion for each of His children; He knows just what you need, and how much. Never forget that He has said, "I will never leave you or forsake you" and "I'm with you always." Believe those promises and then remember: there's no temptation except what is common—and God will always make an exit sign to get you out of it (1 CORINTHIANS 10:13).

Depression means it's time to speak to the Lord your Master. Say to the Lord, "When I'm depressed I learn that You alone are my true LISTENER (v. 6a)—the One Who cares and hears. I choose to believe Your promise and pour out all my troubles to You because You care for me." In David's psalms he often prayed, "Attend to my cry!" Then he poured out all his woes to the Lord. It's truly comforting to know that God *wants* us to load our burdens on Him, as David testified: *Cast your burden on the LORD, and He shall sustain you; He shall never permit the righteous to be moved* (PSALM 55:22). As you tell your troubles to the Lord, you can almost feel the load lightening as you give them over to Him. (Be careful to not take your troubles back, which is worrying— meditating on your problems instead of believing God's promises.)

Also say to the Lord, "When I'm depressed I learn that You alone are my true DELIVERER (v. 6b)—the One Who comes and helps!" Someone once asked me, "What do you think of using medication to treat depression?" I'm not an anti-drug person; nor am I a proponent of living on medication. Ultimately, it is the Lord Who brings us out of depression, but sometimes He does so through the use of medication. For example, years ago when I was at Grace Community Church, there was one fellow who would show up in John MacArthur's office with knives and a dog. When the police arrived to get the guy, John would always say, "Take your lithium!" After the man took his medicine regularly, he'd be back in church the next week sitting in the front smiling.

If you take medication for depression, just be aware that you risk placing your belief in those pills rather than God. Medications cannot affect your spirit, your eternal soul; the only lasting and complete help is from the Lord who brings our refuge to us as our Deliverer—the One Who comes and helps us in our need!

Depression means it's time to trust in the Lord your Redeemer—and worship God. Say to the Lord, "When I'm depressed I learn that You alone are my true OBJECT OF WORSHIP (vv. 7a-b). I choose to believe Your promise to rescue me from my prison so I can worship You even when I don't feel like it." God loves and accepts true worship. So David said, "You are the One I want to worship, but when my soul is in prison I'm not doing very well at that, so I need Your deliverance to worship as You truly deserve."

In John Bunyan's *Pilgrim's Progress*, the key to getting out of the Giant of Despair's castle was the promise. When they started praising the Lord and singing, it got brighter and brighter until the giant tipped over and they escaped. When you feel depressed, it is time to praise; it is time to worship; and it is time to claim the faithful promises of God!

Depression means it's time to rest in the Lord your Provider. Say to the Lord, "When I'm depressed I learn that You alone are my true PROVIDER (7c)—You will surround me with the righteous and bountifully supply me with everything I need!"

CAVE TIMES HELP US APPLY TRUTHS ABOUT OUR GOD.
Now let's look at what David the Caveman confessed as the end result of acting upon the great discoveries about God he'd made in Psalm 57—a crucial psalm for his spiritual nurture and development. Here are the Psalm 57 truths that David applied to his steadfast heart:

God is gracious (PSALM 57:1a; see also EXODUS 33:12–34:6). The Lord is so gracious that He saves us even when we are very sinful—and, of course, He's much more than that!

God is a refuge (PSALM 57:1b). David mentioned this again in Psalm 142:5: *You are my refuge; my portion.* In Psalm 91, God is our shelter, protection, covering, and shade. The cross is our safe harbor—the anchor of our soul (HEBREWS 6:19).

God is able (PSALM 57:2)—He accomplishes all needful things for us. He can deliver us from the enemy without as well as the enemy within us (vv. 4, 6). The solution to victorious living is to keep our focus on God (v. 5).

God establishes (PSALM 57:7a). In Psalm 40 David testified: *He inclined to me,* and *heard my cry* (v. 1); *brought me up out of a horrible pit ... and set my feet upon a rock* (v. 2); and then *put a new song in my mouth* (v. 3).

God makes us praise through sorrow (PSALM 57:7b).

God makes us thankful (PSALM 57:8–9).

God opens an audience to us (PSALM 57:9b).

God is loyal (PSALM 57:10; see also LAMENTATIONS 3). His mercies never fail!

God uses our adoration of His Name (PSALM 57:11). Through our worship, He pulls us up out of the cave times unto Himself!

> Martin Luther once said about David, the psalmist: "David must have been plagued by a very fearful devil. He could not have had such profound insights if he had not experienced great assaults." Luther felt that those who are predisposed to fall into despondency as well as to rise into ecstasy may be able to view reality from an angle different from that of ordinary folk.[105]

Discouragement is no respecter of persons. In fact, discouragement seems to attack the successful far more than the unsuccessful—the higher we climb the farther down we can fall. Therefore, God wants us to learn to not run away from the dark times by giving in to discouragement and depression. Instead, He wants us to flee to Him and let Him unshackle us so that we can praise, worship, trust, and cry out to Him—then see Him deliver us in His perfect timing.

By the way, the Lord let David out of the cave not too long afterward and he later ascended to the greatest successes of his life! But David would never have been the great king he became had he not gone through the Lord's refinement in his "Cave of Troubles."

Sharing Struggles—Sharing Prayers

JUST AS DAVID LEARNED TO minister to his cavemates in their afflictions, our sufferings should draw us closer to other Christians as we share burdens and pray for one another. When that is done faithfully, God can use our hard times to magnify His glory! Look at how such a ministry blessed Paul during a period of intense suffering:

> *For we do not want you to be ignorant, brethren, of our trouble ... :*
> *that we were **burdened beyond measure**, above strength, so that we*
> ***despaired** even of life. Yes, we had the sentence of death in ourselves,*
> *that we should not trust in ourselves but in God who ... **delivered us***
> *from so great a death, and **does deliver us**; in whom we trust that He*
> ***will still deliver us**; you also **helping together** in prayer for us, that*
> *thanks may be given by many persons on our behalf for the gift granted*
> *to us through many* (2 CORINTHIANS 1:8–11).

The word translated "helping together" (Greek *sunopourgeo*) is only used here in the New Testament and is composed of three words: "with, under, work." It is a picture of laborers under the burden, working together to get the job accomplished. Paul was so squashed in spirit that he could not make it on his own. Yes, he had the Lord Who never left him, but he also needed "with, under, work" from others—"helping together" in prayer. So Paul enlisted faithful believers to hold him up before the Lord in his emotional, physical, and spiritual struggles. This was in addition to Paul trusting the Holy Spirit to assist him in prayer and help him carry the load:

> *The Spirit also **helps in our weaknesses**. For we do not know what we*
> *should pray for as we ought, but the Spirit Himself **makes intercession***
> ***for us** with groanings which cannot be uttered* (ROMANS 8:26).

In closing, I exhort you to prayerfully look at 1 Thessalonians 5 where Paul gives one of the clearest descriptions in Scripture of the basic ministry God commands of every believer in Christ's church. In this passage there are probably more imperative commands than in any other paragraph in the Bible:

1. *Comfort each other* ...
2. *edify one another* ...
3. *Be at peace* among yourselves.
4. *Warn* those who are unruly,
5. *comfort* the fainthearted,
6. *uphold* the weak,
7. *be patient* with all.
8. *See that no one renders evil* for evil to anyone, ...
9. *always pursue* what is good both for yourselves and for all.
10. *Rejoice* always,
11. *pray* without ceasing,
12. *in everything give thanks*; for this is the will of God.
13. *Do not quench* the Spirit.
14. *Do not despise* prophecies.
15. *Test* all things;
16. *hold fast* what is good.
17. *Abstain* from every form of evil ...
18. Brethren, *pray* for us.
19. *Greet* all the brethren (1 THESSALONIANS 5:11–22, 25–26).

I pray that you will especially take seriously God's command to *comfort the fainthearted, uphold the weak, be patient with all* (1 THESSALONIANS 5:14). Paul wonderfully described the purpose of this mandated ministry in 2 Corinthians 1:3–7:

Blessed be the God and Father of our Lord Jesus Christ, the Father of mercies and God of all comfort, who comforts us in all our tribulation, that we may be able to comfort those who are in any trouble, with the comfort with which we ourselves are comforted by God. For as the sufferings of Christ abound in us, so our consolation also abounds through Christ. Now if we are afflicted, it is for your consolation and salvation, which is effective for enduring the same sufferings which we also suffer. Or if we are comforted, it is for your consolation and salvation. And our hope for you is steadfast, because we know that as you are partakers of the sufferings, so also you will partake of the consolation.

If you are personally undergoing an extended period of refinement by the Lord, I offer this powerful and comforting reminder:

> *He gives power to the weak, and to those who have no might He increases strength. Even the youths shall faint and be weary, and the young men shall utterly fall, but those who **wait** on the LORD shall renew their strength; they shall mount up with wings like eagles, they shall run and not be weary, they shall walk and not faint* (ISAIAH 40:29–31).

The Hebrew word translated *"wait"* means "hope that renews exhausted strength." Isn't that a beautiful promise to grab hold of? That is what David experienced in Psalm 52:9 when he said, *I will praise You forever … ; and in the presence of Your saints **I will wait** on Your name, for it is good.* So then, no matter what is going on in your life, I exhort you to trust the Lord—for He is GOOD!

There Are No Supersaints

14

Psalms 17, 54, 35-36, 16, 39

Oh, love the LORD, all you His saints! ... Be of good courage, and He shall strengthen your heart, all you who hope in the LORD. —**Psalm 31:23-24**

MOST OF US WHO GREW up in the twentieth century remember this saying: "Look up in the sky, it's a bird, it's a plane, no ... it's Superman!" This superhero with extraordinary abilities and wholesome upbringing fought a never-ending battle for truth and justice. Fans all over the world therefore idolized him—and loved hearing stories of his great feats! But that was only make-believe.

In the real world, many Christians view God's choicest servants like David, Elijah, or Paul as Supersaints. These men actually fought a never-ending battle for truth and justice—*God's* Truth and *God's* justice. And Christians all over the world love to hear stories about their great feats—like when David the shepherd boy slew the evil giant, Goliath; or when Elijah called down God's miraculous power in front of the 850 prophets of Baal; or how the Apostle Paul was so instrumental in the spread of Christianity throughout the Roman Empire.

Yet, when believers fight *"the good fight"*[106] of faith in hard times, Satan tries to rob them of encouragement and strength through the testimonies of these great saints. *"Surely,"* he whispers, *"their God-hearted service is way* beyond what you as an average Christian can expect in your own life." The devil has deceived many into thinking that these giants of faith were made of a different substance—as if the Lord gave them something extra that we didn't get. Or, that some were so special because they had been with Jesus in person, or were at Pentecost.

STRUGGLES COMMON TO ALL

All too often we forget that Scripture declares that everyone is subject to the same passions and struggles. For example, Elijah—that great prophet who embodied all the prophets, who never had to die a physical death, who got to come back and stand on the Mount of Transfiguration with Christ—was a monumental servant of the Lord *"with a nature like ours"* (JAMES 5:17). In other words, Elijah was just like us!

The only other time this word *"with a nature like ours"* was used is when Paul and Barnabas were being besieged and bowed down to by the people of Lystra. As the multitudes started to offer a sacrifice to them, the two men tore their clothes[107] and ran in among the multitude crying out: *"Men, why are you doing these things? We also are men with the same nature as you"* (ACTS 14:15).

Paul and Barnabas refused to let those lost pagans think they were Supersaints—like some sort of special "gods." So they clearly informed the people: "We are just normal men—human, not divine!"

God's greatest servants—David, Elijah, and Paul—were made of the same stuff we are. Their greatness was *of God*, and not of themselves. And Paul even testified to that truth:[108]

> For God, who said, "Let light shine out of darkness," made his light shine in our hearts to give us the light of the knowledge of the glory of God in the face of Christ. But we have this treasure in jars of clay to show that **this all-surpassing power is from God and not from us**
> (2 CORINTHIANS 4:6–7 NIV).

The apostle continued on by giving examples of how God's *"all-surpassing power"* was his source of victory in manifold trials (2 CORINTHIANS 4:8–10). So then, even when Paul's whole world was crashing in all around him, and there seemed to be no escape, though they were not happy times for him— they were rejoicing times in the Lord. *And that is the spiritual secret of God's greatest servants!*

In his classic entitled *Spiritual Depression,* author Martyn Lloyd-Jones explains the difference between rejoicing and feeling happy:

> We must recognize that there is all the difference in the world between rejoicing and feeling happy. The Scripture tells us that we should always rejoice. Take the lyrical Epistle of Paul to the Philippians where he says: "Rejoice in the Lord always and again I say rejoice." He goes on saying it. To rejoice is a command, yes, but there is all the difference in the world between rejoicing and being happy. You cannot make yourself happy, but you can make yourself rejoice, in the sense that you will always rejoice in the Lord. Happiness is something within ourselves, rejoicing is "in the Lord." How important it is then, to draw the distinction between rejoicing in the Lord and feeling happy. Take the fourth chapter of the Second Epistle to the Corinthians. There you will find that the great Apostle puts it all very plainly and clearly in that series of extraordinary contrasts which he makes: "We are troubled on every side (I don't think he felt very happy at the moment) yet not distressed," "we are perplexed (he wasn't feeling happy at all at that point) but not in despair," "persecuted but not forsaken," "cast down, but not destroyed"—and so on. In other words the Apostle does not suggest a kind of happy person in a carnal sense, but he was still rejoicing. That is the difference between the two conditions.[109]

Now let's apply that perspective to an example from David's life. As we move on in this chapter to the last big events of David's "struggling years,"[110] we will see that he and his men fled the cave of Adullam and hid in the wilderness of Judah. Did he feel happy about having no sure place to live, no reliable source of income, and being responsible to take care of hundreds of men as well? Certainly not; God empowered David to be victorious by rejoicing in the Lord in his unending struggles—whether he felt happy or not. Just as that was the spiritual secret behind David's greatness, so it is for those who also seek to be a God-hearted servant.

Now let's look at what went on in David's life after moving out of the cave of Adullam. This was a challenging yet exciting period because God was in the final phase of preparing David to assume the throne as king!

David Had Constant Insecurities and Huge Responsibilities
(1 Samuel 22:5; 23:1–14)

WITH HIS BASIC TRAINING IN the cave of Adullam completed, it was time for David to further apply what God had been teaching him. Thus, the Lord let Saul discover where David and his men were hiding. However, through the prophet Gad, He warned David beforehand to relocate:

> *The prophet Gad said to David, "Do not stay in the stronghold; depart, and go to the land of Judah." So **David departed and went into the forest of Hereth** (1 SAMUEL 22:5).*

David faced constant insecurities and huge responsibilities caring for about 600 men on the run. To make matters worse, the Philistines invaded the city of Keilah and were robbing their threshing floors. When David heard about it, he immediately *inquired of the LORD, saying, "Shall I go and attack these Philistines?"* God told him to go save the city. After David saved the inhabitants of Keilah, Saul heard about it and was delighted as he felt certain David and his men would be trapped inside this city that had only one gate. So he quickly plotted to besiege them, but David heard about Saul's evil plan and sought the Lord's direction:

> *David said [to the Lord], "Will the men of Keilah deliver me and my men into the hand of Saul?" And the LORD said, "They will deliver you." So David and his men, about six hundred, arose and ... **went wherever they could go.** Then it was told Saul that David had escaped from Keilah; so he halted the expedition. And David stayed in strongholds in the wilderness, and remained in the mountains in the Wilderness of Ziph. **Saul sought him** every day, **but God did not deliver him into his hand** (1 SAMUEL 23:12–14).*

Psalm 17, the first psalm in the Bible entitled "A Prayer of David," appears to have been penned during this dangerous period in the wilderness. In spite of his insecurities and enormous responsibilities, David expressed great confidence in the Lord's protection:

A Prayer of David.

1 ***Hear a just cause, O Lord,***
    Attend to my cry;
    Give ear to my prayer which is not from deceitful lips.
2 *Let my vindication come from Your presence;*
    Let Your eyes look on the things that are upright.

3 *You have tested my heart;*
    You have visited me in the night;
    You have tried me and have found nothing;
    I have purposed that my mouth shall not transgress.
4 *Concerning the works of men,*
    By the word of Your lips,
    I have kept away from the paths of the destroyer.
5 *Uphold my steps in Your paths,*
    That my footsteps may not slip.

6 *I have called upon You, for You will hear me, O God;*
    Incline Your ear to me, and hear my speech.
7 *Show Your marvelous lovingkindness by Your right hand,*
    O You who save those who trust in You
    From those who rise up against them.
8 *Keep me as the apple of Your eye;*
    Hide me under the shadow of Your wings,
9 *From the wicked who oppress me,*
    From my deadly enemies who surround me.

10 *They have closed up their fat hearts;*
    With their mouths they speak proudly.
11 *They have now surrounded us in our steps;*
    They have set their eyes, crouching down to the earth,
12 *As a lion is eager to tear his prey,*
    And like a young lion lurking in secret places.

13 *Arise, O Lord,*
    Confront him, cast him down;
    Deliver my life from the wicked with Your sword,

¹⁴ With Your hand from men, O LORD,
   From men of the world who have their portion in this life,
   And whose belly You fill with Your hidden treasure.
   They are satisfied with children,
   And leave the rest of their possession for their babes.

¹⁵ As for me, I will see Your face in righteousness;
   I shall be satisfied when I awake in Your likeness.

David Was Betrayed by Men He Trusted
(1 SAMUEL 23:15–29)

NOT ONLY HAD THE MEN of Keilah planned to deliver David over to Saul—even though he'd just rescued them from the Philistines—but he was also betrayed by men he trusted in the Wilderness of Ziph:

> **The Ziphites came up to Saul** *at Gibeah, saying, "Is David not hiding with us in strongholds in the woods, in the hill of Hachilah, which is on the south of Jeshimon? Now therefore,* **O king, come down** *according to all the desire of your soul to come down;* **and our part shall be to deliver him into the king's hand**" *(1 SAMUEL 23:19–20).*

If you have ever been betrayed or maligned by someone you trusted, you know how David felt when the Ziphites turned against him. He probably thought that his recent rescue of the inhabitants of Keilah would make a difference in how he was viewed, but it didn't.

This time of betrayal prompted David to pen Psalm 54 in which he appealed to the Lord for deliverance and vindication in this betrayal—praising God that He is good and would hear his prayers!

To the Chief Musician. With stringed instruments, A Contemplation of David when the Ziphites went and said to Saul, "Is David not hiding with us?"

*¹ **Save me**, O God, by Your name,*
   *And **vindicate me** by Your strength.*
*² **Hear my prayer**, O God;*
   Give ear to the words of my mouth.
³ For strangers have risen up against me,
   And oppressors have sought after my life;
   They have not set God before them. Selah

⁴ *Behold,* **God is my helper;**
   The L<small>ORD</small> *is with those who uphold my life.*
⁵ *He will repay my enemies for their evil.*
   Cut them off in Your truth.

⁶ *I will freely sacrifice to You;*
   I will praise Your name, O L<small>**ORD**</small>**, for it is good.**
⁷ *For He has delivered me out of all trouble;*
   And my eye has seen its desire upon my enemies.

Did God hear David's prayers? You bet! Here's the really interesting part: just as Saul and his men were encircling David and his men, *a messenger came to Saul, saying, "Hurry and come, for the Philistines have invaded the land!" Therefore Saul returned from pursuing David and went against the Philistines; so they called that place* **the Rock of Escape** (1 S<small>AMUEL</small> 23:27–28).

Don't you just love to see the Lord's sovereignty at work like that? It is so comforting to know that God *works all things according to the counsel of His will* (E<small>PHESIANS</small> 1:11)! Nothing can come into a believer's life without first passing through the Lord's hands—and then He promises to work *"good"* through it (R<small>OMANS</small> 8:28)! So while Saul was off chasing the Philistines who had invaded Israel, **David and his men safely relocated to the Wilderness of En Gedi** (1 S<small>AMUEL</small> 23:29).

David Spared Saul. After King Saul returned from chasing the Philistines, he was informed of David's whereabouts. Saul and his 3,000 choice warriors once again set out to track him down. This is another fascinating part of this whole "cat and mouse game": while Saul was searching for David's hideout, he came to a cave (not knowing that David and his men were hiding in its recesses) and *went in to attend to his needs* (1 S<small>AMUEL</small> 24:3). When Saul's presence was discovered, David's men told David, "Wow! What an opportunity! God's given Saul into your hands this very day!"

Did he heed their unwise counsel? No, he only cut off a corner of the king's robe without Saul knowing it, but even that act pricked David's sensitive conscience:

*He said to his men, "**The L**<small>**ORD**</small> **forbid that I should do this thing to my master, the L**<small>**ORD**</small>**'s anointed***, to stretch out my hand against him, seeing he is the anointed of the* L<small>ORD</small>*." So David restrained his servants* *with these words, and did not allow them to rise against Saul. And Saul got up from the cave and went on his way* (1 SAMUEL 24:6–7).

David then followed Saul out of the cave and told him what had transpired inside—that he had a chance to kill him but didn't. Although King Saul would not give up his throne, he admitted that David was more righteous than he was, and deserved to be Israel's king. Saul then returned home.

While living in the cave at En Gedi, David seems to have written Psalm 35 about the Lord being the avenger of His people. Here are some excerpts from that wonderful Psalm:

> **Plead my cause**, O LORD, with those who strive with me; fight against those who fight against me. … Say to my soul, "I am your salvation." … For without cause they have hidden their net for me in a pit, which they have dug without cause for my life (35:1, 3, 7).
>
> All my bones shall say, "LORD, who is like You, delivering the poor from him who is too strong for him, yes, the poor and the needy from him who plunders him?" … Let them shout for joy and be glad, who favor my righteous cause; and let them say continually, "**Let the LORD be magnified**, who has pleasure in the prosperity of His servant." And my tongue shall speak of Your righteousness and of Your praise all the day long (35:10, 27–28).

Don't you love the liberty David feels to express negative emotions to the Lord? Whenever he voiced complaints and appeals, however, he consistently reigned in his wayward emotions and put his focus on the Lord instead—and that usually caused David to break forth in praise.

Psalm 36, also apparently written at this time, presents a contrast between man's wickedness and God's perfections. After describing the characteristics of the wicked, mid-Psalm David couldn't help but burst forth praising God's infinite attributes:

> Your **mercy**, O LORD, is in the heavens; Your **faithfulness** reaches to the clouds. Your **righteousness** is like the great mountains; Your **judgments** are a great deep; O LORD, You preserve man and beast. How precious is Your **lovingkindness**, O God! Therefore the children of men put their trust under the shadow of Your wings. They are abundantly satisfied with the fullness of Your house, and You give them drink from the river of Your pleasures. **For with You is the fountain of life; in Your light we see light** (PSALM 36:5–9).

David Was Wronged in a Business Deal
(1 Samuel 25)

IN THE WILDERNESS OF PARAN, David and his men encamped near the shepherds of Nabal—a very rich but harsh and evil man who had 3,000 sheep and 1,000 goats. When David heard that Nabal was shearing his sheep, he sent ten young men to greet him, saying on David's behalf:

> "Peace be to you, peace to your house, and peace to all that you have! Now I have heard that you have shearers. Your shepherds were with us, and **we did not hurt them, nor was there anything missing from them** all the while they were in Carmel. Ask your young men, and they will tell you. Therefore, let my young men find favor in your eyes, for we come on a feast day. **Please give whatever comes to your hand** to your servants and to your son David" (1 SAMUEL 25:6–8).

To make a long story short, the scoundrel refused to help. David was so furious that Nabal was paying him evil for good that he immediately planned to wreak revenge on him and his male household. As David and 400 of his men were on their way to Carmel, Nabal's wife, Abigail, intercepted them. Without her husband's knowledge, she hurried to head David off with a peace offering of an abundance of food. She then pleaded with David to not avenge himself because, when he became king, it would be a grief and offense of heart.

Look at how humbly he responded:

> Then David said to Abigail: "**Blessed is the LORD God of Israel, who sent you** this day to meet me! And blessed is your advice and blessed are you, because you have kept me this day from coming to bloodshed and from avenging myself with my own hand. For indeed, as the LORD God of Israel lives, **who has kept me back from hurting you,** unless you had hurried and come to meet me, surely by morning light no males would have been left to Nabal!" (1 SAMUEL 25:32–34).

Once again, God's sovereignty was brought to bear on David's life. Through Abigail, the Lord intervened to keep him from sinning because he'd given place to the devil and planned to repay Nabal's evil with evil. God's way is to *not avenge yourselves, but rather give place to wrath; for … "Vengeance is Mine, I will repay," says the Lord. … Do not be overcome by evil, but overcome evil with good* (ROMANS 12:19, 21).

As it turned out, God quickly punished Nabal's evil. When Abigail told her husband about the food she took to David, he "apparently suffered a stroke and became paralyzed until he died."[111] The Lord then rewarded Abigail for being a peacemaker—David asked her to be his wife!

In the Wilderness of Paran, after facing the danger of his anger toward Nabal "the fool" and seeing God's deliverance, David likely wrote Psalm 53—how to overcome feelings of loneliness when tempted to be bitter over being hurt in a business deal.

To the Chief Musician. Set to "Mahalath." A Contemplation of David.

¹ *The fool has said in his heart,*
    "There is no God."
    They are corrupt, and have done abominable iniquity;
    There is none who does good.

² *God looks down from heaven upon the children of men,*
    To see if there are any who understand, who seek God.
³ *Every one of them has turned aside;*
    They have together become corrupt;
    There is none who does good,
    No, not one.

⁴ *Have the workers of iniquity no knowledge,*
    Who eat up my people as they eat bread,
    And do not call upon God?
⁵ *There they are in great fear*
    Where no fear was,
    For God has scattered the bones of him who encamps against you;
    You have put them to shame,
    Because God has despised them.

⁶ *Oh, that the salvation of Israel would come out of Zion!*
    When God brings back the captivity of His people,
    Let Jacob rejoice and Israel be glad.

David Spared Saul Again. Alerting Saul previously hadn't brought about David's capture, so the Ziphites once again reported David's location to the king (1 SAMUEL 26:1). Like the last time, Saul took off with 3,000 warriors to find David. But David's spies discovered where Saul was encamped, so Abishai volunteered to sneak into the camp at night with David. But, like the last time, David's heart of integrity would not let him slay Saul. Note how God sovereignly protected David—another testimony that his victories were *of God*, and not of himself:

> *"As the* LORD *lives, the* LORD *shall strike him, or his day shall come to die, or he shall go out to battle and perish. The* LORD *forbid that I should stretch out my hand against the* LORD*'s anointed. But please, take now the spear and the jug of water that are by his head, and let us go."* [No one noticed this happening because] *a **deep sleep from the** LORD had fallen on them* (1 SAMUEL 26:10–12).

Afterward, on the top of a hill afar off, David called out to King Saul to inform him that he had again spared his life. Surprisingly, Saul answered: *"May you be blessed, my son David! You shall both do great things and also still prevail."* So David went on his way, and Saul returned to his place (1 SAMUEL 26:25).

In spite of Saul's favorable words, *David said in his heart, "Now I shall perish someday by the hand of Saul. There is nothing better for me than that **I should speedily escape to the land of the Philistines**; and Saul will despair of me, to seek me anymore in any part of Israel. So I shall escape out of his hand"* (1 SAMUEL 27:1).

God had told David to stay in Judah (1 SAMUEL 22:5), but he became so overwhelmed with fear that he disobeyed and fled back to Gath—hoping King Saul would never pursue him there. During the sixteen months David lived in the area, he and his men made regular raids on Achish's enemies and Achish gave them the city of Ziklag to live in.[112] Since his life continued to be full of insecurities and huge responsibilities, David's "up and down" temperament caused him to struggle periodically with emotional upheavals:

> Hunted by Saul, he knew not where to betake himself, at one time seeking refuge among the Moabites, at another in the wilderness of Ziph; … an outlaw hiding himself in the cave of Adullam, and anon a captain in the service of the King of the Philistines; and amid all his projects haunted by the mournful conviction, "I shall now one day perish by the hand of Saul."[113]

Yet, even though David struggled emotionally, he never turned his back on God. Again and again, his songs to the Lord bore witness that he poured his heart out and worshiped anew!

David Lost His Family, Friends, and Finances
(1 Samuel 30)

THIS FINAL BIG EVENT OF his "struggling years" was the greatest challenge David and his men had to face. While they were away from Ziklag, the Amalekites (whom Saul had previously refused to utterly destroy) attacked the city, burned it with fire, and took all their families captive!

When they saw Ziklag's total destruction and that their wives and children were gone, *David and the people* who were with him lifted up their voices and *wept, until they had no more power to weep* (1 SAMUEL 30:4).

If you had been in David's shoes, wouldn't you have felt like this was "the final straw"? How did a maturing David cope with this tragedy?

> *David was greatly distressed,* for the people spoke of stoning him, because the soul of all the people was grieved, every man for his sons and his daughters. *But David strengthened himself in the LORD his God.* ... [Then God told David,] *"Pursue, for you shall surely overtake them and without fail recover all"* (1 SAMUEL 30:6, 8).

As the Lord promised, David recovered all the families plus so much spoil from the enemies of the Lord that he sent some of it to the elders throughout Judah!

While he was so grieved and feeling endangered over the raid on his family and the city of Ziklag, David appears to have penned Psalms 16 and 39—how to overcome feelings of loneliness when threatened with a great loss.

At the end of Psalm 16, David beautifully expressed his absolute confidence in the Lord: *You will show me the path of life; in Your presence is fullness of joy; at your right hand are pleasures forevermore* (v. 11). For David had discovered three very precious things about the Lord:

1. God wanted to arrange his life for him daily.
2. In God's presence he could enjoy intimate companionship with Him for the rest of his days.
3. God's *"right hand"* (which speaks of power and authority) would enable him to joyfully accomplish all His purposes for his life here on earth!

Was David perfect by now? No. Although his heart was fixed on God, he would always struggle with sin just like we do. But because he was such a God-hearted servant, sin penetrated his heart deeply. He couldn't bear being out of fellowship with the Lord he loved so much!

In Psalm 39, David's great lament over sin and the brevity of life was intense. In verse 1 David resolved to keep silent before men: *"I will guard my ways, lest I sin with my tongue; I will restrain my mouth with a muzzle, while the wicked are before me."* But after further meditation on his situation, he felt compelled to speak up:

> *"Lord, make me to know my end, and what is the measure of my days that I may know how frail I am. ... Certainly every man at his best state is but vapor. ... And now, Lord, what do I wait for? My hope is in You. Deliver me from all my transgressions; do not make me the reproach of the foolish. I was mute, I did not open my mouth, because it was You who did it. Remove Your plague from me; I am consumed by the blow of Your hand. ... Hear my prayer, O Lord, and give ear to my cry; do not be silent at my tears; for I am a stranger with You, a sojourner, as all my fathers were. Remove Your gaze from me, that I may regain strength, before I go away and am no more"* (Psalm 39:4–5, 7–10, 12–13).

Just as God purposes loneliness to drive us closer to Him so that He can satisfy and complete us, so it is with chastisement: *"Do not despise the chastening of the Lord, nor be discouraged when you are rebuked by Him; for whom the Lord loves He chastens, and scourges every son whom He receives"* (Hebrews 12:5–6).

In Hebrews 12:11 the Lord then summarized His purpose for chastening: *No chastening seems to be joyful for the present, but painful; nevertheless, afterward it yields the peaceable fruit of righteousness to those who have been trained by it.*

Throughout David's "growing" and "struggling years" the Lord was equipping his *"workmanship"* to accomplish the *good works, which God prepared beforehand that* [he] *should walk in them* (Ephesians 2:10).

THE CONSEQUENCE ENGINE—GOD PUNISHES EVIL AND REWARDS GOOD

God always rewards good and eventually punishes all evil. Now that the Lord had prepared righteous David to serve God's purposes as the next king of His people, Israel, the time had come for King Saul to suffer the consequences of his rebellion (1 SAMUEL 15:23). After the Philistines killed his sons Jonathan, Abinadab, and Malchishua, Saul lay gravely wounded all night on the battlefield. In an ironic twist of fate, at his request, he finally died at the hand of an *Amalekite*—one of God's enemies whom he'd earlier refused to utterly destroy.[114]

When David learned of the death of King Saul and Jonathan, rather than rejoicing that Saul's efforts to kill him were over, he had the young Amalekite executed who had dared to slay *"the LORD's anointed"* (2 SAMUEL 1:15).

David then greatly lamented over the deaths of Saul and Jonathan. So much so that he instructed that they be remembered by all Israel through a war song entitled "The Song of the Bow" (see 2 SAMUEL 1:17–27). The following excerpts from "The Song of the Bow" reveal both the depths of David's integrity before the Lord and his great love for his beloved friend Jonathan:

> [19] *"The beauty of Israel is slain on your high places!*
> *How the mighty have fallen! ...*

> [23] *"Saul and Jonathan were beloved and pleasant in their lives,*
> *And in their death they were not divided;*
> *They were swifter than eagles,*
> *They were stronger than lions.*

> [24] *"O daughters of Israel, weep over Saul,*
> *Who clothed you in scarlet, with luxury;*
> *Who put ornaments of gold on your apparel.*

> [25] *"How the mighty have fallen in the midst of the battle!*
> *Jonathan was slain in your high places.*

> [26] *I am distressed for you, my brother Jonathan;*
> *You have been very pleasant to me;*
> *Your love to me was wonderful,*
> *Surpassing the love of women.*
> [27] *"How the mighty have fallen,*
> *And the weapons of war perished!"*

After this, at the Lord's direction, David and his two wives, his men, and their families relocated to the cities of Hebron. Then *the men of Judah came, and there they anointed David king over the house of Judah* (2 SAMUEL 2:4). After a long war between the house of Saul and the house of David, at age thirty David was finally anointed king over all Israel. He reigned as king a total of forty years: *In Hebron he reigned over Judah seven years and six months, and in Jerusalem he reigned thirty-three years over all Israel and Judah* (2 SAMUEL 5:5).

God had thus rewarded David's faithfulness by keeping the promise made to him while just a teenager: *"You shall shepherd My people Israel, and be ruler over Israel"* (2 SAMUEL 5:2). Although David was no Supersaint, he *was* a one-of-a-kind devoted servant—a man after God's own heart—who became empowered to rejoice in the Lord through life's unending struggles!

15 | The Giant That Slew David Was Lust

2 Samuel 11:1–4

Let him who thinks he stands take heed lest he fall. —**1 Corinthians 10:12**

A S WE MEET DAVID IN this chapter, he is at the top of his career—a successful king, powerful ruler, undefeated general, wealthy businessman, and surrounded on every side by God's blessing.[115] David is writing worship music, serving the Lord in public worship, practicing personal worship, and loving the Lord.

But, there is an incredible postscript to an incredible life that should stop each of us dead in our tracks. Note the phrase that God emphasized in this verse:[116]

> *David did what was right in the eyes of the LORD, and had not turned aside from anything that He commanded him all the days of his life,* ***except in the matter of Uriah the Hittite*** (1 KINGS 15:5).

Although the Lord forgave the sins, and forgot the iniquities, David's consequences and losses were recorded in the Bible—God's "forever settled in heaven" Word.

God not only recorded David's key role in one of the greatest events in history—that climactic moment as a teenaged shepherd boy who victoriously stood alone in battle against the most fearsome warrior of his day—but He also sadly recorded the role David later played in a horrible sequel.

In today's world, books and movies often have sequels. Well, there's a sequel to "David and Goliath" that is perhaps more tragic than the glory of its initial run. You see, less than thirty years after the historic victory over Goliath, David had a disastrous fall. In that sequel known as "David and Bathsheba"—the giant-killer himself was slain by a giant.

But didn't David kill Goliath? Yes, wonderfully by the Lord's power the *humble David* slew God's enemy. However, later on a *proud David* ignored His Word and allowed another giant to come right into God's city, Jerusalem. In fact, David, the man after God's own heart, even welcomed that enemy into his presence. And so, in midlife (perhaps in his early forties), David was slain by the giant called LUST! And that story is forever contained in the Holy Scriptures.

David Slowly Stepped Downward Into Sin

FAR MORE DANGEROUS THAN THE Goliath he faced as a teenager, the giant Lust had crept slowly into David's own inner chambers. In a moment, blinded by his selfish desires, when his guard was down, David was slain. He had been enticed, baited, hooked, and finally reeled in by lust!

David the giant-killer was slain by the giant Lust because he had ignored God and His Word. It is very insightful how this occurred. Note the five dreadful steps downward that led to a disastrous fall which destroyed his life and testimony:

1. David *desensitized* his conscience by incomplete obedience (2 SAMUEL 5:13).
2. David *relaxed* his grip on personal purity (2 SAMUEL 11:1).
3. David *fixed* his heart on physical desires (2 SAMUEL 11:2).
4. David *rationalized* in his mind about wrong decisions (2 SAMUEL 11:3).
5. David *plunged* his life into lustful sin (2 SAMUEL 11:4).

Death, deceit, murder, immorality, spiritual oppression, and poverty and famine of the soul are only a few offspring of this act of momentary pleasure with Bathsheba!

FIRST STEP DOWNWARD:
DAVID DESENSITIZED HIS CONSCIENCE BY INCOMPLETE OBEDIENCE.

David took more concubines and wives from Jerusalem, after he had come from Hebron. Also more sons and daughters were born to David (2 SAMUEL 5:13).

Although David was a great guy who loved the Lord and was writing the Scriptures and songs to worship God, he began to slowly desensitize his conscience by not obeying the Lord completely. And that was the first warning sign of danger ahead.

At this point, David had let himself become involved in socially acceptable things that were unacceptable to God. Initially, it was just carelessness—a slight wandering, a tiny loosening in a socially acceptable area. But I believe that David's sin with Bathsheba was sparked by small disobediences back in the earlier days as he relaxed his grip on the way God asked Him to live.

Watch the unfolding of the story of the deadly little things he allowed into his life. David had already been king for seven years when he *took more concubines and wives from Jerusalem* (2 SAMUEL 5:13). That verse sounds like you are just reading the news—nothing major, nothing bad, it is kind of neutral. In fact, you might even be thinking: *Was it really wrong? Didn't all the men back then do it? Didn't Abraham have multiple wives? You know, Jacob had several wives. Since they were all God's people, was it really so bad?*

If God says it is wrong, it is wrong—even if everybody else does it. Six hundred years after Abraham God told Moses to *write down* His rules for future kings. Deuteronomy 17:15–20 became the code by which the kings were supposed to live. That passage contains God's instructions for His leaders and, by the way, in principle form they are very much something that you should likewise heed if you want to be a man or woman of God.

For example, consider these powerful words in Deuteronomy 17:15:

"You shall surely set a king over you whom the LORD your God chooses; one from among your brethren you shall set as king over you; you may not set a foreigner over you, who is not your brother."

How does that apply to us today? Simply this: we are not to follow anybody that God hasn't picked. In other words, a woman is not to hold a position as leader over our life. Nor, as Paul says in 2 Corinthians, should a believer date, court, get engaged, or married to an unbeliever because God would not choose such a person. It is all tied together. Some might say, "Well, my friend did and the unbeliever got saved." Yes, but for everyone who gets saved, twenty don't, and they have a life of heartache.

Now back to David who, as the second king, would have carefully listened to what the God he loved so much had to say in the only instructions He recorded for the King of Israel. Note what God had to say about multiplying horses:

> *"But he shall not multiply horses for himself, nor cause the people to return to Egypt to multiply horses, for the LORD has said to you, 'You shall not return that way again' "* (DEUTERONOMY 17:16).

Why would that instruction be so important? God had a very good reason. Multiplying horses would cause the people to return to Egypt—a horse breeding area of the world. And if they went back, they would be lured in by the Egyptian's gods, false ways, and immorality! As far as we know, David didn't have any problem with wanting to multiply horses, but he didn't completely obey this next command:

> *"**Neither shall he multiply wives for himself**, lest his heart turn away; nor shall he greatly multiply silver and gold for himself* (DEUTERONOMY 17:17).

David personally disobeyed God when he multiplied wives for himself. A king wasn't to multiply wives because they would turn his heart away from the Lord. David's going along with a socially accepted custom rather than God's directive reminds me of a sign that appears along I-44 in Missouri: **What part of "Thou Shalt Not" is unclear?**

Now look at the next verse:

> *"Also it shall be, when he sits on the throne of his kingdom, that **he shall write for himself a copy of this law in a book**, from the one before the priests, the Levites. **And it shall be with him**"* (DEUTERONOMY 17:18).

The Pentateuch (the first five books of the Bible) has 5,852 verses and nearly 160,000 Hebrew words. At normal speed, it would take a minimum of 900 hours to hand copy the Hebrew letters with ink and quill onto an animal skin or parchment; that is six months of work, non-stop at eight hours a day! To be

"God's man" he had to give up most of his first year as king to do this Bible Study—and even had to carry a copy of the law around with him. For God had clearly laid out His instructions for the king:

> "**He shall read it** all the days of his life, That he may learn **to fear the LORD** his God and be careful **to observe all the words** of this law and these statutes" (DEUTERONOMY 17:19).

Some people may ask: "Where does it say in the Bible that we are supposed to read the Bible all the time?" That is an easy answer because the instructions in verse 19 apply to us as well. As believers, we are supposed to have a personal copy, keep it with us all the time, be meditating on it, and read it all the days of our life. Why? A continued exposure to God's Word causes us to learn about the Lord so that we may live a life that acknowledges our fear of Him.

Now note why God says a king of Israel must obey His instructions:

> "**that his heart may not be lifted above his brethren** that he may not turn aside from the commandment to the right hand or to the left, and that he may prolong his days in his kingdom, he and his children in the midst of Israel" (DEUTERONOMY 17:20).

If a king's heart became "*lifted above his brethren*" he might conclude that he could look over the rooftop of his house at any man's wife he desired—and take her. And that is *exactly* what happened. David's heart became so prideful that he basically said to himself, "Boy, I'm the number one warrior … the giant killer … the wealthiest guy in the land! Since I'm the great king of God's people, I can have whomever and whatever I want—*whenever* I want it!" But GOD had commanded: "*Don't* let your heart be lifted up!"

Because David ignored God's warning, his life moved on without the Lord's protection.

SECOND STEP DOWNWARD:
DAVID RELAXED HIS GRIP ON PERSONAL PURITY.

> It happened in the spring of the year, at the time when kings go out to battle, that David sent Joab and his servants with him, and all Israel; and they destroyed the people of Ammon and besieged Rabbah. **But David remained at Jerusalem** (2 SAMUEL 11:1).

David had let little things slide in his life. Everything seemed to be going so well that he forgot to be on guard, and consequently relaxed his grip on personal purity. That reminds me of what we sometimes see in young children's T-ball and Little League games. At the beginning of the game, those eager ball players are in their positions, ready for anything that comes—especially if they're infielders. They've got that small glove on and they're looking like pros. Then, by about the second inning, they've turned around, no longer watching the game, and start throwing dandelions. *They lost their grip on their position.*

At the height of his life, David **lost his grip on purity** and was simply "playing with dandelions" in the presence of a ravenous lion called Lust! Look at the warnings Peter and Paul gave us so we don't likewise succumb to such temptation:

> *Be sober,* ***be vigilant****; because your adversary the devil walks about like a roaring lion, seeking whom he may devour. ... Therefore let him who thinks he stands* ***take heed*** *lest he fall* (1 PETER 5:8; 1 CORINTHIANS 10:12).

Beware of allowing any unguarded moments in your life, thinking you are safe from sin's reach and it won't bother you anymore. For at that very moment the ravenous devourer himself is crouching and preparing to spring. You and I need to be doing whatever it takes to maintain purity in our lives. That is what David discovered—only it was too late.

In the Sermon on the Mount Jesus told us how serious we must be about sexual sin. Most people dismiss His words as hyperbole, overkill, or something other than He intended. But as we consider this moment in David's life, wouldn't it be wise to read Christ's words again and ponder them personally? Listen with new ears to what He had to say:

> *"You have heard that it was said, '****Do not commit adultery****.' But I tell you that anyone who looks at a woman lustfully has already committed adultery with her in her heart. If your right eye causes you to sin, gouge it out and throw it away. It is better for you to lose one part of your body than for your whole body to be thrown into hell. And if your right hand causes you to sin, cut it off and throw it away. It is better for you to lose one part of your body than for your whole body to go into hell"* (MATTHEW 5:27–30 NIV).

Now consider this excerpt from a magazine article written about this passage by Randy Alcorn, a pastor and author I really respect:

JESUS, THE RADICAL

Why does Jesus paint this shocking picture? I believe
He wants us to take radical steps, to do whatever
is necessary to deal with sexual temptation.

Now, the hand and eye are not the causes of sin. A blind man
can still lust and a man without a hand can still steal. But the
eye is a means of access for both godly and ungodly input. And
the hand is a means of performing righteous or sinful acts. We
must therefore govern what the eye looks at and the hand does.

If we take Jesus seriously, we need to think far
more radically about sexual purity.

The battle is too intense, and the stakes are too high
to approach purity casually or gradually.

Some men fall into mental adultery through lingerie ads, billboards,
women joggers in tight pants, women with low cut blouses or
short skirts, cheerleaders or dancers, movies, TV shows, and
commercials of the beer-and-bikini variety. Some men's weakness
is the Sunday newspaper's ad inserts or nearly any magazine.

So, *stop looking*. And then *stop putting yourself in the position
to look!* ...

Romans 13:14 instructs us to "make no provision for the flesh" (NASB).

It's a sin to deliberately put ourselves in a position
where we'll likely commit sin. Whether it's the lingerie
department, the swimming pool, or the workout room at
an athletic club—if it trips you up, stay away from it.

Proverbs describes the loose woman meeting up with the foolish man after dark (see Proverbs 7:8–9). We must stay away from people, places, and contexts that make sin more likely.

If it's certain bookstores or hangouts, ***stay away from them.***

If cable or satellite TV or network TV, old friends from high school, the Internet, or computers are your problem, ***get rid of them.***

Just say no to whatever is pulling you away from Jesus. Remember, if you want a different outcome, you must make different choices. …

[You may be thinking:] *But you're talking about withdrawing from the culture. What you're saying is too radical.*

No, what I'm saying is nothing. Jesus said, "If it would keep you from sexual temptation, you'd be better off poking out your eye and cutting off your hand." Now that's radical.

Many claim they're serious about purity, but then they say, "No way; I'm not going to give up cable TV," or "I'm not going to have my wife hold the computer password."

Followers of Jesus have endured torture and given their lives in obedience to Him. And we're whining about giving up cable?

When Jesus called us to take up our crosses and follow Him (see Matthew 10:38), didn't that imply sacrifices greater than forgoing Internet access?

How sold out are you to the battle for purity?
How desperate are you to have victory over sin?
How radical are you willing to get for your Lord?
How much do you want the joy and peace that can be found only in Him?" [117] (Emphasis added.)

THIRD STEP DOWNWARD:
DAVID FIXED HIS HEART ON PHYSICAL DESIRES.

*Then it happened one evening that David arose from his bed and walked on the roof of the king's house. And **from the roof he saw a woman bathing**, and the woman was very beautiful to behold* (2 SAMUEL 11:2).

David began to think so much about his sexual desire that it soon became an obsession. As the king, he was in a position which posed a greater temptation than the average man's. You see, in the ancient world kings always built high on a hill so that enemies were at a disadvantage. Living in the biggest and the highest house in Jerusalem therefore gave David a vantage point. As he wandered around at night on the roof, he could look down and around barriers which normally blocked the view of other men. Because of his position in the highest house, David could see over walls, fences, and screens. But, rather than discipline himself to look away from temptation, he engaged in watching, which then became lust-filled staring.

In this period of restlessness with time on his hands, in a moment of listlessness and boredom David wandered the palace and used the highest spot in the city to take a supposed innocent peek at Bathsheba, his neighbor's wife. This woman, who was very beautiful to behold, happened to be bathing at the time.[118]

When David peeked over the wall at his neighbor's house, because Jerusalem at this time was not very big, it's not like he didn't know who lived down there. The king knew his subjects. He knew it was one of his mightiest warrior's homes, and thus knew whose wife lived there, and who she was.

What I want to underline for you is this: There is no such thing as an innocent peek at another man's wife; there is no such thing as an innocent peek at an off-color TV show; there is no such thing as an innocent peek at pornographic materials! Likewise, there is no such thing as an innocent "trying out" of intoxicating alcohol, enslaving cigarettes, debilitating drugs, or premarital sexual relations!

All of these temptations are downward steps to life-crippling habits which can destroy your testimony and usefulness for Christ! It is impossible to flirt innocently with lust! Rather than fixing his heart on the Lord, as he had in the past, David fixed his heart on his physical desires instead. That made his mind start to click and he took another step downward, and away from God.

Temptations abound all around us as well. Because temptation to sin is so powerful, we need help. The best, and the only real help is Christ—the Refuge for the tempted.

Before you might think this message isn't for you, look at James 1:13–15 in two of the major translations:

> *Let no one say **when he is tempted**, "I am tempted by God"; for God cannot be tempted by evil, nor does He Himself tempt anyone. But each one is tempted when he is drawn away by his own desires and enticed. Then, **when desire has conceived**, it gives birth to sin; and sin, when it is full-grown, brings forth death* (NKJV).

> *Let no one say when he is tempted, "I am being tempted by God"; for God cannot be tempted by evil, and He Himself does not tempt anyone. But each one is tempted **when he is carried away and enticed by his own lust**. Then when lust has conceived, it gives birth to sin; and when sin is accomplished, it brings forth death* (NASB).

Note that James (the initial pastor of the first New Testament church, the first leader of the Church of Jerusalem, and our Lord's earthly brother) doesn't say *"if"* but *"when."*

God's Word says temptation is inevitable; temptation is inescapable; and temptation is going to follow us all through our earthly lives. In other words, this chapter's message is for ALL of us. And this message hinges on one word—LUST.

Lust (Greek *epithumia* – "super desires") is dreadful, dangerous, and deadly. Lust is surrounding us and, in various forms, planted within us. Lust is either pursued for pleasure or fled from for righteousness. Remember: youthful lusts that we nurture and feed as young people will chase us throughout our lives (2 TIMOTHY 2:22). So we must decide to flee lust—no matter *what* our age happens to be.

Lust which tempts us to sin against God will cost us far more than we could ever imagine. And that is what David found out!

FOURTH STEP DOWNWARD:
DAVID RATIONALIZED IN HIS MIND ABOUT WRONG DECISIONS.

> So **David sent and inquired about the woman**. And someone said, "Is this not Bathsheba, the daughter of Eliam, the wife of Uriah the Hittite?" (2 SAMUEL 11:3).

David took yet another step downward, away from God, when he started rationalizing in his mind: *Oh well, it's not really that bad. It'll only be this once ... nobody will know ...*

Each of us has an infinite capacity for rationalization—not just David. According to Webster, rationalizing is seeking "to provide plausible but untrue reasons for conduct." And David was about to learn what a horrible thing that sin is! For such sin deceives with all its glittering promises, and destroys with the precision of a surgeon.

Over the years countless men who have descended into sexual sins have been asked the same question: "What could have been done to prevent this?" With haunting pain, most of them have answered nearly the same thing: "If only I had really known, and really thought through and weighed what it would cost me and my family and my Lord, I honestly believe I would never have done it."

In the back of my Bible (the one that is always with me at work, at home, and whenever I travel) I keep a very pointed reminder of the *consequences* of sexual sin. I use the list below as an encouragement to refocus on the Lord and take any steps of wisdom and purity that are necessary at the moment of temptation (in any form in which it strikes). We must always remember to put the focus where Scripture does—on the love of God *and* the fear of God, both of which should act in concert to motivate us to holy obedience.

MY PERSONALIZED LIST OF ANTICIPATED
CONSEQUENCES OF IMMORALITY[119]

TOWARD MY GOD—
- Grieving my Lord; displeasing the One whose opinion most matters.
- Dragging Christ's sacred reputation into the mud.
- Losing my reward and commendation from God.
- Dreading the day that I will have to look Jesus in the face at His judgment seat and give an account of why I did it.

- Forcing God's chastening upon my life in various ways.
- Prompting laughter, rejoicing, and blasphemous smugness by those who disrespect God and the church (2 SAMUEL 12:14).
- Bringing great pleasure to Satan, the enemy of God.

TOWARD MY WIFE AND FAMILY—

- Heaping untold hurt on Bonnie, my best friend and loyal wife.
- Forfeiting Bonnie's respect and trust.
- Giving up my credibility with my beloved sons and daughters: John II, Estelle, James, Julia-Grace, Joseph, Jeremiah, Elisha, and Elisabeth. ("Why listen to a man who betrayed Mom and us?")
- Realizing that if my blindness should continue, or my family be unable to forgive, I could lose my wife and my children forever.
- Bringing years of shame to my family. ("Why isn't Daddy a pastor anymore?"—plus all the cruel comments of others who would invariably find out.)
- Plaguing memories and flashbacks that could taint future intimacy with my wife.

TOWARD MY CHURCH AND MINISTRY—

- Bringing years of shame to my church families I have served all these years.
- Bringing years of shame and hurt to my fellow pastors and elders.
- Bringing years of shame and hurt to my friends, and especially those I've led to Christ and discipled.
- Realizing that guilt is very hard to shake; even though God would forgive me, would I forgive myself?
- Following in the shameful footsteps of men I know of whose immorality forfeited their ministry and caused me to shudder.
- Causing innocent people to suffer around me when they get hit by my shrapnel (like in Achan's sin).

TOWARD MYSELF—

- Disqualifying myself after having preached to others.
- Giving up the things I am called to, and love to do: teach and preach, write, and minister to others. Forfeiting forever certain opportunities to serve God. Years of training and experience in ministry wasted for a long period of time, maybe permanently.

- Being haunted by my sin as I look in the eyes of others, and having it all dredged up again wherever I go and whatever I do.
- Undermining the hard work and prayers of others by saying to our community, "This is a hypocrite. Who can take seriously anything he and his church have said and done?"
- Heaping judgment and endless problems on the person I would have committed adultery with.
- Loss of self-respect, discrediting my own name, and invoking shame and lifelong embarrassment upon myself.

FIFTH STEP DOWNWARD:
DAVID PLUNGED HIS LIFE INTO LUSTFUL SIN.

*Then **David sent messengers, and took her**; and she came to him, and he lay with her, for she was cleansed from her impurity; and she returned to her house* (2 SAMUEL 11:4).

When David plunged his life into lustful sin he forgot to do what he had done in the past, wrote of in the past, and rejoiced over in the past.

David Forgot to Look for God

Look at David's personal testimony in Psalm 139:7–11:

Where can I go from Your Spirit?
Or where can I flee from Your presence?
If I ascend into heaven, You are there;
If I make my bed in hell, behold, You are there.
If I take the wings of the morning,
And dwell in the uttermost parts of the sea,
Even there Your hand shall lead me,
And Your right hand shall hold me.
If I say, "Surely the darkness shall fall on me,"
Even the night shall be light about me.

That Truth is even clearer on this side of the cross. Look at Paul's wonderful promise in 1 Corinthians 10:12–13:

Therefore let him who thinks he stands take heed lest he fall. No tempta-
*tion has overtaken you except such as is common to man; but **God is***
***faithful, who** will not allow you to be tempted beyond what you are*
*able, but with the temptation **will also make the way of escape**, that*
you may be able to bear it.

This is a call to all of us who know and love the Lord to **look for God in times of temptation**—for He's always there!

First, the Apostle Paul gave us hope when he said, *"Such as is common to man."* In other words, no temptation will ever overtake us or spring upon us **except the ones God has already prepared us for in His Word**. There are no new strains of sin viruses, but if the medicine or vaccines (God's promises!) are in the Medicine Chest (God's Word!) and we don't use them, what good are they when we need them?

Jesus said that we must live by " *'every word that proceeds from the mouth of God' "* (MATTHEW 4:4).

- Are you immersing yourself daily in God's Word?
- If not, and you have started to slip in your walk with the Lord, I encourage you to pause right now and renew your vows to get in the Word DAILY so that the Word gets in YOU!

Second, regardless of the type of temptation facing us, we can be sure that **our faithful God will not allow us to be tempted beyond what we are able to take without falling into sin**. God knows our limits and is thus always standing by to protect us by holding open the way of escape so we don't succumb to the devil's snare.

Third, we need to fully grasp that **God is there all the time**. The longer we meditate on 1 Corinthians 10:13, the bigger the shadow looming over it becomes. That shadow is none other than the shadow of the One Who made that promise to us! In order to do everything that verse says, God has to actually manage this project on-site. He is not distant—*He is never closer than when we are tempted!* It is God Who towers over this passage: *God is there all the time.*

Have you allowed that truth to sink into your soul to become a part of your operating system? God has told us that He is faithful. Whenever we think we are alone, we are not alone. He is there all the time, all the way, every time. So we never face the adversary, the prowling lion called the devil, *alone*.

If we had to face temptation all alone, we would be hopelessly defeated. But God has already measured and limited any attack upon us, and He has the best escape route ready if we will only look for it and take it.

What a Mighty God we serve!

Now then, I exhort you to pause and do something before you lose that truth:

- As you bow your head, say in your heart, "Lord, I believe that You never leave me." Then tell Him "Thank You!" that He is there with you right now.

- This is now the hard part! With your heart open before Him, tell Him that the next time you are tempted (you may even want to whisper in your heart to Him the temptation you most fear and often get defeated by)—that you will look for Him.

- Now, look up and say out loud, "I WILL LOOK FOR YOU, GOD, WHEN I AM TEMPTED!"

Warren Wiersbe once told this story about a father whose son was experiencing his first serious conflict at school:

Two or three bullies had been picking on the boy. They had punched the youngster a time or two, pushed him over when he was riding his bike home from school, and generally made life miserable for the lad. And then came the day they told him that they would meet him the next morning and beat him up.

That evening the dad really worked with the boy at home. He showed his son how to defend himself, passed on a few helpful techniques, and even gave him some tips on how he might try to win the bullies over as friends. Before heading to school the next morning, the father and son prayed together, knowing that the inevitable was sure to happen. With a reassuring embrace and a firm handshake, the father smiled confidently and said, "You can do it, son. I know you'll make out all right."

Choking back the tears, the boy got on his bike and began the lonely, long ride to school. What he did not know, however, was that every block he rode was under the watchful eye of his dad … who drove his car a safe distance from his son, out of sight, but ever ready to speed up and assist if the scene became too threatening. The boy had thought that he was all alone—but he wasn't. His loving father had been there the whole time![120]

Now fast forward in your mind to envision the next time you face a surge of temptation to fear, to lust, to be embittered, or to lie. Know that at that instant, in *even greater measure*, the God of the universe is near!

Though often unseen, He is with us!

Christ has already gone ahead of us and was tempted in every way that we are tempted—and triumphed!

He has joined us in every temptation and makes the way of victory marked and open for us.

So then, look for God! He is always faithful!

You might be wondering: "*Where* and *when* should I look for God?"

LOOKING FOR GOD

Always look for the Lord when faced with the various temptations that are never new, but are so unexpected and powerful. And then remember the blessing the following saints of God experienced by looking for Him in their trials—for the Lord offers that to you also:

- **Abraham looked for God on the mountain of despair** (GENESIS 22:1-14). Although he could not understand why all that ever mattered to him was about to be lost, Abraham chose to trust the Lord. He looked to God in his time of despair and found Him faithful! When we look for the Lord as Abraham did, He will supply all our needs as well.
- **Joseph looked for God in the den of passion** (GENESIS 39:1-9). When he was unexpectedly accosted, and blatantly faced with strong physical temptation, Joseph cried out to the God he could not see—but *knew* was there! When we look for God in whatever temptation we face, we'll discover that He sees our plight and will rescue us.
- **David looked for God in his lonely "Cave of Troubles"** (PSALMS 57; 142). Surrounded by complainers, rebels, and runaways with all their struggles and violent tempers, David looked up in his desperate

loneliness and found that the God Who is always faithful was right there with him—all the time! When we also look for God in times of fear and loneliness, God will always be there making a way of escape for us.

- **Jeremiah looked for God in the gloom of failure** (JEREMIAH 16:1–13). When we look for the Lord in our own gloomy times, we will learn that through life's unending struggles God purposes to shape our character.
- **Daniel looked for God in the spotlight of pride** (DANIEL 2:24–28). As the man of the moment, all eyes were on him. Daniel could easily have stolen the moment, taken the prize, and walked away with the accolades of the world—but never God's. When we look for the Lord to give Him the glory for anything we accomplish, as Daniel did, we will find that God has sent us forth for times just like that to put the spotlight and the glory back upon Him—the One Who holds our lives in His hand.
- **Peter looked for God in the fury of the storm** (MATTHEW 14:24–31). When we are sinking because of looking at our circumstances rather than God's faithfulness, we will find God's hand stretched out to save us, like Peter, at the very instant we cry out to Him.
- **Paul looked for God in the grip of pain** (2 CORINTHIANS 12:7–10). When the pain of our trials has a grip upon us, as we look for God we'll find Him to be more than sufficient for us.

So then, first decide that you will learn from David's failure and quickly look for God when temptations come.

David Forgot to Use God's Word

DAVID KNEW SO MUCH OF God's Word—having written down a lot of it *for* Him. But gripped by his lust, David suffered spiritual amnesia. The only hope we have for purity and obedience through temptation is to quote Scripture like Jesus! Remember what Christ's method was in Matthew 4:1–11? Jesus used the Word to combat the devil. He planned and prepared.

Note the very first word that Christ spoke in His temptation; you know it already, *"Man shall not. ..."* This is an insight into the most powerful truth in this passage: JESUS MET AND MASTERED SATAN AS A MAN. He did not face him as God's Son, for that would not have been a match. Jesus met Satan with the same two, and the only two, resources we have—the Word of God and the Spirit of God.

If the Word of God is hidden in our hearts, look at the fruit that will be produced:

- **Like Ezra the psalmist we will say:** *How can a young man cleanse his way? By taking heed according to Your word. With my whole heart I have sought You; oh, let me not wander from Your commandments! Your word I have hidden in my heart, that I might not sin against You!* (PSALM 119:9–11).
- **Like the Apostle Paul we will say:** *Walk in the Spirit, and you shall not fulfill the lust of the flesh* (GALATIANS 5:16).
- **Like the Apostle John we will say:** *Whoever is born of God does not sin; but he who has been born of God keeps himself, and the wicked one does not touch him* (1 JOHN 5:18).
- **We will listen to Jesus who said:** [Grace to you and peace] *from Jesus Christ, the faithful witness, the firstborn from the dead, and the ruler over the kings of the earth. To Him who loved us and washed us from our sins in His own blood* (REVELATION 1:5).

Jesus did not zap Satan with His deity—He flattened him with totally obedient humanity. Jesus had no evil desires Satan could attach to: *"I will no longer talk much with you, for the ruler of this world is coming, and he has nothing in Me"* (JOHN 14:30).

But the real battleground of the devil is our *will*. Jesus had already proclaimed His life's direction as doing the will of God, and not His own (HEBREWS 10:7–9).

"Then I said, 'Behold, I have come—
In the volume of the book it is written of Me—
***To do Your will, O God.'* "**

*Previously saying, "Sacrifice and offering, burnt offerings, and offerings for sin You did not desire, nor had pleasure in them" (which are offered according to the law), then He said, "Behold, I have come **to do Your will, O God.**" He takes away the first that He may establish the second* (HEBREWS 10:7–9).

Doing God's will is another way of saying, *"Walk in the Spirit."*

David Forgot to Run From Lust

LOOK AGAIN AT PAUL'S CLEAR command in that easy-to-find address in God's Word—2 Timothy 2:22: *Flee also youthful lusts; but pursue righteousness, faith, love, peace with those who call on the Lord out of a pure heart.*

Sensuality is easily the biggest obstacle to godliness among men today, and it is wreaking havoc in Christ's church. Godliness and sensuality are mutually exclusive, and those in the grasp of sensuality can never rise to godliness because **the mind controlled by lust has an infinite capacity for rationalization.**

> The man who carries on an act of impurity is not simply breaking a human code, not even sinning against the God who at some time in the past gave him the gift of the Spirit. He is sinning against the God who is present at that moment, against One who continually gives the Spirit. The impure act is an act of despite against God's good gift at the very moment it is being proffered. … This sin is seen in its true light only when it is seen as a preference for impurity rather than a Spirit who is holy.[121]

Satan baits his traps with pleasures that appeal to the old nature, the flesh. But none of his bait appeals to the new divine nature within a Christian. If a believer yields to his old nature, he will hanker for the bait, take it, and sin. But if he follows the leanings of his new nature, he will refuse the bait and obey God.

IF DAVID HAD ONLY KNOWN!

If David had only considered the consequences of his immorality! But He forgot to think about God, Who also is a part of all we do and say and think. Thus, God has another perspective for us to consider: David took the wife (completer) of Uriah to be his own completer. And that is a dangerous thing to do.

By the way, who is completing *you*? Physically and emotionally it MUST be your spouse if you are married—not another person, your work, your hobbies, or things like a habit, videos, pictures, and chats. To complete your life with *anything* but what God has designed and planned for you is to make an idol out of something God has made—and that always brings God's displeasure.

See how clearly David reaped God's displeasure in this passage:

"Why have you despised the commandment of the LORD, to do evil in His sight? You have killed Uriah the Hittite with the sword; you have taken his wife to be your wife, and have killed him with the sword of the people of Ammon. Now therefore, the sword shall never depart from your house, because you have despised Me, and have taken the wife of Uriah the Hittite to be your wife" (2 SAMUEL 12:9–10).

God was so displeased with David's sin that the sword would never depart his house! The pain—the cutting that would tear his family—would relentlessly be the consequence of his sin!

If David had only known what his sin would do to Bathsheba as she watched their child die; as she was reminded every day about the horrible death her husband suffered as he fell under a rain of arrows and lay there in agony dying; as she looked into the faces of her friends and saw behind their smiles the disbelief that she would ever do such a thing.

If David had only known what his sin would do as Uriah's lifeless body was brought back by a military detachment that carried him the forty-four miles from Amman to Jerusalem. Bathsheba watched as his body was washed, anointed, and wrapped for burial in the family tomb—seeing the arrow's deadly marks that spoke of the anguish of his final hours—helpless as his life slowly ebbed from his body. She probably thought about him thinking of her as he died thinking he had died nobly. But instead he was murdered in the deceit of adultery's sinful grip!

If David had only known what his sin would do to Ahithophel, Bathsheba's grandfather, as he advised those who sought to kill David and overthrow his kingdom.

If David had only known what his sin would do to Absalom, Amnon, and Tamar as the lives of his own children were ravaged by lust, murder, and death. He paid a dear price for his sin because **he gave up his credibility** with his sons and daughters. ("Why listen to a man who betrayed Mom and us?")
Here are only some of the consequences of David's sin:

- Ammon raped Tamar. ("But didn't Dad kind of do that?")
- Absalom killed Amnon. ("But didn't Dad kill Uriah?")

- Adonijah took the throne without asking. ("But didn't Dad do something like that?")
- Joab betrayed David and took the side of his enemy. ("But didn't David do that?")

And on and on we could go. Sin has consequences and they are painful! **If only we would rehearse in advance** the ugly and overwhelming consequences of immorality, we would be far more prone to avoid it.

Don't forget to look for God, to use His Word, and to run from lust! God is close. Cry out to Him. He will rescue you every time!

May you and I live each day in the love and fear of God! For if we faithfully walk in the *Spirit*, we will NOT fulfill the lust of the flesh! (GALATIANS 5:16)

How to Flee the Lusts of the Flesh

16

Judges 13-16

Flee also youthful lusts; but pursue righteousness, faith, love, peace with those who call on the Lord out of a pure heart. —2 **Timothy 2:22**

IN A MOMENT, BLINDED BY his own selfish desires, when his guard was down, the man after God's own heart was overcome by the lusts of the flesh. Having ignored the Lord and His Word, David was enticed, baited, hooked, and finally reeled in! And that sin reaped devastating consequences. To this day, his sin is repeatedly made public every time the account of "David and Bathsheba" is rehearsed.

Our Lord, Who is a jealous, holy God, hated David's sin *"in the matter of Uriah the Hittite"* (1 KINGS 15:5). The sin He hated in the Old Testament He hated in the New Testament—and still hates today.[122] What would offend the One Who loves us so much that He wants us to be utterly loyal to Him? The answer is in James 4:4–5:[123]

*Adulterers and adulteresses! Do you not know that **friendship with the world is enmity with God**? Whoever therefore wants to be a friend of the world makes himself an enemy of God. Or do you think that the Scripture says in vain, "The Spirit who dwells in us yearns jealously"?*

The Gradual Slope

WHAT IS *"friendship with the world"*? It is the "lusts of the flesh" chasing after pleasures—the cravings of the body. *These are all of the sensual temptations.* This is lust for another person—the desire to have and enjoy the body of an individual, either mentally or physically, even though such pleasure is illegal and/or immoral. These lusts are fed by going to places where we see uncovered bodies; watching TV and movies displaying various states of immodesty; and searching for images in magazines and online that feed these evil desires.

Often, we are not even aware that we are drifting into this dreadful state. How can that be? Because we *gradually* become friendly with the world by forgetting to ask ourselves questions like these:

- Do I flee the lusts of the flesh—or show interest and good will toward what God hates?
- Am I emotionally attached to anything God hates?
- Do I have affection for something utterly opposed to Him?
- Do I look upon the devil's world of rebellion and lusts hostile toward God with interest, for entertainment, or for pleasure?
- Are God's enemies my favored companions?

LUST STALKS THE AMERICAN BELIEVER

Look at what Paul—the apostle of holy living, the most disciplined man of the first century, the man who wrote more of the New Testament than anyone else—said about this subject:

> *Follow God's example in everything you do just as a much loved child imitates his father. Be full of love for others, following the example of Christ who loved you and gave himself to God as a sacrifice to take away your sins. And God was pleased, for Christ's love for you was like sweet perfume to him. Let there be no sex sin, impurity or greed among you. Let no one be able to accuse you of any such things. Dirty stories, foul talk, and coarse jokes—these are not for you. Instead, remind each other of God's goodness, and be thankful. You can be sure of this: The Kingdom of Christ and of God will never belong to anyone who is impure or greedy, for a greedy person is really an idol worshiper—he loves and worships the good things of this life more than God. Don't be fooled by those who try to excuse these sins, for the terrible wrath of God is upon*

all those who do them. Don't even associate with such people. For though once your heart was full of darkness, now it is full of light from the Lord, and your behavior should show it! Because of this light within you, you should do only what is good and right and true. Learn as you go along what pleases the Lord. Take no part in the worthless pleasures of evil and darkness, but instead, rebuke and expose them. It would be shameful even to mention here those pleasures of darkness that the ungodly do. But when you expose them, the light shines in upon their sin and shows it up, and when they see how wrong they really are, some of them may even become children of light! That is why God says in the Scriptures, "Awake, O sleeper, and rise up from the dead; and Christ shall give you light" (EPHESIANS 5:1–14 TLB).

The NIV Bible captures Ephesians 5:3 so clearly: *But among you **there must not be even a hint** of sexual immorality, or of any kind of impurity, or of greed, because these are improper **for God's holy people.***

If we were to evaluate the lives of average believers in America today, how would they measure up against Paul's admonition in Ephesians 5:1–14 above? Do you think Bible-believing Christians as a whole would be characterized as *"God's holy people"*? How would you respond to those questions concerning your own life testimony?

If we can't honestly testify that as God empowers us we're seeking to live as *"God's holy people,"* then it is possible our lives are slowly being squeezed into the shape our lust-driven world incessantly pressures us to be. The danger then is this: if we welcome the lusts of the flesh into our lives, we can eventually be ensnared by lust and act like unbelievers who are *"lovers of pleasure rather than lovers of God"* (2 TIMOTHY 3:4).

THE DANGERS OF WATCHING EVIL

As an example of how this can happen, I'm going to share the first page of a very blunt magazine article I found to be both convicting and distressing. (It may surprise you!):

Suppose I said, "There's a great-looking girl down the street. Let's go look through her window and watch her undress, then pose for us naked, from the waist up. Then this girl and her boyfriend will get in a car and have sex— let's listen and watch the windows steam up!" You'd be shocked. You'd think, What a pervert!

But suppose instead I said, "Hey, come on over. Let's watch **Titanic**."

Christians recommend this movie, church youth groups view it together, and many have shown it in their homes. Yet the movie contains precisely the scenes I described.

So, as our young men lust after bare women on the screen, our young women are trained in how to get a man's attention.

How does something shocking and shameful somehow become acceptable because we watch it through a television instead of a window?

In terms of the lasting effects on our minds and morals, what's the difference?

Yet many think, **Titanic?** *Wonderful! It wasn't even rated R!*

Every day Christians across the country, including many church leaders, watch people undress through the window of television. We peek on people committing fornication and adultery, which our God calls an abomination.

We've become voyeurs, Peeping Toms, entertained by sin.

Normalizing Evil

The enemy's strategy is to normalize evil. Consider young people struggling with homosexual temptation. How does it affect them when they watch popular television dramas where homosexual partners live together in apparent normality?

Parents who wouldn't dream of letting a dirty-minded adult baby-sit their children do it every time they let their kids surf the channels. Not only we, but our children become desensitized to immorality. Why are we surprised when our son gets a girl pregnant if we've allowed him to watch hundreds of immoral acts and hear thousands of jokes with sexual innuendos?

But it's just one little sex scene.

Suppose I offered you a cookie, saying, "A few mouse droppings fell in the batter, but for the most part it's a great cookie—you won't even notice."

"To fear the LORD is to hate evil" (PROVERBS 8:13). When we're being entertained by evil, how can we hate it? How can we be pure when we amuse ourselves with impurity?

God warns us not to talk about sex inappropriately:

"But among you there must not be even a hint of sexual immorality, or of any kind of impurity ... because these are improper for God's holy people. Nor should there be obscenity, foolish talk or coarse joking, which are out of place" (Ephesians 5:3–4).

How do our favorite dramas and sitcoms stand up to these verses? How about **Seinfeld** and other nightly reruns? Do they contain "even a hint of sexual immorality" or "coarse joking"? If we can listen to late night comedians' monologues riddled with immoral references, are we really fearing God and hating evil?[124] (Emphasis added.)

I hope this has been thought-provoking enough to cause you to want to re-examine your life to make sure you are not slowly being squeezed into embracing the lusts of the flesh—and thus becoming an enemy of God!

As Paul said:

*I beseech you ... by the mercies of God, that you **present your bodies a living sacrifice, holy, acceptable to God**, which is your reasonable service. **And do not be conformed to this world**, but be transformed by the renewing of your mind, that you may prove what is that good and acceptable and perfect will of God* (ROMANS 12:1–2).

God Warns Us Through Examples

BECAUSE WE ARE SO LOVED by God, He wants us to repent of any friendship with the world. He has therefore provided warnings through examples in Scripture to show what will happen to us if we persist in a friendliness-to-the-world mode.

In 1 Corinthians 10:1–5, Paul gave an Old Testament example of Israel's failures during their forty-year journey from Egypt to Canaan. He concluded by saying that *with most of them God was not well pleased*. He then explained:

> *Now these things became our examples*, to the intent that *we should not lust after evil things as they also lusted*. And do not become idolaters as were some of them. As it is written, "The people sat down to eat and drink, and rose up to play." Nor let us commit sexual immorality, as some of them did. ... Now all these things happened to them as examples, and **they were written for our admonition**, upon whom the ends of the ages have come. Therefore **let him who thinks he stands take heed lest he fall** (1 CORINTHIANS 10:6–8, 11–12).

Two more Old Testament saints also set valuable examples for our admonition—David and Samson. **David** was primarily "**a lover of God** rather than lover of pleasure." Because of this, since this God-hearted servant was slain by the giant Lust in an unguarded moment, how much more should the rest of us be on guard against yielding to such sin?

In contrast, **Samson** was a classic example of living as "**a lover of pleasure** rather than lover of God"; his life depicts how through the lusts of the flesh a believer becomes a friend of the world and an enemy of God. He often lived in the lust of the flesh, walked by the lust of the eyes, and responded with the pride of life. In fact, Samson's greatest enemy was himself—and he paid an extremely high cost for his transgressions.

Because we all struggle with the same problem—our flesh—Samson's failures are a stern warning of what can happen if we don't persistently keep our guard up.[125] This traitorous inclination against God called "the flesh" resides within each of us; it never slumbers, and always smolders. Given any amount of fuel—the desires of the body, the desires of the eyes, or the pride of life—and it blazes to life in a conflagration of destruction! For that reason, in this chapter we will examine Samson's tragic life which so clearly pictures the destructive power of sin.

STEPS TO A TRAGIC END

To have grown up with Samson was probably amazing! Surely, his neighborhood pals must have stood in wonder at his immense strength and his enemies would have fled quickly. He was like having a one-man army!

As a young man (probably in his teens), we get the first indicator that Samson was not going the direction the Lord had pointed him. As he began to live by his own desires rather than the Lord's—to serve his own lusts and not God's Words—Samson was in great need of God's grace. Soon a string of women began to parade through his life. Seven times Samson was guided by the lust of his eyes when he saw women that pleased him, and that was a dangerous choice each time.[126]

The final, and deadliest woman, was Delilah.[127] Her name has become synonymous with lust, deceit, betrayal, and ruin. For the price of an enormous bribe, Delilah worked to discover the secret of Samson's strength. In a series of lies he slowly gave clues until she finally wore him down and he confessed his secret. C. H. Spurgeon's summary says it all:

> At last he falls into the hands of Delilah. He foolishly plays with his own destruction. At last he lets out the secret, his strength lay in his locks. Not that his hair made him strong; but that his hair was the symbol of his consecration, and was the pledge of God's favor to him.
>
> While his hair was untouched he was a consecrated man; as soon as that was cut away, he was no longer perfectly consecrated, and then his strength departed from him. His hair is cut away; the Philistines begin to oppress him, and his eyes are burned out with hot iron. How are the mighty fallen!
>
> And now he comes to the very city out of which he had walked in all his pride with the gates and bolts upon his shoulders; and the little children come out, the lower orders of the people come round about him, and point at him—"Samson, the great hero, hath fallen! Let us make sport of him!" What a spectacle!
>
> Why, he must be the sport and jest of every passer by, and of every fool who shall step in to see this great wonder—the destroyer of the Philistines made to toil at the mill.
>
> That he should have lost his eyes was terrible; that he should have lost his strength was worse; but that he should have lost the favor of God for a while; that he should become the sport of God's enemies, was the worst of all.

Samson's soiled life was recorded so clearly to show that practicing sin first blinds us, then slowly binds us with its fetters, and finally, blinded and bound, we must go grinding through life because of sin!

Talk to those who have come to Christ after living in immorality, being on drugs, or immersing themselves in the world of alcohol and bars, and you'll find that such lifestyles were not all the media portrayed them to be. Such a sinful life could never satisfy because it consisted of quickly passing pleasures that slowly bound with cords that were hard to break. Were it not for the power of Christ which freed them of their bondage, they would have miserably ground out an existence as slaves to their sin!

What Was Samson's Problem?

Samson was **dominated by lust**. That passion led him to desire a Philistine woman as a wife, which was strictly forbidden by God's Law. In addition, his passion led him to liaisons with prostitutes (like the one with the woman Delilah who betrayed him for money). Many times men say, "I'm only doing that because I love her!" No, real love can wait to fulfill a legitimate desire; lust can't. Lust always fulfills legitimate desires in an illegitimate way. Do you want to know the difference between love and lust? Can you wait? If you can't, it is lust. Love always waits.

Samson was **driven by pride and revenge**. He was more motivated to strike out at the Philistines over personal affronts than he was by the suffering of the people he was supposed to lead (JUDGES 14:19–20; 15:7–8; 16:28).

Samson was **defeated by himself**. Imagine what Samson, with his great strength and godly heritage, might have been if only he had lived by his commitment to God when he took his Nazarite vow.

The rest of his story shows the tragic end of the believer who would not let God have his way with his life. From Judges 16:20 on, Samson did nothing but lose. What exactly did he lose?

- **Samson lost his hair**—the symbol of his Nazarite dedication. Since his dedication had long since been abandoned, God allowed the outward symbol of it to be taken away from him.
- **Samson lost his strength**—but didn't even know it until he was overpowered: *And she* [Delilah] *said, "The Philistines are upon you, Samson!" So he awoke from his sleep, and said, "I will go out as before, at other times, and shake myself free!" But* **he did not know that the LORD had departed from him** (JUDGES 16:20).

Samson didn't understand how futile it is for a servant of God to try to serve the Lord without being in His will. If we choose to operate in our own strength, God will let us fail in our own strength. If we choose to operate without heeding His warnings, He will let us do so. If we refuse to walk in the Spirit, He'll let us operate that way. However, His consequence engine is inescapable: what we sow, we reap (GALATIANS 6:7).

- **Samson lost his sight**—the Philistines put out his eyes.
- **Samson lost his freedom**—the Philistines bound him with fetters of brass.
- **Samson lost his usefulness to the Lord**—he ended up grinding corn instead of fighting God's battles. What a picture of sin! Remember, sin first blinds, then sin binds, and finally sin grinds. No matter how alluring it looks, sin grinds like gravel in the mouth (PROVERBS 20:17). And this began when Samson despised his blessings and defied his parents!
- **Samson lost his testimony**—he was the laughingstock of the Philistines. Their fish-god Dagon, not the God of Israel, was given all the glory.
- **Samson lost his life**—he had committed sin unto death, He was a castaway, so God had to take him off the scene.[128] His loved ones claimed his body and buried him *"between Zorah and Eshtaol"*—the very place where he had started his ministry (JUDGES 13:25).

Samson's life was disqualified: in heaven he was remembered as a man of faith, but not on earth. Hebrews 11:32 cites him for his faith in God's Word, but apart from this, very little can be said on his behalf.

So then, we've seen that the Scriptures tell us to ponder the examples in the Old Testament. However, we're not Nazarites; we get our hair cut and don't stay away from the fruit of the vine or from being near dead people. Since we aren't in the Old Testament, what is the applicable message for us in the New Testament? Look at Paul's testimony in 1 Corinthians 9:27: ***I discipline my body and bring it into subjection***, *lest, when I have preached to others, I myself should* ***become disqualified.***

In Greek, *"disqualified"* is *adokimos*, which is a very interesting word. In the ancient world, it was a word used in coin making. Individual men would melt gold, pour it into molds, stamp it with a number, and then give it out as currency as they agreed upon how much it weighed.

But people learned early on that if you filed off a little bit of numerous gold coins, you could get coins without working. Therefore, if you found coins with file marks on them, they were considered *adokimos* and were given back saying, "I'm not taking that coin. It's not right because someone shaved off the edges, cut the corners, and ruined its worth!" In other words, it was "disqualified" as a pure coin.

So Paul was saying, "I would be cheating in the holiness department if after I've lived my life, pouring my life into the mold of God's will, I decided to cut corners and say, 'I'm serving God, so I deserve to secretly serve my lust just a little bit because life's hard and, after all, I've got to have a few pleasures.' " If he did that, in the judgment God would say, "This person cut the corners, so We will disqualify his life." That is exactly what Paul feared.

What is the message for us? We ought to meditate on 1 Corinthians 3:9–15 to regularly remind ourselves that the fires of God's judgment will burn away worthlessness from our lives!

Samson's Sin in New Testament Terms

WHAT HAPPENED TO SAMSON IN New Testament terms? To answer that as well as remind us we're called to lifelong consecration to the Lord, this series of verses shows what can lead to a "sin unto death."

We are CONSECRATED: **Just as Samson was, all New Testament believers are consecrated to the Lord.**

*Do you not know that you are the temple of God and that the Spirit of God dwells in you? If anyone defiles the temple of God, God will destroy him. For the temple of God is holy, which temple you are. ... Or do you not know that **your body is the temple** [Greek naos – the sacred chamber where God dwelt] **of the Holy Spirit** who is in you, whom you have from God, and you are not your own? For you were bought at a price; therefore glorify God in your body and in your spirit, which are God's* (1 CORINTHIANS 3:16–17; 6:19–20).

Don't shave off the corners, excuse, or try to justify your actions in order to allow sin in your life. God says that you and I are to be consecrated to Him!

We are ANSWERABLE: **We will answer to God for what we did with our body.**

*Each one's work will become clear; for the Day will declare it, because it will be revealed by fire; it will be revealed by fire; and the fire will test each one's work, of what sort it is. If anyone's work which he has built on it endures, he will receive a reward. If anyone's work is burned, **he will suffer loss; but he himself will be saved, yet so as through fire** (1* CORINTHIANS 3:13–15).

That is why Paul said he was disciplining his body, bringing it into subjection, because he did not want to become disqualified by cutting corners in his walk with the Lord.

We are OWNED: **God is involved in our lives, so He will not stand by as we continue in sin.**

For this reason [those who couldn't control their appetites] ***many are weak and sick among you, and many sleep***. *For if we would judge ourselves, we would not be judged* [by God] (1 CORINTHIANS 11:30–31).

In the Bible, *"sleep"* refers to "death of the body" when the spirit is with Christ. Believers who will not repent will get weak, sick, and die—not because they are at an age when it is normal for death to happen, and it is a glorious home-going, but because they did not deal with their pride, lust, and living for the flesh.

We are LIABLE: **God gives warnings by chastening to prove His love for us.**

*And you have forgotten the exhortation which speaks to you as to sons: "My son, do not despise the chastening of the Lord, nor be discouraged when you are rebuked by Him; **for whom the Lord loves He chastens, and scourges every son whom He receives**"* (HEBREWS 12:5–6).

God will chastise true believers who live by the lusts of the flesh, lust of the eyes, and the pride of life—those who will not separate from the world, who love the world, who make friends with the world. God says:

*If you endure chastening, God deals with you as with sons; for what son is there whom a father does not chasten? But if you are without chastening, of which **all** have become partakers, **then you are illegitimate and not sons** (HEBREWS 12:7–8).*

Every child of God will be disciplined if he continues to live in sin. There are no exceptions—not even for God's servant, David, the man after God's own heart! God will not be mocked; what we reap we shall also sow. Consider this comparison:

*Blessed is the man who walks **not** in the counsel of the ungodly, **nor** stands in the path of sinners, **nor** sits in the seat of the scornful, but his delight is in the law of the LORD, and in His law he meditates day and night. … **Whatever he does shall prosper.** [But] **the ungodly are not so** (PSALM 1:1–4).*

We are RESPONSIBLE: **You can go too far in sin, too often, which is deadly for believers.**

*If anyone sees his brother sinning a sin which does not lead to death, he will ask, and He will give him life for those who commit sin not leading to death. **There is sin leading to death.** I do not say that he should pray about that. All unrighteousness is sin, and there is sin not leading to death (1 JOHN 5:16–17).*

What that unusual language means is this: If you go too far, too long, God will say, "That's enough!" and take you out of the world, just as he did Samson. He sinned unto death, which was a tragic thing.

We are WARNED: **God kills believers who refuse to repent.**

*Indeed I will cast her into a sickbed, and those who commit adultery with her into great tribulation, **unless they repent of their deeds. I will kill her children with death,** and all the churches shall know that I am He who searches the minds and hearts. And I will give to each one of you according to your works (REVELATION 2:22–23).*

God has a time period in which He waits, chastens, weakens, and then sickens. If that does not bring about a godly sorrow leading to repentance, then God takes the life of the believer who will not repent. So then, as a lost person, turn *while you hear His voice.* As a believer, there is no one who has gone too far to miss God's grace if you'll respond *while you hear His voice.* I exhort you to do so before it is too late!

Samson apparently repented of his sin during the grinding at the mill. He was sightless, abused, and made fun of constantly—a center of attraction, like in an amusement park. But while that was going on, God offered him one more chance to act by faith. His hair had begun to grow and Samson remembered his calling. So he asked God for strength to win one more victory over the enemy. God answered his prayer, but in defeating others, Samson lost his own life!

Samson is a strong illustration of friendship with the world through the lusts of the flesh. Samson's life was an example of those who have power to conquer others, but can't conquer themselves:

- He could set the Philistine fields on fire, but was consumed by the fires of his own lust.
- He could kill an attacking lion, but was utterly defeated by the passions of his own flesh.
- He could easily break the bonds men put on him, but the shackles of his own sin gradually grew stronger on his soul.
- He could have led the nation, yet he preferred to work independently. As a result, he left no permanent victory behind.
- He could have been remembered for what he built up, but instead everyone except God only remembers what he destroyed: lions, foxes, fields, gates, soldiers, women's purity, and his own life and ministry.

The life of Samson was recorded in God's Word as a picture of both the destructive power of sin and the restoring power of grace. Although Samson often lived in the lust of the flesh, often walked by the lust of the eyes, and often responded with the pride of life, in the final analysis, because God sees the heart, he was still called a man of faith.

Be a Friend of God and Enemy of the World

How CAN YOU AND I be a friend of God and enemy of the world, the flesh, and the devil? James 4:7–10 gives three instructions to follow if we want to enjoy peace with God instead of war:

1.**Submit to God** (v. 7). This word is a military term that means "get into your proper rank." Unconditional surrender is the only way to complete victory. If there is any area of the life kept back from God, there will always be battles. This explains why uncommitted Christians cannot live with themselves or with other people. "Neither give place to the devil," cautions Paul in Ephesians 4:27. Satan needs a foothold in our lives if he is going to fight against God; and *we give him that foothold.* The way to resist the devil is to submit to God.

2. **Draw near to God** (v. 8). How do we do this? By confessing our sins and asking for His cleansing. "Cleanse your hands, ye sinners; and purify your hearts, ye double-minded." The Greek word translated *purify* means "make chaste." This parallels the idea of "spiritual adultery" in James 4:4. Dr. A.W. Tozer has a profound essay in one of his books, entitled, "Nearness Is Likeness." The more we are like God, the nearer we are to God. I may be sitting in my living room with my Siamese cat on my lap, and my wife may be twenty feet away in the kitchen; yet I am nearer to my wife than to the cat because the cat is unlike me. We have very little in common. God graciously draws near to us when we deal with the sin in our lives that keeps Him at a distance. He will not share us with anyone else; He must have complete control. The double-minded Christian can never be close to God. Again, Abraham and Lot come to mind. Abraham "drew near" and talked to God about Sodom (GEN. 18:23ff), while Lot moved into Sodom and lost the blessing of God.

3. **Humble yourself before God** (vv. 9–10). It is possible to submit outwardly and yet not be humbled inwardly. God hates the sin of pride (PROV. 6:16–17), and He will chasten the proud believer until he is humbled. We have a tendency to treat sin too lightly, even to laugh about it ("let your laughter be turned into mourning"). But sin is serious, and one mark of true humility is facing the seriousness of sin and dealing with our disobedience. "A broken and a contrite heart, O God, Thou wilt not despise" (Ps. 51:17).

If we obey these three instructions, then God will draw near, cleanse us, and forgive us; *and the wars will cease!* We will not be at war with God, so we will not be at war with ourselves. This means we will not be at war with others. "And the work of righteousness shall be peace; and the effect of righteousness quietness and assurance forever" (ISA. 32:17).[129]

The Benefits of Humility

What all this boils down to is this:

God exalts the humble and debases the proud. During his time on earth Jesus repeated this on three separate occasions: "For everyone who exalts himself will be humbled, and he who humbles himself will be exalted" (Luke 18:14; cf. Matthew 23:12; Luke 14:11). The gravity of grace will always channel the rivers of divine favor to the lowly—to those 1) who submit to God, 2) whose soul's momentum is away from the Devil and toward God, 3) who purify their inner and outer lives, 4) who mourn over their sins, and 5) who obey the final summary command, "Humble yourselves before the Lord, and he will lift you up" [JAMES 4:10]. We are not to wait passively for this to somehow happen. We are not to wait for someone else to humble us, nor should we wait for the vicissitudes of life to do it. Rather, self-humbling is *our* Christian duty. We must take inventory of our sinfulness and weakness, then bow in total submission to God, yielding our total being, our dreams, our future, our *everything* to him. It is then that he will pour on the grace—grace upon grace—grace heaped upon grace—"and he will lift you up."[130]

Samson's life is truly a remarkable reminder of God's grace! He descended into the depths of a lust-filled life, and wandered far from his calling and consecration, but the Lord never let go of him. Though his soiled life was recorded, and his defeats were unvarnished and clear for all to see, against the backdrop of Samson's sin is the beauty of grace.

God forgave, restored, and used Samson one last time. In one moment of godly sorrow that led to a repentant prayer of faith, at his darkest hour, the Lord brought him back to the place of blessing. That is the wonder of God's grace—the God of the Second Chance tells us that even if we have lived like Samson, if he could make it, then anyone can make it who will turn in faith, repent, and look to Him for salvation!

GRACE GREATER THAN OUR SIN

Marvelous grace of our loving Lord,
Grace that exceeds our sin and our guilt,
Yonder on Calvary's mount outpoured,
There where the blood of the Lamb was spilt.

Dark is the stain that we cannot hide,
What can avail to wash it away?
Look! there is flowing a crimson tide;
Whiter than snow you may be today.

Marvelous, infinite, matchless grace,
Freely bestowed on all who believe;
All who are longing to see His face,
Will you this moment His grace receive?
Refrain—
Grace, grace, God's grace,
Grace that will pardon and cleanse within;
Grace, grace, God's grace,
Grace that is greater than all our sin.
    —Julia H. Johnston (1849–1919)

How to Sing the Song of a Soul Set Free

17

2 Samuel 11:27-12:14; Psalms 38 and 32

He who covers his sins will not prosper, but whoever confesses and forsakes them will have mercy. —**Proverbs 28:13**

ALL THAT REALLY MATTERS IN life may be reduced to one simple reality:

What does God think of what you are doing, or have done?[131]

In 2 Samuel 11, David's horribly disobedient choices regarding Bathsheba and Uriah prompted the worst days of his recorded life. All that mattered at that moment and for eternity was this: *What did God think of what David had done?* The answer was made abundantly clear in 2 Samuel 11:27:

The thing that David had done displeased the LORD.[132]

In the days, weeks, and months following God's assessment of David's sin, the ornate halls of Jerusalem's royal palace became strangely silent, as if he had lost his voice. David, the most written about person in God's Word, slowly withdrew from what had most characterized him ever since his boyhood on the hills of Judah.

In the past, sweet songs of God's power were often heard coming from the throne room of this victorious warrior. The shepherd-boy-become-king had carried his stringed instrument (a harp or lyre) into the daily life of leading God's people. This man, a living and talking expression of God's heart, was always refreshing others with his praises.

It was a daily treat for the myriads of aides, clerks, and military attachés to hear their king rapturously sing great hymns of worship. Rivers of praise to the Lord flowed down the halls, past the conquered treasures taken from fallen kingdoms, and over the storehouses of consecrated gold and silver heaped for the future temple of God. These songs poured out of David's mouth from a heart filled with the goodness of God. Each song (or psalm) sent from God to David was a great treasure from heaven.

With a heart of abandon, a heart welling up and overflowing with praise and worship, a heart unashamed of coming into God's presence, David led all around him into the Lord's presence as well. David's love for his Good Shepherd was so glorious that people were deeply blessed just to see him, hear him, and feel the warmth and glow of his spirit uplifted to God! Wouldn't you love to have been among those worshipers who heard David sing testimonies like Psalm 21:1?

> The king shall have joy in Your strength, O LORD; and in Your salvation how greatly shall he rejoice!

And rejoice he did—year after year after year as the invincible armies of Israel extended the borders of Israel to the very limits. But then things changed.

David Lost His Song

NO MORE WAS DAVID HEARD singing: *The LORD is my shepherd; I shall not want* (Psalm 23:1). Something was missing; something was greatly wanting in his life. For he no longer sang to his Good Shepherd: *To You, O LORD, I lift up my soul. O my God, I trust in You* (PSALM 25:1–2).

David's soul was cast down, trampled, empty, defiled, and infected with guilt and sin. And so he no longer sang: *The LORD is my light and my salvation; whom shall I fear?* (PSALM 27:1).

David no more walked in the Light or delighted in the joy of his salvation. No longer did he know the fearlessness of the righteous. For the righteous are as bold as a lion, but the wicked run even when nobody is chasing them (PROVERBS 28:1).

What David had done displeased the Lord—*and all that really mattered was what God thought of him.* Consequently, David fell silent. He had lost his song.

- The daily business of the Kingdom of Israel no longer flowed to the songs of heaven.
- The former shepherd's peace and joy no longer touched each worker, aide, and courier. The palace was slowly becoming a wasteland.
- The face of David was dark, no longer aglow with the joy of the Lord. Instead, he was quiet, pensive, and moody.
- The words of David were like honey before, but now they seemed more like his sword at his belt—sharp, cutting, and bringing death to those around him.
- The life-giving expressions of blissful delight that nourished the government of God's people were extinct. What a blessing those songs had been!

What was wrong? David was hiding his sin, and Proverbs 28:13 states: *He who covers his sins will not prosper, but whoever confesses and forsakes them will have mercy.* Thus the only solution for his dreadful condition was repentance.

As David desperately struggled with attacks from within and without, he poured his lonely heart out to the Lord in Psalm 38—an intense lament over the awful sin for which he was being chastised.

A Psalm of David. To bring to remembrance.

*¹ O Lord, **do not rebuke me in Your wrath**,*
  Nor chasten me in Your hot displeasure!
² For Your arrows pierce me deeply,
  And Your hand presses me down.

³ There is no soundness in my flesh
  ***Because of Your anger**,*
  Nor any health in my bones
  Because of my sin.
⁴ For my iniquities have gone over my head;
  ***Like a heavy burden** they are too heavy for me.*

⁵ *My wounds are foul and festering*
   Because of my foolishness.
 ⁶ *I am* **troubled***, I am* **bowed down** *greatly;*
   I go **mourning** *all the day long.*
⁷ *For my loins are full of inflammation,*
   And there is no soundness in my flesh.
⁸ *I am feeble and* **severely broken***;*
   I groan because of the **turmoil of my heart***.*

⁹ *Lord, all my desire is before You;*
   And my **sighing** *is not hidden from You.*
¹⁰ *My heart pants,* **my strength fails** *me;*
   As for the light of my eyes, it also has gone from me.

¹¹ *My* **loved ones** *and my* **friends** *stand aloof from my plague,*
   And my **relatives stand afar off***.*
¹² *Those also who seek my life lay snares for me;*
   Those who seek my hurt speak of destruction,
   And plan deception all the day long.

¹³ *But I, like a deaf man, do not hear;*
   And I am like a mute who does not open his mouth.
¹⁴ *Thus I am like a man who does not hear,*
   And in whose mouth is no response.

¹⁵ *For* **in You, O Lord, I hope***;*
   You will hear, O Lord my God.
¹⁶ *For I said, "Hear me, lest they rejoice over me,*
   Lest, when my foot slips, they exalt themselves against me."

¹⁷ *For I am* **ready to fall***,*
   And my **sorrow is continually before me***.*
¹⁸ *For I will declare my iniquity;*
   I will be in **anguish over my sin***.*
¹⁹ *But my enemies are vigorous, and they are strong;*
   And those who hate me wrongfully have multiplied.
²⁰ *Those also who render evil for good,*
   They are my adversaries, because I follow what is good.

²¹ Do not forsake me, O Lord;
   O my God, be not far from me!
²² Make haste to help me,
   O Lord, my salvation!

Although God was willing to completely forgive and restore David, the high price he had to pay for his sin would ultimately make this period the saddest era of his life.

THE HIGH PRICE OF SIN

What a powerful warning to beware of allowing unguarded moments in our lives—thinking we are safe from sin's reach. For it is at that moment the ravenous devourer is crouching, preparing to spring! But when David remembered this, it was too late.

Note again the steps he took downward into sin as he allowed the giant Lust to slowly creep in:

- **David desensitized his conscience** by incomplete obedience (2 SAMUEL 5:13).
- **David relaxed his grip** on personal purity (2 SAMUEL 11:1).
- **David fixed his heart** on physical desires (2 SAMUEL 11:2).
- **David rationalized his mind** about wrong decisions (2 SAMUEL 11:3).
- **David plunged** into lustful sin (2 SAMUEL 11:4).

As a result, **David destroyed his testimony** by the sin of a moment of stolen pleasure. Death, deceit, murder, immorality, spiritual oppression, and poverty and famine of the soul were only a few offspring of this act of momentary gratification. And those unguarded moments led to the inevitable consequences of sin.

Swollen with the putrid puss of sin, David's wounded soul throbbed with the long-incubated infection of self-righteousness. Due to the deadening effects of sin, the Spirit of God had been quenched, snuffed out, and doused in his life.[133] So when the Holy Spirit became grieved, the spring of David's soul—and the songs that resulted—dried up.

However, the Lord had a plan to deliver him out of the pit he'd dug for himself. When the crushing weight of sin brought David to near collapse, God sent His Word through the prophet Nathan to confront him.

To really experience the wonder of being freed from the vise of sin, let's look at that climactic moment when God gave His joy, His peace, and His new song back to David in 2 Samuel 12:1–14.

Then the LORD sent Nathan to David. And he came to him, and said to him: "There were two men in one city, one rich and the other poor. The rich man had exceedingly many flocks and herds. But the poor man had nothing, except one little ewe lamb which he had bought and nourished; and it grew up together with him and with his children. It ate of his own food and drank from his own cup and lay in his bosom; and it was like a daughter to him. And a traveler came to the rich man, who refused to take from his own flock and from his own herd to prepare one for the wayfaring man who had come to him; but he took the poor man's lamb and prepared it for the man who had come to him."

So David's anger was greatly aroused against the man, and he said to Nathan, "As the LORD lives, the man who has done this shall surely die! And he shall restore fourfold for the lamb, because he did this thing and because he had no pity."

Then Nathan said to David, **"You are the man! Thus says the LORD God of Israel:** *'I anointed you king over Israel, and I delivered you from the hand of Saul. I gave you your master's house and your master's wives into your keeping, and gave you the house of Israel and Judah. And if that had been too little, I also would have given you much more!* **Why have you despised the commandment of the LORD,** *to do evil in His sight? You have killed Uriah the Hittite with the sword; you have taken his wife to be your wife, and have killed him with the sword of the people of Ammon. Now therefore,* **the sword shall never depart from your house,** *because you have despised Me, and have taken the wife of Uriah the Hittite to be your wife.' Thus says the LORD: 'Behold,* **I will raise up adversity against you from your own house;** *and I will* **take your wives** *before your eyes* **and give them to your neighbor,** *and he shall lie with your wives in the sight of this sun. For you did it secretly, but* **I will do this thing before all Israel,** *before the sun.' "*

So **David said** *to Nathan,* **"I have sinned against the LORD."** *And Nathan said to David,* **"The LORD also has put away your sin;** *you* *shall not die. **However**, because by this deed you have given great occasion to the enemies of the LORD to blaspheme, **the child also who is born to you shall surely die**."*

Sin is horrible: it deceives with glittering promises and destroys with deadly accuracy. But, touched by God's grace, when Nathan confronted David, he responded with confession and repentance. Then things changed!

One day, as they did each morning, the generals of King David's cabinet walked the cobbled streets up the winding way to the palace. Upon arriving at the huge stone citadel, they expected to be dismissed again by the frustrated and depressed King of Israel. (His chambers were usually shuttered and silent, unlike the old days when he was up at the dawn.) But before they could get any further, the sound of the sweet songs of David stunned them.

DAVID FOUND HIS SONG AGAIN

With incredulous faces, one by one they looked up, and there he was: the sweet psalmist of Israel, perched on the steps of his throne, harp in hand, face tilted reverently upward, and tears streaming down his face.

He was back. David was back—and so was his song!

Like a spring gushing up in a parched desert, a river of worship once again flowed from David's heart—and the generals gratefully dropped to the floor to drink from it. Like the days of old their hearts began to burn again with adoring love to God!

All work was set aside because worship was their passion. Workers, servants, aides, guests, nobles—soon all took their places in the court of God's king. For David had gotten his song back!

What Happened to David?

AFTER DAVID CONFESSED AND REPENTED of the horrible sin he had been covering up for weeks and months, he wrote a song about what it means to return to God and receive, experience, and possess His forgiveness. I therefore like to call Psalm 32 "The Song of a Soul Set Free"!

When God moves to live within us by His Spirit, outward evidences will begin to be seen. Paul described one of those evidences in his epistles to the church:

[Be] *speaking to one another in psalms and hymns and spiritual songs,*
singing and making melody in your heart to the Lord
(EPHESIANS 5:19).

Let the word of Christ dwell in you richly in all wisdom, teaching and admonishing one another in psalms and hymns and spiritual songs, **singing with grace in your hearts to the Lord** (COLOSSIANS 3:16).

Psalm 32 is the song that marked the return of the rivers of living water to David's soul. The man after God's own heart had returned! Although the consequences of his sin would continue for years, David's joy was back, the peace was back, the fellowship was renewed, and the songs began to flow again. Psalm 32 is probably an expression of David's initial gratitude of liberation—his testimony at the relief of forgiveness:

A Psalm of David. A Contemplation

¹ *Blessed is he whose transgression is forgiven,*
   Whose sin is covered.
² *Blessed is the man to whom the* LORD *does not impute iniquity,*
   And in whose spirit there is no deceit.

³ *When I kept silent, my bones grew old*
   Through my groaning all the day long.
⁴ *For day and night Your hand was heavy upon me;*
   My vitality was turned into the drought of summer. Selah
⁵ *I acknowledged my sin to You,*
   And my iniquity I have not hidden.
   I said, "I will confess my transgressions to the LORD*,"*
   And You forgave the iniquity of my sin. Selah

⁶ *For this cause everyone who is godly shall pray to You*
   In a time when You may be found;
   Surely in a flood of great waters
   They shall not come near him.
⁷ *You are my hiding place;*
   You shall preserve me from trouble;
   You shall surround me with songs of deliverance. Selah

⁸ *I will instruct you and teach you in the way you should go;*
  I will guide you with My eye.
⁹ *Do not be like the horse or like the mule,*
  Which have no understanding,
  Which must be harnessed with bit and bridle,
  Else they will not come near you.

¹⁰ *Many sorrows shall be to the wicked;*
  But he who trusts in the LORD, mercy shall surround him.
¹¹ *Be glad in the LORD and rejoice, you righteous;*
  And shout for joy, all you upright in heart!

What a song his generals and other workers in the royal palace must have heard! Now let's go deeper by looking at the divisions of this psalm.

DAVID DELIGHTED IN SINS FORGIVEN—

Blessed is he whose transgression is forgiven, whose sin is covered. Blessed is the man to whom the LORD does not impute iniquity, and in whose spirit there is no deceit (PSALM 32:1–2).

In verses 1–2 David sang with delight when his sins were forgiven! He used three Hebrew words to describe *"forgiven"*:

1. Forgiveness means our SINS ARE PULLED OFF.
David said this in verse 1: *Blessed is he whose transgression is forgiven.*

"Forgiven" (Hebrew *nawsaw*) literally means "to have our sin lifted off by our Redeemer." Like Pilgrim's burden, it rolls off and into Christ's tomb. We are being crushed by any sins we keep around. They suffocate, smother, and squash the very life of our soul. But there is a Redeemer who can set us free. So to his only Hope, David fled.

Horatio G. Spafford (1828–1888), a man with a heavy load of sin, was saved and later moved to serve the Lord the rest of his days in Jerusalem. He lived in a house on the walls of Jerusalem next to the Damascus Gate as he ministered to Muslim orphans. Note his wonderful confession in the third stanza of his now famous song "It Is Well with My Soul" (1873):

> *My sin—oh, the bliss of this glorious thought!—*
> *My sin, not in part, but the whole,*
> *Is nailed to the cross and I bear it no more,*
> *Praise the Lord, praise the Lord, O my soul!*

2. Forgiveness means being SHIELDED FROM WRATH.

David finished verse 1 with *"whose sin is covered."*

David went on to say a second reality was now his: all of his just punishment had been graciously removed from him and he no longer faced God's wrath. That word *"covered"* (Hebrew *kawsaw*) uses the strong imagery of the Day of Atonement.

On that day the High-Priest took the blood of an animal and sprinkled it onto the mercy seat. Above the mercy seat was the presence of God portrayed by the outstretched arms of the cherubim. Beneath the lid of the ark were the tablets containing God's divine law.

In essence, the blood stood between a Holy God and the sinners who broke His law, averting His wrath. David cried for joy when the wrath of God was turned away from him. So our sins are *"covered"* away by the blood of Jesus shed for us! I love how Charles Wesley describes it:

ARISE, MY SOUL, ARISE

> *Arise, my soul, arise; shake off thy guilty fears;*
> *The bleeding sacrifice in my behalf appears:*
> *Before the throne my surety stands,*
> *Before the throne my surety stands,*
> *My name is written on His hands.*

> *He ever lives above, for me to intercede;*
> *His all redeeming love, His precious blood, to plead:*
> *His blood atoned for all our race,*
> *His blood atoned for all our race,*
> *And sprinkles now the throne of grace.*

Five bleeding wounds He bears; received on Calvary;
They pour effectual prayers; they strongly plead for me:
"Forgive him, O forgive," they cry,
"Forgive him, O forgive," they cry,
"Nor let that ransomed sinner die!"

The Father hears Him pray, His dear anointed One;
He cannot turn away, the presence of His Son;
His Spirit answers to the blood,
His Spirit answers to the blood,
And tells me I am born of God.

My God is reconciled; His pardoning voice I hear;
He owns me for His child; I can no longer fear:
With confidence I now draw nigh,
With confidence I now draw nigh,
And "Father, Abba, Father," cry.[134]
—Charles Wesley (1707–1788)

3. Forgiveness means ALL DEBTS ARE CLEARED OUT.

In verse 2 David said, *Blessed is the man to whom the* LORD *does not impute iniquity.*

"Not counted" speaks of a list of debts no longer held against us. David had become utterly bankrupted by his sin. The heavy bills of his soul were piling up, mounting like a flood and drowning him: desire, deceit, cruel deception, cunning craftiness, and shameless murder. But now, in sheer delight, all the mountain of impossible debt was cleared from his ledger and David could shout: "My sins are gone, and shall not be remembered! God in mercy tenderly forgives!"

The importance of forgiveness is a constant theme of Scripture. There are no less than seventy-five different word pictures about forgiveness in the Bible. They help us grasp the importance, the nature, and the effects of forgiveness. Look at these word pictures:

- To forgive is to turn the key, open the cell door, and let the prisoner walk free.

- To forgive is to write in large letters across a debt, "Nothing owed."
- To forgive is to pound the gavel in a courtroom and declare, "Not guilty!"
- To forgive is to shoot an arrow so high and so far that it can never be found again.
- To forgive is to bundle up all the garbage and trash and dispose of it, leaving the house clean and fresh.
- To forgive is to loose the moorings of a ship and release it to the open sea.
- To forgive is to grant a full pardon to a condemned criminal.
- To forgive is to relax a stranglehold on a wrestling opponent.
- To forgive is to sandblast a wall of graffiti, leaving it looking like new.
- To forgive is to smash a clay pot into a thousand pieces so it can never be pieced together again.

This message is so powerful to all of us who, like David, have had our sins "pulled off" by Christ's work on the cross for us.

DAVID DESPAIRED BECAUSE OF SINS CONCEALED—

When I kept silent, my bones grew old through my groaning all the day long. For day and night Your hand was heavy upon me; my vitality was turned into the drought of summer. Selah (PSALM 32:3–4).

God convicted David. In verses 3–4 he sang in despair when he remembered what it was like when his sins were concealed. In fact, concealed sin actually sickened him: *When I kept silent, my bones grew old.* That is a biblical concept; God's chastisement for sin does sicken Christians. However, every time you get sick doesn't mean you've committed a specific sin. All sickness, decay, and old age are results of the Curse.

In a *Time* magazine article about the great mysteries of the world, aging was identified as one of those mysteries. At age thirty, our DNA starts replicating in a little program that doesn't let the enzyme production continue in a way that utterly renews our body. Therefore, at thirty we start dying. You may have heard that you start dying from birth, but genetically there is a snap at age thirty in the protein and enzyme production and so we start going down.

But God says that it is sin that sickens us until we die. Scientists don't understand why it does that, because they believe if doctors could get inside our bodies and tinker around a bit, we could live forever—our bodies simply wouldn't wear out. What scientists don't realize is that the death process is a consequence of the Fall. So then, it is the Curse that makes us decline and degenerate. But even before age thirty, if we conceal our sin and refuse to repent, God's chastisement will sicken us.

- David's concealed sin saddened him: *through my groaning all the day long.*
- David's concealed sin burdened him: *For day and night Your hand was heavy upon me.*
- David's concealed sin stifled him: *my vitality was turned into the drought of summer* [like sun-parched brown grass when it's 120 degrees in the desert].

Punctuating verse 4 with *"Selah"* was like David saying, "Hey, look at what can happen if you conceal your sin!"

David Delighted in Sins Confessed—

I acknowledged my sin to You, and my iniquity I have not hidden. I said, "I will confess my transgressions to the Lord*," and You forgave the iniquity of my sin. For this cause everyone who is godly shall pray to You in a time when You may be found; surely in a flood of great waters they shall not come near him. You are my hiding place; You shall preserve me from trouble; You shall surround me with songs of deliverance. Selah* (Psalm 32:5–7).

God heard David's confession. In verse 5 David sang of deliverance. He delighted that his sins were cleansed; he despaired when they were concealed; but he was delivered when his sins were confessed. Note how he took personal responsibility for his sin: *I acknowledged my sin to You.* Like Joseph who in a moment of temptation cried out to the God Who saw him (Genesis 39), David acknowledged God's ability to see all things and that nothing was hidden from Him: *My iniquity I have not hidden.*

David acknowledged God's desire to forgive and cleanse away his sins when he said, *"I will confess my transgressions to the* Lord*."* Though there were thousands of priests in Israel, he didn't contact any of them. Instead, he said, "I want to talk to You, Lord." God wants to hear us and forgive us!

David recognized that only God's power could completely remove sin: *You forgave the iniquity of my sin.* He then punctuated it with *"Selah."* He was essentially saying, "WOW, Lord! I can come to You because You are an approachable God!"

God offered David refuge. In verses 6–7 David understood that the Lord is worthy of trust: *For this cause everyone who is godly shall pray to You in a time when You may be found.* He was saying, "God, when it looks like everything is just swirling around me, I can trust You!"

David knew he could rest in the Lord anywhere: *Surely in a flood of great waters they shall not come near him.* It was so refreshing to be able to rest in the Lord: *You are my hiding place; You shall preserve me from trouble; You shall surround me with songs of deliverance. Selah*

Once again David delighted in the Lord! Punctuating verse 7 with *"Selah"* was like saying, "The blessing comes from You, O God!"

DAVID DESIRED THAT SINFUL WAYS BE CRUSHED—

I will instruct you and teach you in the way you should go; I will guide you with My eye. Do not be like the horse or like the mule, which have no understanding, which must be harnessed with bit and bridle, else they will not come near you. Many sorrows shall be to the wicked; but he who trusts in the LORD, mercy shall surround him. Be glad in the LORD and rejoice, you righteous; and shout for joy, all you upright in heart! (PSALM 32:8–11).

God promised to keep David from sin. In verses 8–11 David sang about his desire that his sinful ways be crushed.

- **David now cried, "God, YOU LEAD ME."** He confessed, "When I was running my own life, I blew it—I was sinning. When I was running the show I was sinning. But when You run the show, You bring holiness. I can't do it myself, so please lead me." And the Lord said, "I will instruct you and teach you in the way you should go; I will counsel you with My eye upon you."

- **David now cried, "God, YOU GUARD ME."** He didn't want to be like the horse or mule which have no understanding and need to be harnessed with bit and bridle. Consequently, David prayed, "Guard me, Lord. I don't want to be hard and stubborn and rebellious. Keep me from that!"

- **David now cried, "God, YOU TEACH ME."** Because *"Many sorrows shall be to the wicked,"* he wanted the Lord to teach him when sin looked alluring. Allan Petersen wrote an interesting book called *The Myth of the*

Greener Grass. His book chronicled key Christians in the last fifty years who had given up the power and blessing of God in their ministry and went off to so-called "greener grass." It is so tragic when someone willingly gives up the blessings of God, the power of God, and the intimacy with God to pursue a pleasure that lasts for only a moment (if that long). Proverbs 20:17 says that *afterward his mouth will be filled with gravel.* And Proverbs 9:17 says, *"Stolen water is sweet, and bread eaten in secret is pleasant."* Sin may seem gratifying at first, but it doesn't last. Then the venom and the dregs and the poison of guilt and remorse and destroyed lives follow. Therefore, David said, "Teach me; remind me that the wicked are full of many sorrows."

- **David now cried, "God, YOU SURROUND ME."** David believed that *he who trusts in the LORD, mercy shall surround him.* Hence he said, "Lord, I am not sure I can make it alone; surround me like the bodyguards around a president." I still remember seeing pictures of the attempted assassination of Ronald Reagan. To protect him, his Secret Service men immediately dove on him, tackled him, and surrounded him. And if sinful humans can have that great a desire to protect someone, how much more so will Almighty God protect His own? Therefore He says, "I want to surround you—to clothe you with Christa. [135] Put on My armor, and I will surround you to guard you from sin."

- **David now cried, "God, YOU FILL ME."** Verse 11 captures the joyful song of a soul set free: *Be glad in the LORD and rejoice, you righteous; and shout for joy, all you upright in heart!*

At the end of verses 4, 5, and 7, we saw that David used the emphasis word *"Selah"* which, in today's language, means: "Hey, look at this!" Like David, I also say to you, "Hey, look at this!" Turn your attention from David, and now look at your own heart. Focus for a moment on what God wants from you. Then ask the Lord to examine your heart and enlighten you to answer each of these questions according to what He thinks of your life:

- Have I lost my song like David?
- Did I used to be closer to You, oh God?
- Am I holding onto some sin that displeases You, Lord?
- Is my heart growing restless and cold?

If the Holy Spirit brought conviction on any of those questions, the only right remedy is to confess and forsake the sin that has caused God's displeasure (1 JOHN 1:9). Don't wait like David did—and suffer the consequences that will inevitably come.

Remember: All that really matters in life may be reduced to one simple reality:

What does GOD think of what you are doing, or have done?

The Miracle of Complete Forgiveness

18

Psalm 32

Blessed is he whose transgression is forgiven, whose sin is covered.
—Psalm 32:1

IN THE BACK OF YOUR mind, have you ever wondered whether it is even possible to be completely forgiven and cleansed of *all* your sins? [136] What about truly bad ones that have been hidden from nearly everyone who knows you?

If you are the type of person that no one would ever suspect of having succumbed to strong temptation, and yet you have, complete forgiveness may seem impossible. After all, former drug addicts have a pass, right? They were bad, got saved, and are now set. It is the same for repentant alcoholics, sexual sinners, criminals, and so forth. But what if you have been a faithful church-goer, reared in a Christian home, and have never been into anything really bad? What if you have fallen headlong into sin—the kind where others are tempted to question: *Was that person ever really saved?* Can you be absolutely sure of God's complete forgiveness?

That is where David was before he wrote Psalm 32!

Before his sin with Bathsheba, David had been a living testimony to the grace of God. Even as a young shepherd boy he began telling the world he wanted to live a pure life for the Lord. Look at the disciplines he committed to in Psalm 132:

- Put God ahead of personal comforts (v. 3).
- Maintain a holy habit of devotions (v. 4).
- Make time for the Lord a priority (v. 5).
- Genuinely long for God (vv. 6–7).
- Stay pure (v. 9).

When David became king of Israel, he then laid out his plan for integrity. This became his personal operating system, which was probably the background for his commitments in Psalm 101:

- Live a non-hypocritical life of integrity (vv. 1–2).
- Adhere to a strong personal pact of purity (v. 3a).
- Never allow a buildup of sin (v. 3b).
- Limit exposure to sin (vv. 4–5).
- Hold only to proper heroes (vv. 6–7).
- Clean out whatever displeases the Lord (v. 8).

As wonderful as all those personal, private, and public commitments may have been, by 2 Samuel 11, David had drifted away and gotten out of touch with the Lord. Consequently, he fell headlong into sin.

When the initial consequences of guilt and shame multiplied, David finally came to the end of himself. For he had deeply reflected on his sin: he had one of his most loyal friends murdered, took that friend's wife as his own, and angered her family (which included two of his most trusted bodyguards and one of his most senior advisors). And now God had revealed to the whole world why his baby died, why his loyal friend was killed, and what he had been up to while everybody was out of town.

David longed for God's forgiveness, but in the back of his mind he wondered: *In light of my horrendous sin, is complete forgiveness even possible?*

And that brings us back to Psalm 32—a place to flee to if you find yourself wondering: *Can I ever be completely forgiven of this sin?*

Complete Forgiveness

THE GOSPELS RECORDED THIRTY-SEVEN SPECIFIC miracles Jesus performed during His earthly ministry. If you analyze them, they were wonderful, yet all but one was temporary. For example:

- The paralyzed to whom Jesus restored usage of limbs eventually lost their mobility years later when they died.
- Peter's mother-in-law was set free from a fever but ultimately died of other causes (which may have involved a fever).
- The food Jesus miraculously created to feed thousands was consumed and used up, and then hunger returned the next day.
- The eyes restored to blind Bartimaeus later wore out and dimmed by the time he died.
- The hearing the deaf received was subject to the natural downward slide of the human body and most likely faded even before death.
- The dancing feet the lame possessed after Christ's touch soon turned to a shuffle, and then stopped working altogether as they lay in bed awaiting death when they aged.
- Lepers who received fresh new skin and limbs saw a return to wrinkles, weakness, and finally immobility as circulation, respiration, and digestion were all slowly assaulted by the weight of many years.

THE GREATEST OF ALL MIRACLES

The greatest of Christ's amazing miracles, however, was the one that never faded, never aged, never ended. It was unfaded by time, untouched by health, unaffected by circumstances.

That miracle, the most wondrous of them all, is the one Jesus Christ is still performing in our midst today. It is the miracle I have personally experienced, and it is the same miracle you most likely have experienced too. What is it? The greatest of all Christ's miracles is *complete forgiveness*!

Up until the moments just before Psalm 32, a distraught David was uncertain about total forgiveness. Hence Psalm 32 became his song of testimony—a joyful heart praising God for complete forgiveness.

The miracle of complete forgiveness is a light in a dark place—a hope in a weary land—a promise from the God Who cannot lie! For God has said, "Neither do I condemn you! I am willing to completely cleanse and forgive in the Name of Jesus because of His payment made for your sins!" In the first two verses of Psalm 32, this is literally what David sang:

Oh, the happiness of the man whose rebellion has been forgiven, whose record of failures has been erased. How happy is the man on whose account the LORD does not put his crookedness, and in whose spirit there is no deceit [author's amplified translation].

David had been guilty: he rebelled against God's Law; he failed to meet God's righteous standard; he yielded himself to his crooked nature's control; and he deceitfully covered the whole matter up for nearly a year. So when he received God's complete forgiveness it was so wonderful that he sang Psalm 32! As Kent Hughes has expressed so well:

Total forgiveness is something to celebrate. It is beyond anything positive thinking, therapy, or hypnosis can provide. It is complete, extending to the conscious and unconscious sins in our lives, because God knows all things and because Jesus' blood is infinite.

And anyone can be forgiven, no matter what their sin is, whether they are the torturous commandant of Auschwitz or a serial killer like John Wayne Gacy or the most immoral (or even the most moral) person in America. Total forgiveness is possible through Christ. [137]

TRUE FORGIVENESS

God's forgiveness is always based on sin's penalty being paid. Only an acceptable payment can satisfy the Lord's holy justice. God required a substitute—a perfect sacrifice to die in the sinner's place. The chosen substitute, and the only one who qualified, was Jesus Christ, the Lamb of God. Salvation during both the Old and New Testament times was always based on Christ's sacrifice. When any sinner comes to God, convicted by the Holy Spirit that he cannot save himself from the deserved penalty of God's wrath, God's promise of forgiveness is granted when he believes.

But the modern tragedy is that many Christians are depressed about their sins and failures. They operate under the false notion that God still holds some or all of their sins against them. These misguided believers *forget* what the Scriptures say.

- They forget that because God has taken their sins upon Himself, they are separated from those sins *as far as the east is from the west* (PSALM 103:12).

- They forget God's promise through Isaiah that one day He would wipe out the transgressions of believers *"like a thick cloud." "Return to Me,"* He said, *"for I have redeemed you"* (ISAIAH 44:22).

- They forget that God looked down the corridors of time even before He made the earth and placed the sins of the world on the head of His Son, the Lamb of God *slain from the foundation of the world* (REVELATION 13:8). At Calvary Jesus took the sins of all who would believe an eternal distance away.

- They forget that hundreds of years before Calvary, Micah proclaimed that the Messiah's death would provide a way for complete forgiveness: *Who is a God like You, pardoning iniquity and passing over the transgression of the remnant of His heritage? He does not retain His anger forever, because He delights in mercy. He will again have compassion on us, and will subdue our iniquities. You will cast all our sins into the depths of the sea* (MICAH 7:18–19).

- They forget Christ's promise to never condemn them. When Jesus comes into our lives as Savior and Lord, He says to us what He said to the woman caught in the act of adultery: *"Neither do I condemn you; go, and sin no more"* (JOHN 8:11). *There is therefore now no condemnation to those who are in Christ Jesus. For the law of the Spirit of life in Christ Jesus has* [set you] *free from the law of sin and of death* (ROMANS 8:1–2).

CLEANSING FORGIVENESS

Listen to these profound words expressing the miracle of our complete forgiveness.

Because we continue to sin, we need the continued forgiveness of cleansing; but we do not need the continued forgiveness of redemption.

Jesus told Peter, "He who has bathed needs only to wash his feet, but is completely clean" (JOHN 13:10). Even though we continue to sin, Jesus "is faithful and righteous to forgive us our sins and to cleanse us from all unrighteousness" (1 JOHN 1:9). He forgives all our sins in the sweeping grace of salvation.

That does not mean we will no longer sin, nor that when we do our sins have no harmful effect. They have a profound effect on our growth, joy, peace, usefulness, and ability to have intimate and rich communion with the Father. Thus the believer is called on to ask for forgiveness daily so that he may enjoy not just the general forgiveness of redemption, but the specific forgiveness of daily cleansing, which brings fellowship and usefulness to their maximum.

There are no second class Christians, no deprived citizens of God's kingdom or children in His family. Every sin of every believer is forgiven forever.

God knows how we were, how we now live, and how we will live the rest of our lives. He sees everything about us in stark–naked reality.

Yet He says, "I am satisfied with you because I am satisfied with My Son, to whom you belong. When I look at you, I see Him, and I am pleased." [138]

The greatest miracle is Christ's sacrifice applied to us as believers so we know that in Christ all sins—past, present, and future—are forgiven forever. In Christ all guilt and penalties are permanently removed. In Him we will stand totally guiltless and holy for the rest of eternity. And so, as one great saint of the past said, we confess that:

The Bible is a corridor between two eternities down which walks the Christ of God; His invisible steps echo through the Old Testament, but we meet Him face to face in the New; and it is through that Christ alone, crucified for me, that I have found forgiveness for sins and life eternal. The Old Testament is summed up in the word *Christ*; the New Testament is summed up in the word *Jesus*; and the summary of the whole Bible is that Jesus is the Christ the Son of God. [139]

When God saves, He ultimately takes away all sin, all guilt, all punishment, as David found out:

*Blessed is he whose **transgression is forgiven**, whose **sin is covered**. Blessed is the man to whom the LORD does not impute iniquity, and in whose spirit there is no deceit. When I kept silent, my bones grew old* *through my groaning all the day long. For day and night Your hand was heavy upon me; my vitality was turned into the drought of summer. Selah* (PSALM 32:1–4).

David was the man whose *"transgression is forgiven"* and whose *"sin is covered"*—God having cast it as a millstone into the depths of the sea! And the man whose iniquity and perversion is not reckoned to his account, and whose *guile,* the deceitful and desperately wicked heart, is annihilated, being emptied of sin and filled with righteousness, is a happy man: *He who trusts in the LORD, mercy shall surround him. Be glad in the LORD and rejoice, you righteous; and shout for joy, all you upright in heart!* (PSALM 32:11).

David experienced all this because God's nature is to forgive. The Old Testament abounds with teachings about His forgiveness.

- God described Himself to Moses as *"the LORD, the LORD God, compassionate and gracious, slow to anger, and abounding in lovingkindness and truth; who keeps lovingkindness for thousands, who forgives iniquity, transgression and sin"* (EXODUS 34:6–7 NASB).

- David declared: *For You, Lord, are good, and ready to forgive, and abundant in lovingkindness to all who call upon You"* (PSALM 86:5 NASB).

- In another psalm David reminds us that God pardons all our iniquities: *Who forgives all your iniquities, Who heals all your diseases, … as far as the east is from the west, so far has He removed our transgressions from us* (PSALM 103:3, 12).

- And look at this psalm: *If You, LORD, should mark iniquities, O Lord, who could stand? But there is forgiveness with You, that You may be feared* (PSALM 130:3–4).

- Daniel well said, *"To the Lord our God belong compassion and forgiveness"* (DANIEL 9:9 NASB).

All Sins Are Forgivable

NO MATTER HOW SEVERE THE sin, God can forgive it. The worst conceivable sin would be to kill God's own Son—and that happened while He was on earth for the very purpose of providing salvation from sin and the way to everlasting life. Nothing could possibly be more heinous, vicious, and wicked than that. Of course, killing Him is exactly what men did to the Son of God. Yet, while hanging on the cross and about to die, Jesus prayed and affirmed the forgiving mercy available to even His executioners: *"Father, forgive them; for they do not know what they do"* (LUKE 23:34).

- The *degree* of sin does not forfeit forgiveness, because even killing the Son of God was forgivable.

- Nor does the *volume* of sin end the possibility of mercy. A seventy-year-old profligate who has lived a life of debauchery, stealing, lying, profanity, blasphemy, and immorality is just as forgivable as a seven-year-old who has done nothing worse than normal childhood naughtiness.

- Nor does the particular *kind* of sin cancel grace. In Scripture we find God forgiving idolatry, murder, gluttony, fornication, adultery, cheating, lying, homosexuality, covenant breaking, blasphemy, drunkenness, extortion, and every other kind of sin imaginable. He forgives self-righteousness, which is the deceiving sin of thinking that one has no sin. He even forgives the sin of rejecting Christ; otherwise no one could be saved, because before salvation *everyone,* to some degree, is a Christ rejecter. There is no forgiveness of even the smallest sin unless it is confessed and repented of; but there is forgiveness of even the greatest sin if those divine conditions are met. [140]

From the Garden of Eden onward God has offered forgiveness to all who come to Him! But how are we to get that forgiveness? Paul triumphantly declares that truth for us in Ephesians 1:7:

In Him we have redemption through His blood, the forgiveness of sins, according to the riches of His grace.

Christ Paid the Infinite Price of Sin

ON THE CROSS, CHRIST PURCHASED our redemption, which was the payment of a price or ransom. For guilty sinners, the only price was Christ's own blood, which He poured out on the cross. As the Scriptures repeatedly attest, all humanity is enslaved to sin and powerless to pay for their freedom, but Christ paid for all who would believe in the infinite price it cost Him for us:

[Jesus came] *"to give his life as a ransom for many"* (MARK 10:45 NIV). [Jesus] *entered the Most Holy Place once for all by his own blood, having obtained eternal redemption* (HEBREWS 9:12 NIV).

For you know that it was not with perishable things such as silver or gold that you were redeemed from the empty way of life handed down to you from your forefathers, but with the precious blood of Christ, a lamb without blemish or defect (1 PETER 1:18–19 NIV).

Our redemption cost God the very life of Christ, which was an astounding mystery that puzzled the Old Testament prophets and one the angels long *"to look into."* (See 1 PETER 1:10–12.)

Christ's death to pay the price of our sin is so wonderful that we, the redeemed of all the ages, will be joined by the angels so that together we may sing a new song, as Revelation records:

And they sang a new song: "You are worthy to take the scroll and to open its seals, because you were slain, and with your blood you purchased men for God from every tribe and language and people and nation. You have made them to be a kingdom and priests to serve our God, and they will reign on the earth." Then I looked and heard the voice of many angels, numbering thousands upon thousands, and ten thousand times ten thousand. They encircled the throne and the living creatures and the elders. In a loud voice they sang: "Worthy is the Lamb, who was slain, to receive power and wealth and wisdom and strength and honor and glory and praise!" (REVELATION 5:9–12 NIV).

So then, to see how God accomplished complete forgiveness of our sins through Christ's sacrifice, let's look at our final destination—that wonderful city we are headed toward in heaven! For the Christian life is lived in the *present* tense; we have *today in Christ* the benefits of His work on the cross.

We are forgiven, we are justified (ROMANS 3:24), we are redeemed, we are cleansed, we are kept!

The Future of Forgiven

WHAT AWAITS ALL OF US who have experienced the miracle of complete forgiveness? Hebrews 12 tells us of these precious realities:

We the forgiven will enter the City of the Living God: *But you have come to Mount Zion, to the heavenly Jerusalem, the city of the living God* (HEBREWS 12:22 NIV). Throughout our earthly lives we were pilgrims and strangers who were always waiting for, and longing for, this city God was preparing for us.

Mount Zion, also known as the region of Moriah in Genesis 22, was the location of the city of Melchizedek, the site of Abraham's offering of Isaac and then later the Jebusite stronghold David captured. When David brought the Ark of the Covenant to this place he made Jerusalem the spiritual center of his kingdom—the place of God's presence with His people. Later, as Solomon built the temple and installed the Ark, Zion/Jerusalem became representative of the earthly dwelling-place of God.

As believers we are already citizens of the heavenly Jerusalem and have all the privileges of that citizenship. Remember what Paul wrote: *But our citizenship is in heaven. And we eagerly await a Savior from there, the Lord Jesus Christ* (PHILIPPIANS 3:20 NIV).

As believers we are already seated at the banquet table with Jesus because of our position in Him. Paul wrote that *God raised us up with Christ and seated us with him in the heavenly realms in Christ Jesus* (EPHESIANS 2:6 NIV). So, like Paul, we follow after (keep on plodding along through the trench warfare of life) so that we can arrive at the goal already ours through the upward call of Christ Jesus!

We the forgiven will see the countless angels: Y*ou have come to thousands upon thousands of angels in joyful assembly* (HEBREWS 12:22 NIV). At last we get to meet all those who watched over us while we went through this life—God's mighty flaming *ministering spirits sent to serve those who will inherit salvation* (HEBREWS 1:14 NIV).

Moses tells us that *"myriads of holy ones"* attended the giving of the Law (DEUTERONOMY 33:2 NIV); from Daniel we hear that *thousands upon thousands attended him* [the Ancient of Days—God]; *ten thousand times ten thousand stood before him* (DANIEL 7:10 NIV). And David said, *The chariots of God are tens of thousands and thousands of thousands* (PSALM 68:17 NIV).

So seldom do we even reflect upon God's special ministering angels who are, as Kent Hughes writes,

> ... passing in and out of our lives, moving around us and over us just as they did Jacob of old. Sometimes they protect God's elect—for example, the "tall men in shining garments" who surrounded Mr. and Mrs.

John G. Paton years ago in the New Hebrides—or the "tall soldiers with shining faces" who protected missionary Marie Monsen in North China—or, on another occasion, the "huge men dressed in white with flaming swords" who surrounded the Rift Valley Academy—and on another the "hundreds of men dressed in white, with swords and shields" who stood guard over a hut shielding Clyde Taylor, who would one day found the National Association of Evangelicals.

Olive Fleming Liefeld in her book *Unfolding Destinies* tells how two young Auca Indians, Dawa and Kimo, heard singing after witnessing the martyrdom of the five missionaries in the jungles of Ecuador: "As they looked up over the tops of the trees they saw a large group of people. They were all singing, and it looked as if there were a hundred flashlights."

But the grand emphasis of our passage is not so much the angels' care of us, but rather our joining them in festal assembly. The word translated "joyful assembly" was used in ancient culture to describe the great national assemblies and sacred games of the Greeks. Whereas at Mount Sinai the angels blew celestial trumpets that terrified God's people, we are to see ourselves on Mount Zion as dressed in festal attire and worshiping in awe side by side with these shining beings!" [141]

We the forgiven will join the saints of all time: *the church of the firstborn, whose names* [fellow believers] *are written in heaven* (HEBREWS 12:23 NIV). Hebrews tells us that Jesus is not ashamed to call us brothers and sisters, so with Him we are sharing in the inheritance promised to us by God the Father.

In the ancient world all the rights of inheritance go to the firstborn. Because we are purchased by Christ and completely forgiven, we are *"co-heirs with Christ"* (ROMANS 8:17 NIV).

Bishop Westcott says we are "a society of 'eldest sons' of God." There are no second or third or fourth sons and daughters in the church. We all get the big inheritance! Plus, our names are written in heaven along with those who are already there. In other words, we are all the Body of Christ! They are there awaiting our arrival as Christ escorts us home one by one until His entire family has safely made it home. Then Christ can celebrate communion with His whole family present!

We the forgiven will be with our Almighty God: *You have come to God, the judge of all men* (HEBREWS 12:23 NIV). At last we come before the God of the Universe! What an awesome moment to be transported before Him!

The writer of Hebrews has already said, *Nothing in all creation is hidden from God's sight. Everything is uncovered and laid bare before the eyes of him to whom we must give account* (HEBREWS 4:13 NIV). Plus, he said that God is dreadfully powerful: *"It is mine to avenge; I will repay," and again, "The Lord will judge his people." It is a dreadful thing to fall into the hands of the living God"* (HEBREWS 10:30–31 NIV).

But in Revelation we learn that we will be led by the nail-scarred hand of Jesus to meet our heavenly Father—because Jesus paid it all. This is our *highest delight*—to gather before God! It is a miracle of grace!

Look at what Jesus says will happen then: *"I will confess his name before My Father and before His angels"* (REVELATION 3:5). Try to envision this awesome scene in your mind as you come face to face with Jesus:

> Picture yourself being taken by the hand by the Lord Jesus, led up past the marshaled ranks of the angels, up along the golden boulevards of glory, up past the cherubim and the seraphim, up, up to the throne of God Himself and then hearing the Lord Jesus call you by your name as He presents you in person as His well-beloved child!

> Then listen to the Father say, "Bring the best robe and put it on him." Think of it—a robe of white, bright as the day, pure as the light—like when the Lord Jesus was transfigured on the mount and His raiment became white as the light.

What a reward for all who have been completely forgiven—to have a robe like that draped around our shoulders and be invited to walk the shining ways of glory in light-transfigured clothes. We will have joined all the saints of all the ages—home at last with our God! Doesn't that make you want to joyfully burst forth singing the beloved hymn "Face to Face"?

FACE TO FACE

Face to face with Christ, my Savior,
Face to face—what will it be,

When with rapture I behold Him,
Jesus Christ Who died for me?
Only faintly now I see Him,
With the darkened veil between,
But a blessèd day is coming,
When His glory shall be seen.

What rejoicing in His presence,
When are banished grief and pain;
When the crooked ways are straightened,
And the dark things shall be plain.

Face to face—oh, blissful moment!
Face to face—to see and know;
Face to face with my Redeemer,
Jesus Christ Who loves me so.

Refrain—
Face to face I shall behold Him,
Far beyond the starry sky;
Face to face in all His glory,
I shall see Him by and by!
 —Carrie E Breck (1855–1934)

We the forgiven will at last be perfected: *to the spirits of righteous men made perfect* (HEBREWS 12:23 NIV). As saints of heaven, we join in the assembly of the perfected ones, the justified, the sanctified, and now at last—the glorified ones. The hope and longing of our entire earthly struggle has been realized. We are finally free from sin in all its hideous power and presence!

We are sharing in that power of an endless life, but by God's absolutely amazing plan, we get to partake of it together with all the saints of all the ages! Though some will have preceded us by thousands of years God tells us in Hebrews 11:40 *that only together with us would they be made perfect* (NIV). The Old Testament saints waited for centuries for the perfection we received when we trusted Christ, because that came only with Christ's death: *By one sacrifice he has made perfect forever those who are being made holy* (HEBREWS 10:14 NIV). Because of Christ's work we are not one whit inferior to the patriarchs—for through Christ we are all equal in righteousness!

We the forgiven will be with Jesus our Savior: *Jesus the mediator of a new covenant* (HEBREWS 12:24 NIV). The writer of Hebrews uses the name given to God the Son at His birth. He is seen in Hebrews as the One Who destroyed the devil—*"him who holds the power of death"* (HEBREWS 2:14 NIV); and Who was made like us and has felt our temptations. He is Jesus Who invites us to boldly come to the very throne of God and find grace and mercy. Jesus is the One through Whom all things are promised us and given us, and He sustains all things. So here we come to Him Who is our all in all, as Dennis Jernigan so beautifully says in the following chorus: [142]

> *You are my strength when I am weak;*
> *You are the treasure that I seek—You are my all in all.*
>
> *You took my sin, my cross, my shame,*
> *Rising again, I take your name—You are my all in all.*

We the forgiven will finally enjoy His complete forgiveness: [because of] *the sprinkled blood that speaks a better word than the blood of Abel* (HEBREWS 12:24 NIV). Those completely forgiven come to eternal forgiveness because of *Christ's blood.* The blood of Abel cried from the ground demanding vengeance, but the blood of God the Son will forever proclaim that we are completely forgiven at an infinite price—the love of God Who gave His only Son to die in our place!

The miracle of complete forgiveness is what Jesus said we are to celebrate in heaven forever! Such total forgiveness, which David experienced and joyfully sang about in Psalm 32, is nicely expressed in this great hymn:

WONDERFUL GRACE OF JESUS

> *Wonderful grace of Jesus, Greater than all my sin;*
> *How shall my tongue describe it, Where shall its praise begin?*
> *Taking away my burden, Setting my spirit free,*
> *For the wonderful grace of Jesus reaches me.*
>
> *Refrain—*
> *Wonderful the matchless grace of Jesus,*
> *Deeper than the mighty rolling sea;*
> *Higher than the mountain, sparkling like a fountain,*
> *All sufficient grace for even me;*

Broader than the scope of my transgressions,
Greater far than all my sin and shame;
O magnify the precious name of Jesus, Praise His name!
        —Haldor Lillenas (1885–1959) [143]

So then, God's Word tells us that those who come to Christ are miraculously and completely forgiven! The writer of Hebrews says it is now ours in Christ for we have come (*right now!*) to these seven realities:

- To the City of God
- To myriads of angels
- To fellow-believers
- To our awesome God
- To at last be glorified
- To Jesus our Savior
- To complete forgiveness

If this greatest miracle of all time does not create a wellspring of thanksgiving in our hearts and make us want to march to Zion—what will? [144]

19 | David's Road Map: The Pathway Back to God

Psalm 51

Create in me a clean heart, O God, and renew a steadfast spirit within me.
—**Psalm 51:10**

DAVID FELL SO FAR, so fast, and he didn't even realize it until the dullness of his soul spread to every inch of his spiritual life. [145] Soon his cold and lonely heart was combined with his tormented soul and trapped in a painfully chastened body. And he stayed at the bottom like that for almost a year.

Does that length of time surprise you? After all, think of whom it was that had fallen so far away from the God he passionately loved and served. For David was a man who

- received God's Word directly through inspiration,
- knew the indwelling presence of God the Spirit,
- had the direct line to God's throne by way of prophets,
- could enter the very tent of God built to the Lord's specifications,
- perhaps held the very scrolls Moses had written down,
- may have seen the stone tablets of the Law that were kept in the Ark of the Covenant, and

- had seen God's supernatural protection month after month in hand-to-hand combat. David was never defeated on the battlefield and, as far as we know, never even wounded in spite of the tens of thousands of weapons that had at some time been aimed at him by those who hated him and wanted him dead.

David was a man who knew God, experienced God's presence, loved God, sang scores of songs inspired by God, wrote chapters of the eternal Word of God—and yet he seemed to lose touch with God for a YEAR!

Just Going Through the Motions

AMAZINGLY, DAVID HID THIS WELL as he went through the motions of being the king. After all, he was still God's leader—the sweet psalmist of Israel, head of the family line that would never end, and the one through whom the Christ would come. But like an engine without fuel or an electronic device with no power, those blessings and benefits meant nothing when he walked away from the Lord and stayed away for a long time.

To the casual observer, it may have looked like David had gotten away with sin. But David was God's man and He would never let His choice servant get by with sin. In reality, during the interval David kept quiet, he was tormented from within and without—as seen in Psalm 38, which was a prayer of intense lament during chastening.

Psalm 32, which I like to call "The Song of a Soul Set Free," was probably an expression of his initial gratitude over the relief of forgiveness. That song shows what really went on in David's heart during this distressful period. The self-inflicted stress of those many months was completely debilitating to him:

> When I kept silent, my bones grew old through my groaning all the day long. For day and night Your hand was heavy upon me: my vitality was turned into the drought of summer (PSALM 32:3–4).

If we could have visited the court of David during that nearly year of hidden sin, we would have seen him literally aging before our eyes!

Coming Back to God

ONLY GOD COULD RELIEVE DAVID'S cold, distant, lonely tormented heart by granting complete forgiveness and restoration of his joy, peace, and security.

Hence Psalm 51 is all about David, who had been so far away, coming back to the Lord. It stands as a paradigm of prayers for forgiveness of sins—a divinely inspired road map to the path back to God. [146]

Out of the 327 words in Psalm 51, thirty-five times David used "I," "me," or "my" (shown in bold below) to repeatedly say, "I am guilty!" Doing so was his acknowledgement of God's perspective that we are all sinners (ROMANS 3:10–12, 23). [147]

To the Chief Musician. A Psalm of David when Nathan the prophet went to him, after he had gone in to Bathsheba.

¹ *Have mercy upon **me**, O God,*
According to Your lovingkindness;
According to the multitude of Your tender mercies,
*Blot out **my** transgressions.*
² *Wash **me** thoroughly from **my** iniquity,*
*And cleanse **me** from **my** sin.*

³ *For **I** acknowledge **my** transgressions,*
*And **my** sin is always before **me**.*
⁴ *Against You, You only, have **I** sinned,*
And done this evil in Your sight—
That You may be found just when You speak,
And blameless when You judge.

⁵ *Behold, **I** was brought forth in iniquity,*
*And in sin **my** mother conceived **me**.*
⁶ *Behold, You desire truth in the inward parts,*
*And in the hidden part You will make **me** to know wisdom.*

⁷ *Purge **me** with hyssop, and **I** shall be clean;*
*Wash **me**, and **I** shall be whiter than snow.*
⁸ *Make **me** hear joy and gladness,*
That the bones You have broken may rejoice.
⁹ *Hide Your face from **my** sins,*
*And blot out all **my** iniquities.*

¹⁰ *Create in **me** a clean heart, O God,*
   *And renew a steadfast spirit within **me**.*
¹¹ *Do not cast **me** away from Your presence,*
   *And do not take Your Holy Spirit from **me**.*

¹² *Restore to **me** the joy of Your salvation,*
   *And uphold **me** by Your generous Spirit.*
¹³ *Then **I** will teach transgressors Your ways,*
   And sinners shall be converted to You.

¹⁴ *Deliver **me** from the guilt of bloodshed, O God,*
   *The God of **my** salvation,*
   *And **my** tongue shall sing aloud of Your righteousness.*
¹⁵ *O Lord, open **my** lips,*
   *And **my** mouth shall show forth Your praise.*
¹⁶ *For You do not desire sacrifice, or else **I** would give it;*
   You do not delight in burnt offering.
¹⁷ *The sacrifices of God are a broken spirit,*
   A broken and a contrite heart—
   These, O God, You will not despise.

¹⁸ *Do good in Your good pleasure to Zion;*
   Build the walls of Jerusalem.
¹⁹ *Then You shall be pleased with the sacrifices of righteousness,*
   With burnt offering and whole burnt offering;
   Then they shall offer bulls on Your altar.

Psalm 51, designed primarily for public reading and worship, is one of the most treasure-laden psalms in the Bible. It was part of the regular songs of the tabernacle, then the temple, and now the church. Inspired by the Spirit of God, written by David, the song has been lifted up before God as a memorial to His great love that made Him able and willing to forgive men such as David.

The structure of Psalm 51 was intended for effective communication in public assembly and worship. Note the emphasis and how it changed:

- **David took the blame.** In verses 3–9, David emphasized his responsibility for his sin, but God was not mentioned by name.

- **God was his desire.** In verses 10–19, the Holy God against Whom David sinned was emphasized twenty times, but sin and sinner were only mentioned once.

The primary lesson of this psalm is that ALL SIN is AGAINST GOD—not simply a personal defeat. If you believe that your sin is only a defeat you experience, sin becomes manageable and thus something to just learn to live with. But that would be a serious misconception for the following reason:

When the church has a superficial view of sin, this attitude affects everything the church believes and does. If men and women are basically good and not sinners under the wrath of God, then why preach the Gospel? Why send out missionaries? For that matter, why did Jesus even die on the cross? If people are good, then what they need is counseling and consoling, not convicting; we should give them encouragement, not evangelism. [148]

David, however, understood that sin is against GOD (v. 4). But because David's sins were forgiven, countless other believers have been comforted that their sins can also be forgiven by following the same pathway back to God.

Now look at how David laid bare his soul as he sought restoration from the Lord.

The Pathway Back to God

GOD INSPIRED DAVID TO SHOW four steps that will lead us back to God when we feel defeated by sin:

STEP 1—Understand that all sin is against God. (PSALM 51:1–4)
- The Lord can renew our relationship. (v. 1)
- The Lord can wash us clean. (v. 2)
- The Lord can remove the roadblock. (v. 3)
- The Lord can utterly forgive. (v. 4)

STEP 2—Take personal responsibility for our sin. (PSALM 51:5–9)
- As sinners we are all spiritually destitute (v. 5).
- As sinners we need truthfulness. (v. 6)
- As sinners we need cleansing. (v. 7)
- As sinners we need joyfulness. (v. 8)
- As sinners we need fellowship with our God. (v. 9)

STEP 3—Believe that only God can cleanse and restore us.
(PSALM 51:10–13)

- God wants to wash our hearts. (v. 10) [See also HEBREWS 9:14; 10:22.]
- God wants to restore our walk in the Spirit. (v. 11)
- God wants to renew the fruit of the Spirit. (v. 12)
- God wants to prepare us for further ministry. (v. 13)

STEP 4—Seek God and repent. (PSALM 51:14–19)

- Call sin what it is [e.g., David murdered Uriah]. (v. 14)
- Talk to God [e.g., David had dried up spiritually in Psalm 32]. (v. 15)
- Experience true contrition, not mere externalism. (vv. 16–17)
- Begin zealous worship anew and afresh. (vv. 18–19)

I Am Guilty

(Psalm 51:1)

"I AM GUILTY. I WAS wrong. I am sorry. Please take from me the just punishment I deserve!" So began the greatest song about the love of God a desperate David experienced when he was overwhelmed. For in a moment, he went from absolute gloom and heaviness of soul to the joy of having his sins lifted off!

The spiritual scales that had slowly taken the color and light from his life were removed. His soul, now flooded with light and peace, began again to drink deeply from the wells of his salvation. His cold heart was warmed; his tormented soul was set free; and he was no longer trapped in a painfully chastened body. David had left the bottom where he had stayed for almost a year!

How did David get back on track? And even more pressing for each of us is this: How can *we* come back to God when we've sinned and grown cold and distant?

David began at quite a different reference point from that of modern psychotherapists or social workers who usually begin with "our inner experience. They invite us to try to face up to our moral problems, to recognize how our misdeeds affect society for the worse or how we have even broken society's laws." [149]

But David swept beyond all these human and moral considerations and looked straight at the Almighty Holy God he had sinned against. By confessing that he was guilty, David was coming back to God Who alone can renew a relationship broken by sin: *Have mercy upon me, O God, according to Your loving kindness; according to the multitude of Your tender mercies, blot out my transgressions* (PSALM 51:1).

David appealed to God's love and compassion as he petitioned the Lord to forgive him by grace and cleanse him from his sin. Mercy is to *not* get what we deserve and grace is to *get* what we don't deserve. Mercy withholds; grace outpours.

> God's attributes of **unfailing love** (chesed) for His servant and His **compassion** for the helpless, were the basis for David's appeal for mercy. Even the verb **have mercy** was a prayer for **God** to act in accord with His nature. It is also a recognition that David did not deserve forgiveness. God's forgiveness is by His grace alone. [150] (Emphasis added.)

If you want swift, immediate, and relationship-restoring help from God, start with that simple guilty plea. A David-type response to God in the New Testament is in Luke 18:13: *"And the tax collector, standing afar off, would not so much as raise his eyes to heaven, but beat his breast* ["kept on" — imperfect active], *saying, 'God, be merciful to me a sinner!' "*

God just can't resist this type of heart cry to Him! The Greek tenses tell us that the publican couldn't stop saying this; it was an ongoing longing of his heart. Like the publican who wouldn't even lift his face toward God, but just said, *"God, be merciful to me,"* we can also come back to God in this manner.

Such a cry of acknowledgment of our sin is very humbling. In fact, the very way we started is how we are to continue: *As you have therefore received Christ Jesus the Lord, so walk in Him* (COLOSSIANS 2:6). The word *"received"* in Colossians 2:6 is the very same word for salvation that appears in John 1:12: *As many as received Him, to them He gave the right to become children of God.* In other words, the humble contrition that brought us salvation also brings us back to God whenever we sin.

Let's remember again that each of us came, just as we were, and humbly fell at His feet pleading for mercy!

Just As I Am

THE HUMBLE APPROACH WE NEED when we come to Jesus was beautifully seen in the story behind one of the best known hymns in America. It took place in 1822 when a visiting evangelist was invited to a very large and prominent home in London where a choice musical was to be presented.

The musician was Charlotte Elliott, who was born in Clapham, England. As a young person she had lived a carefree life, gaining popularity as a portrait artist, musician, and writer of humorous verse. At age thirty, however, her health began to fail rapidly, and soon she would become a bedridden invalid for the remaining years of her life. With her failing health came great feelings of despondency. The visit that night by the noted Swiss evangelist, Dr. Caesar Malan, proved to be a turning point in Charlotte's life. [151]

After Charlotte finished thrilling the audience with her singing and playing, the evangelist threaded his way through the crowd gathered around her. When he finally had her attention, he said, "Young lady, when you were singing, I sat there and thought how tremendously the cause of Christ would be benefited if you would dedicate yourself and your talents to the Lord. But," he added, "you are just as much a sinner as the worst drunkard in the street, or any harlot on Scarlet Street. But I am glad to tell you that the blood of Jesus Christ, God's Son, will cleanse you from all sin if you will come to Him." In a very haughty manner, she turned her head aside and said to him, "You are very insulting, sir." And she started to walk away. He said, "Lady, I did not mean any offense, but I pray that the Spirit of God will convict you."

That night this young woman could not sleep. At two o'clock in the morning she knelt at the side of her bed and received Christ as her Savior. And then she sat down and wrote the words of this favorite hymn—a prayer of repentance:

JUST AS I AM

Just as I am, without one plea,
But that Thy blood was shed for me,
And that Thou bidd'st me come to Thee,
O Lamb of God, I come!

Just as I am, and waiting not
To rid my soul of one dark blot,
To Thee whose blood can cleanse each spot,
O Lamb of God, I come!

Just as I am, tho' tossed about
With many a conflict, many a doubt,
Fightings and fears within, without,
O Lamb of God, I come, I come.

Just as I am, poor, wretched, blind—
Sight, riches, healing of the mind,
Yea, all I need in Thee to find—
O Lamb of God, I come, I come.

Just as I am—Thou wilt receive,
Wilt welcome, pardon, cleanse, relieve;
Because Thy promise I believe,
O Lamb of God, I come!
    —Charlotte Elliott (1789–1871)

And that is the basis on which all of us must come to Christ. [152]

Throughout the remainder of her life, Miss Elliott yearly celebrated the day on which her Swiss friend had led her to a personal relationship with Christ, for she considered it to be her spiritual birthday. Although she did not publish this hymn until 1836, fourteen years after her conversion experience, it is apparent that she never forgot the words of her friend, for they form the very essence of this hymn.

Wash Me

(Psalm 51:2)

THE NEXT SECTION OF PSALM 51 is so very important, if not at this moment, then in the not-too-distant future when we need to seek cleansing for sin. When it comes to our spiritual side, our minds, our consciences, and the part of us which is eternal—only the Lord can WASH US CLEAN. That is what God explains through this inspired record of David's prayer. Note his very clear cry at the end of verse 1: *Blot out **my transgressions***. And then in verse 2 he prayed: *Wash me thoroughly from **my iniquity**, and cleanse me from **my sin***.

David made three requests for cleansing: *"blot," "wash,"* and *"cleanse."* What did David want cleansed out of his life? There are not only three words for cleansing, but also three types of stains being washed away: *"transgressions," "iniquity,"* and *"sin."*

The three verbs David used for removing his sins are a comprehensive look at how deeply we are stained and how completely Christ can clean us up:

1. **Blot out** (Hebrew *machah* – "wipe or blot out"). David compared his sins to a human record that needed to be erased. In the New Testament Paul also used this idea in Colossians 2:14 when he reported that Christ **wiped out** *the handwriting of requirements that was against us, which was contrary to us. And He has taken it out of the way, having nailed it to the cross.*

The word Paul used (Greek *exaleipho* – "to wipe off") is like erasing a blackboard. Ancient documents were commonly written either on papyrus, a paper-like material made from the bulrush plant, or vellum, which was made from an animal's hide. The ink used back then had no acid in it, so it did not soak into the writing material. Since the ink remained on the surface, it could be wiped off if the scribe wanted to reuse the material.

Paul was saying that God has "wiped off" our certificate of debt, having nailed it to the cross. Not a trace of it remains to be held against us. Our forgiveness is complete. When David asked God to wipe out the record of his sins, God erased them and David rejoiced.

2. **Wash away** (Hebrew *kabac* – "thoroughly wash"). The word David used compared forgiveness with washing clothing (often viewed as an extension of a person), so he was saying, "Lord, completely wash me like dirty clothes that need a complete cleansing." [153]

> *We are all like an unclean thing, and all our righteousnesses are* **like filthy rags**; *we all fade as a leaf, and our iniquities, like the wind, have taken us away* (Isaiah 64:6).

> *Grace to you and peace … from Jesus Christ, the faithful witness, the firstborn from the dead, and the ruler over the kings of the earth. To Him who loved us and* **washed us** *from our sins in His own blood* (Revelation 1:5).

3. **Cleanse** (Hebrew *taher* – "clean as not to contaminate others"). This word stressed the need for ceremonial cleansing so that David's sin would not keep him or others from being able to approach God. David did not want to hinder anyone else by what he had done. For

sin contaminates everything—our souls, our lives, our homes, and our society. David was therefore crying out, "Lord, cleanse away the contamination so that no one else gets defiled by my sin!"

What sin was David talking about? Sin is such an offense to God that He used fifteen different words in the Hebrew Old Testament just to describe it. Three major Hebrew word groups communicate the concept of sin in the Old Testament, and each of them was used in Psalm 51—David's prayer of confession.

David now saw his life from God's perspective, and so he knew that the Lord had to deal with these areas of sin. When David's adultery stole his neighbor Uriah's little ewe lamb for his already overflowing "banquet table" he defied the rules God had laid down.

First, David said, "**Lord, I am guilty of resisting or defying Your rule in my life,** and that is sin. I need You to blot out **my transgressions**." God has established certain boundaries in this life: physical laws, moral laws, and spiritual laws. And anytime we attempt to step over them, we suffer the consequences. That kind of sin is always called *"transgression."*

The word the Holy Spirit guided David to use is such a powerful picture of how God looked upon David's sin. It was a *"transgression"* (Hebrew *peshah* – "a going away, a departure, a passing over a boundary, doing what is prohibited, or a rebellion against God and His authority"). This is a picture of how our actions are a direct affront against the Lord Himself. That is why David started off his prayer of repentance by saying, "Against You, and You alone, I have sinned!"

Second, David said, "Lord, I am guilty of **twisting, warping, defacing, or distorting Your image in my life**, and that is sin. I need You to wash me thoroughly from **my iniquity**." He was saying, "I am iniquitous on the inside." *"Iniquity"* (Hebrew *hawon*) means "corrupt or twisted, twisted out of shape, or crooked." This word pictures what sin does to us inside as it warps and ruins us. It is an "inward crookedness, perversity; that which is altogether wrong." You can't excuse it; you can't offer some sort of apology; you can't in any way condone it.

Thirdly, David said, "Lord, I am guilty of **falling short of Your perfection and missing Your mark in my life**, and that is also sin. I need You to cleanse me from **my sin**." The word for *"sin"* (Hebrew *chattath*) is the same as *hamartia* in Greek—"coming short" or "falling short," as in an arrow falling short of its target. The target is God's Law; consequently, sin is missing the mark on His target. This is a picture of failing to measure up to God's divine Law.

Sin must be *cleansed*, removed from God's sight. It is odious and abominable to Him, and must be put out of His sight. David's song in Psalm 32 also describes this cleansing as the blessing of one *"whose sin is covered"* (v. 1). The word David used for sin being *"covered"* by God is the same word used for the Ark of the Covenant in the tabernacle, covered by the mercy-seat. It is also used for the earth covered by the Flood, and the Egyptians covered by the depths of the sea.

When God takes away our sins, they are buried and unable to return. As Spurgeon commented on this point in Psalm 51, "What a cover must that be which hides away forever from the sight of the all-seeing God all the filthiness of the flesh and of the spirit!"

Think about it: when David stood at the other end of Nathan's bony finger pointed directly in his face, he was guilty and he knew it. In fact, David had broken every law in the book, God's Book.

DAVID BROKE ALL TEN COMMANDMENTS

In reality, when David sinned with Bathsheba he broke all of God's Ten Commandments. How had he broken them all? In two ways: first, by his actions; and second, by God's standards. The following is an abbreviated list of God's standards in Exodus 20:1–17:

Have no other gods (v. 3): David allowed the giant Lust to be the "god" to which he bowed in obedience.

Do not make a carved image (v. 4): The image of the naked Bathsheba bathing was so deeply engraved on David's lustful soul that he forgot even the God he loved for that momentary pleasure of sin.

Do not take the Name in vain (v. 7): David took the holy Name of God in vain whenever he said he was "God's man" and yet lived like the devil.

Remember the Sabbath (v. 8): After he allowed lust to rule, David didn't keep the Sabbath or any other day holy for God.

Honor your father and mother (v. 12): David dishonored them and all his family when he sank into such wicked and premeditated sin.

Do not murder (v. 13): Although David did not directly kill Uriah, he gave orders to Joab to make it happen.

Do not commit adultery (v. 14): That was the clearest of all David's law breaking.

Do not steal (v. 15): David stole the wife of his neighbor and trusted friend, Uriah.

Do not lie (v. 16): David's false response was a lie when the messenger came with the ghastly news of Uriah's death; and every day he lived in sin was a lie he deceptively covered.

Do not covet (v. 17): David coveted his neighbor's wife so greatly that he stole her and then killed her husband to lie in sexual sin with her.

So then, David was a guilty sinner who had actually broken all of God's Ten Commandments. But, in reality, so have we. By God's standards, we, too, are guilty of breaking them all: *For whoever shall keep the whole law, and yet stumble in one point, he is guilty of all* (JAMES 2:10).

The good news is that Jesus died for guilty sinners. As we look at the rest of Psalm 51 we will see how David asked for the sacrificial death of Another to be counted for him (*"purge me with hyssop"*). That is why Christ's death for us sinners is so precious—and powerful!

Purge Me
(Psalm 51:7)

AS SINNERS WE ARE ALL defiled internally and need cleansing. So David cried: *Purge me with hyssop, and I shall be clean; wash me, and I shall be whiter than snow* (v. 7). He was saying, "I am so aware of my utter filthiness on the inside compared with Your holiness, oh God! I now see myself as I am, and desperately need You to purify me! I need You to **purge me with hyssop**— sprinkle Christ's atoning blood upon me. Give me the reality which ceremonies symbolize. Nothing but His blood can take away my bloodstains; nothing but His cleansing can cleanse me."

Verse 7 should also be read as the voice of faith: *Purge me with hyssop, **and I shall be clean.*** David was saying, "There is such power in Christ's sacrifice that my sin will vanish away. I will be accepted back into the assembly of

God's people—and by grace into God's holy presence! But not just ceremonially clean, I also need real spiritual purification of soul and spirit, my deepest parts, so **wash me, and I shall be whiter than snow.**" Snow stays white only briefly; soon it gathers dirt, smoke, and dust, and then it melts and disappears in a muddy mess. But God offers an endlessly kept purity. He has promised to *"save to the uttermost"* (see HEBREWS 7:24–25).

You really have to go to Calvary to find the explanation of David's cry to *"purge me with hyssop,"* as J. Vernon McGee writes:

On the cross the Son of God said, "My God, My God, why have You forsaken Me?" (Matthew 27:46). Why did He say that? Because God cannot by any means clear the guilty. He cannot. He never will. And when the Lord Jesus Christ, who knew no sin, was made sin for us on the cross—when He was delivered for our offenses that we might be made the righteousness of God in Him—God had to treat Him as He must treat sin.

Remember that God spared Abraham's son, but God did not spare His own Son when He had my sin and your sin upon Him. He had to slay Him, because God cannot pardon the guilty. Let's be clear on that. God hates sin and He will punish sin. By no means will He clear the guilty.

On the cross Jesus also said, "Father, forgive them" (Luke 23:34). How can He forgive them? How can He extend mercy to thousands? How can He forgive iniquity? How can He forgive David? And how can He forgive you and me? The Bible is clear on this: "In Him we have redemption through His blood, the forgiveness of sins, according to the riches of His grace" (Ephesians 1:7).

And every time you find forgiveness in the New Testament, the blood of Christ is responsible. God never forgives sin apart from the death of Christ. Never. God is not forgiving sin because He is a big-hearted old man sitting on a cloud. He forgives sin because His Son paid the penalty.

And now, with open arms, He can say to you, "I can extend mercy to you because My Son died in your place." Oh, David knew the way into the heart of God. [154]

So when David said *"Purge me with hyssop"* he was crying out to God: "Apply Christ's sacrificial death on me!" In God's sight, David was a debtor owing an impossible debt his sins had run up against God. He was a guilty convict, legally convicted as having broken God's law. Since adulterers were supposed to be stoned, as far as God was concerned—David was dead in his sin.

When David saw himself in Psalm 51 as God saw him (a guilty, convicted sinner), the man who broke all the commandments found complete forgiveness.

We are also guilty and convicted sinners, having stumbled in at least one point, so we are guilty of breaking all of God's Law. But the good news of the Gospel is exactly this truth: Christ died for sinners. He died in the place of guilty sinners. And all who receive His gift through His Son will confess that—

God the Innocent died for me the guilty.
God the Offended died for me the offender.
God the Holy died for me the sinful.
God the Just died for me the unjust.
God the Perfect died for me the imperfect.

Do You Know Your Critical Need?

CHRIST'S DEATH IS ONLY FOR the guilty, only for the hopelessly stained, and only for the helplessly lost. It is in that condition, like David's, that we find God's grace.

All sinners (that is, everyone who has ever lived on planet Earth, except Jesus Christ) have seven basic needs described in the Bible. Briefly summed up, a lost sinner needs forgiveness, justification, regeneration, reconciliation, adoption, redemption, and sanctification.

Critical Need #1—Forgiveness: *Because of our sin, we like David are all debtors; so we need forgiveness.*

Christ died to take away the hopeless debt we owe to God because of our sin. With His own life, He paid the price of eternal death—**that's forgiveness.** (See PSALM 32:1–2; EPHESIANS 1:7; ROMANS 8:1.) Have you, like David, experienced the relief of knowing that **all your sins— past, present, and future—are GONE?**

Critical Need # 2—Justification: *Because of our sin, we like David are all guilty convicts in God's sight; so we need justification.*

Christ died for us as guilty convicts; He destroyed any record of our having committed a crime when He took our place in the punishment—**that's justification!** A sinner stands before God as accused, but is declared righteous by Christ's imputed righteousness. (See PSALM 51:3–4; ISAIAH 53:6; ROMANS 5:1.) Have you, like David, experienced the peace of justification—**all guilt removed, all punishment forever taken away** from God's sight?

Critical Need #3—Regeneration: *Because of our sin, we like David are all dead in our trespasses and sin; so we need regeneration.*

Christ died to take dead and rotting spiritual corpses and make them vibrant, full of endless life, and brand new—**that's regeneration!** (See EPHESIANS 2:1; JOHN 10:10; HEBREWS 7:16B.) Have you, like David, experienced **the power of an endless life?** Are you partaking every day of the powerful indwelling presence of the very Lord God Almighty?

Critical Need #4—Reconciliation: *Because of our sin, we like David are all enemies of God; so we need reconciliation.*

Christ died to make friends out of His enemies—**that's reconciliation!** A sinner stands before God as an enemy and is made a friend by His peace. (See ROMANS 8:7 and 5:10.) Have you, like David, experienced **the wonder of friendship with God?**

Critical Need #5—Adoption: *Because of our sin, we like David are all strangers to God; so we need adoption.*

Christ died to make strangers a part of His family—**that's adoption!** A sinner stands before God as a stranger and is called a son by His choice. (See EPHESIANS 2:12; GALATIANS 4:4–6.) Have you, like David, experienced **the joy of being adopted into Christ's family?**

Critical Need #6—Redemption: *Because of our sin, we like David are all slaves to unrighteousness; so we need redemption.*

Christ died to make slaves free forever—**that's redemption!** A sinner stands before God as a slave and is granted freedom by His ransom. (See JOHN 8:34, 36.) Have you, like David, experienced the thrill of being **liberated, set free, rescued by God forever?**

Critical Need #7—Sanctification: *Because of our sin, we like David are all defiled; so we need sanctification.*

Christ died to take our soiled, spotted, wasted lives and make them clean, focused, and fruitful—**that's sanctification!** (See ROMANS 6:13b; ROMANS 12:1–2; 1 CORINTHIANS 6:19–20; 1 THESSALONIANS 5:23.)

There are two sides to the coin of salvation. To best understand what God has done, let me contrast justification and sanctification. Because we are saved (justified) this is how we should live (sanctified).

- **Justification** is what Christ *did* for me on the cross; **sanctification** is what Christ *is doing* in me because of the cross.
- **Justification** is immediate and was *completely finished* in me the instant I was saved; **sanctification** is an *ongoing process* until I meet Jesus face to face at death or His coming.
- **Justification** is activated the moment I trust in the Person of Christ Jesus and His *finished* sacrifice of the cross; **sanctification** *grows* with each obedient choice I make empowered by the Holy Spirit.
- **Justification** is my *position* declared right in God's sight; **sanctification** is my *practice* made right by becoming more conformed to His image.

Have you, like David, experienced **the stability of coming under new management—God's?** Do you know the thrill of looking at your life and sensing His control? Do you see your hands as extensions of His? Your voice as a channel for Him to speak? Your days as no longer belonging to you but to be lived unto Him Who loved you and gave Himself for you?

David Took the Blame—And Repented
(Psalm 51:8–19)

BECAUSE CHRIST DIED TO SAVE sinners from their sins and to rescue them from death, destruction, despair, and doom, in Psalm 51 David asked for and received mercy and grace from the cross. He acknowledged before a holy God, "I am guilty; I have sinned against You alone. Purge me by the cleansing power of Christ's death—Who gave Himself for me!" Accepting the blame for his sin and repenting gave David a new beginning with the God of the Second Chance—Whom he needed so desperately.

When David repented he needed joyfulness: *Make me hear joy and gladness, that the bones You have broken may rejoice* (v. 8). As sinners we lose our joy. David was saying, "I have lost my song—I don't hear Your joyful song anymore!"

When David repented he longed for fellowship with God: *Hide Your face from my sins, and blot out all my iniquities* (v. 9). In Eden we saw Adam and Eve hiding from God because sin separated and blinded them to God's presence. So David wanted the sin that blinds and separates to be taken away—he wanted God more than any sin!

David knew that only God could give him a new beginning: *Create in me a clean heart, O God, and renew a steadfast spirit within me* (v. 10). This word *"create"* speaks of what only God can do by His gracious power. We must never think that God's forgiving grace, wonderful as it is, either permits or encourages us to go on sinning: *"Shall we go on sinning so that grace may increase?"* asked Paul. He answered, *"By no means! We died to sin; how can we live in it any longer?"* (ROMANS 6:1–2 NIV).

David knew that only God could restore his walk in the Spirit: *Do not cast me away from Your presence, and do not take Your Holy Spirit from me* (v. 11). The days that had stretched into the weeks and months of that spiritual wasteland David had just experienced were so bad that he never wanted to revisit that time again. He was very aware that the Holy Spirit's sweet influence that had formerly come upon him and filled his heart with joy, with songs, and with peace that made him a blessing had been pulled back.

David knew that only God could renew the fruit of the Spirit: *Restore to me the joy of Your salvation, and uphold me by Your generous Spirit* [sustain me with a willing spirit] (v. 12). Remember that the fruit of the Spirit is love and JOY. It is not something we get by moving to a nicer home and neighborhood—that is so temporary. It is not something we get by buying something we really want—that is so brief. It is not something we get by accomplishing some deed of greatness—that is so fragile. It is an internal fruit born by the Spirit of God that grows deeper and deeper inside of us.

David was saying, "Bring back the fruitfulness of Your Spirit in my life. I am going to focus on Your work; I want You to wash my heart. I want You to restore my walking in the power of Your Spirit. I want You to renew His fruit growing in me!"

David knew that only God could prepare him for further ministry: *Then I will teach transgressors Your ways, and sinners shall be converted to You* (v. 13). He was saying, "When I let You, God, do all this—wash my heart, restore my walk in the Spirit, renew the Holy Spirit's fruit in my life—You prepare me for further ministry."

Sometimes when we hit the bottom and are deep into sin, we tend to think: *It's all over! I can't do anything—I'm useless now.* But look at what David was saying, "Wow! I am going to come back and get to serve You again!" Although he didn't go back when he was still in sin, because there was quite a long period of time involved, God had worked through the process and it utterly cleansed David and filled him again with joy.

David sought God by calling sin what it is: *Deliver me from the guilt of bloodshed, O God, the God of my salvation, and my tongue shall sing aloud of Your righteousness* (v. 14). We must repent of sin: turn from it, change our mind about it, want to get rid of it, get uncomfortable about it. Rather than say, "I have sinned," a lot of people will say, "I have made a mistake" or "I didn't do that as well as I should have." We don't like to humbly confess when we've sinned. Why? Because to say, "I've sinned," means that we have to agree with God. So then, all that is within us—our flesh and our pride—rebels against such humble repentance.

But David called his sin what it really was when he said, "Deliver me from blood guiltiness." Wait a minute. Did David literally kill Uriah? No, an Ammonite archer shot arrows and did it for him. But it was really David who killed Uriah: David sent him there and then ordered Joab to send Uriah to the front lines to get him killed. Thus, when David truly turned to God, he repented by unabashedly praying, "Deliver me from blood guiltiness. I killed Uriah. God, forgive me of that. Cleanse me and renew me."

David wanted to talk to God: *O Lord, open my lips, and my mouth shall show forth Your praise* (v. 15). In Psalm 32, those months of hiding his sin had dried David up physically and spiritually. When we are attached to our sin, we become strangely silent toward God. That is what Psalm 32 was all about. David had dried up spiritually. He just closed his mouth; he wasn't talking to God anymore. In fact, when he lost his song, he felt too empty inside to be interested in talking to anyone.

But when we call sin what it is, and repent, we have to start talking to God. We have to open our lips and say like David said, "God, open my mouth back up. Don't let me hang around down here in the lowlands. Let my mouth declare Your praise again!" When we are downhearted, if we will just start praising God for Who He is, what He has done, and what He means to us, God will restore our joy.

David wanted to experience true contrition, not mere externalism: *For You do not desire sacrifice, or else I would give it; You do not delight in burnt offering. The sacrifices of God are a broken spirit, a broken and a contrite heart—these, O God, You will not despise* (vv. 16–17).

You see, it would have been easy to have taken a lamb to the tabernacle and have it killed in his place. It would have been easy to have brought a guilt offering, or a sin offering. But God says, "I don't want you to merely do something externally. I want you, on the inside, to have a broken spirit."

God's view is this: *Lament and mourn and weep. Let your laughter be turned to mourning and your joy to gloom* (JAMES 4:9). Why is that so important? As Paul pointed out, *godly sorrow produces repentance leading to salvation, not to be regretted; but the sorrow of the world produces death* (2 CORINTHIANS 7:10).

Godly sorrow is when we say to the Lord, as David did, "God I have sinned against You. I have broken Your righteous standard. Against You I have _____ [name the sin]." In contrast, **the sorrow of the world** is over what happens to us, such as: "Oh no, I've lost my health"; "Oh no, I've lost my job"; "Oh no, I have a sexually transmitted disease"; "Oh no, I'm pregnant" (or whatever else is relevant in your life). That is not a godly sorrow because it does not bring repentance.

So David was saying, "I'm not going to just admit to my sin; I will confess it. I am going to experience true contrition, not mere externalism. Therefore, I won't simply offer some little lamb—I am going to be broken hearted inside over my sin against God!"

David wanted to chase after God to begin zealous worship anew and afresh: *Do good in Your good pleasure to Zion; build the walls of Jerusalem. Then You shall be pleased with the sacrifices of righteousness, with burnt offering and whole burnt offering; then they shall offer bulls on Your altar* (vv. 18–19).

What he was finally saying is this: "God, now that I am back with You, I am going to zealously follow Your program. I am going to zealously praise You in Zion. I am going to zealously bring my offerings to You—not as a token, but from a true heart!"

In summary, Psalm 51 is one of the greatest examples in the Bible of God's forgiving love! David sinned; he was chastened and convicted; and then he turned back to God in humble, contrite repentance to receive the cleansing only the Lord can give. And then God put a new song in David's heart—"The Song of a Soul Set Free"—so that the king of His people, Israel, could once more be empowered to faithfully walk in the Spirit to worship and serve the King of Kings and Lord of Lords!

If you have ever felt far away from God, then you can relate to David.

If you have ever sinned deeply and paid a heavy price, then you can relate to David. If you are presently at church in body only, and your heart has been cold, dull, burdened, and distant, then you can especially relate to David. And, just as it was for David, God stands waiting with open arms to welcome you back, for the power of God is available to restore your relationship with the Lord through your humble, contrite repentance.

If the Holy Spirit has spoken to your heart, convicting you of your need to repent, I exhort you to come back to God NOW. Just as David sang often to the Lord, I encourage you to humbly, contritely, and prayerfully sing the words of the following song to God. Then, like David, chase after the Lord to begin zealous worship anew and afresh—and receive complete forgiveness, joy, peace, and security once more!

LORD, I'M COMING HOME

I've wandered far away from God,
Now I'm coming home;
The paths of sin too long I've trod,
Lord, I'm coming home.

I've wasted many precious years,
Now I'm coming home;
I now repent with bitter tears,
Lord, I'm coming home.

I'm tired of sin and straying, Lord,
Now I'm coming home;
I'll trust Thy love, believe Thy Word,
Lord, I'm coming home.

My soul is sick, my heart is sore,
Now I'm coming home;
My strength renew, my hope restore,
Lord, I'm coming home.

I need His cleansing blood, I know,
Now I'm coming home;
O wash me whiter than the snow,
Lord, I'm coming home.

Refrain—
Coming home, coming home,
Nevermore to roam,
Open wide Thine arms of love,
Lord, I'm coming home.
  —William Kirkpatrick (1838–1921)

20 | Overcoming Personal Attacks and Abuse

2 Samuel 15:13-37; 16:1-14; Psalms 3 and 63

You, O LORD, are a shield for me, my glory and the One who lifts up my head.
—**Psalm 3:3**

THERE IS PROBABLY NO MORE touching, poignant moment in all the incredible life of David than the scene in 2 Samuel 15:13–37. [155] In your mind, try to picture the country people and hear their loud wails as they view this somber procession:

> A band of loyal commanders is walking in formation in full armor as they protectively surround the King of Israel—now deposed by a rebellious son, driven from his throne, banished from his city.

> King David is walking head down, tears dropping silently to the ground. His face is wet; his eyes are swollen and red; his head is covered as he trudges heavily down the slopes of Zion toward the brook called Kidron.

> Stepping across the stones as the water swiftly runs across them, the steep upward incline of the path points David's feet toward the

Mount of Olives, now green with countless olive trees. Nearby where David walked and wept is a garden called Gethsemane where the Son of David would one day also walk and weep—both of them because of the sins of others.

David, the one who had faced lions and bears and armies and giants, stumbled out of his beloved Jerusalem with eyes blurred by his own tears. He is fleeing for his life. He had left everything: behind him is the Ark of God; behind him is the Tent of God's Presence; behind him is Zion, the City of His Great God; behind him are the trophies of all his battles—the treasures amounting to the largest personal fortune in gold and silver ever amassed by anyone. So, as David walked, he wept and covered his head.

Can't you just feel the depths of sorrow David was suffering?

Inescapable and Painful Consequences

As WE LOOK AT THE final years of David's life, from God's perspective his suffering began with his fall into sin with Bathsheba. Everything from 2 Samuel 11–12 (Bathsheba) to 1 Kings 2 (David's death) was touched, affected, and colored by that event. As a result of David's sin with Bathsheba, he would now reap the great pain of a son's betrayal, the verbal abuse by Shimei, and finally the physical abuse and death threats of Absalom.

Because we should never isolate the psalms that flow from a period of David's life from the inspired record of that period, I recommend you write these words over Psalms 32, 38, and 51: "Unguarded moments lead to sin." There are lessons to be learned from David that are very difficult but so necessary. For the Apostle Paul's words still ring across the twisted wreckage of so many lives that litter the highway of the redeemed: *Whatever a man sows, that he will also reap* (GALATIANS 6:7).

Although we often forget about it, both halves of this verse impact all of us. In reality, most Christians find we may still be reaping the unpleasant long-term consequences of past bad choices while at the same time, as forgiven sinners, we are probably also sowing to the Spirit for a future positive harvest.

One thing is certain, however—sin *always* pays back with boredom, guilt, shame, loneliness, confusion, emptiness, loss of purpose, and loss of rewards. For example, that was happening to David when he failed the Lord in Gath (Psalm 34), escaped, and consequently felt lonely and abandoned (Psalm 13).

His bad choices had led to guilt and shame which produced numbing loneliness, profound confusion, emptiness, and a complete loss of purpose. But then David found God's pathway out of the pits (PSALM 40).

The negative consequence engine for the Christian should never be thought of as punishment because Jesus has already been fully punished for the believer's sins. Neither is it to be confused with God's corrective discipline of his wayward sons and daughters (see HEBREWS 12:6–17).

David was forgiven: *"The LORD also has put away your sin"* (2 SAMUEL 12:13). But forgiveness never seems to take away the consequences of the sin. So when he wrote Psalm 51, it was not only in the joy of assured forgiveness, but also in evident painful remorse and agony. David grieved over the awfulness of his sin: *"Against You, You only, have I sinned, and done this evil in Your sight"* (PSALM 51:4). He also had to endure the coming years of painful consequences, yet he did so with peace and settled faith in the goodness and wisdom of God.

In 2 Samuel 12:1–6 is an amazing explanation of just how much David's sin would cost him. Nathan the prophet told David he would have to make restitution four-fold. In the context of Nathan's parable about the rich man (David), the poor man (Uriah), and the ewe lamb (Bathsheba), we know from Exodus 22:1 that God's Law demanded four-fold restitution.

The penalty for stealing and slaughtering an ox or a sheep was not death, but restitution. However, in Nathan's parable, the wrongful taking and using of the *"lamb"* (Bathsheba) pointed to David's adultery and subsequent murder of Uriah. Under the Mosaic Law, both sins, adultery (LEVITICUS 20:10) and murder (LEVITICUS 24:17), were punishable by death. So when David pronounced his judgment on the rich man of Nathan's parable, David was condemning himself to death.

It is very possible that the four-fold restitution God required may be related to the tragic events of David's final years. For instance, it could be an allusion to the death of four of David's sons: Bathsheba's first son (2 SAMUEL 12:18); Amnon (2 SAMUEL 13:28–9); Absalom (2 SAMUEL 16:14–15); and Adonijah (1 KINGS 2:25).

There is also a possible allusion to the four disasters marking the final days of David's reign:

1. Ammon's rape of his sister Tamar (2 SAMUEL 13:1–22) and his death at the hand of his brother Absalom (2 SAMUEL 13:23–33).

2. Absalom's treasonous rebellion (2 SAMUEL 15:1–18:8) and death at the hand of Joab (2 SAMUEL 18:9–19:8).

3. Sheba the Bichrites rebellion (2 SAMUEL 20:1–22) and the plague following David's numbering of the people (2 SAMUEL 24:1–25).

4. The plot of Adonijah to grasp the throne, endangering Solomon and Bathsheba (1 KINGS 1:1–53).

What a lesson David becomes to us of the goodness and justice of the Lord! God's grace is free, but the cost of sin is high—as John MacArthur writes:

Every sin I as a Christian commit is forgiven in Jesus Christ. But no sin is ever right or good, and no sin ever produces anything right or good. The price for doing some things is terribly high, terribly unprofitable. Sin never brings profit; it always brings loss.

David was a man after God's own heart and was greatly used of the Lord in leading Israel and even in writing Scripture. But David was not exempted from the consequences of his sin. He committed adultery with Bathsheba and she became pregnant. He then arranged for her husband to be killed in battle and took her as his own wife. "But the thing that David had done was evil in the sight of the Lord" (2 SAMUEL 11:27).

Through His prophet Nathan, God told David that because of his sin, "the sword shall never depart from your house. … I will raise up evil against you from your own household," and "the child also that is born to you shall surely die" (12:10–11, 14).

David paid for those sins almost every day of his life. Several of his sons were rebellious, jealous, and vengeful, and his family life was for the most part a tragic shambles. [156]

In spite of David's family life being a "tragic shambles," he still faced the consequences of his sins in a godly way. For part of genuine repentance is the grace to go forward—no matter what life may bring.

When Memories Turn Bitter

To FACE THE HATRED OF pagan Philistines was one thing, but the hatred of your own son is quite another. To have a murderous father-in-law is devastating, but to have a murderous child is beyond words. So David was speechless as his tears ran and the wailing sobs of his friends rose in crescendos about him.

Could it get any worse for David? Such thoughts must have been on his mind as the saddest day of his life unfolded. Because Satan often attacks when we are at our weakest point, life was about to get much worse for David.

David's thoughts raced back and forth from all the battles he had fought to save the Israelites from their enemies. And now he was being betrayed by their children who became the very army that had joined his son to kill him.

David then recalled how he had rescued his own son Absalom so many times. Before he was old enough to even realize it, he had kept young Absalom from Saul's hand. Later he risked his life to attack the raiding bands of the desert peoples and rescue Absalom from their grasp. David also remembered bringing young and handsome Absalom up to Jerusalem, the City of David, Zion, the City of God. How it had thrilled David's heart to build a home and see his wives and children happy and secure in the home God provided. But nothing would ever be the same again. Tamar was raped by Amnon, so Absalom killed Amnon. And now Absalom was seeking to kill his own father. Nothing was right anymore—nothing could ever make this all go away.

Back and forth flew David's thoughts, his painful questions: *Why do the people turn away from me so quickly? Why does my own son hate me? Why does God allow all this?*

And then, as David looked around at his mighty men marching like a wall of strength around him, that space once occupied by the bravest of the brave—Uriah—was empty. The same Uriah who went to his death at David's deceitful bidding and murderous plot did so because he was loyal to the death for David, and always had been. David's thoughts raced back over the years and smote him with renewed contrition as he was once more reminded of his sin against the Lord. And now David was suffering the consequences.

Do This When Attacked, Slandered, and Abused

SOMEWHERE IN THE MIDST OF being lost in his thoughts, mingled with tears, a barefoot David heard trouble coming. Before he saw him, he heard the hatred of his curses. Coming up from Bahurim, the first village on the downward slope of the Mount of Olives, was the figure of an angry man. This distant relative of Saul's was bitter to the point of blindness. With the poison of a venomous serpent on his tongue, curses, dust, and rocks flew from the one-man-army named Shimei. With every means possible he tried to attack David while he was the most vulnerable possible.

Isn't that how temptations often come? The devil—in alliance with our flesh, the world around us, and the demons—always tries to get us at our weakest moment. And this was perfect timing: David was physically, emotionally, mentally, and humanly at his weakest and lowest point. But much to Satan's disappointment, David was not at his lowest point spiritually.

David's responses in 2 Samuel 16:10–12 are the most beautiful example of how to handle such attacks. Although his suffering was part of the inevitable consequences of his sin, God was still watching to see what choices he would make. Either David would respond in a selfish and thus sinful way, or he would respond in a godly and glorifying way.

The good news is that David responded consistently for God, both before Bathsheba and after Bathsheba. He was still God's man—one who had slipped into sin, repented, and then "walked the walk" from there on out. For even when he faced the painful consequences of sin, he could still praise God, glorify his Savior, and experience His all-sufficient grace more than ever.

As we review this sad and painful day step-by-step we can mine eight wonderful truths to live by when we also suffer as David did. Here is the summary of what God captured for us in 2 Samuel 15:13–37 and 16:1–14. Look at how God was glorified in David's painful consequences:

1. When David was at the bottom, God came with help.

*Then the king said to Ittai the Gittite, "Why are you also going with us? Return and remain with the king. For you are a foreigner and also an exile from your own place. In fact, you came only yesterday. Should I make you wander up and down with us today, since I go I know not where? Return, and take your brethren back. Mercy and truth be with you." But Ittai answered the king and said, "As the LORD lives, and as my lord the king lives, **surely in whatever place my lord the king shall be, whether in death or life, even there also your servant will be**" (2 SAMUEL 15:19–21).*

2. When David was at his weakest point, he waited for God's strength.

*Then the king said to Zadok, "Carry the ark of God back into the city. If I find favor in the eyes of the LORD, **He will bring me back and show me both it and His dwelling place**" (2 SAMUEL 15:25).*

Note that David did not try to defend himself. Because he left his burdens with the Lord, he didn't have to take matters into his own hands. David did not grasp after things, even when they were rightfully his. That is the strength and serenity we can have from the Lord. It is unusual and magnificent to see such strength—for it only comes from the Lord!

David knew that the Lord was with him; he didn't need a box covered with gold to remind him. He had the Lord Himself, so he was willing to leave the Ark of God in the Tent of God's Presence and go out of the city trusting in God and God alone!

3. **When David was at the lowest moment of his life, he lifted his heart in worship.**

*So David went up by the Ascent of the Mount of Olives, and wept as he went up; and he had his head covered and went barefoot. And all the people who were with him covered their heads and went up, weeping as they went up. Now it happened **when David had come to the top of the mountain**, where **he worshiped God**—there was Hushai the Archite coming to meet him with his robe torn and dust on his head* (2 SAMUEL 15:30, 32).

David trusted God's control; he relied upon it and prayed for it. So rather than give in to fear, in faith he worshiped the Lord instead. God's servants can, and should, worship even when life is tough, difficult, and almost looking like it is impossible to go on. This same spirit can flow from us if we, like David, will bow in worship when the bitter tears of sorrow and grief fall across our lives.

4. **When David was least in control of his circumstances, he entrusted his situation to the Lord.**

*Then someone told David, saying, "Ahithophel is among the conspirators with Absalom." And David said, "**O LORD, I pray, turn the counsel of Ahithophel into foolishness!**"* (2 SAMUEL 15:31).

People often share reports that can either lead us to fear or prompt us to prayer. David chose to lift his heart in prayer to the Lord at this evil report!

5. **When David was attacked, he realized God had adversaries to arise for His own purposes.**

*Now when King David came to Bahurim, there was a man from a family of the house of Saul, whose name was Shimei ... coming from there. He **came out cursing** continuously as he came. And he **threw stones at David** and at all the servants of King David* (2 SAMUEL 16:5–6).

*Then Abishai the son of Zeruiah said to the king, "Why should this dead dog curse my lord the king? Please, let me go over and take off his head!" But the king said, "What have I to do with you, you sons of Zeruiah? So let him curse, because the LORD has said to him, 'Curse David.' Who then shall say, 'Why have you done so?'" And David said to Abishai and all his servants, "See how my son who came from my own body seeks my life. How much more now may this Benjamite? **Let him alone,** and let him curse; **for so the LORD has ordered him*** (2 SAMUEL 16:9–11).

After his brief worship stop, David trudged onward. But then, on top of all else, insult was added to injury as Shimei kicked David when he was down. He sprayed him with curses, dust, and stones. But the man after God's own heart kept going until he was at last safely across the Jordan River and in the wilderness camp to be made for the night.

David simply entrusted his personal adversaries to the Lord because he knew God "raises up" and "puts down." Since adversaries are allowed by God, he wanted to respond correctly. For the Lord often allows us to be attacked by various adversaries just to reveal what is really in our hearts.

6. **When the painful abuse was overwhelming him, David fled to the Lord for hope.**

*"**It may be** that the LORD will look on my affliction, and **that the LORD will repay me with good** for his cursing this day"* (2 SAMUEL 16:12).

David knew God cared, that He saw his troubles, and could cause all these things to work together for good. Thus, David consistently entrusted his personal sufferings to the Lord.

7. **Even when David's situation looked hopelessly impossible, God was managing everything.**

*Absalom and all the men of Israel said, The counsel of Hushai the Archite is better than the counsel of Ahithophel. For **the LORD had appointed to defeat** the good counsel of **Ahithophel**, to the intent that the LORD might **bring evil upon Absalom** (2 SAMUEL 17:14 KJV).*

When we let God take care of us, and entrust our personal vengeance to the Lord, He can accomplish what we never could to remedy the situation: *"Vengeance is Mine, I will repay," says the Lord* (HEBREWS 10:30). So allow the Lord to recompense your enemies. David had many enemies and adversaries, but he let the Lord deal with them all.

8. **At just the exact moment God planned, David's needs were met.**

*Now it happened, when David had come to Mahanaim, that **Shobi ... brought** beds and basins, earthen vessels and wheat, barley and flour, parched grain and beans, lentils and parched seeds, honey and curds, sheep and cheese of the herd, **for David and the people who were with him** to eat. For they said, "The people are hungry and weary and thirsty in the wilderness"* (2 SAMUEL 17:27–29).

God worked behind the scenes in the hearts of people to provide just what David needed to continue on. So a servant of the Lord must always entrust his personal needs to the Lord.

Worship God—Even Through Tears

WHAT WAS JOAB, THE COMMANDER-IN-CHIEF of all David's armies, doing during this time? He was working feverishly in his preparation to protect David. Guards were posted, and troops were stationed. Concentric rings of defenses were planned and prepared so that the 600 seasoned soldiers who marched out with David were arrayed to face any army or enemy that might attack on this very vulnerable night.

Joab, worried that a frontal assault by Absalom's army could overwhelm his perimeter, was tense as he came back to camp. He considered taking David deeper into the wilderness, or finding some other spot. With his head spinning with all these thoughts, he greeted David.

For the first time in hours Joab got to see David all alone and sensed something was completely different about him. Gone were the red, swollen eyes of the morning. Back were the clear, bright eyes he remembered from so many years of fighting alongside this giant of a man. David was calm, peaceful, and actually joyous as he began to tell Joab what the Lord had done in his heart. Incredulous, Joab smiled, shook his head, and hurried off to check the defensive positions one more time.

When Joab returned, he was struck with an even more amazing sight. David was on the ground, an animal skin unrolled in front of him, and with pen and ink in hand he was busily writing—just like Joab remembered from those days in the Cave of Adullam when David wrote Psalms 57 and 142; and just like he remembered in those days of fleeing from King Saul when David wrote Psalms 17, 54, 35–36, 53, 16, and 39. And now his king was at it again!

Once finished, David held up the scroll to the fading light of the evening sky. He read it over, quietly sang the words to a tune he'd just made up, rolled it up, tied a cord about it, and tucked it into his cloak. David had just written another psalm. And then he turned, unrolled his sleeping bag, laid down, and was soon sound asleep. In the very presence of his enemies, in the middle of the camp that could be over run at any moment—David slept. And Joab marveled again at this man after God's own heart.

Where we decide to turn in our most desperate moments, and how we face what we never wanted or dreamed of happening, reveals what is really on the inside of us. And what came out of David at this excruciating time was a song that was so good God forever recorded it in heaven. Because it pleased the Lord, his song was better than any of today's "top of the charts," "top of the billboard," or even a "gold" or "platinum." Here is the exact record of the worship flowing from David that day:

A Psalm of David when he fled from Absalom his son.

¹ LORD, *how they have increased who trouble me!*
Many are they who rise up against me.
² *Many are they who say of me,*
"There is no help for him in God." Selah

³ *But You, O LORD, are a shield for me,*
My glory and the One who lifts up my head.

⁴ *I cried to the* LORD *with my voice,*
    And He heard me from His holy hill. Selah

⁵ *I lay down and slept;*
    I awoke, for the LORD *sustained me.*
⁶ *I will not be afraid of ten thousands of people*
    Who have set themselves against me all around.

⁷ *Arise, O* LORD*;*
    Save me, O my God!
    For You have struck all my enemies on the cheekbone;
    You have broken the teeth of the ungodly.
⁸ *Salvation belongs to the* LORD*.*
    Your blessing is upon Your people. Selah

Psalm 3 is an amazing psalm because it actually introduces us to the book of Psalms. It is the first in the Bible called a psalm, and it is the first psalm noted as written by David. It is also the first psalm giving us a divinely written setting in the first verse of the Hebrew text.

Psalm 3 is set in the context of battles. If you trace through the verses you will find the setting to be about seven different indications of warfare and battlefields:

Verse 1: David was facing "foes" (NIV); "adversaries" (NASB).
Verse 3: David needed a "shield" (NKJV).
Verse 6: David saw them deployed like an army—"set against me" (NASB/NKJV); "drawn up against me" (NIV).
Verse 7: David called them "enemies" (NKJV).
Verse 7: David cried "Arise, O LORD" and used the actual formula from Numbers 10:35 for entering battle.
Verse 8: David spoke of armies; the word "people" in this verse can also be used for an army (NKJV).
Verse 8: David sought victory implied by the word "deliverance" (NIV), and deliverance from the Lord is a war cry.

Psalm 3 divides up the message God gave through David by the use of the word *"Selah"* at the end of verses 2, 4, and 8. *"Selah"* means "lift up" and is a musical term for crescendo. It means "Boom it out," "Crank it up," or

"Punctuate that with emphasis." In other words, David was saying, "Hey, look at THIS!" And so when you see the word *"Selah,"* God wants you to stop and ask yourself: *What do I think of that?*

In verse 2 David said, *Many are they who say of me, "There is no help for him in God." Selah*—**Boom! Stop and consider this. What do you think of that?** So David paused and thought about it and found a lifetime of definite proof God cared for him.

In verse 4 David said, *I cried to the LORD with my voice, and He heard me from His holy hill. Selah*—**Boom! Stop and consider this. What do you think of that?** So David reflected upon his steadfast hope and confident faith that God had rescued him in the past and would continue to do so.

In verse 8 David said, *Salvation belongs to the LORD. ... Selah*—**Boom! Stop and consider this. What do you think of that?** So David reflected upon the truth that God alone can save us from all our deepest troubles.

These uses of *"Selah"* make three very clear divisions which are the message points of this psalm.

First, Like David, We Will All Face Battlefields
(Psalm 3:1–2)

EVERY ONE OF US WILL face a variety of battles daily. Think about the workplace, which is largely cut-throat these days. As more and more people compete for fewer and fewer good jobs, with less and less job security, enduring personal attacks and abuse are the norm. Competition prompts the ungodly use of weapons such as lying, slander, gossip, misrepresentation, bribes, stealing, falsification, and blame shifting—all to gain personal advancement. How many enemies does it take to make your life miserable? Just one who is *persistent.*

Our battlefield may not be the workplace, it may be our home. Even though you and I will never face an army led by our son seeking to destroy us and take our throne, we may someday face personal attacks, slander, and abuse through the hatred of our children. They may betray what we stand for and even seek to undermine our family unity, or discredit and destroy us as parents.

Some of us may have to deal with personal attacks, slander, or abuse from a husband or wife who has turned against us with no warning, deserted us, and seeks to harm or torment us by breaking the lasting promise made in marriage.

Still others may face parents who turn against them, abandon them, or are slanderous and abusive against their very own children. Life is hard; sin is horrible; and people seem more than willing to harm others easily. So that is why David said, *"Selah*—**Stop, look around, and think about your battle!"**

Second, Like David, We Will All Make Choices

(Psalm 3:3–4)

DAVID WAS SUCH A GODLY example because he turned his attention away from his problems and focused on God. Suddenly, everything would then be put into proper perspective. David did this by holding tightly to a truth about God. For example, because God had been a shield in the past for David, he could truly say: *You, O LORD, are a shield for me* (PSALM 3:3). He told the Lord, "You *are* my glory, the One I want to please, the One worth living for, praising, and honoring!"

David addressed God by the name "LORD," which is "Yahweh" or "Jehovah." The significance is that this is the name for the covenant-keeping God. In other words, He is "the God Who keeps His Word." So David could say, "Lord, You Who keep Your Word, You Who brings to pass the promises You have made, be the shield around me You have promised to be, and have always been."

This exposed the spiritual secret that kept David strong even through his darkest hours: he knew and trusted the Lord. This trust had stayed constant with him long before his rule as king. So he reminded himself that the Lord could be trusted and counted upon as *"the One who lifts up my head"* (PSALM 3:3)—just as in the days when the Amalekites plundered David's home, stole his property, and took his family hostage (1 SAMUEL 30:1–6). What did David do then? He **strengthened himself in the LORD his God** (1 SAMUEL 30:6).

When David was in so much grief he couldn't even look up, he felt the gentle hand of his loving Lord under his chin, lifting his head. Only the Lord can encourage us to the depth needed to heal a broken heart. Only He can lift our heads when they are cast down. David knew that, sought that, wanted that—and experienced that. So now in this saddest of hours he declared God as being the One Who encouraged and strengthened him.

Sin always beats us down; God always lifts us up. Others may ignore us; God always answers us. In other words, David said, *"Selah—***Stop and look at this. Let that truth settle down on your heart.***"* For God always lifts, and God always answers. So think about the Lord Who can be trusted rather than looking at all the problems. *Anxiety* is "meditating on problems," but *peace* is "believing His promises." The latter is what David chose.

Third, Like David, We All Need Sleep

(Psalm 3:5–8)

AT THE END OF ONE of the most grievous days of his life, David rested in the Lord: *I lay down and slept; I awoke, for the LORD sustained me* (PSALM 3:5). Sleep is a gift from God to help prepare us to start over again tomorrow—refreshed and renewed. It is also a picture of how much we need God, and even more, how we receive His salvation. Sleep should decimate any pride we have in our own power or might, and humble us to think how weak and needy we really are.

Sleep is not an accident; God is the designer and promoter of sleep. As believers who look at life through the lens of God's Word, we need to see sleep as having the very signature of God written across it. When God designs something, it is very special and has specific purposes He wants us to know about:

- Sleep means work must stop.
- Sleep means a day must end.
- Sleep means our strength has been depleted and must be renewed.
- Sleep means our minds have become weary and must be refreshed.
- Sleep means our bodies have gotten exhausted and must be restored.
- Sleep means we have limitations that must be faced.
- Sleep means we have a dependence that must be acknowledged.
- Sleep means we must deny self-sufficiency, as Psalm 121 tells us.

One of the clearest reasons for sleep is to remind us of this truth: God is God and we are not. We are helpless, limited, and dependent. But that is not all. Sleep can also be one of the most beautiful reminders of what true saving faith looks like.

In a few hours, when it is your time to sleep, think of what you will do. You will end activities, conversations, and even your consciousness of life around you as you lay the full weight of your body on an object that can hold you up (usually a bed). Then as you lay down you must choose to completely trust that something else other than yourself will hold you up while you are no longer able to take care of yourself. That is pure faith.

So sleep is when we relax fully because we no longer need to take care of ourselves. We are held up by something else, so we give in to sleep. As one author so beautifully states: "Throughout the night as you sleep, Someone else is sustaining you. This is a picture of what it's like to belong to Christ." [157]

As you crawl into your bed tonight, pause to remember to lift your heart in worship to God Who holds your soul in the sweet comfort of lying secure in His arms. Tell the Lord you are also resting your life in Him. Whisper that you completely need Him, trust in His care, and ask Him to get rid of any pride you may have built up throughout the day.

That is the supreme peace David felt as he laid down in the presence of his enemies and slept. Thus he said, *"Selah—***Stop and consider this. Sleep is lying secure in God's peace."** So should we, humbly, and in complete dependence upon our Lord.

Like David, We All Have Problems

ONE WORD IN PSALM 3 weighed heaviest on David, and it appears in the attribution line: A Psalm of David when he fled from Absalom his **son**.

All of this unforeseen and painful trial was because of David's own son. What could lead to a son to rape his own sister? Or what would incite a son to murder his own brother? Or, as we see here, what could drive a son to try to murder his own father? One word answers all three—sin! Sin led Amnon to rape Tamar; sin prompted Absalom to murder Amnon; and sin drove Absalom to seek his father's death.

Since time began, parents in every generation have faced the heartache of children who do not follow the Lord, and even turn away from Him. What comfort is there for those whose hearts have been broken many times over? What hope is there after all the years we loved them, earnestly prayed for them, read God's Word to them, nurtured them in the ways of the Lord, and sought to guide them as best we could? Here are some truths that comfort our hearts— and the hearts of the many parents we have encouraged over the years:

- Absalom's rebellion was *no surprise to God.* Every day of our life (PSALM 139) was written in His book—even the darkest of days!

- Absalom's rebellion was *an opportunity for God to see David's response.* Our response is what matters to God most. He is watching and waiting for what we will do, to whom we will turn. And when we turn to Him, our Lord is glorified.

- Absalom's rebellion must have *driven David to pray* for what he may have thought impossible—Absalom's return to the Lord and to David.

- Absalom's rebellion *opened to David a situation* where only God could encourage him (1 SAMUEL 30:6b)!

- Absalom's rebellion *filled David with hope* as he remembered that God wasn't ever through with him as long as he lived—and neither is He ever through with our wayward child.

- Absalom's rebellion *reminded David* that he had a perfect heavenly Father, and then he saw his own imperfections reflected by his son.

- Absalom's rebellion must have *humbled David* as he remembered how often he also had failed his children (PSALM 130:3)—and failed to respond correctly to his perfect Father.

- Absalom's rebellion must have *rebuked David* because he expected so much obedience from his imperfect parenting, yet he gave his heavenly Father such imperfect obedience—even though God's parenting was perfect!

- Absalom's rebellion *made David believe* more and more each day what only God is able to do: touch their hearts, soften their hearts, and turn their hearts back to Him (EZEKIEL 36:26–27)—and to us.

- Absalom's rebellion *showed David God's never ending grace* as each wave of fear and sorrow rolled over him, and he found his feet firmly planted on the Solid Rock (PSALM 40:1–2)!

I hope these truths will give you strength when the parenting path gets rough—whether for a moment, a few weeks or months, or even for the rest of your life. Beloved, God is faithful, so never stop trusting Him, and never cease waiting upon Him. Faithful prayer, in step with God's plan in His Word, is God's most powerful key to unlock children's hearts as we disciple them for Christ. The battle for our children's souls is won "one prayer at a time." Remember: *"Is anything too hard for the LORD?"* (GENESIS 18:14)!

For as long as your children have breath, keep on seeking God's face on their behalf! David did, and regardless of how much sorrow and pain Absalom's betrayal caused him, he still continued his lifelong pattern of worshiping God.

David Used Every Means to Pursue God

WE NEED A NEW GENERATION of God-hearted, Spirit-empowered, Christ-seeking worshipers like David who earnestly pursue the Lord in all circumstances—like when David penned this song of worship in the hot, empty, lifelessness of the bleak and hostile desert while being chased by his son, Absalom (most likely the context) of Psalm 63:

A Psalm of David when he was in the wilderness of Judah.

¹ *O God, You are my God;*
Early will I seek You;
My soul thirsts for You;
My flesh longs for You
In a dry and thirsty land
Where there is no water.
² *So I have looked for You in the sanctuary,*
To see Your power and Your glory.

³ *Because Your lovingkindness is better than life,*
My lips shall praise You.
⁴ *Thus I will bless You while I live;*
I will lift up my hands in Your name.
⁵ *My soul shall be satisfied as with marrow and fatness,*
And my mouth shall praise You with joyful lips.

⁶ *When I remember You on my bed,*
I meditate on You in the night watches.
⁷ *Because You have been my help,*
Therefore in the shadow of Your wings I will rejoice.
⁸ *My soul follows close behind You;*
Your right hand upholds me.

⁹ *But those who seek my life, to destroy it,*
Shall go into the lower parts of the earth.
¹⁰ *They shall fall by the sword;*
They shall be a portion for jackals.

11 *But the king shall rejoice in God;*
   Everyone who swears by Him shall glory;
   But the mouth of those who speak lies shall be stopped.

We need believers like David who used every tense of life to describe his pursuit of the Lord. Even a quick glance at this psalm in your English Bible shows an ancient Hebrew pattern: David used seven different means in verses 3–6 to praise and worship God (seven as in a complete set):

1. David used **his lips** to speak of God's kind and true love: *Because Your lovingkindness is better than life, **my lips** shall praise You* (v. 3).
2. David harnessed **his tongue** to bless the God he loved: ***I will** bless You while I live* (v. 4a).
3. David used **his hands** to point to the God he sought and loved: *I will lift up **my hands** in Your name* (4b).
4. David used **his will** to intentionally make a declaration of God's worthiness: ***My soul** shall be satisfied as with marrow and fatness* (v. 5a).
5. David again spoke with **his mouth** to lift praises to the God he loved: *And **my mouth** shall praise You with joyful lips* (v. 5b).
6. David used **his mind** to remember: *When **I remember** You on my bed* (v. 6a).
7. David used **his intellect** to meditate upon God's character: *I **meditate** on You in the night watches* (v. 6b).

David was saying, "I am using all the faculties that God gave me in seeking Him." Is that pursuit of God echoed in your heart today?

Since childhood we have been taught that we have far more capacity in our brains than we ever use. Most doctors say the average human barely uses 10 percent of his brain. So we are continually challenged by our culture to never stop learning to use a few extra percentage points through life; but in a vastly more strategic way, God is saying through David—***Why not start employing more and more of your capacity to worship God?*** Regularly use your lips, your tongue, your hands, your will, your mouth, your mind, and your intellect *to the max* in seeking to offer worship to God!

Only God Can Satisfy

ONE OF THE MOST FUNDAMENTAL truths from Psalm 63 is that God can satisfy us to the very core of our existence and being. That is David's three-thousand-year-old testimony, and he was as human as anyone can get.

David's life reflected every virtue and every vice. He struggled with fear, depression, and lust, and yet he sang with abandon, worshiped with a passion, and meditated into the very throne room of God. So we can each identify with his struggles and learn from his relentless pursuit of God.

David's life has shown us the precious lifelong opportunity we can have of pursuing God. God is an exhaustless supply of new satisfaction; He is a well that never runs dry, a spring that always wells up with fresh and life-giving waters. Every desire, even the deepest, can be satisfied by Him. And, as Augustine said those well remembered words 1600 years ago, "Our hearts are restless till they find rest in Thee." [158]

David repeatedly testified to the fact he was *completely satisfied* **by God**, **with God**, and **in God**. He experienced what the Lord has offered and promised to each of us—He can't hold Himself back from those who seek Him! God is always looking throughout the earth for anyone who focuses his heart's desires upon Him. And He has promised to be found by those who seek Him with all their heart. So David testified: "Yes, that is what I have experienced!"

Look at verse 3 again: *Because Your lovingkindness is better than life, my lips shall praise You.* In other words, David was saying, "**Life is good—but God is better!**"

Now that is something all of us can relate to and decide upon. David declared that life is good, and most of us would agree. In reality, life is so good people cling to it with a tenacity surpassing all other desires. In fact, we will do anything to save ourselves from death, humanly speaking. For example, at gun point we will give up every dollar we have to not be killed. Or, we will agree to the most painful surgery and other medical procedures to try to stave off cancer's advance, to the point of amputation of parts of our body if that will give us hope of more days to live.

Satan's assessment of Job reminds us that this is always the case with humans: *Satan answered the LORD and said, "Yes, all that a man has he will give for his life"* (JOB 2:4).

For almost everyone, life is the most precious and treasured possession. But verse 3 tells us that even though life is good, and God made it wonderful, *God Himself is better*. Why? Because no matter how carefully we guard our life, it can be lost.

Our bodies will wear out or get ravaged by some disease or trauma—and die. Life, as good as it is, still ends. But God will never end; His love will never fade away or get traumatized or diseased. So David said, "God is better because of His lovingkindness—His faithful, steady, and unwavering love." That is the love of God He has covenanted to us. It is safe, sure, and reliable. God's love is inseparable from us who receive it.

God has told us as clearly and forcefully as is possible in human language—nothing can remove His promised "better than life" love!

For I am persuaded that neither death nor life, nor angels nor principalities nor powers, nor things present nor things to come, nor height nor depth, nor any other created thing, shall be able to separate us from the love of God which is in Christ Jesus our Lord (ROMANS 8:38–39).

When we stop and think about it, isn't it hard to believe that we neglect and spend so little time cultivating something that is "better than life"—and instead spend the majority of our time pursuing, protecting, and seeking to prolong what is a distant second?

Enjoy God!

GOD OFFERS ENDLESS SATISFACTION—completion on a supreme level to enjoy and enlarge on a daily basis. I therefore encourage you to pause and, like David, with your lips, tongue, hands, will, mouth, mind, and intellect convey to the Lord just how much you want to enjoy Him!

One way I do that, when struck by thoughts like these, is to break right out in song; whether I am in the study before my open Bible, or riding in the car listening to the Dramatized Bible on my iPod, or walking and meditating on memorized verses—I right then grab for the reality of endless joy in His presence. And so I often sing praise choruses like "More Precious Than Silver" because the Lord is truly "more costly than gold," "more beautiful than diamonds," and "nothing I desire" compares to Him! [159]

A lifelong personal pursuit of worshiping God is not only what God came to earth seeking (John 4), and what we will be doing forever as Revelation 4 onward teaches us, it is also what we are to be doing now. The definition of true believers as worshipers is at the heart of the church: *For we are the circumcision, who worship God in the Spirit, rejoice in Christ Jesus, and have no confidence in the flesh* (PHILIPPIANS 3:3).

But with all that truth, reality is often much less, isn't it? We often move deeper in our studies—but not closer to the Lord.

We often have more contact with the Truth—but less touch with God's power in our own personal lives.

We have more and more relationships at church, in groups, and in activities—but less and less depth.

And outside the church, the world is going faster, life is getting harder, and spiritual lives need deepening. Could it be that the difference is because the three-thousand-year-old secret of David is largely missing in believers' lives today? I pray that you have come to the place, like David, where you can wholeheartedly claim: Nothing I desire compares with You!

Living Deliberately for God—No Coasting Allowed | 21

Psalm 31

In You, O LORD, I put my trust. —**Psalm 31:1**

PSALM 31 CONFRONTS EACH OF us with a serious question: "Am I seeking the Lord deliberately with all my heart—or just coasting along spiritually?" [160]

Do you recall God's epitaph for David's life? In nine words He summarized all that David was on earth: [161]

David ... served God's purpose in his own generation (ACTS 13:36 NIV).

As we begin our look at Psalm 31, we find David's personal resolve which captures why God thought so highly of him:

In You, O LORD, I put my trust (PSALM 31:1).

The order of this psalm's opening words was carefully crafted: David directed our thoughts toward the Lord before he spoke of himself. God was the deliberate focus of his opening verse, his psalm, and his entire life.

Psalm 31 is David's reflective song about the dangers and painful consequences of coasting through our spiritual lives. David had carefully lived for the Lord most of his life. He had seen the hand of God so clearly as a lad facing Goliath. He had felt the presence of God as a young man fleeing from King Saul, and, as a man, he had experienced the numerous blessings of God when leading the armies of Israel as king.

But somewhere along the way David disengaged his heart. His passion was no longer in the Lord; surrounded by so many blessings he had started to just coast spiritually. He went through all the motions, said all the same words, but neglected to guard his own heart.

In those unguarded moments he crashed. Everything in his spiritual life halted abruptly and stayed in neutral for nearly a year following his grievous sin against God involving Bathsheba.

In the spiritual woodshed of God's chastening, David learned that sin paid a heavy wage of consequences and no longer would his life be the same. He found out the hard way that he couldn't live on yesterday's manna or last month's spiritual disciplines and get away with it.

After his repentance and restoration, however, David changed. He was different not because he had lost something, but because he now lived with acute awareness of God's complete forgiveness which gave him a second chance. That caused him to live life so much more deliberately than ever before.

Beware of Coasting Spiritually

ONE OF THE GREATEST DANGERS for a mature believer is that we disengage our engine (our hearts) and start coasting spiritually by slacking up on seeking the Lord with all our being. We soon begin feeding our souls on yesterday's blessings, last week's devotions, and last month's ministry. And then we pass up worshiping, neglect spiritual disciplines, and slowly drift away from ministry.

This serious risk warrants regular soul searching on our part: *Am I just coasting along in my walk with the Lord? Or, am I truly seeking God with my whole heart?*

In Psalm 31, through David's painful lessons we will be challenged to live life deliberately—intentionally living in a way that, as much as possible, is for the glory and purpose of the Lord our God. We will learn how to avoid coasting and the costly consequences of an unguarded heart.

Because Psalm 31 contains a kaleidoscope of settings, scholars are divided as to who wrote it. However, most seem to think the author was probably David reflecting back across the seasons of his life. I view this psalm as being written by David:

- after the events of 1 Samuel 11–12 (David's sin and repentance),
- after the year of painful chastisement recorded in Psalm 32,
- after the magnificent prayer of repentance and return of Psalm 51, and
- after the painful dash to the wilderness by David—away from his rebel son Absalom, as recorded in Psalm 3.

I believe David penned Psalm 31 as reflections upon his choice to return to God and henceforth deliberately build upon the lessons learned in both triumphs and failures. [162] As part of his soul searching, he looked back over his life to pinpoint exactly when he stopped seeking the Lord with his whole heart. After reflecting upon God's hand in his life in the past, he resolved to once again faithfully make intentional choices, careful steps, and measured responses to each event he would have to face as an outcome of his having coasted spiritually.

This resolution is seen so clearly by David's initial response in Psalm 3 to Absalom's rebellion. He wept, worshiped, fled, and cried to God for help— all very carefully. The strong lesson David learned from his failures and sins convinced him he must spend the rest of his days living wholeheartedly for the Lord!

WITH ALL MY HEART

After his personal crash, David was careful. He guarded his heart, harnessed his moments, and established a new focus for his spiritual life. His renewed longing for the Lord could be summarized in the words of this short chorus I remember learning at camp:

With all my heart I want to love You Lord,
And live my life each day to know You more.
All that is in me is Yours completely;
I'll serve You only, with all my heart.

The dictionary's definition of the word *deliberately* is quite applicable to our Christian walk with the Lord:

De·lib·er·ate·ly *adv.* With careful consideration, or deliberation; circumspectly; warily; not hastily or rashly; slowly; as, a purpose *deliberately* formed; as words and actions said or done on purpose. A life not hurried.

Is that where you are with God today? Or are you coasting? The following adds even further insights into this concept of living deliberately:

A Short Definition: intentional
Some Antonyms: A person who does not act deliberately acts—by chance, indeterminately, unintentionally, unmethodically, unsystematically, unwittingly.

In Psalm 3 David discovered anew how to face abuse and danger in a godly manner plus sleep peacefully in the face of both. This was the first lesson God taught him through the consequence of Absalom's rebellion.

The next lesson learned through this consequence led David to tell the Lord, "No longer will I spiritually coast through life! I am intentionally renewing my walk with You!" David purposed to never again give into boredom as he did the night he peeked over the rooftops looking for something to interest him. Nor would he walk defenselessly into unplanned situations. And never more would he allow unguarded moments to lead him into an instant of passion and a lifetime of heartaches.

In other words, living deliberately for God meant intentionally neglecting anything that would hinder his walk with the Lord, as Romans 6 commands.

Living deliberately for God means choosing to live—
- *by careful consideration* as we count the cost, as Jesus said in Luke 14:28.
- *circumspectly,* as Paul said in Ephesians 5:15.
- *warily* of the devil, our prowling adversary, as Peter said in 1 Peter 5:8.
- *not hastily or rashly,* as James warned in James 1:19.

Living life intentionally, on purpose, and deliberately for God became the theme of Psalm 31 as David drew inspired lessons from three eras of his life—"running," "not running," and "again running":

1. Psalm 31:1–8 reflects lessons David learned in his ***running-from-Saul years.***
2. Psalm 31:9–11 reflects lessons David learned in his ***not-running-from-Bathsheba year.***
3. Psalm 31:12–22 reflects lessons David learned in his ***running-from-Absalom years.***

Let's now walk through this wonderful psalm section by section to see the lessons David learned from his troubles that helped him walk the rest of his days for the glory and purpose of the Lord his God.

Lessons from David's Running-from-Saul Years

In You, O LORD, I put my trust; let me never be ashamed; deliver me in Your righteousness. Bow down Your ear to me, deliver me speedily; be my rock of refuge, a fortress of defense to save me. For You are my rock and my fortress; therefore, for Your name's sake, lead me and guide me. Pull me out of the net which they have secretly laid for me, for You are my strength (PSALM 31:1–4).

David seems to have started this psalm by reflecting upon all his years on the run from King Saul, fleeing from one cave to another, from one wilderness fort to another.

This period is when David discovered that only God was the place where we could safely rest. In verse 1, when he said *"I put my trust"* (Hebrew *chacah* – Strong's #2620, meaning "to seek refuge; to trust"), he used four different nouns to describe how the Lord was his place of safety. His security in God is seen in his usage of the following words:

- Verses 2, 4—*"rock"* and *"strength"* (Hebrew *maowz* – Strong's #4581, meaning "fortress, stronghold, strong").
- Verse 2—*"refuge"* (Hebrew *tsuwr* – Strong's #6697, meaning "cliff, rock wall").
- Verses 2, 3—*"fortress of defense"* and *"fortress"* (Hebrew *matsuwd* – Strong's #4686, meaning "fortress"). [163]
- Verse 3—*"rock"*; this is a different word than verse 2's *"rock"* (Hebrew *sehlah* – Strong's #5553, meaning "rock, stronghold," as in Psalm 18).

David used every word in the Hebrew language he could find to sing of the security he found in his great God during his years of running from King Saul. Such graphic pictures symbolized both comfort and help in a time of desperation. Saul's vast superiority in both numbers and strength were blunted by David's God-given ability to hide in and out of the many caves, canyons, and rocks of the wilderness.

As David looked back, he drew lessons from that period of intense fear on the run from Saul. Because his hope now rested more firmly in the Lord, rather than run from his problems with Absalom, he purposed to walk forward in the strength of the Lord.

This is very clear even in the word order David used: the *"In You, O LORD"* precedes the *"I put my trust."* God was being put first as the source, the target, and the point of all David intended to do from then on. Before, when David had stepped out on his own, he fell deep into sin with Bathsheba. But no more. Serving his beloved Lord faithfully was now his heart's greatest desire.

Even more specifically, however, it seems David was reflecting upon one of the darker days of those years—when he had asked God if he should rescue his fellow Jews of Keilah, a town in Judah, from attack by their enemies. Although David delivered them, as 1 Samuel 23:1–13 records, they betrayed David. Had God not intervened on his behalf, they would have turned him over to Saul's murderous intentions.

Perhaps David may have wanted to make the city of Keilah his safe fortress against Saul, but it turned out to be a false hope and a worthless refuge. God wanted David to learn that as those natural outcroppings gave him a safe haven all those years, so the supernatural presence of the Lord, Who was always there and always able to protect, was his real Rock, Refuge, and Fortress. So David often referred to God this way in Psalms 18–19; 28; 61–62; and 71.

David filled Psalm 31 with statements to the Lord that **"You are ..."**; then he applied them to his need by saying to himself by faith—**" ... then be . ..."**

This practice is well worth developing: each time you're in the Word, stop when you find a Truth about the Lord; repeat the Truth back to Him in the "You are ..." form. Next, pause and by faith say, "Please be ..." For example, you could say to the Lord:

- God, You are a *Rock;* please be *my* Rock.
- God, You are *Strength;* please be *my* Strength.
- God, You are a *Refuge;* please be *my* Refuge.
- God, You are a *Fortress of Defense;* please be *my* Fortress of Defense.

Forming such a habit is how we can derive the greatest comfort and strength from God's Word as we learn to apply what He *is* to our lives.

This next verse contains another treasure. See if you recognize it.

Into Your hand I commit my spirit; You have redeemed me, O Lord
God of truth (Psalm 31:5).

After three and one half years of public ministry, after six long hours of
horrific suffering on the cross, Jesus lifted His head one last time, pulled
Himself up on the spikes, and cried out David's initial words in Psalm 31:5 as
His final words on earth (Luke 23:46)!

Those same words also found their way into the hearts and lips of many
notable saints of the past. For example, those who stood at the bedside of the
following great saints as they died have reported that, like Christ, they spoke
Psalm 31:5a as their last words on earth:

- Saint Bernard of Clairvaux (1090–1153), author of the words to the
  now famous song entitled "Jesus the Very Thought of Thee," died
  quoting this verse.
- John Hus (1369–1415) was burnt at the stake in Constance by the RCC
  [Roman Catholic Church] for believing and preaching justification by
  faith alone. At the end of the ceremony condemning Hus to death by
  fire, the presiding bishop uttered this chilling condemnation, "And now
  we commit thy soul to the devil." To which John Hus calmly was heard
  to say by those who loved him and stood by him to the end, "I commit
  my spirit into Thy Hands, Lord Jesus Christ; unto Thee I commend my
  spirit, which Thou hast redeemed!"
- Martin Luther (1483–1546), who wrote "Blessed are those who die not
  only *for the Lord* as martyrs; not only *in the Lord* as all believers; but
  likewise *with the Lord*, as breathing forth their lives in these words:
  'Into Thy Hands I commend my spirit.' " And so on his death bed
  in February 18th 1546 that great reformer confidently left this world
  faintly uttering those words of triumph! [164] (Emphasis added.)

In this next passage David expressed his trust in the Lord by affirming
truths he held on to in dangerous times:

*I have hated those who regard useless idols; but **I trust in the Lord.***
I will be glad and rejoice in Your mercy, for You have considered my
trouble; You have known my soul in adversities, and have not shut me
up into the hand of the enemy; You have set my feet in a wide place
(Psalm 31:6–8).

Four truths in verses 6–8 gave David special strength, as James Boice explains: [165]

1. David trusted in the fact that **God was well aware of all his trouble** (31.7a "*I will be glad and rejoice in Your mercy, For You have considered my trouble*"). God was aware and close by in every bit of his agony.

2. David trusted in the fact that **God responded to his anguishing soul** (31.7b "*You have known my soul in adversities*"). When God sees something we are struggling with it is not merely that He just notices it, He also responds and comes to help us in our time of need.

3. David trusted in the fact that **God did not hand him over to his enemies** (31.8a "*And have not shut me up into the hand of the enemy*"). God will keep us from falling and is very near to us in time of need. He promises that we are more than conquerors through Him who loves us.

4. David trusted in the fact that **God set his feet in a wide place** (31.8b "*You have set my feet in a wide place*"). Since God is faithful, always had been—David knew that all he needed to do was trust in Him! The memory of a past deliverance can bear the fruit of a present confidence. [166]

Lessons From David's Not-Running-from-Bathsheba Year

Have mercy on me, O Lord, for I am in trouble; my eye wastes away with grief, yes, my soul and my body! For my life is spent with grief, and my years with sighing; my strength fails because of my iniquity, and my bones waste away. I am a reproach among all my enemies, but especially among my neighbors, and am repulsive to my acquaintances; those who see me outside flee from me (PSALM 31:9–11).

David moaned in these verses that his sin with Bathsheba was just not worth it! His moment of stolen pleasure was repaid with months of unbearable tortures. Look at how many ways David described all he went through: "*trouble,*" "*wasting with grief,*" "*years of sighing,*" "*strength fails,*" "*bones waste away,*" "*reproach,*" "*repulsive,*" "*fled from.*"

None of those woes was recorded in either 2 Samuel or 1 Chronicles where David's biography was written by God. They appear only in the Psalms he wrote—his personal diary. Because David was excruciatingly aware of sin's high cost, he now purposed to avoid headlong plunges into sin.

Lessons From David's Running-from-Absalom Years

*I am forgotten like a dead man, out of mind; I am like a broken vessel. For I hear the slander of many; **fear is on every side**; while they take counsel together against me, they scheme to take away my life. **But as for me, I trust in You, O Lord**; I say, "You are my God"* (PSALM 31:12–14).

The fearsome times of being chased and hunted to the death is described by David using a curious word in Hebrew. In verse 13 he said *"fear is on every side,"* which is the translation of the Hebrew word *magormisbib*. Jeremiah used this same phrase six times to describe those final days as Judah was besieged and destroyed by the relentless Babylonian armies (6:25; 20:3–4, 10; 46:5; 49:29; LAMENTATIONS 2:22).

My times are in Your hand; deliver me from the hand of my enemies, and from those who persecute me. Make Your face shine upon Your servant; save me for Your mercies' sake. Do not let me be ashamed, O LORD, for I have called upon You; let the wicked be ashamed; let them be silent in the grave. Let the lying lips be put to silence, which speak insolent things proudly and contemptuously against the righteous (PSALM 31:15–18).

Pay particular attention to the beginning of verse 15: *My times are in your hand.* Why is that so important? Because David was confident that every part of his life was held by God. Wherever we are on the path of life, we should likewise affirm this same Truth with David.

OUR TIMES ARE IN GOD'S HANDS
- The **times of our youth**, when others make decisions for us, are in God's hands. He guides, directs, protects, and works all things together for our good.
- The **times of our career** are in God's hands—every choice, every victory, every defeat, all our accomplishments, all our possessions, all

our troubles and triumphs. He is guiding them, and if we will just let Him, He will fashion all our life for His glory.

- The **times of our decline** are in God's hands—when our days run out, and our starting of new projects ceases, even then God holds those days and wants to bless them with His presence and power. He cares for us and wants to make those final years the *best of all* (PSALM 92).

  Remember that God is never surprised; nothing gets past the boundaries of His good, acceptable, and perfect will (ROMANS 12:2). Because God is working for our good in all things (ROMANS 8:28), He wants us to be content in what He allows to come our way (PHILIPPIANS 4:11).

WHATEVER GOD DOES IS GOOD

Oh, how great is Your goodness, which You have laid up for those who fear You, which You have prepared for those who trust in You in the presence of the sons of men! You shall hide them in the secret place of Your presence from the plots of man; You shall keep them secretly in a pavilion from the strife of tongues. Blessed be the LORD, for He has shown me His marvelous kindness in a strong city! For I said in my haste, "I am cut off from before Your eyes"; nevertheless You heard the voice of my supplications when I cried out to You (PSALM 31:19–22).

George Gallup once found in his research that "highly religiously motivated" people had a much higher quality of life—fewer divorces, less strife with others, and more involvement helping out. But all those factors only present a tiny perspective of what God's goodness brings to the lives of His children.

Most of what God does is unseen by outsiders. His constant comfort in time of need is unknown to them. So is the indescribable rapture we find in those moments we truly connect with God in worship and praise. Those outside Christ can never know the assuring strength of His presence felt in the darkest of times and places. They have never felt the strength of seeing immediate as well as long-awaited answers to prayer—when we are struck with the fact our awesome God heard us and has responded.

THE BEST IS YET TO COME

But all of this, great as it may seem, is nothing compared to what the Lord is preparing for His children in eternity! As David said early on in life (PSALM 23:5–6), what we have now is wonderful, but what is yet to come is the best.

Look at these wonderful insights Alexander MacLaren (1826–1910), a Baptist pastor in Scotland, preached on Psalm 31:19–20:

> Here we see, sometimes, the messengers coming with the one cluster of grapes on the pole. There we shall live in the vineyard. Here we drink from the river as it flows; there we shall be at the fountain-head. Here we are in the vestibule of the King's house, there we shall be in the throne room, and each chamber as we pass through it is richer and fairer than the one preceding. Heaven's least goodness is more than earth's greatest blessedness. All that life to come, all its conditions and everything about it, are so strange to us, so incapable of being bodied forth or conceived by us, and the thought of Eternity is, it seems to me, so overwhelmingly awful that I do not wonder at even good people finding little stimulus, or much that cheers, in the thought of passing thither. But if we do not know anything more—and we know very little more—let us be sure of this, that when God begins to compare His adjectives He does not stop till He gets to the superlative degree and that *good* begets *better*, and the better of earth ensures the *best* of Heaven. And so out of our poor little experience here, we may gather grounds of confidence that will carry our thoughts peacefully even into the great darkness, and may say, "What Thou didst work is much, what Thou hast laid up is more." And the contrast will continue for ever and ever; for all through that strange Eternity that which is wrought will be less than that which is laid up, and we shall never get to the end of God, nor to the end of His goodness. [197]

Now note that the last two verses of Psalm 31 are different than verses 1–22 where David addressed the Lord. He concluded by challenging all who will listen to learn from his lessons in life's unending struggles:

> *Oh, love the Lord, all you His saints!* For the Lord preserves the faithful, and fully repays the proud person. Be of good courage, and He shall strengthen your heart, all you who hope in the Lord (PSALM 31:23–24).

David challenged us—**Love the Lord like I do:** *Oh, love the Lord, all you His saints!* (31:23). The Lord knows our deepest desires and responds to them.

David challenged us—**Trust the Lord like I do:** *For the Lord preserves the faithful* (31:23b). God always looks at our hearts.

David challenged us—**Fear the Lord like I do:** For God *fully repays the proud person* (31:23c). Don't mess with the Lord! Never forget that He has built into this universe the inescapable laws of the consequence engine.

David challenged us—**Wait for the Lord like I am:** *Be of good courage, and He shall strengthen your heart* (31:24a). "Fear not" is the most repeated negative prohibition in God's Word, and He means it. Fear is the devil's playground. Fear disables us, debilitates us, and robs us of joy and peace. Whenever you are tempted to fear, ask for and receive God's heart-strengthening treatments. As much as you would seek a cardiologist for blockages, seek the Great Physician for His all-sufficient strength (2 Corinthians 12:9).

David challenged us—**Hope in the Lord like I will:** *All you who hope in the LORD* (31:24b). Here David uses that great Hebrew word (*yachal*) which denotes "trusting hope." This is the hope Job, David, Ezra, and Jeremiah all clung to as they trusted God through their darkest days, longest nights, and most uncertain times. Here is a reminder of the depth of their trusting hope:

Job testified: *Though he slay me,* **yet will I trust in him**: *but I will maintain mine own ways before him* (JOB 13:15 KJV).

David confessed: *Why art thou cast down, O my soul? and why art thou disquieted in me?* **hope thou in God**: *for I shall yet praise him for the help of his countenance. ... Why art thou cast down, O my soul? and why art thou disquieted within me?* **hope thou in God**: *for I shall yet praise him, who is the health of my countenance, and my God. ... Why art thou cast down, O my soul? and why art thou disquieted within me?* **hope in God**: *for I shall yet praise him, who is the health of my countenance, and my God. ... But* **I will hope continually**, *and will yet praise thee more and more* (PSALM 42:5, 11; 43:5; 71:14 KJV).

Ezra prayed: *And take not the word of truth utterly out of my mouth; for* **I have hoped** *in thy judgments. ... ZAIN. Remember the word unto thy servant,* **upon which thou hast caused me to hope**. *... They that fear thee will be glad when they see me; because* **I have hoped in thy word**. *... CAPH. My soul fainteth for thy salvation: but* **I hope in thy word**. *... Thou art my hiding place and my shield:* **I hope in thy word**. *... I prevented the dawning of the morning, and cried:* **I hoped in thy word** (PSALM 119:43, 49, 74, 81, 114, 147 KJV).

Jeremiah remembered: *This I recall to my mind,* **therefore have I hope.** *It is of the* LORD's *mercies that we are not consumed, because his compassions fail not. They are new every morning: great is thy faithfulness. The* LORD *is my portion, saith my soul;* **therefore will I hope in him.** *The* LORD *is good unto them that wait for him, to the soul that seeketh him* (LAMENTATIONS 3:21–25 KJV).

In light of God's exceeding great goodness, have you said in your heart and at the center of your will, "Lord, You are first"?

In light of the fact that all your times are in Almighty God's loving hands, whose plans for you are perfect, have you said in your heart and at the center of your will, "Lord, You come ahead of me, my plans, my desires, my way"?

If you've been coasting spiritually by feeding your soul on yesterday's blessings, last week's devotions, and last month's ministry, I exhort you, like David, to choose a new focus for your spiritual life: Live deliberately for God. No coasting allowed!

As an aid to renew your longing for God, these words provide precious truths to meditate upon for just such a moment:

JESUS, THE VERY THOUGHT OF THEE

Jesus, the very thought of Thee
With sweetness fills my breast;
But sweeter far Thy face to see,
And in Thy presence rest.

No voice can sing, no heart can frame,
Nor can the memory find
A sweeter sound than Jesus' name
O Savior of mankind!

O Hope of every contrite heart!
O joy of all the meek!
To those who fail, how kind Thou art!
How good to those who seek!

But what to those who find? Ah! this,
No tongue or pen can show
The love of Jesus, what it is
None but His loved ones know.

    —St. Bernard of Clairvaux (1090–1153)

Ending Well— Living Purposefully for God | 22

Psalm 71

When I am old and grayheaded, O God, do not forsake me, until I declare
Your strength to this generation, Your power to everyone who is to come.

—Psalm 71:18

JESUS HAS CLEARLY EXPRESSED WHAT He would like to say to each of us when we arrive safely home to dwell with Him forever: *"Well done, good and faithful servant"* (MATTHEW 25:21)! [168] Christ's *"Well done"* is the ultimate prize for living purposefully for God—even in our waning years when old age and all that entails has come upon us.

The older we get, the harder it is to hide what is really going on inside our hearts and minds. Consequently, we become more and more transparent with our feelings and fears. And God designed it that way. For as the clay pot of our body cracks, He wants the treasure of Christ within us to spill out to encourage others in their own unending struggles.

Paul referred to this when he explained his difficulties as an apostle of Jesus Christ. Writing to the church at Corinth, he said, *We have this treasure in earthen vessels, that the excellence of **the power may be of God** and not of us* (2 CORINTHIANS 4:7). [169]

That is why David's final words spoke of the power of the Holy Spirit within him (2 SAMUEL 23:2). God's grace and power, through His precious Spirit, is our only source of strength to live and die this way—even when life is as rough as Paul's explanation in this passage following the *"treasure"* verse:

On every side being in tribulation, but not straitened; perplexed, but not in despair; persecuted, but not forsaken; cast down, but not destroyed; at all times the dying of the Lord Jesus bearing about in the body, that the life also of Jesus in our body may be manifested, for always are we who are living delivered up to death because of Jesus, that the life also of Jesus may be manifested in our dying flesh, so that, the death indeed in us doth work, and the life in you. And having the same spirit of the faith, according to that which hath been written, 'I believed, therefore I did speak;' we also do believe, therefore also do we speak; knowing that He who did raise up the Lord Jesus, us also through Jesus shall raise up, and shall present with you, for the all things are because of you, that the grace having been multiplied, because of the thanksgiving of the more, may abound to the glory of God; wherefore, we faint not, but if also our outward man doth decay, yet the inward is renewed day by day; for the momentary light matter of our tribulation, more and more exceedingly an age-during weight of glory doth work out for us—we not looking to the things seen, but to the things not seen; for the things seen are temporary, but the things not seen are age-during (2 CORINTHIANS 4:8–18, *Young's Literal Translation*).

THE PURPOSE-LESS LIFE

The concept of ending well by living purposefully for God is illustrated nicely in this contrast between two very different women. The first, an elderly woman who lived in a nursing home in Great Britain in the 1940s, looked only at herself. As her life was coming to a close, remembering only what she'd had and lost, she drowned in her troubles, grief, and losses. After the woman died, a nurse packed up her personal possessions and found a poem she'd written about her life. Its quality so impressed the staff that copies were distributed to all the nurses in the hospital. Here's how this first woman viewed her life:

GRUMPY OLD WOMAN

What do you see nurse, What do you see?
What are you thinking When you look at me?
A grumpy old woman, Not very wise,
Uncertain of habit With far away eyes.

Who dribbles her food And makes no reply;
Then you say in a loud voice, "I do wish you'd try."
Who seems not to notice The things that you do,
And forever is losing A stocking or shoe …

I'll tell you who I am, As I sit here so still,
As I move at your bidding, As I eat at your will.

I'm a small child of ten With a father and mother,
And brothers and sisters Who love one another.

A girl of sixteen, With wings on her feet;
Dreaming that soon, A lover she'll meet.

A bride soon at twenty My heart gives a leap;
Remembering the vows That I promised to keep.

At twenty-five, I have young of my own,
Who need me to build A secure and happy home.

A woman of thirty, My young now grow fast,
Bound together with ties That forever should last.

At forty, my young ones Have grown up and gone;
But my man is beside me To see I don't mourn.

At fifty, once more … Babies play 'round my knees;
Again we know children, My loved ones and me.

Dark days are upon me, My husband is dead
I look at the future, I shudder with dread;

> For my young are all rearing, Young of their own,
> And I think of the years And the love I have known.
>
> I am an old woman now, Nature is cruel,
> 'Tis her jest to make old age Look like a fool.
>
> The body, it crumbles, Grace and vigor depart,
> There is now a stone Where I once had a heart …
>
> I think of the years All too few, gone too fast,
> And accept the stark fact That nothing can last … [170]

A touching poem; but more than that, it was a life with the wrong focus because she ended up losing the blessing God offered to David and all who are in Christ.

PURPOSE-FILLED LIVING

In contrast, the second woman, who had just as many trials as the first, became a great blessing to others by viewing all her hardships through the lens of God's Word. Songwriter Civilla D. Martin (1869–1948) wrote of this saint's life early in the spring of 1905:

> My husband and I were sojourning in Elmira, New York. We contract-ed a deep friendship for a couple by the name of Mr. and Mrs. Doo-little—true saints of God. Mrs. Doolittle had been bedridden for nigh twenty years. Her husband was an incurable cripple who had to propel himself to and from his business in a wheel chair.

> Despite their afflictions, they lived happy Christian lives, bringing inspiration and comfort to all who knew them. One day while we were visiting with the Doolittles, my husband commented on their bright hopefulness and asked them for the secret of it. They read us this verse:

> *Are not two sparrows sold for a penny? Yet not one of them will fall to the ground apart from the will of your Father in heaven. And even the very hairs of your head are all numbered. So don't be afraid; you are worth more than sparrows.* (MATTHEW 10:29–31)

Then, Mrs. Doolittle's reply was simple: "His eye is on the sparrow, and I know He watches me." The beauty of this simple expression of boundless faith gripped the hearts and fired the imagination of Dr. Martin and me.

The hymn "His Eye Is on the Sparrow" was the outcome of that experience.

1. Why should I feel discouraged, why should the shadows come, why should my heart be lonely and long for Heav'n and home, when Jesus is my portion? My constant Friend is He: His eye is on the sparrow, and I know He watches me; His eye is on the sparrow, and I know He watches me.

2. "Let not your heart be troubled," His tender word I hear, and resting on His goodness, I lose my doubts and fears; tho' by the path He leadeth but one step I may see: His eye is on the sparrow, and I know He watches me; His eye is on the sparrow, and I know we watches me.

3. Whenever I am tempted, whenever clouds arise, when songs give place to sighing, when hope within me dies, I draw the closer to Him; from care He sets me free; His eye is on the sparrow, and I know He watches me; His eye is on the sparrow, and I know He watches me.

Refrain: I sing because I'm happy, I sing because I'm free, for His eye is on the sparrow, and I know He watches me. [171]

What a difference it makes to see our life as God's plan that we willingly submit to day by day!

The prophet Habakkuk, who wrote one of the most hope-filled paragraphs in the Bible, understood this vital principle. Twenty-seven hundred years ago, when Israel was in a steep decline and headed for national ruin, defeat, and deportation to Babylon, he wrote the following:

Though the fig tree may not blossom,
Nor fruit be on the vines;
Though the labor of the olive may fail,
And the fields yield no food;
Though the flock may be cut off from the fold,

And there be no herd in the stalls—
Yet I will rejoice in the LORD,
I will joy in the God of my salvation (HABAKKUK 3:17–18).

The key to finishing life by ending well like this is the long term cultivation of godly habits. Life is a constant stream of choices, and each choice we make has a consequence. The consequences of godly habits are good; the consequences of ungodly habits are bad. Life is really that simple, and David in Psalm 71 knew that.

God Can Be Trusted in All Seasons of Life

AS WE TURN OUR FOCUS to Psalm 71, we are looking at the words of someone who ended well—someone whom God prompted to pause and look back over his life. At its writing the author was old, had lived through much pain, and was facing the weaknesses of old age with all its challenges, blessings, and curses.

Some have questioned the authorship of Psalm 71, but if it wasn't David, the only other possibilities would be Samuel or Jeremiah. If it was Samuel, it was most likely David who captured the thoughts from his wonderful mentor and friend and put them down on parchment to sing of God's great faithfulness. If it was Jeremiah, then there is also a hint of the troubles he confessed in Lamentations as well as the hope he declared in 3:23: *Great is Your faithfulness.*

I believe that David has the strongest case for authorship because this has been almost universally agreed upon from ancient times. The Bible of Christ's day (the Septuagint) says so, as do most Jewish sources. In the Hebrew Bible, Psalm 71 is joined to Psalm 70, also written by David. In addition, the first three verses of Psalm 71 were taken directly from Psalm 31 that David wrote while fleeing from Absalom.

Most amazing, though, is the fact that Psalm 71 quotes over fifty times from twenty-six psalms, eighteen of which are psalms David wrote: 3, 5, 7, 18, 22, 23, 31, 32, 34–36, 40, 51, 56, 57, 60, 63, and 86. So reading Psalm 71 is probably listening to the voice of God pointing out David's resolves for life.

Regardless of which channel God used to deliver this psalm to us, it is a powerful testimony to the One we can trust in all seasons of life. For even at our weakest times when age, infirmity, and incapacity are mounting—our great God is faithful and will not fail us even when we fail Him!

David Called Us to Live Life Intentionally for God

Psalm 71 is more than just a strong comfort for the years ahead; it is also the distillation and crystallization of some underlying resolves or purposes David had learned to live by in his long and eventful life.

Much like the books written by the titans of business and finance that give their leadership secrets and principles which drove these men and women to great successes in their careers—Psalm 71 is David's testimony guided by the mighty hand of God, through the infinite Spirit of God, of what in life is worth repeating.

David's testimony in this psalm distilled the purposes of his life. He confessed those underlying truths that had guided him well and would keep him strong no matter what else he faced to the end of life.

If you are young and the weaknesses of old age are far away, this psalm has something for you as well. It is the call to live life intentionally for God so that when the days speed by and life is getting short, you can say you are ending well because you have lived purposefully for Him.

Why is this so important? You and I live in an aimless culture driven by the latest fads and events. We also see trends in the church by the fads and events believers reflect. One trend I watch is what books make big splashes because best-selling books among Christians are indicators of common needs and desires.

For example, below are the titles of five mega-selling books written by believers in the last forty years. No matter what you may think about the authors or their books, they reveal where God's children are in their spiritual pilgrimages.

- In 1971, Ken Taylor's *Living Bible* (over 40 million copies sold) was a big statement that many people wanted to understand the Bible.
- The same year, Hal Lindsey's *Late Great Planet Earth* (28 million copies sold) was an indicator that many believers also wanted to understand the future as God had laid it out in His Word.
- In 1995, Tim LaHaye's *Left Behind* series (over 62 million and counting) has been a renewed statement of a new generation of people wanting to know what God's Word says about the future.
- The surprise of the year 2000 was Bruce Wilkinson's book *The Prayer of Jabez* (sold 13 million copies overnight); those sales were a cry from many believers that they really wanted to experience prayer. At a Bible conference where I spoke, a woman stood at the final meeting and gave

a public testimony. She said, "I have been praying the Prayer of Jabez over my family for years, but now I have verses from the Bible to use to focus my prayers for my family."

- Rick Warren's 2002 *Purpose Driven Life* (selling an astonishing 24 million copies) is a statement that many people are really interested in finding out how to live life for what matters to God.

But the best-selling book in all history, *The Holy Bible*, is where we find the Truth to answer these and all other deep cries of our hearts. And Psalm 71 deals with some of the troubles common to living on planet Earth. For troubles are always with us—as Job said almost 5,000 years ago (JOB 5:7). Either we are just getting through some, in the middle of some, or headed into some. Consequently, every day is an opportunity to either focus on ourselves—our troubles, problems, misfortunes, woes—or to focus on God and His plans, promises, purposes, and faithfulness to guide our lives to the very end.

Someone has well said that life is not really mountains and valleys where we have all good times (mountains) and all bad times (valleys); rather, life is more a parallel line of railroad tracks. One side is all of our unending struggles; the other side is all of God's goodness being worked out in our lives.

Bottom line is that the Lord wants us to view all our trials through the lens of His Word—and that is exactly what David did in Psalm 71.

Viewing the Present Through the Lens of God's Word
(Psalm 71:1–13)
IN PSALM 71, A PSALM of intentional abiding, David first surveyed the challenges everyone faces in old age. In a series of verses which blend God's faithfulness and promises, he reflected upon the problems of aging, such as the following:

Confusion increases as we age. David reminded us in verses 1–2 that as we get older, our minds get slower, and it is easier to get confused. Life moves so fast these days that when our minds and bodies slow down, it is hard to keep pace. This can prompt confusion. Too many choices, too fast a pace, and too short a period to process needed information to make a decision can prompt confusion and indecisiveness as to what to do.

When confusion increases what should we do? We should declare our unwavering choice to form these godly habits:

- **Like David, flee to the Lord for hope instead of living in confusion:** *In thee, O Lord, do I put my trust: let me never be put to confusion* (Psalm 71:1 KJV).

- **Like David, cry out to the Lord before giving in to temptation:** *Deliver me in Your righteousness, and cause me to escape; incline Your ear to me, and save me* (Psalm 71:2).

Insecurity increases as we age. In Psalm 71:3–8, David pointed out that an increase of insecurity is another challenge of growing older. Like confusion, insecurity shows up periodically from childhood; it just gets bigger and bigger the older and weaker we get. Elderly people commonly feel like they are no longer needed, and often are in the way. Combined with all the other weaknesses of life, a sense of feeling unwanted breeds an increased insecurity.

David warned, however, that God will not allow us to persist in the enticing sins of old age: a lust for comfort and convenience, a greed for recognition, and covetousness for security. God used David to remind us that the sins of old age can erase Christ's "Well done!" Remember Solomon: he started out well but failed in the end because he refused to obey God in his waning years.

The increased insecurities of aging are usually prompted by fears like the fear of pain, abandonment, rejection, death, losing control, failure, uncertain future, shame and embarrassment, strangers, losses, worrying about what people think of you, and aging itself.

How does God deliver us from fear? He does so by instilling in us a greater fear—the fear of God. What is the fear of God? From references to *"the fear of the Lord"* that appear throughout the Psalms, below is a distilled description of what this "greater fear" means:

- Having reverence and respect for God as the all-powerful Leader of all else.
- Having certainty of inescapable accountability for behavior to God.
- Practicing the personal awareness of the presence of a Holy God.
- Humbly following His leadership by obeying His Word. [172]

When insecurity increases what should we do? We should declare our unwavering choice to form these godly habits:

- **Like David, resist fear by running into God's Refuge:** *Be my strong refuge, to which I may resort continually; You have given the commandment to save me, for You are my rock and my fortress* (PSALM 71:3). Rather than let fears paralyze us, we should trust God's Word over the fears.

- **Like David, ask for God's help before becoming bitter:** *Deliver me, O my God, out of the hand of the wicked, out of the hand of the unrighteous and cruel man* (PSALM 71:4). We should turn our hurts over to the Lord to handle.

- **Like David, keep remembering the faithfulness of God:** *For You are my hope, O Lord GOD; You are my trust from my youth* (PSALM 71:5). We should choose to believe God's faithfulness.

- **Like David, remember to praise God that He has a plan for our lives:** *By You I have been upheld from birth; You are He who took me out of my mother's womb. My praise shall be continually of You* (PSALM 71:6). We should seek God's plan every day.

- **Like David, let our lives be a testimony for the Lord:** *I have become as a wonder to many, but You are my strong refuge* (PSALM 71:7). In all circumstances, we should do what's right because it's right in God's eyes.

- **Like David, praise God so much that no time is left for complaints:** *Let my mouth be filled with Your praise and with Your glory all the day* (PSALM 71:8). We should praise often.

Weakness and troubles increase as we age. David also noted in Psalm 71:9 that *weakness increases* as we grow older. How true! Finances decrease and deplete as does our physical, emotional, and mental strength. Our senses dim, our minds dull, and our hopes diminish. Everything in our physical world weakens from bones to teeth, from circulation to stamina, from sight to hearing. Nothing in our physical world escapes this slow (or rapid) decline.

John Wesley (1703–1791), a giant among eighteenth-century servants of the Lord, wrote this on his eighty-sixth birthday in a diary he kept for most of his adult life:

June 28. This day I enter on my eighty-sixth year. I now find I grow old:

1. My sight is decayed, so that I cannot read a small print, unless in a strong light.
2. My strength is decayed, so that I walk much slower than I did some years since.
3. My memory of names, whether of persons, or places, is decayed, till I stop a little to recollect them.

What I should be afraid of, is, if I took thought for the morrow, that my body should weigh down my mind, and create either stubbornness, by the decrease of my understanding, or peevishness, by the increase of bodily infirmities; But thou shalt answer for me, O Lord my God. John Wesley.

Another realm David mentioned in Psalm 71:10 is that *troubles increase* as we age. David mentioned his enemies were as much present at the end of his life as they were at the start and throughout. And so we will also discover the older we get. From troubles with mobility to troubles with relationships, life will be filled with tribulation. It will become harder to get up, get around, sleep, hear, remember, and even trust.

Anxiety will be easily accessed, fears will multiply, and bitterness will be near at hand. Enemies imagined and enemies experienced will then all run together.

There will be emotional troubles (some struggle with lifelong depression), financial troubles (some have constant financial needs and hardships), family troubles (some have hurtful children or burdensome and ungrateful parents for many years)—and all these troubles will feel heavier to bear the weaker we get.

When weakness and trouble increases what should we do? We should declare our unwavering choice to form these godly habits:

- **Like David, trust God to the end of life:** *Do not cast me off in the time of old age; do not forsake me when my strength fails* (PSALM 71:9).

- **Like David, trust in the Lord's ability to rescue us:** *For my enemies speak against me; and those who lie in wait for my life take counsel together, saying, "God has forsaken him; pursue and take him, for there is none to deliver him." O God, do not be far from me; O my God, make* *haste to help me!* (PSALM 71:10–12). In a modern sense David trusted God as much as in 911, so take all fears to the Lord in prayer.

Aloneness increases as we age. David noted in Psalm 71:11–13 that *aloneness increases*. In younger years there are endless avenues to pursue. Time flies, friends flow around us, and plans are laid out far into the future for this and that. Life is filled with classrooms, bus and car rides, work meetings, gatherings as parents; as members and participants we just can't keep up with it all.

But slowly the calendar clears, friends decrease, travel abates, and we find ourselves increasingly alone. Being alone is a lifelong condition, but it seems to sting more when coupled with increased troubles, insecurities, weaknesses, and confusion.

As some people age, they look back on **their past** and only remember what they had and lost or never had and wanted. That is a debilitating choice. Some aged people look on **their present** as a basis to complain and bewail their aches, pains, and problems. That is also a debilitating choice. Other elderly persons choose to not look at **their future** because they fear death and are afraid of dying. That, too, is a debilitating choice.

In Psalm 71, David **looked back at the past** and saw God's hand of faithfulness and power; he **looked around in the present** and saw God's plans for him and started anew and afresh declaring that is what he would do; and then he **looked ahead to the future** and saw all that God wanted him to do until he went home to dwell in the house of the Lord forever. That is the way to end well by living purposefully!

When aloneness increases what should we do? We should declare our unwavering choice to form this godly habit:

- **Like David, never give up:** *Let them be confounded and consumed who are adversaries of my life; let them be covered with reproach and dishonor who seek my hurt. But I will **hope continually**, and will **praise** You yet **more and more*** (PSALM 71:13–14). We should never be quitters even if alone, neglected, sick, ignored, rejected, maligned, and forgotten by everyone in the world EXCEPT GOD.

Viewing the Future Through The Lens of God's Word
(Psalm 71:14–24)

IN PSALM 71:14–24 DAVID SHIFTED his focus from his troubles and turned the spotlight on the other track of life. In the first thirteen verses he used the present tense twenty-three times. But in these final verses David used the future tense twelve times in eleven verses! He declared his intentions in a "from now on I will" form saying, "I will trust …; I will rest …; I will believe … ." In other words, David was saying, "God has been faithful in the past; He is faithful in the present moment; and He will be faithful in the future! For God has promised to care for me."

But what does it mean to end well? Is it being healthy to the last breath? No. Does it mean being surrounded by comforts to the last moments? No. Does it mean getting everything done that we wanted to do? No.

Ending well was defined by David as being able to keep our focus on the other rail upon which we travel through life—God's plans for us, which are good; God's promises, which are sure; and God's presence, which is real.

How do you get a handle on all those truths? By God's grace, take them one at a time and make them action statements by faithfully doing them as David did:

- **Like David, hope always in God—no matter what:** *But I will hope continually, and will praise You yet more and more* (PSALM 71:14). No complaining; we should trust the Lord to be working for good in our lives even as we age.

- **Like David, bring God into the conversation often:** *My mouth shall tell of Your righteousness and Your salvation all the day, for I do not know their limits* (PSALM 71:15). When was the last time you brought the things of God into a conversation? We should never stop talking about God's goodness, for that is what genuine Spirit-prompted fellowship is focused upon doing.

- **Like David, humbly depend on the Lord:** *I will go in the strength of the Lord GOD; I will make mention of Your righteousness, of Yours only* (PSALM 71:16).

What could keep us from living purposefully to end well like David? Let's look at some **attitudes** that steal our fruitfulness and rob us of rewards:

Beware of Exceptionism. First, we won't end well unless we resist the attitude of thinking our life, situation, or current struggles are an exception to God's Word. We must not excuse ourselves from doing anything for heaven due to our past, pain, poverty, or poor self-image because the attitude of exceptionism can erase Christ's "Well done!"

Beware of Superiority. Unless we resist the habit of assuming our own superiority, we won't end well. This is when we constantly think we are more right than anyone else. God will not tolerate any attitude that builds us up by tearing others down.

Beware of Promoting Ourselves. If we are to end well, we must resist the constant impulses to promote ourselves. Just as God resists the proud, so He will resist the tendency to take credit for things that were really the ideas or the work of others—and most of all were for God's glory, and not ours.

Beware of Grudge Bearing. If we don't resist the ease with which we hold a grudge over slights we've been guilty of committing ourselves, we won't end well.

Beware of Rationalizing. We won't end well unless we resist our uncanny ability to rationalize, justify, and excuse what we do and say while at the same time, and even over the same issues, being unsympathetic and judgmental with others.

Beware of Unmortified Pockets of Pride. Unless we resist all the unmortified pockets of pride in our lives, we won't end well. Pride is the root of all sin because pride competes with God for control and glory. What do pockets of pride look like? They arise when we are proud of our intellect, achievements, giftedness, or even our goodness. Pockets of pride can erase Christ's "Well done!" Remember: Lot was righteous yet lost it all because he thought he could stand and he fell into sin instead. [173]

Now back to David's Psalm 71 resolves to live purposefully for God to the end of his life. The Lord wants us to declare our unwavering choice to form these godly habits:

- **Like David, have a lifetime commitment to the Lord:** *O God, You have taught me from my youth; and to this day I declare Your wondrous works* (PSALM 71:17). Remember to thank God for being so faithful.

- **Like David, serve God by finding young people to invest in:** *Now also when I am old and gray headed, O God, do not forsake me, until I declare Your strength to this generation, Your power to everyone who is to come*

(PSALM 71:18). David had learned to serve the Lord even when he was out of season, past his prime, and old and gray.

God wants us to pass on the faith to His younger children. I know of few people who do this, but those who do never cease to find the joys the Lord brings when we intentionally seek out young people and try to influence them to seek and follow the Lord.

- **Like David, never stop experiencing God daily:** *Your righteousness, O God, is very high, You who have done great things; O God, who is like You?* (PSALM 71:19). We should never stop pursuing God in a deepening experience of knowing Him—just like a friend of mine who, at almost 100 years old, was still learning a new verse each week, as he had since the Lord got hold of him in his late sixties.

- **Like David, view affliction as a blessing:** *You, who have shown me great and severe troubles, shall revive me again, and bring me up again from the depths of the earth* (PSALM 71:20). We should welcome pain and suffering as refining tools to shape our lives. Affliction is a gift from God—like Ezra, Job, Joni Erikson Tada, Phillip Yancey, and many other suffering saints have so gloriously testified.

- **Like David, let the Lord be in charge:** *You shall increase my greatness, and comfort me on every side* (PSALM 71:21).

- **Like David, never stop using music in personal worship:** *Also with the lute I will praise You—and Your faithfulness, O my God! To You I will sing with the harp, O Holy One of Israel* (PSALM 71:22).

John Piper once wrote of using the simple singing of a song over and over again to deliver a demonized woman in his congregation. He also affirmed:

> The Holy Spirit is our great hope against Satan. But how does the Holy Spirit fill and empower us? Ephesians 5:18–19 says, "Be filled with the Holy Spirit, addressing one another in psalms and hymns and spiritual songs, making melody to the Lord with all your heart." The fullness of the Holy Spirit is experienced as a heart filled with singing. So if we fight Satan by the fullness of the Spirit, we fight him with song. [174]

If you have read Dick Eastman's book, *The Hour That Changes the World*, you may recall Mary Slessor, who worked in China for many years. She used to say, "I sing the Doxology and dismiss the devil." And Amy Carmichael said, "I believe truly that Satan cannot endure it and so slips out of the room—more or less—when there is a true song." [175]

- **Like David, stay enthusiastic for the Lord:** *My lips shall greatly rejoice when I sing to You, and my soul, which You have redeemed* (PSALM 71:23). Forget stereotypes of uselessness in old age—don't ever stop serving and singing and shouting for Christ!

- **Like David, let God invade all of our lives:** *My tongue also shall talk* [Hebrew *hagah* – "meditate"] *of Your righteousness all the day long; for they are confounded, for they are brought to shame who seek my hurt* (PSALM 71:24).

So then, looking forward to Christ's "Well done!" means pointing our lives at ending well—no matter what age we happen to be at the moment. Living purposefully for God means making specific choices to—in the power of God's Spirit—form holy habits like David who penned Psalm 71 as a prayerful testimony of how to be a godly servant of the Lord to the end of life.

Because no one knows how long we have before our Master returns, Jesus said we must faithfully do His work until He comes. The best way to do that is to live presently in the way we want Him to find us when He comes (rapture) or calls (death) in the future. David's sixteen resolves in Psalm 71 explain how to do that.

PLANS FOR GROWING OLD IN GODLINESS

To profit most from this lesson, I encourage you to personalize David's list by beginning each resolve saying, "Lord, by Your grace I will—

- **Flee to You for hope** as my troubles threaten to drown me."
- **Cry out to You for help** before I give in to temptations."
- **Trust Your Word over my fears** before I get paralyzed by them."
- **Seek You about my hurts** before I get bitter."
- **Keep reminding myself** of Your faithfulness for all of my life."
- **Seek Your plan** for my life each day."
- **Use my mouth so often for praise** that there's no room left to complain."

- **Trust in Your ability to rescue me** more than any EMS, doctor, or calling 911."
- **Never give up** even when all alone, forgotten by most, and out of circulation for the rest of my days."
- **Never stop looking** for people to share a testimony of Your goodness in my life."
- **Humbly depend** on You, oh Lord."
- **Seek out** younger people and pass on to them my testimony of Your goodness and great faithfulness."
- **Never stop pursuing You** in a deepening experience of knowing You daily."
- **Welcome pain and suffering** as Your perfect tools for shaping my life."
- **Forsake the stereotypes of the uselessness of** 'old timers.' "
- **Let You invade my whole day**, not just the start or finish, but all of it!"

Before we conclude this precious study of Palm 71, one of the last two songs David wrote, I would like to remind you of another fellow believer who ended well—David Livingstone.

David Livingstone (1813–1873), who had drawn great courage from Psalm 56 when he first arrived in Africa, came to the end of his life while deep in the swamps of that country, alone with a few native carriers. His feet were covered with bleeding ulcers, his body was completely exhausted, and he was bleeding internally. As a doctor, he realized his end was near. The last entry in his journal was simply: "Knocked up quite." But he was not *really* alone—and Livingstone knew it. A lifetime of godly habits had led him to still end his day in prayer no matter how ill he felt.

As the darkness fell over the swamp that night, the shadow of a sixty-year-old man was silhouetted against the canvas of his tent. The flickering candle cast a golden aura inside as he knelt next to a small wood-and-canvas cot. Rhythmic tropical rain lightly pelted the tent as he prayed beside his bed. The prayer was one he had written in his journal many years before. If you were able to hear what God heard that night, his prayer may have sounded very much like the words that Faye Springer and Steve Lopez wrote many years ago in their chorus, "Lord, Send Me Anywhere":

O Lord since Thou hast died, To give Thyself for me,
No sacrifice would seem too great, For me to make for Thee.

I only have one life, and that will soon be past;
I want my life to count for Christ, What's done for Him will last.
I follow Thee my Lord, And glory in Thy Cross;
I gladly leave the world behind, And count all gain as loss.

Lord send me anywhere, Only go with me;
Lay any burden on me, Only sustain me.

Sever any tie, Save the tie that binds me to Thy heart.
Lord Jesus my King, I consecrate my life Lord to Thee!

Outside the tent, the native porters, guides, and cooks who had followed this man for nearly twenty years through the jungle heard the low sound of his voice communing with God, as he always had done before bed. Then the candle flickered out and they also retired to sleep through the rainy night.

The next morning the cold and stiff body of David Livingstone was still kneeling beside the cot when his beloved native brothers found him. He was so thin from countless bouts with malaria that his skin, darkened by the years of Equatorial African sun, loosely draped over the bones of his earthly tent, now vacant. His spirit had soared immortal, making its flight from the darkness of a disease-ridden, weak, and failing body to the realm of light and life in the presence of Jesus his King to Whom he had consecrated his life. [176]

That is ending well.

Ending well has nothing to do with comfort, health, or security. It has everything to do with godly habits empowered by the Holy Spirit. Had God let David Livingstone down by allowing him to die alone, sick, and in such desperate conditions? No, a thousand times no! Into that tiny tent, as Livingstone weakly knelt by his tiny cot, the Good Shepherd had come to take His faithful servant home! As David Livingstone prayed, Christ's gentle everlasting arms had wrapped around him, and into his ears He whispered, "I will never leave you or forsake you." And then David Livingstone heard Him say, "It is time for you to come home. I'll carry you there; we'll go through that valley of darkness, but don't fear any evil because I am with you. You are coming to dwell in My house forever. Well done, My good and faithful servant!"

David Livingstone looked at his entire life through the lens of Scripture.

He believed God, trusted His Word, and found both to be true every time he tested them. Livingstone looked at all his pains and struggles as part of God's plan. That is why his faithful friends, the native porters, carried his body 1,500 miles to the coast to send it back to England by steamer. And that is why one of them stood at his funeral in Westminster Abbey. And that is also why these words were engraved upon Livingstone's tomb stone:

> For thirty years his life was spent in an unwearied effort to evangelize the native races, to explore the undiscovered secrets, to abolish the desolating slave trade of Central Africa. [177]

I am confident that both men—David, the man after God's own heart, and David Livingstone, the missionary who served God faithfully against all odds—would heartily agree with Thomas Obadiah Chisholm's (1886–1960) beautiful lyrics based upon Jeremiah's Lamentations 3:22–23—"Great Is Thy Faithfulness." In fact, it's conceivable that both of these God-hearted servants would gladly have praised God's unfailing compassions with words like these just before their spirits took flight to their eternal rest!

> *Great is Thy faithfulness, Great is Thy faithfulness,*
> *Morning by morning new mercies I see;*
> *All I have needed Thy hand hath provided—*
> *Great is Thy faithfulness, Lord, unto me! Amen.* [178]

23 | Gracefully Heading Toward Home

i Kings 2; Psalms 23 and 116

Though I walk through the valley of the shadow of death,
I will fear no evil; for You are with me. —**Psalm 23:4**

IT IS HARD TO FULLY comprehend how much lasting impact one single human life can accomplish. [179] Just think of David's brief lifetime!

Three thousand years ago David lived and died—yet today millions and millions of people read, quote, memorize, gather comfort and hope, and sing the words he wrote in nearly half the Psalms.

Three thousand years ago David lived and died—yet today billions and billions of people think about, revere, love, and desire the city he founded and built as the Capitol of God's people. That city is regularly in most newspapers, TV news reports, and Internet news sites. In fact, the two final wars on this planet[180] will both be fought over control of David's city, which is also God's city—Jerusalem!

So David's life has accomplished something that still touches most people daily. That is astounding, and just one more reason it has taken an entire book to view David's life through the lens of Scripture. And now we are coming to the conclusion of his life on earth.

When David came to the end of his long and event-filled life, it was not a worn-out body that caused his death; nor was it the lack of medical care. It was God's appointed time. Consider these words of Job who lived nearly 5,000 years ago:

> *"Man who is born of woman is of few days and full of trouble. He comes forth like a flower and fades away; he flees like a shadow and does not continue. … Since his days are determined, the number of his months is with You; You have appointed his limits, so that he cannot pass"* (JOB 14:1–2, 5).

Our lifetime is not set by how carefully we have guarded our health through diet and exercise (yet God commands us to be disciplined and not reckless in our physical lives); nor is our lifetime extended by physicians (though God commends to us proper health care). Our length of days has been determined by God alone.

When King David was aged 70, he knew his appointed time with the Good Shepherd was near:[181]

> Now **the days of David drew near that he should die**, and he charged Solomon his son, saying: "**I go the way of all the earth**; be strong, therefore, and prove yourself a man" (1 KINGS 2:1–2).

As David gracefully headed toward home, he modeled how to end well—spiritually, materially, and physically. We can learn much from this unique God-hearted servant!

David Was Spiritually Prepared for Death

BECAUSE DAVID WAS SAVED, REDEEMED, **and spiritually prepared, he was gracefully unafraid of death.** Since he had taken time to plan for it, he could initiate talk about his death. Therefore, he was both open and exemplary in his instruction with his son, Solomon (and probably many others). And, by God's Spirit, even to us.

David was certain about the destination of his soul; he knew he was redeemed—bought and paid for by God. As a result, he confidently declared his entire life was held by God's hands: *Into Your hand I commit my spirit; You have redeemed me, O LORD God of truth* (PSALM 31:5).

Jesus Himself reflected this certainty as He went to the cross. Remember: At His final moment, He calmly voiced those same words of David's:

And when Jesus had cried out with a loud voice, He said, "Father, 'into Your hands I commit My spirit.' " Having said this, He breathed His last (LUKE 23:46).

Spiritual certainty like David's comes from faith in what Christ's sacrificial death on the cross accomplished. The writer of Hebrews also noted that part of Christ's work at Calvary was to deliver His children from the fear of death:

Inasmuch then as the children have partaken of flesh and blood, He Himself likewise shared in the same, that through death **He might destroy** *him who had the power of death, that is, the devil,* **and release those who through fear of death were all their lifetime subject to bondage** (HEBREWS 2:14–15).

If you have been born again, Jesus has released you from the fear of death. Christ's work is finished; the power of death is destroyed; the price of sin is paid; and the power of an endless life is yours in Christ.

This exquisite reality reminds me of Fanny Crosby's (1820–1915) wonderful words in "All the Way My Savior Leads Me." That blind poet, hymnist, and saint triumphantly affirmed her hope in Christ as *"the resurrection and the life"* (JOHN 11:25):

All the way my Savior leads me;
Oh, the fullness of His love!
Perfect rest to me is promised
In my Father's house above.

When my spirit, clothed immortal,
Wings its flight to realms of day,
This my song thro' endless ages:
Jesus led me all the way;

This my song thro' endless ages:
Jesus led me all the way.

A secured spiritual life, being certain our immortal spirit is safely sealed and kept by God, is the first element of ending well when we head toward our eternal home.

David Was Materially Prepared for Death

BEFORE HIS DEATH, DAVID GRACEFULLY surrendered the ownership of all his material possessions to God. He chose to avoid the normal things that tie most people down to the planet Earth:

> *"Indeed **I have taken much trouble to prepare** for the house of the LORD one hundred thousand talents of gold and one million talents of silver, and bronze and iron beyond measure, for it is so abundant. I have prepared timber and stone also, and you may add to them"* (1 CHRONICLES 22:14).

One of the most amazing elements of David's life is how he viewed his immense wealth that exceeded half the monetary gold-valued wealth of the entire world of his day. Some economists say that today's total of all monetary wealth (loans, stocks, bonds, deposits, etc.) is in the realm of 250 trillion dollars. By comparison, David would be worth over 125 trillion dollars in the twenty-first century. Now that is wealthy! Yet, no one ever thinks of him as wealthy unless they study that part of his life.

What amazes me is what he did with his wealth. David carefully gathered it, safely stored it, and then consciously gave it away to the Lord. The record of that final gifting to God by way of his son Solomon is very touching in and of itself. But seen in the light of all David experienced and captured in the Psalms we see this pattern: he wanted his stored-up time of his life, measured by his accumulated wealth, to reflect his great love for God.

Wealth is like stored time from the past. Our present use of wealth saved from the past is a way to give part of those years, now gone, to the Lord. When David took *"much trouble to prepare,"* this amounted to the premeditated murder of any materialistic desires in his heart. So while David was alive, he very carefully directed his wealth into the hands of God.

David had learned what Jesus spoke so forcefully about in His Sermon on the Mount: money is the monitor of a person's heart. At any time in life, our view of money reflects the condition of our heart. The entire section of Matthew 6:19–24 is all about one area of life—who owns our material possessions—us or God. Jesus said:

*"**Do not** lay up for yourselves treasures on earth, where moth and rust destroy and where thieves break in and steal; **but lay up** for yourselves **treasures in heaven**, where neither moth nor rust destroys and where thieves do not break in and steal. **For where your treasure is, there your heart will be also**. ... No one can serve two masters; for either he will hate the one and love the other, or else he will be loyal to the one and despise the other. **You cannot serve God and mammon** [money]"* (MATTHEW 6:19–21, 24).

The graceful preparation of personal wealth before death has been a challenge to every generation of Christ's church. For example, a wealthy Christian plantation owner once invited John Wesley to his home. The two rode their horses all day, but only saw a small part of all the man owned. At the end of the day the plantation owner proudly asked, "Well, Mr. Wesley, what do you think?" After a moment of silence, Wesley replied, "I think you're going to have a hard time leaving all this." The plantation owner was attached to the world he was in, but Wesley was attached to the world he was going to.

It is very hard for believers to die when their wealth is not surrendered to Christ's control. Those who lay up treasures on earth spend their lives backing *away* from their treasures—to them, death is loss. In contrast, the ones who lay up treasures in heaven look forward to eternity; they are moving *toward* their treasures—to them, death is gain. David died gracefully because he took so much trouble to surrender the control of all his material possessions to God as tools in the Lord's hands.

God's ownership of everything is the reference point for all who serve the Lord. Century by century the greatest of His servants have said nearly the same thing about their wealth. They each battled with materialism and put it to death by conscious obedience to Christ's claims upon their lives and material possessions—whether little or much. Listen to their voices affirming Christ's words and David's:

And so it is that when a man walks along a road, the lighter he travels. Let temporal things serve your use, but the eternal be the object of your desire. —Thomas A. Kempis (1380–1471)

I have held many things in my hands and I have lost them all. But whatever I have placed in God's hands, that I still possess. —Martin Luther (1483–1546)

Whatever good thing you do for Him, if done according to the Word, is laid up for you as treasure in chests and coffers, to be brought out to be rewarded before both men and angels, to your eternal comfort.
— John Bunyan (1628–1688)

I value all things only by the price they shall gain in eternity.
—John Wesley (1703–1791)

I place no value on anything I possess except in relation to the kingdom of God. —David Livingstone (1813–1873)

He is no fool who gives what he cannot keep to gain what he cannot lose.
—Jim Elliot (1927–1956)

G. Campbell Morgan, a great Bible teacher in Britain a hundred years or so ago, also wrote:

You are to remember with the passion burning within you that you are not the child of today. You are not of the Earth, you are more than dust; you are the child of tomorrow, you are of the eternities, you are the offspring of Deity.

The measurement of your lives cannot be circumscribed by the point where blue sky kisses green earth. All the facts of your life cannot be encompassed in the one small sphere upon which you live. You belong to the infinite.

If you only make your fortune on the Earth—poor, sorry, silly soul— you have made a fortune, and stored it in a place where you cannot hold it. Make your fortune, but store it where it will greet you in the dawning of the new morning.[182]

God's kingdom and control over all of life was the reference point for David and these saints just mentioned. In Acts 13:36 (David's epitaph), Paul stated that David wanted to fulfill God's purposes, and so he did. David and these heroes of the faith saw all else in light of the kingdom. They were compelled to live as they did, not because they treasured *no things*, but because they treasured the *right things*.

David had paid a high price to prepare materials for the advancement of God's kingdom. In his lifetime he was generous with his wealth. He gave, encouraged, and supported many in his realm. But behind all he did was his long-term strategy to be involved in what God was doing that would extend beyond his lifetime. He distilled down moments of his life into wealth that would be used as he directed in the promotion of God's goals. In other words, he amassed building materials for Solomon to use for the Lord's glory.

If we diligently prepare the materials, others after us may build. God asks all of us to live obediently in this life. But within that obedience come choices, and David's choices blessed the Lord and brought an endless reward. The fact he wrote and sang nearly half the worship psalms for the Lord is powerful! His entire life was involved with worship and praise, singing and teaching of God's wonders. And so should ours be.

Because David was saved or redeemed, he was prepared for death spiritually. By surrendering the ownership of his life and treasures back to God, he was prepared for death materially. Finally, what made David unafraid was his confidence that death was simply the way out of planet Earth into the dwelling God had prepared for him.

David Was Prepared Physically for Death

DAVID GRACEFULLY VIEWED DEATH AS an appointment with his Good Shepherd. To him, death was not an unknown; it was not a mystery—and this confidence began when he, as a youth, penned Psalm 23 with its very profound content.

Even at a tender age, David envisioned life as a long walk behind the Good Shepherd as he headed toward spending the night in His Shepherd's home, safe and secure. In other words, for David life meant walking *behind* the Shepherd; the end of life meant being *secured* by the Shepherd; and eternity meant spending it blissfully *with* the Shepherd!

In the fourth verse of Psalm 23 we see the truth lived out by David as he breathed his last: *Yea, though I walk through the valley of the shadow of death, **I will fear no evil; for You are with me**; Your rod and Your staff, they comfort me.*

Our greatest enemy—death—was disarmed before David. He could dine (a wonderful picture of his fellowship with the Lord) even in the presence of death, the end of all we know of this earthly part of life. Psalm 23:5–6 explains why he was so secure, serene, and blessed:

You prepare a table before me in the presence of my enemies; You anoint my head with oil; my cup runs over. Surely goodness and mercy shall follow me all the days of my life; and **I will dwell in the house of the LORD** *forever.*

David knew he had reservations in heaven. After all, that was where his beloved Lord lived—and a wonderful place had been readied to welcome him. So in glad faith David followed his Guide through life into the valley, through the shadows, and safely home.

Many times I have shared these same words as I've stood at bedsides in hospitals, emergency rooms, and hospices. Although the pains associated with death are not removed, the fear of it IS—by faith and trust in Jesus. For all who know Jesus, death is simply a pre-arranged date in which the Good Shepherd will escort us through the Valley of Death's shadow. The exact moment has already been decided by the One Who does *"all things well"* (MARK 7:37). For *it is appointed unto men once to die, but after this the judgment* (HEBREWS 9:27). Neither we nor He shall ever be early or late.

When a loved one dies, whether we make it there in time or not, the Good Shepherd does. He will arrive exactly on schedule, take His beloved child by the hand, and then walk him or her safely home. In light of this, David did not fear death; he spoke openly, with hope and confidence, about his appointment with His Good Shepherd Jesus Who was coming to get him soon!

LIKE DAVID—FEAR NO EVIL

Fear of death, as we saw in Hebrews 2:14–15, was something we were all born with. In Romans 7 Paul pointed out that such fear is part of our flesh which we'll struggle with throughout life. But the more we focus on the character and promises of God, as David did, the more peaceful the ride to the end of life will become.

For example, consider this touching story from the *Autobiography of John Todd*:

In October 1800 John Todd was born in Rutland, Vermont. Soon afterward his parents moved to Killingworth, Connecticut. When John was six years old, both his parents died. A kind-hearted aunt in North Killingworth agreed to take John and give him a home. He was brought up by her and lived in her home until he left to study for the ministry.

In middle life his aunt became seriously ill and feared she would die. In great distress she wrote John Todd a pitiful letter in which she asked what death would be like. Would it mean the end of everything, or is there beyond death a chance to continue living, loving, and growing? Here is the letter John Todd sent his aunt in reply:

It is now thirty-five years since I as a little boy of six was left quite alone in the world. You sent me word that you would give me a home and be a kind mother to me. I will never forget the day when I made the long journey of ten miles to your house in North Killingworth. I can still remember my disappointment when instead of coming for me yourself, you sent Caesar to fetch me.

I well remember my tears and anxiety as perched high on your horse and clinging tight to Caesar I rode off to my new home. Night fell before we finished the journey, and as it grew dark, I became lonely and afraid. "Do you think she'll go to bed before we get there?" I asked Caesar anxiously. "Oh, no," he said reassuringly. "She'll stay up for you. When we get out of this here woods, you'll see her candle shinin' in the window."

Presently we did ride out into the clearing, and there, sure enough, was your candle. I remember you were waiting at the door, that you put your arms close about me and that you lifted me—a tired and bewildered little boy—down from the horse. You had a fire burning on the hearth, a hot supper waiting on the stove. After supper you took me to my room, heard me say my prayers, and then sat beside me till I fell asleep.

You probably realize why I am recalling all of this to your memory. Someday soon God will send for you to take you to a new home. Don't fear the summons, the strange journey or the dark messenger of death.

God can be trusted to do as much for you as you were kind enough to do for me so many years ago. At the end of the road you will find love and a welcome awaiting and you will be safe in God's care. I shall watch you and pray for you till you are out of sight and then wait for the day when I shall make the journey myself and find my Savior and you waiting at the end of the road to greet me.[183]

Todd's testimony reminded me of a special verse in Psalm 116: *Precious in the sight of the* LORD *is the death of His saints* (v. 15)! Have you ever viewed death as your Lord and Savior does?

The Best Way to Die (or Live)— Looking Forward to Heaven

ALTHOUGH NONE OF US KNOWS the exact date of our appointment with Jesus Christ to take us home to heaven, we do know that what lies ahead is far superior to anything we could ever envision. For even now He is preparing a beautiful mansion for us so we can be with Him (JOHN 14:2).

What will it be like in heaven? It will be a joyous and satisfying place! The joy of heaven's inhabitants is pictured by the scenes of praise in the book of Revelation, the white-robed conquerors waving palm branches (Revelation 7:9), and the guests at a wedding supper (REVELATION 19:1–9). This is buttressed by the imagery of some of Jesus' parables where attaining heaven was compared to attending a banquet (LUKE 14:15–24) or entering into the joy of one's Master (MATTHEW 25:21, 23).

From the perspective of life in this world, heaven is the object of human longing and the goal of human existence. The book of Hebrews even employs the imagery of a quest to express this reality:

> *All these people were still living by faith when they died. They did not receive the things promised; they only saw them and welcomed them from a distance. And they admitted that they were aliens and strangers on earth. People who say such things show that **they are looking for a country of their own*** (HEBREWS 11:13–14 NIV).

In addition to being the goal of a quest, heaven is the reward for earthly toil, as in Paul's picture of himself as having *"finished the race"* and looking forward to *"the crown of righteousness"* (2 TIMOTHY 4:7–8). We see this imagery again in Peter's vision of *"the Chief Shepherd"* conferring the unfading *"crown of glory"* on those who have served God faithfully (1 PETER 5:4). There is also the glorious picture of believers having *"come to Mount Zion, to the heavenly Jerusalem, the city of the living God"* where there are *"thousands upon thousands of angels in joyful assembly"* (HEBREWS 12:22 NIV).

Images of satisfaction emerge from the pictures in Revelation of saints being guided by a divine Shepherd who *will lead them to springs of living water. And God will wipe away every tear from their eyes* (REVELATION 7:17 NIV).

Furthermore, they have continual access to the tree of life with its twelve kinds of fruit, yielding its fruit each month (REVELATION 22:2).

Heaven is also portrayed as a rest after labor: those who die in the Lord "*will rest from their labor, for their deeds will follow them*" (REVELATION 14:13 NIV). Similarly, there remains "*a Sabbath-rest for the people of God,*" so believers are exhorted to "*make every effort to enter that rest*" (HEBREWS 4:9–11 NIV).

Does this "*rest*" mean we won't be doing any work in heaven? Contrary to the secular idea that heaven involves saints floating on clouds, polishing their halos, that great preacher, Dr. W. A. Criswell, writes:

> Does rest mean nothingness? No! By "rest" we mean deliverance from sin, temptation, weakness, failure, and defeat. We shall rest in God's grace and love and in the joy of our heavenly assignments. The very word *rest* implies the word *labor*, which is in [REVELATION 14:13]. We shall work without weariness; we shall still be refreshed after the toil of the day and of the century and even of the forever.... Service and unfailing rewards are basic themes of Christ's teaching. [See MATTHEW 24:45–47.][184]

> There are two possessions we shall carry into the forever, beyond the grave: (1) our character, since we are redeemed by the blood of the Crucified One, and (2) our capacity, since we are endowed by the Lord God Himself. Shall these gifts from the creative hand of God be wantonly wasted, discarded in uselessness and forgetfulness? Shall we be consigned to a forever of idleness and nothingness? No, a thousand times no![185]

Have you ever wondered how we will know each other when we get to heaven? Dr. Criswell has shared this precious insight:

> We shall know each other in heaven by intuitive knowledge, which is a gift of God. Moses and Elijah appeared on the Mount of Transfiguration (Luke 9:30–31). How did Peter, James, and John know them? ... They knew them by intuitive knowledge. ... Intuitive knowledge will introduce us to everybody: "Many shall come from the east and west, and shall sit down with Abraham, and Isaac and Jacob, in the kingdom of heaven" (Matt. 8:11). ... We shall sit down and visit with the saints and have all eternity in which to enjoy their fellowship. ... We shall not know less of each other in heaven; we shall know more.

We shall possess our individual names in heaven. We shall be known as individuals. You will be you; I shall be I; we shall be we. Personality and individuality exist beyond the grave.[186]

O. M. Mitchell, a great astronomer, believed that we will be able to move back and forth between the galaxies and that he would therefore get to continue his studies in the heavens. That is exciting to contemplate! And Dr. Criswell apparently agrees:

Our home will be a mansion in the new Jerusalem, the City of God. From that home we are going to govern God's entire universe. ... God is going to give us assignments according to how we have been faithful in serving Him here on this earth. I've often thought that when we go through space in that new creation and in our new bodies, we will travel instantaneously. ... What I am able to do in my mind, I will be able to do in my spiritual body. It is going to be an inheritance of the whole universe, and we will enjoy it all.[187]

Will our intellect be challenged in heaven? Dr. Criswell insightfully writes:

Yes. Our vision will be broadened, our appreciation deepened, and our understanding everlastingly expanded. It is going to be wonderful what God is going to make us capable of doing in heaven. We shall understand then, as we do not understand now, what it meant for God the Father to give His only begotten Son.[188]

Seeing heaven and all its splendor will be amazing; hearing the millions of voices, thunders, and chants of the angels will be awesome—but the greatest and richest part will be to see Jesus Christ, and then hear Him confess our name before His Father as His good and faithful servant!

What a wondrous entrance into heaven you and I can look forward to and fix our hopes upon!

The Son of David

DAVID CAME TO THE HOPE of a wondrous entrance into heaven by trusting and following the Good Shepherd, Whom the New Testament acknowledges as being *"the Son of David"*: *The book of the genealogy of Jesus Christ,* **the Son of David***, the Son of Abraham* (MATTHEW 1:1).

The *"Son of David,"* later named Jesus (MATTHEW 1:21), is Christ's introduction in Matthew. The parallels between David's life and the Son of David's—Christ the Lord's life—are very striking.

Note again that Christ's last words as He died in our place were David's in Psalm 31:5: *And when Jesus had cried out with a loud voice, He said, "Father,* **'into Your hands I commit My spirit.'** *" Having said this, He breathed His last* (Luke 23:46).

At the end of his own life David said, *"When the waves of death surrounded me, the floods of ungodliness made me afraid. The sorrows of Sheol surrounded me; the snares of death confronted me* (2 SAMUEL 22:5–6). Those very words are also what Christ Jesus used in the description of His pathway to death: *Then He said to them, "My soul is exceedingly sorrowful, even to death. Stay here and watch with Me"* (MATTHEW 26:38).

But the lessons from Christ's death do not stop there. Many of us miss a wonderful insight the Gospels capture—the last song Jesus is recorded as having sung in preparation for His death.

What did Jesus sing as He faced death? A Psalm song was mentioned in Matthew 26:30: *And when they had **sung a hymn**, they went out to the Mount of Olives.* (See also MARK 14:26.) This translated a Greek word that literally means "hymning." Since this was the Passover Seder, the hymn being sung must have been one of the Hallel (or "praise") Psalms recited at festivals, Psalms 113–118 or 136.[189]

Throughout the Last Supper Passover Seder, Jesus would have led the disciples in singing these seven Psalms. Traditionally, Psalms 113 and 114 were sung before the meal, and the rest afterward. At different points of the Passover feast these psalms were sung in sections; at the very end *The Great Hallel*, Psalm 136, was then sung. (That was the hymn Jesus and His disciples sang before they went out to the Mount of Olives.) The fourth of the Hallel Psalms, the middle of the seven (the place of importance in the Hebrew mind when listing seven items), is Psalm 116.

During the evening before Christ's death we thus know that the disciples heard Jesus sing Psalm 116—the one Psalm structurally emphasized. What makes this insight extra special is that Jesus Christ Himself, the eternal King of Kings and Lord of Lords, sang Psalm 116 to His very own disciples—a song filled with such powerful meaning as He faced death. Ending well by fearing no evil is the equivalent of dying gracefully—and no one died more gracefully than Jesus!

The word for "hymning"—what Jesus and His disciples did as they headed out and began walking to Gethsemane—is the same word Paul used for singing from the depths of the jail in Philippi:

*And when they had **sung a hymn**, they went out to the Mount of Olives* (MATTHEW 26:30).

*But at midnight Paul and Silas were praying and **singing hymns** to God, and the prisoners were listening to them* (ACTS 16:25).

*"I will declare Your name to My brethren; in the midst of the assembly I will **sing praise** to You"* (HEBREWS 2:12).

Jesus sang as he walked *to* the cross; Paul and Silas sang as they suffered *for* the cross; and Hebrews 2:12 says that Christ is present as we sing to celebrate His death for us *on* the cross.

Christ—Our Deliverer
(Psalm 116)

JUST AS DAVID SANG OF the Good Shepherd walking him through the Valley of Death's shadow in Psalm 23, so the Good Shepherd sang of God's power and grace as He Himself headed to die "the death of deaths" as the Lamb of God to take away the sin of the world.

The first truth we learn in Psalm 116 is that the pains of death are *very personal*. Only Jesus couldn't sleep as He faced death; the disciples couldn't stay awake. So we know that Psalm 116 is a very personal Psalm (the first person pronoun is used thirty-seven times and the Lord's Name fifteen times).

The second truth we find in Psalm 116 is that death is a time when we must be *very intentional*. Like David and Christ, we must purposefully choose to do and say what pleases God as we face our home-going. For that reason, the psalmist said "I will" eight times in Psalm 116:1–19.

¹ *I love the LORD, because He has heard*
    My voice and my supplications.
² *Because He has inclined His ear to me,*
    *Therefore **I will** call upon Him as long as I live.*

³ *The pains of death surrounded me,*
> *And the pangs of Sheol laid hold of me;*
> *I found trouble and sorrow.*

⁴ *Then I called upon the name of the* LORD:
> *"O* LORD, *I implore You, deliver my soul!"*

⁵ *Gracious is the* LORD, *and righteous;*
> *Yes, our God is merciful.*

⁶ *The* LORD *preserves the simple;*
> *I was brought low, and He saved me.*

⁷ *Return to your rest, O my soul,*
> *For the* LORD *has dealt bountifully with you.*

⁸ *For You have delivered my soul from death,*
> *My eyes from tears,*
> *And my feet from falling.*

⁹ ***I will*** *walk before the* LORD
> *In the land of the living.*

¹⁰ *I believed, therefore I spoke,*
> *"I am greatly afflicted."*

¹¹ *I said in my haste,*
> *"All men are liars."*

¹² *What shall I render to the* LORD
> *For all His benefits toward me?*

¹³ ***I will*** *take up the cup of salvation,*
> *And* **[will]** ***call*** *upon the name of the* LORD.

¹⁴ ***I will*** *pay my vows to the* LORD
> *Now in the presence of all His people.*

¹⁵ *Precious in the sight of the* LORD
> *Is the death of His saints.*

¹⁶ *O* LORD, *truly I am Your servant;*
> *I am Your servant, the son of Your maidservant;*
> *You have loosed my bonds.*

¹⁷ ***I will*** *offer to You the sacrifice of thanksgiving,*
> *And* ***will call*** *upon the name of the* LORD.

¹⁸ *I will pay my vows to the* L*ORD*
        Now in the presence of all His people,
¹⁹ *In the courts of the* L*ORD's house,*
        In the midst of you, O Jerusalem.

Praise the L*ORD!*

Psalm 116 also reminds us of Christ's favor which lasts for a lifetime. Note that the past, present, and future are all covered by Christ's grace. In the past he "prayed" (vv. 1, 4); in the present he "loves" (v. 1); and in the future he "will call" (v. 2).

Jesus may have also used Psalm 116:13 in the Last Supper Communion as He said in the words of this Psalm: *I will take up the cup of salvation, and call upon the name of the* L*ORD.* The third cup of the Passover meal may have been this cup.

We can only drink the cup of salvation because Christ already drank the bitter cup for us by taking our sin, our cross, our shame, and rising again. So we bless His Name as we drink the cup of blessing:

The cup of blessing which we bless, is it not the communion of the blood of Christ? The bread which we break, is it not the communion of the body of Christ? (1 C*ORINTHIANS* 10:16).

*So Jesus said to Peter, "Put your sword into the sheath. Shall I not **drink the cup** which My Father has given Me?"* (J*OHN* 18:11).

Finally, what other lessons can you and I learn from the Psalm 116 song Jesus sang as He headed toward His death? Since the pains of death are very personal, we can expect to feel lonely at times—as Jesus did. He felt lonely in Gethsemane when only He couldn't sleep, and then, as our sin-bearer on the cross, He had to face divine wrath and the ultimate loneliness—alienation from God—to destroy the works of Satan to set us free (which includes the fear of death).

But because Christ already faced divine wrath for us, we will not have to experience the ultimate loneliness: *For He Himself has said, "**I will never leave you nor forsake you"** (*H*EBREWS* 13:5). So, like David, we can find great comfort in this Truth! Even though we may *feel* lonely at times, we will never be truly ALONE.

Listed below are some additional insights to encourage you in your own home-going preparation—

You will not feel lonely at death if you follow these guiding principles from Psalm 116:

- Always remember that God hears you (v. 1).
- Pour out all your fears and needs to the Lord (v. 2).
- Remember that troubles and sorrows are neither wrong nor avoidable (v. 3). Every great saint since the Garden of Eden (except Enoch and Elijah) has died in pain of one form or another. Jesus died most painfully. It is not wrong or sinful to have troubles and sorrows—it is normal, and part of God's plan.
- Seek the Lord's aid when life hurts (v. 4).
- Continually praise God for His mercy and goodness that will follow you all the way home (vv. 5–7).
- Make it a habit to walk with God daily (vv. 8–10). The One Who walks through life with you is the same One Who will take you through the Valley of Death's shadows. And the shadows of death are all you will have to face because Jesus said that whoever lives and believes in Him will never die!
- Drink from Jesus Christ's cup of salvation (vv. 12–13). Believers never die!
- Seek to obey God in all things (v. 14). Jesus said that His sheep hear His voice and follow Him; He gives them endless life, even when their body dies.
- Serve the Lord faithfully, because this is what saints are going to be doing forever (vv. 15–16). Like David, desire to end well by being a God-hearted servant!
- Thank and praise the Lord—no matter what—for, as David continually said, God is GOOD (vv. 17–19).

Perhaps you're wondering: Does all this *really* work? The answer resounds through the centuries—yes! This is the very best way to live—and the very best way to die!

Like David, We Should Prepare for Our Home-Going

*These all **died in faith**, not having received the promises, but having seen them afar off were assured of them, embraced them and confessed that they were strangers and pilgrims on the earth* (HEBREWS 11:13).

Do you remember how the saints at Smyrna experienced martyrdom for Christ's sake (Revelation 2)? Their faithfulness unto death was a sweet-smelling savor to God. Unless Christ returns soon, you and I must face the inevitability of death. Will your home-going be a sweet-smelling savor to the Lord because you've been serving Him faithfully?

By a few simple preparations, you can be a great blessing to your family and friends who stay behind after you've gone home to be with Jesus. If you have never done this, I encourage you to plan out the testimony you'd like to share at your funeral. This is really very simple: take out a sheet of paper and label it "My Home-Going Celebration." Write out a brief description of how you came to Christ, and of your hope in His salvation. Then share some of your favorite verses, songs, and hymns—and even a special word to bless loved ones you're leaving behind. If you do this, like Abel you will "speak" even after you've gone home with the Lord (HEBREWS 11:4).

To further prepare, consider these seven godly examples of how to die with grace:

1. **Jacob looked for the Land of Promise to the end of his life.** When he was close to death, Jacob called Joseph to his side and said, *"Now if I have found favor in your sight, … deal kindly and truly with me. Please do not bury me in Egypt, but let me lie with my fathers"* (GENESIS 47:29–30). When Jacob was a young man, God had promised that his people would someday have a Land of Promise, but Egypt was not that land. Jacob therefore asked to be laid to rest in the actual land God was giving to his descendants. For he had followed his Shepherd all the way, and trusted his Redeemer to save him from his sins (GENESIS 48:15–16). Have you thanked the Lord lately for His grace that is greater than all your sins?

2. **Joseph died pointing to the faithfulness of God.** He told his brethren, *"I am dying; but God will surely visit you, and bring you out of this land to the land of which He swore to Abraham, to Isaac, and to Jacob"*

(GENESIS 50:24). In the ancient world, when someone was failing in health and was coming to the end of life, the family would gather around and listen to their last words. Inheritances were then divided up. Joseph died pointing his family to the Lord's promises: "God will surely come to your aid, for He is faithful and will do what He said."

3. **David died exhorting his family to follow God.** When he was about to die, David charged Solomon his son saying: *"I am about to go the way of all the earth,"* he said. *"So be strong, show yourself a man, and observe what the LORD your God requires: Walk in his ways, and keep his decrees and commands, his laws and requirements, as written in the Law of Moses, so that you may prosper in all you do and wherever you go"* (1 KINGS 2:2–3 NIV). David earned the right to exhort his family spiritually because he had lived a godly life. Lot, however, did not. His family laughed and mocked him, saying that he was scoffing (GENESIS 19:14). To make our last moments on earth really count, it is so important to get ready to *die* by first *living* for Christ.

4. **Stephen died praising God.** While he was being stoned he prayed, *"Lord Jesus, receive my spirit." Then he fell on his knees and cried out, "Lord, do not hold this sin against them." When he had said this, he fell asleep* (ACTS 7:59–60 NIV). What an incredible testimony of dying faith! Stephen was radiant and worshiping as he was offering his spirit into the presence of the Lord!

5. **Peter died reminding the saints about the Word of God.** He said, *I will always remind you of these things, even though you … are firmly established in the truth you now have. … It is right to refresh your memory as long as I live in the tent of this body, because I know that I will soon put it aside* (2 PETER 1:12–14 NIV). Jesus had told Peter that someday his hands would be stretched out, and he would be crucified (JOHN 21:18). History tells us that Peter was crucified upside down because he had declared his unworthiness to die like Jesus did.

6. **Paul died finishing the plan laid out for him by God.** When death was near, he said, *I have fought the good fight, I have finished the race, I have kept the faith. Now there is in store for me the crown of righteousness, which the Lord … will award to me on that day—and … to all who*

have longed for his appearing (2 TIMOTHY 4:6–8 NIV). Paul faithfully followed the course God laid out for him. When his last days were spent in the maximum security Mamertine Prison in Rome, he did not protest or try to get out. Instead, he placidly sat there and wrote letters, knowing he had faithfully completed what God asked him to do and was prepared to go to heaven.

7. **Christ died pointing the way for another to come to God.** Jesus told one of the criminals being crucified: *"Today you will be with Me in Paradise"* (LUKE 23:43). Is Jesus *your* hope? If you died today, would you be with Him in Paradise? Are you spiritually ready?

Have you pondered the direction your own life has taken? Perhaps you might regretfully say, "I wish I could do it over so that I could have pointed my life the right way sooner." Paul well understood regrets because he had many of his own. However, you can be comforted from what he said about this:

*Brethren, I do not count myself to have apprehended; but one thing I do, **forgetting those things which are behind** and **reaching forward** to those things which are ahead, I press toward the goal for the prize of the upward call of God in Christ Jesus* (PHILIPPIANS 3:13–14).

Forget what is behind and start living afresh for the Lord *now*: *For our citizenship is in heaven, from which we also eagerly wait for the Savior, the Lord Jesus Christ* (PHILIPPIANS 3:20).

Like Paul, finish the course Christ has laid out for you. And you will experience a great calm by following God's will daily. This is the very best approach to be ready to head home—whether at the Rapture or by a personal escort from your Good Shepherd.

Like David, Make a Choice to End Well

A FEW YEARS BACK I ordered a small computer memory upgrade over the Internet and received an e-mail asking me to track it. I had never done this sort of thing, so I hit the proper key and got this message: "Your package was put in a truck in Philadelphia and headed for the airport at 7:31." I thought: *Oh, that's great!*

I checked later in the day, and this time I read: "Your package has now arrived at the Philadelphia airport." I tracked that package's whereabouts each day until finally, as I checked it for the last time, the doorbell rang and the delivery man was actually dropping it at the door.

I then thought to myself: *We think nothing of tracking packages, but God says:*

"I have sealed you with My Spirit;
I have written My Name upon your heart;
I have addressed your soul with the very address of heaven.
When the time comes for you to go home—I am sending My Son to come and pick you up and bring you safely home.

Also, I'm tracking everything you've done on earth, and the part that is eternal is going to follow you—it's going to arrive with you in heaven."

When you come face to face with Jesus, what will you bring with you to lovingly offer the Lamb of God? What are you sending ahead to heaven?

Are you getting ready to meet Jesus, your Good Shepherd? Are you trusting Him to deliver you from all evil?

When life winds down, strength gets exhausted, and the end is in sight for you, will you look back on life like Solomon did in Ecclesiastes—in bitterness, seeing all as vanity, and ending in emptiness? Or will you look back on life like David—in hopefulness, having had a lifelong growth in experiencing God, and ending well by fearing no evil?

The choice is completely yours: each day you are writing the script that will be your life's eternal summary. The very best way to live is by loving, following, trusting the Good Shepherd—ending well by looking forward to heaven! May the Lord's grace enable you to wholeheartedly sing the following words with great joy!

My Jesus, I Love Thee

My Jesus, I love Thee, I know Thou art mine;
    For Thee all the follies of sin I resign;
My gracious Redeemer, my Savior art Thou;
    If ever I loved Thee, my Jesus, 'tis now.

I love Thee because Thou hast first loved me,
    And purchased my pardon on Calvary's tree;
I love Thee for wearing the thorns on Thy brow;
    If ever I loved Thee, my Jesus, 'tis now.

I'll love Thee in life, I will love Thee in death,
*   And praise Thee as long as Thou lendest me breath;*
And say, when the death dew lies cold on my brow;
*   If ever I loved Thee, my Jesus, 'tis now.*
—William R. Featherston (1846–1873)

24 | Embracing God— A Long Obedience in Seeking the Lord

2 Samuel 22; Psalm 18

I will love You, O LORD, my strength. The LORD is my rock and my fortress and my deliverer; my God, my strength, in whom I will trust. — **Psalm 18:1–2**

WE'VE BEEN WALKING THROUGH DAVID'S life for many chapters—from his lonely childhood to his struggling years on-the-run from King Saul; from his triumphs on the battlefield to the defeats of his unguarded moments; from his consequence years to the final challenges of his home-going—all through the inspired record God gave to us. And, although it's been 3,000 years since David's time, his fervor for life and deep desire to embrace God through his long obedience in seeking the Lord can still thrill our souls![190]

David's life was carved into the bedrock of God's Word for a wonderful purpose. Through his godly responses in life's unending struggles, the Lord was giving Divine Truth to help us learn how to overcome trials in our own lives. In the thirty-one psalms the Holy Spirit inspired David to write during his greatest struggles, he captured how the Lord was his Refuge. But of all those wonderful psalms, I'm praying that Psalm 18 will become the most meaningful and precious to you!

I have dearly loved this study of David's life because of the way God's grace is so visibly brought forward as the grace that saves, the grace that forgives, and the grace that gives new beginnings each day and every hour.

For grace says, "I, the Lord God, am committed to finishing what I have started in your life! Even though I am going to keep cleansing you as often as needed, I will love you no matter what you do. Nothing can make Me love you any more or any less!" That means you and I must be—

Seeking God When Imperfect

DAVID'S WHOLE TESTIMONY DECLARED THAT it doesn't take perfection to please God. One of the reasons it has taken so long to study his life is that it requires time to cement in our hearts and minds that God does not demand nor expect perfection. **To please God:**

- **You don't have to be fearless**—*David was often afraid and had to flee to the Lord.* Remember that the next time you are afraid!

- **You don't have to be perfect**—*David was smitten by guilt and confessed his sins to the Lord.* Remember that the next time you are stained by sin!

- **You don't have to have a perfect marriage**—*David had marriage problems he gave to the Lord.* Remember that the next time you are weeping over the stress and pain in your relationship with your partner!

- **You don't have to have perfect children**—*David has no recorded children who followed the Lord to the end of their life.* Remember that the next time you feel the harsh blast of your children's disobedience, disrespect, or ingratitude!

- **You don't have to be constantly serene**—*David was often depressed and had to sometimes crawl back to the Lord.* Remember that the next time you feel too discouraged to even get out of bed, go to work, or look another person in the eye!

But to please God we *do* have to experience God's grace—and David's entire life was covered with grace. For he was imperfect; sometimes David flat out failed the Lord while at other times he was fearful, depressed, or troubled. But God always looked upon him not as he was, but as he would be. The Lord saw his heart, knew his deepest desire, and forgave all the rest.

Through it all, in spite of it all, and in it all, this God-hearted servant said from start to finish: "I love the Lord!" So when we stopped at David's deathbed, we witnessed his hope and peace as he walked with his beloved Good Shepherd through the Valley of Death's shadow—fearing no evil.

In both heartaches and joys, David's deep passion for God drew him to seek the Lord with an embracing kind of love. So I am praying that his last psalm, Psalm 18, will become a part of your long-term spiritual investment strategy for how to love the Lord, trust the Lord, and seek the Lord for as long as you live. May God empower you, like David, to form a lifelong habit of—

Embracing God

PSALM 18:1 IS THE FULL-HEARTED expression of love to the One Who was more than life itself to David:[191]

> *I will love You, O LORD, my strength.*

The word translated *"love"* (Hebrew *racham* – Strong's #7355, used forty-seven times) is a rare verb form of a word group that expresses tender intimacy. David's word choice was intended to express very strong devotion—like Mary's love on Resurrection Morning when she longed to dearly hug Jesus (JOHN 20:17).

The word *racham* was always used in the Old Testament in a positive sense about God, and by God, to express His love for His people. It is a word which speaks of a love that draws someone close and hugs him—a love which yearns for someone who has been away for awhile and can't wait to welcome him back with a hugging, embracing love.

Psalm 18:1 was the sole time in the Bible that this term for a "hugging, embracing love" was used by a person describing love for God.

In other words, David was the only person in the Old Testament to take this word for God's love of His children and turn it around to use it to express his own personal love for the Lord. So this was very much a part of the reason why God said that David had a heart for the Lord.

In essence, David was saying in verse 1, "Lord, I love You so much that I am passionately drawn to You; I long to run and throw my arms around You to show the immensity of my love for You!" That is "embracing love"—a "seeking love"—a description of David's own heart after God.

For a great blessing, before you go any further, I encourage you to open your Bible and read all fifty verses of Psalm 18—David's reflections on a lifetime of deep love for his all-satisfying God. When you've finished, I hope you will feel inspired to lift your heart, your face, and your voice up to the Lord and sing one of your favorite praise choruses as a gift of worship to Jesus.

Psalm 18 can be summarized as one long testimony to God's great faithfulness—a Shelter, Stronghold, and Sure Foundation to all who will trust in Him. So I call this final aspect of David's life his "long obedience in seeking God." That is what was most evident about David: he continually sought the Lord and served His purposes for almost his entire life. And—

Seeking God Builds a Life God Rewards

IN HEBREWS 11:6 GOD SAID that He is *a rewarder of those who diligently seek Him*. A life God *greatly* rewards is a life with a long history of pursuing or seeking God. Seeking the Lord and loving Him with all his heart was David's lifelong pursuit. He sought the Lord while facing giant enemies like Goliath, through protracted battles with foreign armies, and even when fleeing his own son. But during all his personal struggles and fears, one Person never left him—the Lord.

The sheer volume of information God has given about David offers an incredible opportunity to sift through those chapters and see what a long obedience looks like. That is perhaps the greatest way David's life can impact us—by calling us to walk in the power of the Spirit to serve the Lord God in the same faithful and loving manner.

PSALM 18—DAVID'S LONG-TERM INVESTMENT RECORD

The wording of Psalm 18 appears not only in the book of Psalms as David's *personal testimony* but also in 2 Samuel 22 as the *historical record* of his final words. His psalm is like an investment record, recorded by God, of the deposits made in David's account throughout his long life. This is similar to a long-term investment of our money, which is the best way to go in today's financial world. Let me explain a little further, and then I'll make my point.

Money, like time, is given to us to invest—not merely to spend. More than half of Jesus' thirty-plus parables spoke about money. Money drives the economy of our world, motivates the majority of the workers of this country, and is the target most use to measure their success and happiness.

Those who have obtained great wealth always talk about the power of long-term, compounded investments. When we lived and served at a church in New England we saw the reality of long-term wealth's growing power. For six years we lived in a lovely New England parsonage built around 1828 for the pastor of the Quidnessett Church. Those who donated the money to build that house were part of the E. I. DuPont family. After it was built, one $25 share of stock in the DuPont Company was provided—the dividends to be reinvested to maintain the house on an allocation made annually from that account's value.

When we moved into the home in 1988, 160 years later, the house was lovely, and the acre of grounds looked like a botanical garden. As for the maintenance account, it had grown to be worth nearly $1,000,000! The unbroken compounding of the dividend yield, stock splits, and appreciation of each share through the ups and downs of the Civil War, World War I, the Great Depression, World War II, the Korean and Viet Nam Wars, and onward had turned the original $25 into a million dollars, even after all the expenses were paid for the upkeep of the house.

What an amazing power there is in compounded investment in the long-haul of American financial history. Financial planners tell us that real wealth is found in long-term investments. Even Solomon recognized that wealth hastily gained is elusive (PROVERBS 28:20).

So then, Psalm 18 was God's long-term investment record of the deposits in David's account—written after a lifetime of facing enemies at every turn. As a shepherd, David faced enemies in the form of wolves and lions. Then he stood against the Philistines of both the Valley of Elah (Goliath) and those who were around him while on King Saul's staff. So enemies abounded for years before his marriage.

As King Saul's son-in-law, David saw his enemies multiplied when Saul and the armies of Israel were continually hunting him to kill him. Then, when David was crowned King, he not only had to face the Philistines but also the combined armies of all the pagan nations surrounding the Land of Israel.

Finally, when David was older and nearing the end, the pagan nations were joined by those of his own children who sought his throne and had become his enemies as well. However, though David never seemed to have stopped facing enemies, in his last recorded words he extolled the Faithful God Who had delivered him from murderous Saul, pagan armies, and even wayward sons. And throughout these challenges, David described his intimate walk with God by possessively saying, "The LORD is my ... ." Like David testified, God will not be distant in your relationship with Him if you—

Make Scripture Personal

DAVID VERY PERSONALLY EXPRESSED HIS lifelong seeking of the Lord when he used *"my ..."* nine times in Psalm 18:1–2:

> *I will love You, O LORD, **my** strength. The LORD is **my** rock and **my** fortress and **my** deliverer; **my** God, **my** strength, in whom I will trust; **my** shield and the horn* [Hebrew *keren* – "power"] *of **my** salvation, **my** stronghold.*

His expressions—*"my strength," "my rock," "my fortress," "my deliverer," "my God, my strength," "my shield," and "my salvation, my stronghold"*—are a set of seven metaphors to describe God as He aided David in the military times as his *"strength," "shield,"* and *"horn."* During his years on the run God was a *"rock," "fortress," "deliverer,"* and *"stronghold"* for David.

After telling the Lord in verse 1 that he loved Him so much he wanted to huggingly embrace Him, David exhausted the Hebrew language in the next forty-nine verses in an attempt to explain all that God had been to him throughout his life. But most of those expressions surrounded the way David related to God as his *"Rock":*

- *The LORD is **my rock** and my fortress and my deliverer* (v. 2a);
- *My God, **my strength*** (Hebrew *tsuwr* – "rock"), *in whom I will trust; my shield and the horn of my salvation, my stronghold* (v. 2b).
- *For who is God, except the LORD? And who is **a rock**, except our God?* (v. 31).
- *The LORD lives! Blessed be **my Rock**! Let the God of my salvation be exalted* (v. 46).

By calling the Lord his *"Rock,"* David drew upon his knowledge of the desert where the fragile life of plants and animals was often clustered in areas of shade around the rocks. He was acknowledging that he had only made it through the dangerous deserts of his life by the shadow of God as his Rock of Protection and Shade. As he fled from enemies like Saul and Absalom, God became David's Rock of Refuge—a rock-solid foundation beneath him when everything else in his life was unstable.

David's testimony reminds me of the great hymn "Rock of Ages." In England, around the year 1763, while Ben Franklin was busily flying kites in thunderstorms here in America, a young pastor by the name of Augustus Toplady (1740–1778) was traveling home when a violent thunderstorm struck. Here is the popular recounting of the birth of that wonderful song:

Lightning briefly illuminated the primitive, rock-hewn landscape of Burrington Combe in Somerset. It was followed by a deep growl of thunder, and then rain lashed mercilessly down, pouring bubbling streamlets down the craggy sides of primeval cliffs which rise up some 250ft. to the Mendip Heights on one side, and into Cheddar Gorge on the other.

The curate of Blagdon, a nearby village, had been travelling along the road near the cliffs when the storm struck and dashed into a cave for shelter. He had been fortunate to find this hiding-place so quickly, and while waiting for the storm to pass he began to muse on the idea of the *"rock of faith"* being a shelter from the *"storms of life."*

The words for a hymn began to form in his mind but, according to the legend that still persists, he had no paper in his pocket to write down the words. Looking down he saw a playing card, considered a sinful thing by the young cleric. Nevertheless, he picked it up and began to write one of the world's best-loved hymns which was first published in the Gospel Magazine in 1775, some 12 years after Toplady wrote it.[192]

> *Rock of Ages, cleft for me,*
> *Let me hide myself in thee;*
> *Let the water and the blood,*
> *From thy riven side which flowed,*
> *Be of sin the double cure,*
> *Cleanse me from its guilt and pow'r.*
>
> *Not the labour of my hands*
> *Can fulfil thy law's demands;*
> *Could my zeal no respite know,*
> *Could my tears for ever flow,*
> *All for sin could not atone;*
> *Thou must save, and thou alone.*
>
> *Nothing in my hand I bring,*
> *Simply to thy Cross I cling;*
> *Naked, come to thee for dress;*
> *Helpless, look to thee for grace;*

Foul, I to the fountain fly;
Wash me, Saviour, or I die.

While I draw this fleeting breath,
When my eyelids close in death,
When I soar through tracts unknown,
See thee on thy judgement throne;
Rock of Ages, cleft for me,
Let me hide myself in thee.

So then, when you meet Jesus in prayer and the Word, make it personal. Never cease to tell Him: "Thank you for being my Salvation, my Cleansing, my Redeemer, and my Rock of Ages!"

Now let's look back on David's life to see what God saw in His servant that was so endearing—his remarkable habit of looking for the Lord wherever he was. For in the midst of a hard, stressful, constantly demanding life of unending struggles, David made regular, long-term investments in seeking God. Such a long obedience in seeking God means—

Seeking God All Through Life

MANY OF DAVID'S DISCOVERIES ABOUT the Lord's faithfulness were made in times of acute loneliness, as recorded in the thirty-one psalms written during these life stages: his growing years, struggling years, strong years, and waning years. His inspired testimony in each of these stages captured how to overcome loneliness in every facet of life.

Loneliness in all its many forms has but one purpose: since God made us for Himself, He longs to satisfy and complete us by using our righteous responses in loneliness to draw us closer and closer to Him. That is where "obedience in seeking the Lord" comes in—and David gracefully modeled this for us.

David refused to allow bitterness to fester. Rather than focus on his problems, he chose to seek the Lord by responding righteously in his struggles, ever yearning to draw nearer to his God. The more the Lord satisfied David's deep desire for intimacy with Him, the more David's love for Him abounded until it blossomed into the "hugging, embracing love" of a man after God's own heart!

You will see such growth in the following panorama of David's life through key verses from the psalms he likely penned in each stage. For the greatest blessing, I encourage you to meditate on these verses by relating them to what was going on in David's life at the time. Then, as the Lord leads, ask Him to help you apply needed truths to your own life. If you do this, you'll discover priceless spiritual treasures from the depths of the heart God so valued in David.

A PANORAMA OF DAVID'S LIFE THROUGH
THIRTY-ONE OF HIS PSALMS

David suffered intense loneliness in his growing years—

He was overlooked, ignored, and disliked by his family
(1 Samuel 16–18).

- **Psalm 19:** *Let the words of my mouth and the meditation of my heart be acceptable in Your sight, O LORD, my strength and my Redeemer* (v. 14).
- **Psalm 23:** *The LORD is my shepherd; I shall not want* (v. 1).
- **Psalm 8:** *O LORD, our Lord, how excellent is Your name in all the earth!* (v. 9).
- **Psalm 132:** *Let us go into His tabernacle; let us worship at His footstool. … And let Your saints shout for joy* (vv. 7, 9).
- **Psalm 101:** *I will sing of mercy and justice; to You, O LORD, I will sing praises* (v. 1).

David suffered intense loneliness in his struggling years—

He faced family conflict and danger as he fled from King Saul's wrath (1 SAMUEL 19:11–18; 20:35–42).

- **Psalm 59:** *To You, O my Strength, I will sing praises; for God is my defense, my God of mercy* (v. 17).
- **Psalm 11:** *In the LORD I put my trust; how can you say to my soul, "Flee as a bird to your mountain"?* (v. 1).
- **Psalm 64:** *The righteous shall be glad in the LORD, and trust in Him. And all the upright in heart shall glory* (v. 10).

He had lost his job and was separated from his family when he fled to Ahimelech the priest (1 SAMUEL 21:1–9).

- **Psalm 52:** *I will praise You forever …; and in the presence of Your saints I will wait on Your name, for it is good* (v. 9).

He moved to a new location under duress and faced multiple trials at Gath (1 SAMUEL 21:10–12 AND 13–15).

- **Psalm 56:** *Whenever I am afraid, I will trust in You. In God (I will praise His word), in God I have put my trust; I will not fear. What can flesh do to me? (vv. 3–4).*
- **Psalm 34:** *I will bless the LORD at all times; His praise shall continually be in my mouth. My soul shall make its boast in the LORD; the humble shall hear of it and be glad. Oh, magnify the LORD with me, and let us exalt His name together (vv. 1–3).*

He felt abandoned as he fled Gath, but grew in the Lord as he lived and worked with a troubled crowd in the cave of Adullam (1 SAMUEL 22:1–4).

- **Psalm 13:** *How long, O LORD? Will You forget me forever? How long will You hide Your face from me? … I have trusted in Your mercy; my heart shall rejoice in Your salvation. I will sing to the LORD, because He has dealt bountifully with me (vv. 1, 5–6).*
- **Psalm 40:** *I waited patiently for the LORD; and He inclined to me, and heard my cry. He also brought me up out of a horrible pit, out of the miry clay, and set my feet upon a rock, and established my steps (vv. 1–2).*
- **Psalm 70:** *Let all those who seek You rejoice and be glad in You; and let those who love Your salvation say continually, "Let God be magnified!" (v. 4).*
- **Psalm 57:** *My heart is steadfast, O God, my heart is steadfast; I will sing and give praise. … For Your mercy reaches unto the heavens, and Your truth unto the clouds. Be exalted, O God, above the heavens; let Your glory be above all the earth (vv. 7, 10–11).*
- **Psalm 142:** *Bring my soul out of prison, that I may praise Your name; the righteous shall surround me, for You shall deal bountifully with me" (v. 7).*

He faced constant insecurities and huge responsibilities as he and his men hid from King Saul in the forest of Hereth (1 SAMUEL 22:5; 23:1–14).

- **Psalm 17:** *I have called upon You, for You will hear me, O God; incline Your ear to me, and hear my speech. Show Your marvelous lovingkindness by Your right hand, O You who save those who trust in You from those who rise up against them (vv. 6–7).*

He was betrayed by men he trusted—not only the men of Keilah but also the Ziphites (1 SAMUEL 23:15–29; 1 SAMUEL 24).

- **Psalm 54:** *I will freely sacrifice to You; I will praise Your name, O LORD, for it is good. For He has delivered me out of all trouble; and my eye has seen its desire upon my enemies* (vv. 6–7).
- **Psalms 35–36:** *Let them not rejoice over me who are wrongfully my enemies; nor let them wink with the eye who hate me without a cause. … How precious is Your lovingkindness, O God! Therefore the children of men put their trust under the shadow of Your wings* (35:19; 36:7).

He was wronged in a business deal but God delivered him from his anger against Nabal "the fool" (1 SAMUEL 25).

- **Psalm 53:** *There they are in great fear where no fear was, for God has scattered the bones of him who encamps against you; You have put them to shame, because God has despised them* (v. 5).

He suddenly lost his family, friends, and finances in the raid on Ziklag (1 SAMUEL 30).

- **Psalm 16:** *I have set the LORD always before me; because He is at my right hand I shall not be moved* (v. 8).
- **Psalm 39:** *"LORD, make me to know my end, and what is the measure of my days, that I may know how frail I am. … Certainly every man at his best state is but vapor. … And now, Lord, what do I wait for? My hope is in You"* (vv. 4, 5, 7).

David suffered intense loneliness in his strong years—

He was tempted and failed miserably when he sinned with Bathsheba (2 SAMUEL 11:27–12:14).

- **Psalm 38:** *I am ready to fall, and my sorrow is continually before me. For I will declare my iniquity; I will be in anguish over my sin. … Do not forsake me, O LORD; O my God, be not far from me! Make haste to help me, O Lord, my salvation!* (vv. 17–18, 21–22).

- **Psalm 32:** *Blessed is he whose transgression is forgiven, whose sin is covered. ... Many sorrows shall be to the wicked; but he who trusts in the* LORD, *mercy shall surround him. Be glad in the* LORD *and rejoice, you righteous; and shout for joy, all you upright in heart!* (vv. 1, 10–11).

He was painfully chastised and then restored (2 Samuel 12).

- **Psalm 51:** *For I acknowledge my transgressions, and my sin is always before me. Against You, You only, have I sinned, and done this evil in Your sight—that You may be found just when You speak, and blameless when You judge. ... Create in me a clean heart, O God, and renew a steadfast spirit within me. ... The sacrifices of God are a broken spirit, a broken and a contrite heart—these, O God, You will not despise* (vv. 3–4, 10, 17).

He had to face the inevitable consequences of his sin, but when attacked, slandered, and abused, he still sang of his confidence in the Lord (2 SAMUEL 15:13–16:14).

- **Psalm 3:** *But You, O* LORD, *are a shield for me, my glory and the One who lifts up my head. I cried to the* LORD *with my voice, and He heard me from His holy hill. Selah* (vv. 3–4).
- **Psalm 63:** *O God, You are my God; early will I seek You; my soul thirsts for You . ... Because Your lovingkindness is better than life, my lips shall praise You. Thus I will bless You while I live; I will lift up my hands in Your name. My soul shall be satisfied ... and my mouth shall praise You with joyful lips* (vv. 1, 3–5).
- **Psalm 31:** *In You, O* LORD, *I put my trust; let me never be ashamed; deliver me in Your righteousness. ... For You are my rock and my fortress; therefore, for Your name's sake, lead me and guide me. ... Into Your hand I commit my spirit; You have redeemed me, O* LORD *God of truth. ... Oh, love the* LORD, *all you His saints! For the* LORD *preserves the faithful, and fully repays the proud person. Be of good courage, and He shall strengthen your heart, all you who hope in the* LORD (vv. 1, 3, 5, 23–24).

David suffered intense loneliness in his waning years—

He had to come to terms with old age and impending death, but his humble obedience led to joy as he used his last years for God's glory (2 Samuel 22–23; 1 Kings 1–2).

- **Psalm 71:** *Be my strong refuge, … for You are my rock and my fortress. … O God, You have taught me from my youth; and to this day I declare Your wondrous works. Now also when I am old and grayheaded, O God, do not forsake me, until I declare Your strength to this generation, Your power to everyone who is to come. … Your righteousness, O God, is very high, You who have done great things; O God, who is like You? … My tongue also shall talk of Your righteousness all the day long …* (vv. 3, 17–19, 24).
- **Psalm 18:** *I will love You, O LORD, my strength. The LORD is my rock and my fortress and my deliverer; my God, my strength, in whom I will trust; my shield and the horn of my salvation, my stronghold. … The LORD lives! Blessed be my Rock! Let the God of my salvation be exalted* (vv. 1–2; 46).

David's incredible heart for the Lord continually gushed up rivers of worship even from the parched ground of difficult days! In every stage of life God empowered him to turn his fears into opportunities to trust Him even more. And so God's servant—this unique man after God's own heart—in his very last recorded words launched his psalm of praise with this wholehearted declaration of devotion: *I will love You, O LORD, my strength.*

I pray that you will long, like David, for—

More Love, O Christ!

The *Shema,*[193] the Jewish confession of faith, begins with:

*"Hear, O Israel: The LORD our God, the LORD is one! You shall **love the LORD** your God **with all your heart, with all your soul,** and **with all your strength**"* (DEUTERONOMY 6:4–5).

As the king of God's people, David would have had his own copy of these verses as a result of hand-copying the Pentateuch,[194] which he was also commanded to read *"**all the days of his life**, that he may learn to fear the LORD his God and be careful **to observe all the words** of this law and these statutes"* (DEUTERONOMY 17:19).

David's passion for God's Word and deep desire to love Him with all his heart, soul, and strength was the fruit of embracing God through a long obedience in seeking the Lord. But were it not for David's life being covered with God's grace, none of this would have been possible. We must never forget that his greatness was ultimately of God—not of himself (2 CORINTHIANS 4:6–7 NIV). As John MacArthur has pointed out:

> Only divine grace can enable our hearts to love God in the first place. Scripture clearly teaches this. … So unless God Himself draws us to Christ, we would never love Him on our own (JOHN 6:65). "We love because he first loved us" (1 JOHN 4:19).

> The apostle Paul prayed for the Philippians, "And this is my prayer: that your love may abound more and more in knowledge and depth of insight" (PHILIPPIANS 1:9). So it is certainly appropriate to pray that God would deepen and enrich our love for Christ, for only He can do it.[195]

Elizabeth Prentiss, the hymn-writer of "More Love to Thee, O Christ," earnestly prayed for the empowerment to love Christ more and more—no matter the cost! For she, like David, craved intimacy with the Lord, as her words clearly reveal:

> *More love to thee, O Christ, more love to thee!*
> *Hear thou the prayer I make on bended knee;*
> *This is my earnest plea, more love, O Christ, to thee,*
> *More love to thee, more love to thee!*

> *Once earthly joy I craved, sought peace and rest;*
> *Now thee alone I seek; give what is best:*
> *This all my prayer shall be, more love, O Christ, to thee,*
> *More love to thee, more love to thee!*

> *Let sorrow do its work, send grief and pain;*
> *Sweet are thy messengers, sweet their refrain,*
> *When they can sing with me, more love, O Christ, to thee*
> *More love to thee, more love to thee!*

Then shall my latest breath whisper thy praise;
This be the parting cry my heart shall raise,
This still its prayer shall be, more love, O Christ, to thee,
More love to thee, more love to thee!

Knowing the background behind the writing of that song makes her prayer even more precious—and challenging! John MacArthur continued:

> Elizabeth Prentiss ... wrote this hymn during a time of deep grief after two of her children died in infancy very close together. Her "earnest plea" in the midst of such overwhelming trials was not that the trials would be removed or that the pain would be eliminated, but that patience would have its perfect work: "that you may be mature and complete, not lacking anything" (JAMES 1:4). That is the heart-cry of true faith.

> Stanza 2 is a beautiful testimony that describes how trials refine the believer's perspective: "Once earthly joy I craved." ... But this is not a mere *earthly* joy. Earthly joys are always temporary and transient. ... The testimony of the hymn-writer is that Christ Himself is a blessing vast superior to any earthly joy, and that is where the sorrowful heart finally learns to find its *true* joy: "Now thee alone I seek."

> ... This hymn poetically echoes the message of James 1: "Sweet are thy messengers." Remember, the "messengers" the hymn-writer has in mind are "sorrow," "grief," and "pain." Again, these are in no way "sweet" in and of themselves. But when their effects on our hearts actually increase our love and our longing for Christ, the final result is unspeakably sweet.

> ... The closing stanza looks forward to the end of life, realizing that a prayer like this hymn is never fully answered this side of heaven. No matter how deep and rich our love for Christ grows in this life, we will always feel the need for deeper, more perfect love. And that will be true until the moment when we see Him face to face and are made perfect (1 JOHN 3:2). Then even our love for our glorious Savior will finally be perfect, and the prayer of this hymn will at last be answered in full.[196]

Until then, we, too, should earnestly plead: "More love, O Christ, to Thee." But we must depend upon *God who works in* [us] *both to will and to do for His good pleasure* (PHILIPPIANS 2:13) to work this "hugging, embracing love" for Christ in us! For only God can satisfy to the very core of our existence and being!

David was as human as anyone can get because he reflected every vice and virtue. He struggled with fear, depression, and lust—yet he sang with abandon, worshiped with a passion, and meditated into the very throne room of God. How was the latter possible?

The God of New Beginnings is an exhaustless supply of satisfaction; He is a well that never runs dry, a spring that always wells up with fresh and life-giving waters. Every desire, even the deepest, can be completely satisfied by Him! In light of all that David has modeled for us throughout the Scriptures, could there ever be a greater or more worthy desire than to embrace God through a long obedience in seeking the Lord? No—a thousand times no!

That was David's 3,000-year-old spiritual secret of success in serving God's purposes in his own generation! And by God's grace it can be yours and mine as well!

My Closing Prayer for You: Father in Heaven, from the depth of our beings, from the center of all we are, we want to be found worthy when we stand before You face-to-face; we want to be there clothed in Your righteousness. We don't know when You are going to come or call us home. It could be that the days written in Your Book may end for us even this week. We therefore pray that we would live a life that is true and right—for You, Lord Jesus. We pray that You, Holy Spirit, will put Your finger into our hearts and point out any untoppled idols, unforsaken sins, and unrestrained areas of flesh in our lives. Lord, when You come or call for us, we don't want to be found living, talking, acting, or doing any of those things which displease You. May we make such choices while we're thinking about getting ready to stand before You with all the redeemed, with all the angelic hosts, saying, "Holy, holy, holy, Lord God Almighty." We love You, Lord! Captivate our hearts so that we, like David, will cry out with all that is within us: *I will love You, O LORD, my strength. The LORD lives! Blessed be my Rock! Let the God of my salvation be exalted!* In the blessed Name of Jesus I pray. Amen.

STUDY GUIDE QUESTIONS

CHAPTER 1: THE SECRET OF ETERNAL REWARDS

1. Through biographical portraits in the Scriptures, God identified who is (and isn't) His servant. Consider your own life. How do you think God would characterize your life since you became a born-again Christian? How would your family, friends, and associates describe your service for God?

2. Read 1 Samuel 13:14; Acts 13:22; 1 Kings 15:5; Acts 13:36. In your own words, define the spiritual secret that made David so unique in God's eyes. How can that spiritual principle become an ever-growing reality in your own life?

3. In 1 Samuel 16:13, what was David's empowerment for spiritual success? Will God give you the same empowerment for His service? (See JOHN 14:13–17, 26; 16:13–14; ROMANS 8:14–16, 26–27.) Describe how the Holy Spirit is your Helper.

4. Just as God did in His servant David's life, He wants to use you for His glory through these characteristics:

- your unchangeable features
- your disciplined life
- your available life
- your empowerment by the Holy Spirit
- your righteous actions
- your humility in service
- your ministry of comfort
- your diligent work
- your disciplined habits
- your giving your life back to Him
- your remembering His hand in your life
- your honoring His Name
- your dedication of personal treasures and trophies to Him
- your costly sacrifices for Him

Pray over each characteristic. What areas do you need to improve through the power of the Holy Spirit? One or more of these characteristics will probably be harder for you to achieve than the rest. Therefore, in your daily Bible reading be alert to verses applicable to each area needing growth. Memorize those verses, and pray them back to the Lord, for He always honors His Word.

5. Just as the Apostle Paul encouraged Timothy to be, David was an example *in word, in conduct, in love, in spirit, in faith, in purity* (1 TIMOTHY 4:12). How many saints do you know who have been such an example? What do you admire most about them? The next time you have a chance, ask each of them what his spiritual secret of success has been. How does that secret of success compare with David's—the man after God's own heart?

CHAPTER 2: HOW NOT TO WASTE YOUR LIFE LIKE SAUL

1. God says that better is *the day of death than the day of one's birth* (ECCLESIASTES 7:1). This verse provides a sobering reminder that a *"good name"* is what really matters in life. When your time on earth is over, and you face Christ's analysis of how you ran the race of faith, who you *really* are will become known. Only a life truly devoted to Christ's purposes will hear His treasured "Well done!" To avoid

wasting your life like King Saul, meditate on this principle regularly and ask God to keep you focused on what counts for eternity.

2. Who you are spiritually is far more important than what you look like. King Saul was a prince of a man outwardly, but a demon of a man inwardly, as evidenced by his ungodly character traits:

   - Saul sought the people's praises instead of God's.
   - Saul's kingdom was demonized at his own hands.
   - Saul was cruel and selfish.
   - Saul was bitter.
   - Saul excused himself of sin.
   - Saul was full of fear.
   - Saul was at war with God.

   Do you see any of these sinful character traits in your own life? Is who you are inwardly consistent with how you present yourself to others outwardly? If not, what does God want you to do about it?

3. David's life contrasts with Saul's because David had godly character traits:

   - David sought God's praises.
   - David was kind and giving.
   - David was forgiving.
   - David accused himself of sin.
   - David was full of boldness.
   - David was at peace with God.

   Which of these characteristics has the Holy Spirit been developing in you? Which still need work?

4. Although David was a man after God's own heart, he wasn't perfect— just forgiven. At times he could be impatient, depressed, distressed, fearful, hopeless, tempted, and even angry or wrathful. So then, what was it about David that still made him "God's man"?

5. By 1 Samuel 15, Saul was exhibiting signs of having rejected the Lord to serve himself. Look back through this chapter and retrace Saul's pathway to rejection by God. As you read, ask the Holy Spirit to identify any sins you need to repent of. Make a list of those sins, and then faithfully pray for His divine grace to overcome them.

6. The New Testament clearly condemns the ungodly character traits seen in Saul's life. Read what God has to say about such traits in these verses: Matthew 16:24–27; 23:12; Luke 18:13–14; John 14:21; 1 Corinthians 6:19–20; 2 Corinthians 10:18; 2 Timothy 3:5; James 4:4. Each of the negatives also teaches a positive principle for living. What are these principles?

7. Saul's choice to serve himself rather than the Lord reaped eternal disgrace. He had money, muscles, and charisma, but he didn't have integrity, humility, and a servant's heart. Consequently, his fruitless spiritual life affected far more than him. Make a list by name of all the people affected by your spiritual walk with the Lord. Refer to this list regularly to remind yourself of how deep your obligation is to live an obedient, Word filled life; pray regularly for your example as well as for the persons on your list.

CHAPTER 3: THE POWER OF LITTLE CHOICES

1. Life constantly involves choices, and all choices have consequences; some can even impact many generations to come. Consider Isaac's firstborn son, Esau, who *for one morsel of food sold his birthright* (HEBREWS 12:16). In Hebrews 12:17, what was his consequence for being a man who lived for his appetites?

2. Esau was a foolish man who rejected God's covenant and never repented, yet Scripture records that he prospered. Sometimes the prosperity of the wicked and their seeming escape from judgment can tempt the believer to doubt whether obeying the Lord is worthwhile— to doubt the value of a Word filled life. Why do you suppose God allows the wicked to prosper? What does Psalm 73 say about the prosperity of the wicked compared to the value of obedience to God?

3. Sin left unchecked grows and grows like a deadly cancer. Esau's godless and profane family line continued unbroken up to the time of Christ. In fact, Esau's grandson Amalek fathered the Amalekites. The Amalekites had a ferocious, plundering, merciless culture of murder and wickedness, and God vowed to utterly destroy them. After centuries of patience, the God Who Waits gave King Saul a clear directive regarding Amalek. How did Saul respond to the Lord's edict in 1 Samuel 15:3?

4. God was so hard on King Saul because he was unwilling to hate sin and obey the Lord by turning away from that which caused it. In 1 Samuel 15:23, what was his consequence for being a self-serving man rather than a God-hearted servant?

5. Seeing God's wrath upon sin sometimes makes us uncomfortable, and it should. But in that discomfort we should respond in gratitude that the Lord Jesus was willing to bear God's wrath for our sins by dying in our place at Calvary. Read Psalm 22:1–21, David's prophetic description of the crucifixion of Christ. In light of the extreme price Christ paid to purchase your salvation, have you committed to being a God-hearted servant through the Holy Spirit's empowerment?

6. Our salvation is not dependent upon our good deeds, for no one can go to heaven based upon his own merits. (See ROMANS 3:10–18, 23; 6:23.) Nevertheless, the works of God's children are either pleasing or displeasing in His eyes. Read 1 Corinthians 3:11–15. What future event should motivate your choices daily? If you were to suddenly face Jesus Christ today, how do you think He would categorize your works? Based upon John 15:5–8, how would you define the spiritual secret to hearing Christ's "Well done!"?

CHAPTER 4: OUR SURE REFUGE IN LONELINESS

1. Loneliness is no respecter of persons. From the greatest to the least of us, all will experience such pain at one time or another. In Genesis 2:18a God had something to say about the problem of aloneness. What was it? What was His solution for Adam?

2. In Genesis 3, Adam and Eve experienced the most dreadful form of loneliness. What is it? Why did it occur?

3. When you have been lonely in the past, to whom or to what have you turned for comfort? Did that person, thing, or activity provide relief? Was the relief permanent, or did it leave you feeling lonely again?

4. Though loneliness is not easy, through your righteous responses to God He wants to draw you closer to Him—to complete you. In what three ways does Psalm 19 reveal that David found hope, comfort, and closeness when he felt lonely? Memorize Psalm 19:14. Meditating upon this verse can help you relate properly to God when you feel lonely.

5. David applied Psalm 19's truths to what he penned in Psalm 23, a prayer song for the lonely. To get the most value from this familiar psalm, during your quiet time with your Good Shepherd pray each of its phrases back to Him. As you pray, meditate on the meaning of each. Repeat this as often as needed until Psalm 23 becomes a part of you.

- *The LORD is my shepherd*: Lord, when I'm lonely—shepherd me.
- *I shall not want*: Lord, when I'm lonely—satisfy me.
- *He makes me to lie down in green pastures*: Lord, when I'm lonely—calm me.
- *He leads me beside the still waters*: Lord, when I'm lonely—lead me.
- *He restores my soul*: Lord, when I'm lonely—restore me.
- *He leads me in the paths of righteousness for His name's sake*: Lord, when I'm lonely—sanctify me.
- *Yea, though I walk through the valley of the shadow of death*: Lord, when I'm lonely—walk close to me.
- *I will fear no evil*: Lord, when I'm lonely—protect me.
- *For You are with me*: Lord, when I'm lonely—remind me of Your presence.
- *Your rod and Your staff, they comfort me*: Lord, when I'm lonely—console me.
- *You prepare a table before me in the presence of my enemies*: Lord, when I'm lonely—fill me with Your peace.
- *You anoint my head with oil*: Lord, when I'm lonely—fill me with Your Spirit.
- *My cup runs over*: Lord, when I'm lonely—fill me to overflowing.
- *Surely goodness and mercy shall follow me all the days of my life*: Lord, when I'm lonely—surround me.
- *And I will dwell in the house of the LORD forever*: Lord, when I'm lonely—point me heavenward.

CHAPTER 5: HOW TO STAND ALONE FOR GOD

1. Acts 13:36 contains David's epitaph, written by God Himself: ***David had served God's purpose in his own generation*** (NIV). Based upon your walk with the Lord, have you thought about what epitaph God might write to commemorate your life? After you've died, what would you want others to remember most about you?

2. In 1 Samuel 17, the story of David and Goliath reveals David's godliest characteristic—his entire purpose and motivation for life. What was it? Briefly write out how you would describe your own purpose and motivation for living. Then ask yourself, *Is my description in line with God's purpose for me as set forth in Scripture?*

3. David could stand alone for God because he had God-consciousness. What does this mean?

   David could stand alone for God because he had perseverance. How did he persevere?

   David could stand alone for God because he had a divine perspective. What was this perspective?

   Do you ever feel like you are fighting your spiritual battles all alone? Read Romans 8:31–39. How should you view your present challenges and obstacles in light of what God says in this passage?

4. Read Psalm 8, David's hymn of victory over Goliath. What principle, expressed in both verses 1 and 9, explains why God will surely grant His people victory? Compare Psalm 8 to Hebrews 2:6–9, 14–15. What victory has the Lord Jesus already won on your behalf?

5. Because David had spiritual discipline, he put God ahead of his personal comforts. Read Psalm 132:2–5. Do you have any comforts keeping you from spending time with God? How can you better discipline your time to put God first in your life?

6. In Psalm 132 (and many other psalms) we see David's delight in corporate worship. In Hebrews 10:24–25, what does God say about the importance of His church and its ministry? Are you a faithful church member? Do you wholeheartedly participate in listening to the sermons, singing songs, and praying, or are you merely attending physically? Do you fellowship with believers outside of church for spiritual encouragement? Why is all this so important in end times?

7. Psalm 101 lists David's resolutions, or spiritual disciplines, for living the Christian life:

   - **David sought personal integrity**: *I will behave wisely in a perfect way. Oh, when will You come to me? I will walk within my house with a perfect heart* (101:2).

- **David made a personal pact of purity**: *I will set nothing wicked before my eyes; I hate the work of those who fall away; it shall not cling to me* (101:3).
- **David chose to limit his exposure to evil and things that would displease the Lord**: *A perverse heart shall depart from me; I will not know wickedness* (101:4).
- **David kept his eyes on the faithful**: *My eyes shall be on the faithful of the land, that they may dwell with me; he who walks in a perfect way, he shall serve me* (101:6).
- **David had a lifelong plan to purge evil from around him**: *Early I will destroy all the wicked of the land, that I may cut off all the evildoers from the city of the LORD* (101:8).

Do you lack any of these resolutions? If so, what can you do to develop those disciplines? If you are young in the faith, do you know a mature believer from whom you can learn?

CHAPTER 6: FINDING STRENGTH IN HARD TIMES

1. David experienced nearly every form of loneliness:
   - He endured family conflict and danger.
   - He lost his job and was separated from his family.
   - He faced the unexpected twist of duress in a new location.
   - He felt abandoned by God and then had to live and work with a troubled crowd.
   - He had constant insecurities and huge responsibilities.
   - He was betrayed by men he trusted.
   - He was wronged in a business deal.
   - He suddenly lost his family, friends, and finances.
   - He was tempted and failed miserably.
   - He was painfully chastised and then restored.
   - He had to suffer the inevitable consequences of his sin.
   - He had to come to terms with old age and impending death.

Can you identify with any of these lonely trials? In 2 Corinthians 1:3–5, what does God want to accomplish through you as a result of your suffering?

STUDY GUIDE QUESTIONS | 403

2. In Psalm 59, David recorded his three-step pathway through loneliness when Saul sent men to watch his house in order to kill him: (1) vv. 1–8; (2) vv. 9–15; and (3) vv. 16–17. Briefly describe each of those steps.

    Do you see how those steps represent God's pathway to victory in any trial?

3. Follow this chapter's admonition to personalize Psalm 59 for yourself. Adapt these prayers by expanding them with your specific needs for God's defense, mercy, protection, rule, and refuge. Be sure to read the verses before you pray.

    - Verse 9: Pray, "Be **my** defense."
    - Verse 10: Pray, "Deliver mercy to **me**."
    - Verse 11: Pray, "Be **my** shield."
    - Verse 13: Pray, "Rule over **my** life."
    - Verses 16–17: Pray, "Be **my** refuge in times of trouble."

4. Psalm 11 is about faith in the Lord's righteousness; and Psalm 64 is about the oppression of the wicked. Which verse from each psalm most clearly expresses the song's theme? Which verses seem to hold the greatest promise of God's comfort? Highlight those verses in your Bible, and then turn to them in lonely times.

5. This chapter mentions three verses about the Lord's presence:

    - "*I am with you always, even to the end of the age*" (MATTHEW 28:20).
    - "*My Presence will go with you, and I will give you rest*" (EXODUS 33:14).
    - "*Call His name Immanuel,*" which is translated, "*God with us*" (MATTHEW 1:23).

    Memorize at least one of these verses. Meditate on the verse(s) whenever you are feeling all alone.

6. Here are some practical things you can do to resist loneliness:

    - Meditate on truths about the Lord (like the verses in question 5 above).
    - Resist false guilt; remind God of your need to be reassured of His presence.
    - Change the changeable, such as your attitude about your circumstances. (See COLOSSIANS 3:1; 1 THESSALONIANS 5:16–18.)

What other truths have you learned about the Lord upon which you can meditate? Do you ever experience episodes of false guilt? If so, what kinds? How can that guilt be resisted? Is there anything about your attitude toward loneliness that God wants changed?

CHAPTER 7: HOW TO SURVIVE AN UNEXPECTED JOB LOSS

1. If you've ever faced sudden unemployment, you should be able to identify with how David felt during his very trying time. After all, he'd always been a hard worker, his whole financial and family security was tied to his job, and then God threw him a "curve ball." Read Psalm 52:1b to see how David "hit a home run" for "God's team" by how he responded to the Lord in his unexpected affliction. What was David's response?

2. In Psalm 52:2–4, David recorded that his enemy loved to use his razor-like tongue to destroy him. In each of the six phrases of verses 2–4, a different description of an evil use of the tongue was named. What are they?

   Later, David's son Solomon said this about the tongue: ***Death and life are in the power of the tongue*** (PROVERBS 18:21; cf. JAMES 3:6–10). What do you think Solomon meant by that? How might that biblical principle apply to your own situation?

3. While unemployed and feeling insecure, David learned that people can be mean and even take pleasure in hurting others. Read Psalm 52:5–7. What did David believe would happen to the wicked who do not make God their strength?

4. In Psalm 52:8, David testified to what will happen if you do make God your strength: *I am like a green olive tree in the house of God; I trust in the mercy of God forever and ever.* The phrase *"a green olive tree"* implies security and productivity. Reword this verse as an application to your present circumstance.

5. According to Psalm 52:9a, what can you depend upon while you are jobless? If you are currently unemployed, is your need for a job causing you to trust in yourself or in God?

Memorize Psalm 52:9b: *I will wait on Your name, for it is good.* Meditate on the truth that the Hebrew word translated *"wait"* actually means "hope that renews exhausted strength." Pray this verse often to the Lord, Who is *"good."*

6. If you've lost your job, perhaps you are concerned about your finances. Psalm 37:23–25, also written by David, is an encouraging passage to meditate upon.

   The steps of a good man are ordered by the LORD,
   And He delights in his way.
   Though he fall, he shall not be utterly cast down;
   For the LORD *upholds him with His hand.*
   I have been young, and now am old;
   Yet I have not seen the righteous forsaken,
   Nor his descendants begging bread.

   How many of the righteous had David seen forsaken? How many of the children of the righteous had to beg bread? Does this promise apply to you also?

7. If you are having difficulty finding a job, you probably have extra time on your hands. Have you prayed about using your spare time to bless others? For example, you could volunteer your skills to help out at your church. You might also volunteer to meet a need of an elderly or handicapped shut-in, to minister to a very ill person, to comfort someone recently bereaved, or to help out a struggling single parent. (Suggestions: paint or make repairs around the house, run an errand, provide a meal, help out with transportation to church, or just visit the lonely.) Simply ask God to guide you in preparing a "to do" list to accomplish specific blessings for those He places on your heart.

CHAPTER 8: HOW TO SURVIVE LIFE'S UNEXPECTED TWISTS

1. Just because you love and serve the Lord doesn't mean you will miss the storms and skids of life. Read Psalm 61:2. How did David handle feeling overwhelmed? What promises did God make in 1 Corinthians 10:13 and Philippians 4:6–7 for when you go through trials?

2. Psalm 56 was David's cry to God when he was imprisoned by the Philistines, his fearsome enemies. Have you wondered how David survived the intense loneliness of that horribly foreign place? Psalm 56 reveals that he made nine resolves.

    - Three times David resolved to trust in God (vv. 3, 4b, 11a).
    - Three times David resolved to praise God's Word (vv. 4a, 10a, 10b).
    - Twice David resolved to not fear or become afraid (vv. 4c, 11b).
    - Once David declared, *God is for me* (v. 9).

    Personalize David's resolves by combining his three choices plus the declaration in verse 9 into one sentence expressing your own faith in the Lord.

3. What phrase did David repeat in verses 4 and 10? In troublesome times, what did he find to praise God about? If you are experiencing troublesome times, make a list of things for which you too can praise the Lord.

4. David Livingstone drew great comfort from David's courage in Psalm 56. During a fearful time when Livingstone was tempted to abandon his calling, he recalled Psalm 56:3: ***Whenever I am afraid, I will trust in You.*** Memorize this verse, and meditate upon it. Resist Satan by praying this verse when he hurls his fiery darts of fear at you.

5. It is enriching to see how an Old Testament truth is quoted in the New Testament. Compare the New Testament verses below with their Psalm 56 counterparts.

    - Read Hebrews 13:6 (cf. PSALM 56:4, 11). What can you boldly say because of Christ?
    - Read Romans 8:31 (cf. PSALM 56:9). Which of your enemies do you need to fear?
    - Read John 8:12 (cf. PSALM 56:13). What promise did Jesus make in this verse?

6. When David escaped from Gath, he had bottomed out emotionally. Yet, even though he had acted out of fear before King Achish, David knew God was watching and understood how greatly he needed deliverance. His heart for the Lord, even in tribulation, is clearly seen in these phrases from Psalm 34:

I will bless the LORD at all times (v. 1a).

Oh, magnify the LORD with me (v. 3a).

I sought the LORD (v. 4a).

This poor man cried out (v. 6a).

Oh, taste and see that the LORD is good (v. 8a).

Oh, fear the LORD! (v. 9a).

The eyes of the LORD are on the righteous (v. 15a).

The LORD redeems the soul of His servants (v. 22a).

Which of these phrases best captures your own heart toward God when facing unending struggles? Are you remembering to comfort others with the same comfort God has given you in your trials? (See 2 CORINTHIANS 1:3–4.)

CHAPTER 9: HOW TO OVERCOME FEELINGS OF BEING ABANDONED BY GOD

1. As a believer, regardless of the extent of your spiritual maturity, it is possible to reach a point so low that you feel everyone—even God— has abandoned you. That was David's desperate condition when he wrote Psalm 13. In verses 1–2, what two words were repeated four times to express the anguish of his soul? Have you ever cried out in anguish to the Lord as David did? If so, how did God respond?

2. David frankly admitted to God that he felt abandoned by Him. There is no shame in telling God you doubt Him, as long as you express those doubts in order to ask for wisdom and faith. Read James 1:2–7. What is God's view of trials? What does He promise to give you when you ask Him? What does He say about doubting?

3. To rise above the downward pull of his emotions, all David had to do was to look up and talk to the Lord—the One he thought had abandoned him. Rather than give in to anxiety, which is nothing more than meditating on problems, David chose to turn to the Lord for His solution. Read Joshua 1:8 to find the secret to making your way prosperous and successful. What is it?

4. To habitually look up to God rather than down at your troubles, learn to praise the Lord in every circumstance. The verses below were penned by David during difficult times. Select one or more of them to memorize and meditate upon. Whenever you are tempted to focus on your troubles rather than God, recite the verse(s) in praise to the Lord.

> *The LORD is my shepherd; … I will fear no evil; for You are with me (PSALM 23:1, 4).*

> *To You, O my Strength, I will sing praises; for God is my defense, my God of mercy (PSALM 59:17).*

> *In the LORD I put my trust; how can you say to my soul, "Flee as a bird to your mountain?" (PSALM 11:1).*

> *The righteous shall be glad in the LORD, and trust in Him (Psalm 64:10).*

> *I will wait on Your name, for it is good (PSALM 52:9).*

> *Whenever I am afraid, I will trust in You (PSALM 56:3).*

> *Oh, taste and see that the LORD is good; blessed is the man who trusts in Him! (PSALM 34:8).*

> *I will sing to the LORD, because He has dealt bountifully with me (PSALM 13:6).*

5. Prayer was David's turning point when he felt dejected and abandoned. Look at Psalm 34:4: *I sought the LORD, and He heard me, and delivered me from all my fears.* In Psalm 13:1–2, David cried out four times to God because He was so silent, and then he prayed: *Consider and hear me, O LORD my God; enlighten my eyes* (v. 3). In Psalm 13:6 he concluded: *I will sing to the LORD, because he has dealt bountifully with me.* Even David, the man after God's heart, had to learn that the Lord answers prayers in one of three ways: "Yes," "No," or "Wait."

Read 1 John 5:14–15. What guideline has God given you regarding the type of prayers He will hear and grant? Did David's prayers in Psalm 34 and 13 meet this requirement? Do your own prayers reflect God's standard?

CHAPTER 10: HOW TO GET OUT OF THE PITS OF LIFE

1. When David allowed his mind and emotions to rule over his spirit, he descended into despondency and began living life in the pits. Even though coming back to God didn't instantly solve all his problems, it did provide the pathway and solution needed. Read Psalm 40:1–3. As David waited patiently for the Lord, in what ways did God show His pathway back to Him? Will He do the same for you?

2. In Psalm 40:4–5, David voiced His renewed trust in God as he remembered all His wonderful works. Reflect back on all the Lord has done for you, and then reaffirm your own trust in the Lord.

3. Psalm 40:6–8 and Hebrews 10:5–9 can help us better understand Psalm 40. The writer of Hebrews revealed that 40:6–8 contained a promise of Christ in the Old Testament, which the Lord Jesus fulfilled: *I delight to do Your will, O my God, and Your law is within my heart* (v. 8). If you are in the pits right now, nothing can keep you there if you desire to do God's will with all your heart. So invite the Lord to help you remove any hindrances in the way of renewing your submission to Him.

4. As David looked back over his life of loneliness, desperation, sorrow, and fear, one truth clearly stood out as he was inspired to pen Psalm 40:9–12: God is righteous. The main New Testament book on righteousness is Romans, which identifies these vital areas that matter for eternity:

    - **God is righteous** in declaring us as hopeless in our **sin** (CH. 1–2).
    - **God is righteous** in providing for our **salvation** (CH. 3–5, 9–11).
    - **God is righteous** in demanding our **sanctification** (CH. 6–8).
    - **God is righteous** in bestowing gifts for our **service** (CH. 12–16).

    Think about this: Can there ever be an area of your life where you can justly claim that God isn't being righteous in how He is dealing with you? How should that affect your response to Him in tough times?

5. Psalm 40:13–17 reveals that life was so bad that David cried out to God to hasten to help him, yet he could still rejoice in the Lord while in the pits. The bottom line in life is this: Whom do you want

to please? Either you are striving to please God or seeking to please yourself. One way or another you will get what you really want. What do you *really* want?

6. Psalm 113 shows how to pray and praise the Lord in all circumstances. God wants you to pray and praise systematically, reverently, confidently, humbly, and meditatively. Real victory will come each time you respond to troubles in a way that exalts God through whatever He chooses to do with you in the pits of life. For as David said, **Blessed is that man who makes the LORD his trust** (Psalm 40:4). How do you think God wants you to apply that verse to your own life?

CHAPTER 11: LIVING LIFE SUCCESSFULLY IN A CAVE OF TROUBLES

1. When David arrived at the cave of Adullam, he entered an emotional and physical furnace of adversity. Soon he was babysitting more than four hundred malcontents day and night. In 1 Samuel 22:1–4, God identified three types of men who came to David for help. Name the three types.

2. Even though David had just come out of living life in the pits, he was called by God to live and work with this crowd of cantankerous, needy men who had invaded his life. This proved to be the turning point in David's life—the time when his character was refined more than in any other period. Read Psalm 57:1. What was David's response to what God chose to do with him in this calamitous time?

3. To teach David how to conquer his problems and at the same time minister to the needs of these desperate men, the Holy Spirit came upon him to write down the secret to overcoming afflictions while not letting his own life and emotions be dragged down by others who were suffering. Read 57:7 to find the key to victory in such situations. What is that key?

4. A heart to minister when engulfed in hard times is a heart that is *"steadfast"* (NKJV) or *"fixed"* (KJV). Because David's heart was anchored in the Lord, he was now prepared to meet the needs of others. Never forget that God comforts in tribulation to equip you to

comfort others. Read 2 Corinthians 1:6–7. Do you see how these verses reflect the type training God gave David in his "Cave of Troubles"? Are you sensing that the Holy Spirit has been teaching you similarly?

5. When we are at our depths, God is inviting us to His heights! As Romans 5:3–4 states, we should *glory in tribulations, knowing that tribulation* [trouble] *produces perseverance* [patience]; *and perseverance,* [proven] *character; and character, hope* [unshakable confidence in Jesus Christ]. Read James 1:2–4. Do you see the similarity between these passages in Romans and James? Why is it possible to *"glory in tribulations"* and *"count it all joy"* when enduring trials?

6. While living in the cave of Adullam, David came to grips with the fact there is another dimension the world generally doesn't see: living in a "Cave of Troubles" is an ongoing spiritual warfare. The Apostle Paul thus warned believers to **never** *give place to the devil* (Ephesians 4:27). Read Ephesians 6:10–13; memorize and meditate upon verses 10–11 as a reminder of what you must do to keep strong in the Lord.

CHAPTER 12: THE CERTAINTY OF GOD'S CONSEQUENCE ENGINE

1. After his "Cave of Troubles" period, David went on to the most fruitful years of his life with an unbroken string of spiritual and material triumphs. By Psalm 57 he had learned this important law of the spiritual universe: *there is an unavoidable consequence for every act.* Read Galatians 6:7–9. Memorize and meditate upon this passage as a reminder that every choice you make will reap some type of consequence. What does God promise if you persevere in *"doing good"*?

2. The Lord always rewards good and punishes evil. He continually takes note of everything going on; nothing escapes God's notice—especially a person's motives. Read 1 Corinthians 4:5. Is it possible for you to accurately know why others do things? Does God see every person's heart motive? Will He eventually deal with wrong motives?

3. Galatians 6:7 clearly points out that *whatever a man sows, that he will also reap.* Both halves of this verse impact all of us. For example, perhaps you are still reaping the long-term consequences of past bad

choices. And yet, as a forgiven sinner you are probably also sowing to the Spirit for a future positive harvest. Are you consistently sowing to your *"flesh"* or *"to the Spirit"* (Galatians 6:8). What does Galatians 6:8 say are the consequences of each choice?

4. Like negative consequences, the effects of the positive consequence engine at work in your life will not usually show up immediately. So then, when will the biggest payoff for a faithful follower of Christ actually happen? (See Matthew 6:19–21.)

5. You only have two choices in life: pleasing God or pleasing self. You also have only two building materials: what will last and what will not. Only positive choices energized by the grace of God and His Spirit will produce lasting building materials. Read 1 Corinthians 3:13–15. If you are a born-again Christian, what will happen if your works endure God's test by fire? Will you lose your salvation if your works are burned up?

6. In God's sight, there is nothing at all in you (in your natural life) which is able to please Him. But as a believer, since your old self died with Christ, through Christ's indwelling power you can now live in a way pleasing to God. Read and meditate upon Galatians 2:20. Ask the Lord for His divine grace to live victoriously for His glory!

CHAPTER 13: LIFE IN THE MINOR KEY: IS DEPRESSION SIN?

1. Like David, as well as most of us, the men named below were all spirit-filled saints who struggled with negative emotions. Consider these confessions:

   - **Moses:** *"I am not able to bear all these people alone, because the burden is too heavy for me"* (Numbers 11:14).
   - **Elijah:** *"It is enough! Now, LORD, take my life!"* (1 Kings 19:4).
   - **Hezekiah:** When facing a terminal illness *he turned his face toward the wall ...* [and] *wept bitterly* (2 Kings 20:2a, 3b).
   - **Job:** *"Why did I not die at birth? Why did I not perish when I came from the womb?"* (Job 3:11).
   - **Ezra:** *My soul clings to the dust; revive me according to Your Word* (Psalm 119:25).

- **Jeremiah:** *"See, O Lᴏʀᴅ, that I am in distress; my soul is troubled; my heart is overturned within me"* (Lamentations 1:20).
- **Jonah:** *"It is better for me to die than to live"* (Jonah 4:8).
- **Paul:** *Our flesh had no rest but we were afflicted on every side: conflicts without, fears within* (2 Corinthians 7:5 NASB).

Without exception, each of them found the same cure for depression that Ezra sought in Psalm 119:25. What was it?

2. David was at the depth of loneliness after being on the run for years and having to hide in a desolate cave with a crowd of malcontents. He could have either wallowed in self-pity and sin or used his time alone to grow in the Lord. David chose God's way; and the Holy Spirit inspired him to write Psalm 142. Read verses 1–2. What was the very first thing David did? In verse 2, what did he do next? Did you note how freely he told the Lord what was troubling him?

3. Read Psalm 142:3–4, which contains common symptoms of depression during hard times. What are they? If you have been troubled with despondency, here are some practical steps to help you break free:

   - **Deal with sin**. Read Ephesians 4:27 and 1 John 1:9. Are you applying these truths daily? Is something blocking your fellowship with the Lord that you need to repent of?
   - **Share your burdens with the Lord**. Read Psalm 103:14; 55:22; 1 Peter 5:7. Could there ever be anything in your life that God doesn't care about?
   - **Abandon self-pity**. Read Luke 9:23. Ask the Lord to help you *run with endurance the race that is set before* [you], *looking unto Jesus, the author and finisher of* [your] *faith* (Hebrews 12:1–2).

4. When David felt abandoned by everyone, he drew closer to God and declared: *I cried out to You, O Lᴏʀᴅ: I said, "You are my refuge"* (Psalm 142:5). Suddenly, David knew that, because GOD cared for him, the Lord was his way out of his despondency and troubles. Upon whom or what are you depending when you feel overwhelmed? Are you using your times of feeling alone to draw closer to God? Have you been praying Psalm 142:5 back to the Lord?

5. Read Psalm 142:6–7. When David appealed to the Lord for deliverance in his afflictions, what reason did he give for such a plea? Was it merely for personal relief from his distress? Or for a far greater purpose?

6. Rather than give in to depression, God wants to help you take your focus off yourself and reach out to other Christians by sharing burdens and praying for one another. Read 1 Thessalonians 5:14–22. Ask the Lord for divine grace to implement such a ministry in your own life— regardless of your circumstances.

CHAPTER 14: THERE ARE NO SUPERSAINTS

1. There are no Supersaints. God's greatest servants—men like David, Elijah, and Paul—were made of the same stuff we are. Their greatness was *of God*, and not of themselves. Read John 15:5; 1 Corinthians 1:26–31. Personalize those verses by writing a paraphrase of how they apply to your own walk with the Lord.

2. David and his men delivered the city of Keilah from the Philistines, but the inhabitants informed Saul, so he sought David daily. Read the end of verse 14 in 1 Samuel 23. What phrase identifies God's sovereignty at work in this situation? Now read Ephesians 1:11–12; Romans 8:28. What do these verses tell you about God's sovereignty? Do you look for and gratefully acknowledge His sovereign hand at work in your life?

3. The Ziphites betrayed David, and his small army was being encircled by Saul's, but God saw to it that Saul had to leave to fight the Philistines. After escaping to the Wilderness of En Gedi, David penned Psalm 54 to thank God for deliverance. Memorize and meditate upon verse 6b. Are you likewise remembering to praise God continually— telling Him that He is GOOD—even when life *seems* bad?

4. The Ziphites again made David's whereabouts known, and Saul "happened" to wander into a cave, not knowing of David's presence. Because David spared his life, the king returned home. In Psalm 35 David presented his just case before a righteous Judge, going from complaints to prayer to praise. Read Psalm 35:27–28. At the end of verse 27, how did David refer to himself? In verse 28, what was David's response to God's intervention on his behalf?

5. Nabal paid back David's good with evil, and David became angry. But God delivered David from that temptation, and he was inspired to write Psalm 53—how to overcome feelings of loneliness when tempted to be bitter over being hurt in a business deal. Read 53:1–3. In light of this passage, should it surprise you if you are likewise wronged or otherwise mistreated?

6. Saul's "cat and mouse" pursuit continued until David once again spared Saul's life. Afterward David fled in fear to Gath and made a deal with Achish to live in Ziklag in exchange for making raids on the king's enemies. But after the Amalekites burned Ziklag and captured the wives and children of David and his men, his army became so grieved they threatened to kill him. According to 1 Samuel 30:6, what did David do in this crisis? Where do you instinctively turn when facing a crisis?

7. Psalm 16:11 is a beautiful expression of David's absolute confidence in the Lord. He discovered three precious things about God. What are they? How does that verse apply to your life?

8. David's lament in Psalm 39 over sin and the brevity of life was intense. Hebrews 12:5–6 points out that God's chastening of us is out of love. What does God tell us in Hebrews 12:11 about His purpose for chastening?

CHAPTER 15: THE GIANT THAT SLEW DAVID WAS LUST

1. Far more dangerous than the Goliath David faced as a teenager, the giant Lust had crept into David's own inner chambers. In a moment, blinded by his own selfish desires, when his guard was down, David was slain. Note again the five dreadful steps downward that led to his disastrous fall:

   - David *desensitized* his conscience by incomplete obedience.
   - David *relaxed* his grip on personal purity.
   - David *fixed* his heart on physical desires.
   - David *rationalized* in his mind about wrong decisions.
   - David *plunged* his life into lustful sin.

   Read 1 Peter 5:8; 1 Corinthians 10:12. In light of these verses, is it possible that David's downward spiral into sin could happen to you? What might you be doing that would make you more vulnerable to temptation?

2. Read through the "Jesus, the Radical" article in chapter 15. Ask the Holy Spirit to convict you of any areas in your life that may be warning signs of slippage in your walk with the Lord. Make a list of those areas, and then pray for divine grace to overcome each of them.

3. Lust is dreadful, dangerous, and deadly. Lust surrounds us in the twenty-first century and, in various forms, is planted within us. Lust is either pursued for pleasure or fled from for righteousness. If you nurture youthful lusts, they will chase you for a lifetime. Read and memorize 2 Timothy 2:22. What does God expect of you?

4. Life for the Christian is a continual spiritual warfare, so never let your guard down. Read 2 Corinthians 10:3–5. The mighty weapon that can tear down Satan's *"strongholds"* is **the sword of the Spirit, which is the word of God** (Ephesians 6:17). And at the end of verse 5, the Apostle Paul gave the secret to prevent *rationalizing* in your mind about wrong decisions. What is it?

5. David plunged his life into lustful sin because he forgot to do what he had done in the past, wrote of in the past, and rejoiced over in the past.

   - **David forgot to look for God.** Read 1 Corinthians 10:13. What promise did God make that would have given David victory over his temptation? How does that apply to your own struggles?
   - **David forgot to use God's Word.** Read Matthew 4:1–11. How did Jesus combat the attacks of the devil? Does He want you to do the same? What spiritual discipline is necessary to win such a victory?
   - **David forgot to run from lust.** Read 2 Samuel 12:9–10. Because of David's sin, what was his lifelong consequence? Read Galatians 6:7. Is it ever possible to evade God's consequence engine? So then, how should you live?

CHAPTER 16: HOW TO FLEE THE LUSTS OF THE FLESH

1. When you began to read through chapter 16, did you stop and honestly ask yourself these questions?

   - Do I flee the lusts of the flesh—or show interest and good will toward what God hates?

- Am I emotionally attached to anything God hates?
- Do I have affection for something utterly opposed to Him?
- Do I look upon the devil's world of rebellion and lusts that are hostile toward God with interest, for entertainment, or for pleasure?
- Are God's enemies my favored companions?

Ephesians 5:3 captures God's heart on this topic so clearly: *But among you there must not be even a hint of sexual immorality, or of any kind of impurity, or of greed, because these are improper for God's holy people* (NIV). Read 1 Peter 1:15–16. What does God command of His children?

2. Go back and prayerfully re-read the very blunt magazine article at the beginning of this chapter. As you read, ask the Holy Spirit to examine your life and point out any areas in which you may have become ensnared and don't realize it. Now read Romans 12:1–2. What does God want you to do next?

3. Through examples in Scripture God has revealed what can happen if you remain a friend of the world. Samson was a classic example of that because he lived as a "lover of pleasure rather than lover of God" and the Lord had to chastise him severely. In Judges 16:20, Samson was over-confident and succumbed to Delilah's temptation because he was unaware of what the Lord had done. What was it?

4. When the power of God's presence seems missing, it is wise to examine your life to see whether you have been ensnared by an ungodly world view. For instance, have any of these thoughts ever crept into your mind?

- Look out for Number One!
- Don't get mad—get even!
- You only go around once—so go for the gusto!
- If it feels good—DO it!
- Everyone else is doing it, why shouldn't I?

Read Ephesians 4:25–30. What are some worldly characteristics that grieve the Holy Spirit? Now read verses 31–32. What is the way to avoid grieving the Holy Spirit by acting like the world?

5. Read 1 Corinthians 3:9–15. Meditate often on this passage as a

reminder that one day the fires of God's judgment will examine your works. Only what you've done for Christ will last. Upon what foundation are you building?

6. How can you be the friend of God and therefore an enemy of the world, the flesh, and the devil? If you want to enjoy unbroken peace with God instead of war, follow these steps:

   - **Submit to God** (James 4:7). Are you keeping any area of your life back from God? If so, there will always be battles. Don't forget Paul's caution in Ephesians 4:27!
   - **Draw near to God** (James 4:8). How does verse 8 say to do this?
   - **Humble yourself before God** (James 4:9–10). Read James 4:6; Proverbs 6:16–17a. What does God think of pride? In James 4:10, what does God promise to do if you humble yourself?

7. If you obey God's instructions in James 4:7–10, God promises to draw near to you, cleanse you, and forgive you. You will not be at war with God, nor will you be at war with yourself or others. Read Isaiah 32:17 to discover the long-term fruit of such obedience.

CHAPTER 17: HOW TO SING THE SONG OF A SOUL SET FREE

1. All that really matters in life is this reality: What does God think of what you are doing, or have done? In 2 Samuel 11:27, God clearly recorded what he thought of David's horribly disobedient choices regarding Bathsheba and Uriah. He probably fell into sin because he neglected to pray Psalm 139:23–24, as he used to. What was that prayer? Does the spirit of David's prayer represent your own heart toward the Lord?

2. When David let his guard down, he no longer walked in the Light or delighted in the joy of his salvation. What went wrong? David was hiding his sin. Read Proverbs 28:13. What does God say will happen if you try to hide your sin? What will happen if you confess and forsake your sin?

3. As David desperately struggled with attacks from within and without, he poured his lonely heart out to the Lord in Psalm 38—an intense lament over the awful sin for which he was being chastised. For a summary of the anguish David felt, read Psalm 38:1, 4, 6, 8, 17–18,

21–22. Do you see how his suffering is a powerful warning to beware of allowing unguarded moments in your life—thinking you are safe out of sin's reach?

4. After David confessed to and repented of the horrible pit of sin he had been covering up, he wrote a song about what it means to return to God and receive, experience, and possess His forgiveness. Thus Psalm 32 could be called "The Song of a Soul Set Free"—an expression of David's initial gratitude of liberation and relief of forgiveness. Read Psalm 32:1–2. Is the Holy Spirit speaking to your heart about anything for which you need forgiveness?

5. In Psalm 32:3–4 David sang in despair over how terrible it felt when his sins were concealed. In fact, his concealed sin actually sickened him. Read verse 5 to find out how he was delivered when he took personal responsibility for his sin. If you are suffering from health problems, could it be related to hidden sin in your life? If so, what does God want you to do about it?

6. Read Psalm 32:8. What did God promise to do for David? Will He do the same for you?

7. According to Psalm 32:10–11, what valuable life lesson had David learned through what he suffered because of his sin against God? Have you experienced this same grace in your own life?

CHAPTER 18: THE MIRACLE OF COMPLETE FORGIVENESS

1. Prior to writing Psalm 32, David wondered: *In light of my horrendous sin, is complete forgiveness even possible?* Under the Holy Spirit's inspiration, he gave a joyful conclusion in Psalm 32:1–2. Memorize and meditate upon these verses. If you have sin you've been covering up, I exhort you to confess and forsake it now. (Should Satan ever try to put a guilt trip on you because of confessed and forgiven sin, resist him by quoting these verses.)

2. How could the Lord justly grant complete forgiveness for David's awful sin regarding Bathsheba and Uriah? Read Ephesians 1:7 and Romans 8:1–2 to find out why. Does this apply to you as well?

3. In Christ all sins—past, present, and future—are forgiven forever, and all guilt and penalties are permanently removed. In Him you will stand totally guiltless and holy for the rest of eternity. However, when you sin, God expects you to follow 1 John 1:9 to stay in fellowship with Him. What does He say you need to do?

4. No matter how severe the sin, God can forgive it. In Psalm 86, David again testified of the Lord's readiness to forgive. Read Psalm 86:5. Note David's reference to God being *"good."* Have you realized just how many times David stated that truth in songs throughout his endless struggles? Is the goodness of God the theme of your heart as well?

5. What awaits you in the future if you have experienced the miracle of complete forgiveness? Hebrews 12 tells of these precious realities:

   - Because you're forgiven, you will enter the city with foundations.
   - Because you're forgiven, you will see countless angels.
   - Because you're forgiven, you will join the saints of all time.
   - Because you're forgiven, you will be with Almighty God.
   - Because you're forgiven, you will at last be perfected.
   - Because you're forgiven, you will be with Jesus your Savior.
   - Because you're forgiven, you will finally enjoy His ultimate complete forgiveness!

   Since Jesus paid it all on your behalf, what does Revelation 3:5 say He will do when you are led by Christ's nail-scarred hand to meet your heavenly Father?

CHAPTER 19: DAVID'S ROAD MAP: THE PATHWAY BACK TO GOD

1. Only God could relieve David's cold, distant, lonely tormented heart by granting complete forgiveness and restoring his joy, peace, and security. Hence Psalm 51 is about David coming back to God. Read Psalm 51:1–4. What was his first step toward restoration of fellowship with God? Read Luke 18:13. Do you see a parallel between the tax collector's response and David's?

2. When David took personal responsibility for his sin in Psalm 51:5–9, he was taking the next step toward restoration. Which verse reveals that he recognized having a sin nature since birth? What did David say was the remedy for sin?

3. Did it surprise you to learn that when David sinned with Bathsheba he was breaking all of God's Ten Commandments? Read James 2:10. Based upon this verse, does the Lord consider the breaking of any particular commandment as more grievous than the others? Or is all sin equally offensive to a righteous God?

4. Psalm 51:10 clearly expresses David's belief that only the Lord could cleanse and restore him: *Create in me a clean heart, O God, and renew a steadfast* ["right" – KJV] *spirit within me.* The word translated *"steadfast"* in verse 10 (Hebrew *kuwn* – Strong's #3559) is the same word translated *"steadfast"* in Psalm 57:7: *My heart is steadfast* ["fixed" – KJV], *O God, my heart is steadfast; I will sing and give praise* (Psalm 57:7).

   Do you recall that Psalm 57 was a turning point in David's life because of how greatly God refined his character during his "Cave of Troubles" period? Why do you think the Holy Spirit inspired David to use the same key word in Psalm 51:10 as he did in Psalm 57:7? What did David need most in his life? Do you need this too?

5. Read Psalm 51:12–13. What did David desperately pray for in his time of need? Did David expect God to develop a ministry in him after his fellowship was restored with the Lord? What biblical principle applies to your own life as well?

6. The final step to restore fellowship with his beloved Lord was to earnestly seek Him and repent. Read Psalm 51:14–19, especially noting verse 17. What spirit in David was proof of his genuine repentance? Compare verse 51:17 with James 4:7–10. Has your heart been staying tender toward God, or have you strayed from the Lord's path? If the latter is true, what spirit does God want to see in you?

7. In Psalm 51:18–19 David was essentially saying, "God, now that I am back with You, I am going to zealously bring my offerings to You—not as a token, but from a true and steadfast heart." So David then freely praised and worshiped the God who had been more than life itself to him!

Let's review the steps he took back to God:

- David acknowledged that all sin is against God (Psalm 51:1–4).
- David took personal responsibility for his sin (Psalm 51:5–9).
- David believed that only God could cleanse and restore him (Psalm 51:10–13).
- David sought God and repented (Psalm 51:14–19).

If your heart has been cold, dull, burdened, and distant, will you now follow the same path David took to restore the joy of his salvation?

CHAPTER 20: OVERCOMING PERSONAL ATTACKS AND ABUSE

1. When David penned Psalm 51, it was not only in the joy of assured forgiveness, but also in painful remorse and agony. Read Psalm 51:4a to refresh your mind on how David grieved over the awfulness of his sin. But even though he was forgiven, he still had to endure painful consequences for the rest of his life. Read Psalm 51:4b. What was David's perspective on God's judgment of his sin?

2. Second Samuel 15:13–37 records that David wept as he fled from his son Absalom. And yet, he still *"worshiped God"* (v. 32). David's ultimate trust in the Lord, regardless of the circumstances, reminds me of Job. Read Job 13:15a. This God-inspired spirit of supreme confidence in the Lord was evidenced in both of these great saints. Will God give you similar confidence in difficult times?

3. David's responses to Shimei's attacks, slanders, and abuses in 2 Samuel 16 are a beautiful example of how to react in a godly manner when mistreated. Read 2 Samuel 16:10–12. Which verse reveals David's sweet submission to the will of God? How did David express hope that God might bring *"good"* out of his pain? Read Romans 8:28. What does the Lord promise to those who love God?

4. As David fled from Absalom, what came out of him in Psalm 3 revealed what was really inside of him, and it was so good that God forever recorded it in heaven. The uses of *"Selah"* in Psalm 3 made some very clear divisions which are the message points of this song.

- **Read Psalm 3:1–2**—Like David, you will face battlefields daily. Life is hard; sin is horrible; and many people are more than willing to harm others easily. That is why David said, "*Selah*—**Stop, look around, and think about your battle!**" What are your personal battlefields?

- **Read Psalm 3:3–4**—Like David, you will make choices. Sin will beat you down, but God will always lift you up. Others may ignore you, but God will always answer you. So David said, "*Selah*—**Stop and look at this. Let that truth settle down in your heart.**" Where is your focus? On God, or on your troubles? Remember: *Anxiety* is "meditating on your problems," but *peace* is "believing His promises."

- **Read Psalm 3:5–8**—Like David, you need sleep. Sleep not only refreshes and renews but also reminds you that God is God, and you are not. For sleep is when you relax fully because you no longer need to take care of yourself. Thus David said, "*Selah*—**Stop and consider this. Sleep is lying secure in God's peace.**" So then, as you drift off to sleep lift your heart in worship to the God who holds your soul in the sweet comfort of lying secure in His arms!

5. Psalm 63 was likely penned as a song of worship in the hostile desert when chased by his son Absalom. David used every tense of life to describe his loving pursuit of the Lord Who completely satisfied him. Read Psalm 63:3. Memorize and meditate upon this key verse which essentially teaches that **life is good—but God is better!**

   If you truly believe that God's love is *"better than life,"* how should that affect how you spend our time? Have you committed to a lifelong personal pursuit of worshiping and loving God?

CHAPTER 21: LIVING DELIBERATELY FOR GOD— NO COASTING ALLOWED

1. When David disengaged his heart from following hard after God, he *coasted spiritually* because his passion was no longer in the Lord. But after his repentance and restoration, he changed. Read Psalm 31:1a. Those eight words reflect David's personal resolve, which is why God

thought so highly of him. In whom or what do you trust? Based on what they've observed in your life, how would your family and friends answer that question about you?

2. Psalm 31 is likely David's reflective song about his choice to return to God and deliberately build upon lessons learned in his triumphs and failures. Verses 1–8 reflect his running-from-Saul years when David discovered that he could safely rest only in God. Read verses 2–4. What graphic pictures did he use to symbolize why the Lord was a safe Refuge in times of desperation? Do you view God that way when going through tough times?

3. Read Psalm 31:5a. Under what circumstances were those words spoken in the New Testament? Read Luke 24:6a. Why were those words so crucial to your salvation? (See 1 Corinthians 15:17–22.)

4. In Psalm 31:9–11, David was looking back on his not-running-from-Bathsheba year. Read verses 9–11, and then list ways he suffered as a result of his sin. Was his moment of stolen pleasure worth what he reaped because of it?

5. The lessons David learned in his running-from-Absalom years are recorded in Psalm 31:12–22. In verse 13, he confessed that *"fear is on every side"*—and then expressed the remedy for fear in verses 14–15a. What was it? Are you likewise confident that every part of your life is held by God?

6. Read Psalm 31:19. Which phrase best depicts David's consistent heart attitude toward God in the psalms he penned during his unending struggles? Do you agree with David even in your hard times?

7. The last two verses of Psalm 31 are different than verses 1–22 where David addressed the Lord. He concluded by challenging other believers to learn from both his triumphs and failures. Read Psalm 31:23–24. As you read, note these challenges:

    - Love the Lord like I do (v. 23).
    - Trust the Lord like I do (v. 23b).
    - Fear the Lord like I do (v. 23c).
    - Wait for the Lord like I am (v. 24a).
    - Hope in the Lord like I will (v. 24b).

If you've been coasting spiritually by feeding your soul on yesterday's blessings, last week's devotions, and last month's ministry, are you now ready to choose a new focus for your spiritual life by living deliberately for God—no coasting allowed?

CHAPTER 22: ENDING WELL— LIVING PURPOSEFULLY FOR GOD

1. As the clay pot, the tent we live in, cracks and tears, God wants the treasure of Christ within us to spill out to encourage others in their own unending struggles. What does 2 Corinthians 4:7 say is our only source of strength to live and die this way?

2. Twenty-seven hundred years ago, when Israel was in a steep decline and headed for national ruin, defeat, and deportation to Babylon, the prophet Habakkuk wrote one of the most hope-filled paragraphs in the Bible. Read Habakkuk 3:17–19. Do you see any parallel between Israel's dire situation then and the "doom and gloom" predictions of our own country's steep decline and national ruin? How does God want you to respond to an uncertain future—personally and nationally?

3. Finishing life by ending well is the result of a long term cultivation of godly habits. Psalm 71, a song of intentional abiding, contains comfort for the years ahead as well as some underlying resolves or purposes David had learned to live by. Read verses 1–13, which can help you view the present through the lens of God's Word. What biblical principles in these verses particularly apply to your own life situation?

4. Read Psalm 71:14–24. These verses can help you view the future through the lens of God's Word. What do you believe is David's overall theme of this passage? Which verses most reflect your own attitude toward the future?

5. Ending well has nothing to do with comfort, health, or security. It has everything to do with godly habits empowered by the Holy Spirit. What habits in David's life conformed to Matthew 4:4 and Hebrews 11:6? Are these evident in your own life?

CHAPTER 23: GRACEFULLY HEADING TOWARD HOME

1. Jesus said, *"Which of you by worrying can add one cubit* [about 18 inches] *to his stature?"* (Matthew 6:27). The Greek phrase *"add one cubit to his stature"* can also refer to adding time to one's lifespan. Because our length of days has been determined by God alone, there is nothing we can do to change the inevitable. Even Job understood this truth. Write a modern paraphrase by personalizing Job 14:5.

2. God said that *it is appointed for men to die once, but after this judgment* (Hebrews 9:27). However, through Christ's death on the cross, He has given us victory over *"the sting of death"* (1 Corinthians 15:56–57). Read Hebrews 2:14–15. What else did Jesus accomplish for us at Calvary?

3. As David gracefully headed toward home, he modeled how to end well.

   - David was **spiritually** prepared for death because he was certain about the destination of his soul. Upon what did he base this conviction?

   - David was **materially** prepared for death because he had gracefully surrendered the ownership of all his possessions to God. David's view of money reflected the condition of his heart. What does the way in which you manage the material possessions entrusted to you by the Lord say about what matters to you? Who would other people think owns your possessions, you or God?

   - David was **physically** prepared for death because he viewed it as an appointment with his Good Shepherd. Psalm 23:4–6 explains why he could be so secure, serene, and blessed. Upon what did he base his peace?

4. Have you pondered the direction your own life is taking? If you have regrets, what did the Apostle Paul say to do about them? To find the answer, read Philippians 3:13–14. Memorize these verses, and meditate upon them. Then, when Satan shoots his fiery darts of doubt or remorse at you, resist him by praying Philippians 3:13–14 back to God!

5. Like David, have you given careful thought to preparing for your home-going? What simple preparations can you make to be sure you are a special blessing to family and friends who stay behind after you've gone home to be with Jesus?

CHAPTER 24: EMBRACING GOD—A LONG OBEDIENCE IN SEEKING THE LORD

1. David's entire life was covered by God's grace (unmerited favor), proving that it doesn't take perfection to please God. But to please the Lord we do have to *experience* His grace—the grace that saves, the grace that forgives, and the grace that continually gives us new beginnings. David wrote Psalm 18 after reflecting back upon all God had meant to him. Take a moment to think about your own life, and then write a personal testimony of how the Lord has shown His marvelous grace to you.

2. When David suffered intense loneliness during his four challenging stages in life, the Holy Spirit inspired him to write thirty-one psalms to capture how Christ was his continual Refuge. Look again at this chapter's panorama of these big events and the selected verses from those psalms. If you are suffering from some similar experience(s), make a list of verses that especially minister to your heart. Memorize the verses, meditate upon them, and frequently pray them back to God to find renewed strength.

3. David's final recorded words, Psalm 18, began with a full-hearted expression of his love for God: *I will love You, O LORD, my strength* (v. 1). The word translated *"love"* is a rare verb form of a word group that expresses tender intimacy. It is the sole time in the Bible that this term for a "hugging, embracing love" was used by a person describing love for God. That is the kind of love Christ seeks from you.

   How is your spiritual temperature today? Are the fires of your passion for Christ burning brightly? Or have the embers cooled and you've lost your *"first love"* (Revelation 2:4)? What is *"first love"*?

   - *"First love"* will prompt you to patience—like the love experienced by Jacob as he labored seven years for his bride, Rachel (Genesis 29:20).

   - *"First love"* will prompt you to worship—like David's love that overflowed from the shepherd boy's heart into a worshipful psalm rather than complain about sitting out in the weather while his brothers stayed home (Psalm 19).

- *"First love"* will prompt you to give your treasures—like Mary of Bethany who broke the alabaster box of ointment and poured it out for Christ (Matthew 26:7).

- *"First love"* will prompt you to thanksgiving—like the woman who wept at Christ's feet, washed them with her tears, and wiped them with her hair (Luke 7:37).

- *"First love"* will prompt you to sit at Jesus' feet and just love Him—like Mary of Bethany when she worshiped at Christ's feet while Martha was "busy about the house" serving (Luke 10:38–41).

- *"First love"* will prompt you to love His coming—like Paul who longed for Christ's return, yet faithfully kept doing what Christ wanted him to accomplish (Philippians 1:21–26).

- *"First love"* will prompt you to love His Word—like the Berean Christians demonstrated by their insatiable desire to read and know God's Word (Acts 17:11).

Giving Christ the love and attention He desires is not only possible, but it is also essential if you are to avoid grieving His Holy Spirit. Write out an expression of your own love for the Lord, offering it to Him as an act of worship.

4. David was a man after God's heart because of his long obedience in seeking the Lord—deeply desiring to embrace the One Who was more than life itself to him. By the power of the Holy Spirit, David lived by Deuteronomy 6:5 (cf. Matthew 22:37; Luke 10:27). For an awesome blessing, memorize and meditate upon Deuteronomy 6:5; and then pray daily for the divine grace to love Christ as He seeks—and deserves—to be loved!

5. In writing, summarize your understanding of David's three-thousand-year-old spiritual secret of success in serving God's purposes in his own generation.

Bathsheba and The God of the Second Chance

Where sin abounded, grace abounded much more. —**Romans 5:20**

IN A STUDY OF THE life of David, God's servant, the woman Bathsheba clearly stands out in biblical history. She is not only mentioned in the Old Testament eleven times, but, for a very special purpose, her name is also recorded in the New Testament.

Out of the hundreds of women described in His Word, God has singled out and highlighted five mothers who have each been placed in the pathway through which Christ came. And Bathsheba is one of them.

Women weren't highly regarded in ancient times; they lived in a man's world. This fact made life very difficult for them. Yet, the Lord profiled these five courageous and gifted women because they were on God's team. Their lives were part of His plan to bring a ray of light to herald the sunrise on the night of sin that had come into our world. Through their line, the promised Savior was supernaturally born!

Have you ever studied the women whom God chose to surround Christ's coming to earth? I am talking about the highly unusual presence of five women included in His genealogy in Matthew 1. It is interesting that no women are listed in any of the genealogical records of the Old and New Testaments except for Matthew's. Here is the list of the five special mothers in the line awaiting the coming of the Promised One:

*The book of the genealogy of Jesus Christ, the Son of David, the Son of Abraham: Abraham begot Isaac, Isaac begot Jacob, and Jacob begot Judah and his brothers. Judah begot Perez and Zerah **by Tamar,** Perez begot Hezron, and Hezron begot Ram. Ram begot Amminadab, Amminadab begot Nahshon, and Nahshon begot Salmon. Salmon begot Boaz **by Rahab,** Boaz begot Obed **by Ruth,** Obed begot Jesse, and Jesse begot David the king. David the king begot Solomon **by her who had been the wife of Uriah.** ... And Jacob begot Joseph the husband of **Mary, of whom was born** Jesus who is called Christ* (MATTHEW 1:1–6, 16; emphasis added).

Just five women in a long list of genealogical records—Tamar, Rahab, Ruth, Bathsheba, and Mary—and all have something in common. Each was the subject of moral scandal; each of them would be what we may call "stained by sin."

Since we've been studying the life of David, our focus in this lesson will be upon *"her who had been the wife of Uriah"*—Bathsheba. Bathsheba is a Hebrew name that means "daughter of an oath, promise, or covenant." Don't you find it interesting that that name belonged to a woman who *didn't* keep her oath, promise, and covenant?

What first comes to mind when you hear the name Bathsheba? Most often, it is the sin of adultery David and Bathsheba committed against God and their marriage covenants, oaths, and promises. But did you also think of any of these consequences?

BECAUSE BATHSHEBA FAILED TO KEEP HER PROMISES—

- Her loyal and faithful husband Uriah, betrayed by the king he served, was left to die under a barrage of arrows.
- She had to watch the army of Israel bringing Uriah's body into Jerusalem after carrying him back the forty-four miles from where he fell in battle.
- She had to stand at the funeral for a fallen war hero and know that deep within her womb was the growing life whose conception prompted the murder of her own husband.
- A tiny grave held her infant son who died by God's judgment.
- In the years that followed, whenever a place or person reminded her of the youthful days of meeting and marrying Uriah—she painfully remembered afresh why he died.

When Bathsheba ("daughter of a promise") married Uriah ("the Lord is my light") they became a wonderful picture of all the best God offers in this life. But after one very bad choice, whenever we think of Bathsheba we are reminded that when we fail to keep our oaths, promises, and covenants—God does not.

Bathsheba will always remind us that there are dire and inescapable consequences for sin. Because she failed to keep her promises, she is forever associated with David and their sin. And because of the consequences that come from that sin, Bathsheba was stained and her life marred.

No Stain Is Too Deep for God's Grace

HAS GOD'S WORD STOPPED YOU yet and made you soberly think about where your life, habits, and secret thoughts are headed? Some people may think: *Oh, I could do that and no one would ever find out. We know how to cover our tracks!* But the Scriptures say that whatever you sow, you will reap (GALATIANS 6:7-8); and whatever you whisper in secret will be shouted from the rooftops (MATTHEW 10:27). That is clearly what happened to Bathsheba!

Some say that Bathsheba was simply in the wrong place at the wrong time. (See 2 Samuel 11 and 12 for her full story.) Even so, look at all these areas in which we could call her "defeated":

- She was unwise to have washed herself unclothed outside of her home.
- She was immodest in her display.
- She responded to David's interest in her, even though she was another man's wife and David was another woman's husband.
- She muffled her heart's warning as God's conviction was upon her conscience.
- She stifled the virtuous vows she made of lifelong loyalty to Uriah.
- She ignored the fact that God had given her a wonderful, courageous, and loyal warrior husband.
- She yielded herself to passion, and the sin that would follow.

Think again about what Bathsheba reaped from all that defeat. Her husband, Uriah, was murderously slain, and the baby she had conceived by David choked out his life in death. Bathsheba and David—the grieving, sorrowing mother and the murderous, adulterous father—faced great sadness. And, after Nathan spoke to David about his sin, the world would forever know that Bathsheba was a defeated woman; her sin became monumental for all time. In fact, even numerous movies have been made about her illicit romance, which was both public and shameful.

But is that the end of the story? No, for Bathsheba's name in the opening paragraph of the New Testament reminds us of the One Who came, as Paul says in Romans 5:20: *But where sin abounded, grace abounded much more.*

On this side of the cross, Bathsheba is a forgiven sinner and, according to God's perfect plan, she became a beautiful portrait of His grace, as we saw in Matthew 1:6: *David the king **begot Solomon by her** who had been the wife of Uriah* (emphasis added).

What did placing Bathsheba in Christ's genealogy do? God graciously lifted her out of her pit of defeat. Through that God was saying, "Here's a woman who is unworthy, who is a sinner. Though she's done many things wrong, I'm going to let her be one through whom I will bring Christ into this world." (God also poured out His grace upon David and Solomon, from whom we've received a great deal of our Scripture to learn about what it means to live wisely—to be someone after God's own heart.)

Jesus loves to forgive and cleanse. He is waiting today, as He was in Revelation 2–3, for us to hear His voice, repent of our sin, and let Him wash us clean. Revelation 1:5 says that Jesus wants us to know Him as the One Who *loved us, and washed us* [KJV] *and freed us* [NIV] *from our sins.* No stain of the past, no sin of our youth, no failure in our home or marriage is too deep for the God of the Second Chance.

No failures are permanent with Him. I therefore exhort you to take your burdens to the Lord right now; bow before Him, and start over. You may be estranged from your mother, father, children, or grandchildren—but Jesus can help. So bring that deep pain and sorrow to Him right where you are and place it at His feet. For the Christian life is simply a series of "start overs" offered freely to us from the God of New Beginnings.

The good news is that *God is able to make all grace abound toward you, that you, always having all sufficiency in all things, may have abundance for every good work* (2 CORINTHIANS 9:8). Regardless of your present circumstances, there is hope in Christ for the future! By God's grace, you can partake of "The Promise." You can trust Him, your Savior, to wash away whatever sin has been dragging you down—He will remove it as far as the east is from the west—so that He can look upon you in the righteousness of Christ!

As long as you trust Christ to be your strength, you will never walk alone! For, as Annie Johnson Flint (1866–1932) testified in "He Giveth More Grace":

His love has no limit; His grace has no measure,
His power has no boundary known unto men;
For out of His infinite riches in Jesus,
He giveth, and giveth, and giveth again! [197]

ENDNOTES

CHAPTER 1: *The Secret of Eternal Rewards*

1   This chapter is drawn from messages presented the morning and evening of 8 January 2006 plus the evening of 15 January 2008, which are parts 1, 2, and 3 of the David's Spiritual Secret series and parts 30, 31, and 32 of the Christ Our Refuge series. These messages are available in their entirety at http://www.dtbm.org.

2   Emphasis added to verses in this chapter.

3   David appears in 141 chapters which are the following: Ruth 4 (1 chapter); 1 Samuel 16–1 Kings 2 (42 chapters); 1 Chronicles 2–4, 6–7, 9–29 (25 chapters); Psalms (73 chapters). In 1 Samuel 13:14 and Acts 13:22 David is "the man after God's own heart." Altogether, he is mentioned by name 1,085 times. (Note: These statistics are from the KJV Bible.)

4   Daniel Iverson, "Spirit of the Living God" (Moody Bible Institute, 1963).

5   Elisabeth Elliot, *Passion and Purity: Learning to Bring Your Love Life Under Christ's Control* (Old Tappan, NJ: Fleming Revell, 1984), p. 43.

6   Avis B. Christiansen, "Only One Life to Offer" (Singspiration Music, 1937).

CHAPTER 2: *How Not to Waste Your Life Like Saul*

7   This chapter is drawn from messages presented the morning and evening of 5 February 2006 plus the mornings of 19 February 2006 and 26 February 2006, which are parts 6, 7, 8, and 9 of the David's Spiritual Secret series and parts 35, 36, 37, and 38 of the Christ Our Refuge series. These messages are available in their entirety at http://www.dtbm.org.

8   Emphasis added to verses in this chapter.

9   Adapted from Ray Vander Laan, Stephen Sorenson, and Amanda Sorenson, *Faith Lessons on the Promised Land: Leader's Guide* (Grand Rapids, MI: Zondervan, 1999), p. 136.

10   Linden D. Kirby, *Footprints in the Holy Land: A Devotional Guide* (Grand Rapids, MI: Discovery House Publishers, 1998), p. 154.

CHAPTER 3: *The Power of Little Choices*

11   This chapter is drawn from messages presented the morning and evening of 5 March 2006, which are parts 11 and 12 of the David's Spiritual Secret series and parts 40 and 41 of the Christ Our Refuge series. These messages are available in their entirety at http://www.dtbm.org.

12   Emphasis added to verses in this chapter.

13   Hebrews 12:16.

14   Abraham was born 2166 B.C.; Isaac was born 2066 B.C.; Esau and Jacob were born 2006 B.C. Esau married at age 40 in 1966 B.C., had a son, and then grandson named Amalek. The Exodus was 1446 B.C. and the attack of Amalek was soon afterward in Exodus 17:8. From Esau's marriage to that cowardly attack was about 550 years (1966 B.C. to 1446 B.C. = 550 years).

15   This section on Amalek was adapted from J. Vernon McGee, *Thru the Bible With J. Vernon McGee*, (Nashville, TN: Thomas Nelson Publishers, 2000), electronic edition, in loc.

16   John F. MacArthur Jr., *The Vanishing Conscience: Drawing the Line in a No-Fault, Guilt-Free World* (Dallas, TX: Word Publishing, 1997).

17   See also Galatians 6.7; Romans 2.6; Genesis 18:25.

18   MacArthur, *The Vanishing Conscience*, electronic edition at 1 Samuel 15.

19   This material on First Samuel in this section was adapted or quoted from McGee, *Thru the Bible*, electronic edition at 1 Samuel.

20   McGee, *Thru the Bible*, electronic edition at 1 Samuel 15.

21   Ronald F. Youngblood, ed., *Nelson's New Illustrated Bible Dictionary* (Nashville, TN: Thomas Nelson, 1997), electronic edition, in loc.

22   Youngblood, *Nelson's New Illustrated Bible Dictionary*, electronic edition, in loc.

23   John W. Peterson, "God's Final Call" (John W. Peterson Music Company, n.d.).

CHAPTER 4: *Our Sure Refuge in Loneliness*

24   This chapter is drawn from messages presented the mornings of 24 July 2005 and 11 September 2005, which are parts 7, 19, and 26 of the Christ Our Refuge series. These messages are available in their entirety at http://www.dtbm.org.

25   John F. MacArthur Jr., *The MacArthur Study Bible* (Nashville, TN: Thomas Nelson, 2006), p. 1225.

26   Emphasis added to verses in the rest of this chapter.

27   This chapter is drawn from a message presented on the evening of 8 June 1997, which is part of the David's Spiritual Secret series.

28   See Matthew 11:28–30.

29   MacArthur, *MacArthur Study Bible*, p. 762.

30   See John 14:1–4.

31   Colossians 3:2.

CHAPTER 5: *How to Stand Alone for God*

32   This chapter is drawn from messages presented the mornings of 22 January 2006 and 29 January 2006, which are parts 4 and 5 of the David's Spiritual Secret series and parts 33 and 35 of the Christ Our Refuge series. These messages are available in their entirety at http://www.dtbm.org.

33   Emphasis is added to verses in this chapter.

34   Discover the Book Ministries offers tours of the Holy Land. See the schedule for these tours at http://www.discoverthebook.org.

35   See Luke 16:10.

36   See Ephesians 6:10–11.

37   Randy C. Alcorn, *The Purity Principle* (Sisters, OR: Multnomah Publishers, 2003).

38   Ephesians 2:10.

39   Vander Laan, *Faith Lessons*, pp. 140–141.

CHAPTER 6: *Finding Strength in Hard Times*

40   This chapter is drawn from messages presented the mornings of 31 July 2005, 11 September 2005, and 13 November 2005, which are parts 8, 19, and 26 of the Christ Our Refuge series. These messages are available in their entirety at http://www.dtbm.org.

41   John 1:11.

42   Charles R. Swindoll, *Growing Strong in the Seasons of Life* (Portland, OR: Multnomah Press, 1983), p. 140.

43   Superscriptions like this appeared thirty-one times at the head of Psalms in older Bibles. But newer versions do not normally include them. Superscriptions establish the setting of a psalm, which is like putting you on the map of David's life.

44   Emphasis added to verses in this chapter.

45   See Psalm 139.

46   MacArthur, *MacArthur Study Bible*, p. 751.

CHAPTER 7: *How to Survive an Unexpected Job Loss*

47   See Hebrews 6:18–20.

48   This chapter is drawn from a message presented the evening of 31 July 2005, which was from part 9 of the Christ Our Refuge series and part 30 of the What's Next for Planet Earth series. These messages are available in their entirety at http://www.dtbm.org.

49   1 Samuel 21:1–9.

50   *BBC News*, 18 April 2005, http://news.bbc.co.uk/2/hi/europe/4456087.stm (accessed 20 August 2008).

51   1 Samuel 20:33.

52   For more on this wonderful topic, see my book *Discipline Yourself in Godliness* (Tulsa, OK: Müllerhaus Publishing, 2007). The book is available at http://www.discoverthebook.org.

53   I recommend that you write "1 Samuel 21:1–9" at the beginning of Psalm 52, and then add this note after verse 1: "David lost his job."

54   Emphasis added to verses in this chapter.

55   In 1 Samuel 22:19, all the inhabitants and livestock at Nob were also slain. Only Abiathar, a son of Ahimelech, escaped and joined David's flight from Saul.

56   *Selah* is a pause for emphasis and contemplation.

57   When the Hebrew Old Testament was translated into Greek, in a version called the Septuagint, *hupomeno* (Strong's #5278 – "endure") was used as the equivalent for the Hebrew word *qavah* (Strong's #6960), translated as "wait" in both Psalm 52:9 and Isaiah 40:31.

CHAPTER 8: *How to Survive Life's Unexpected Twists*

58   This chapter is drawn from messages presented the morning and evening of 6 August 2005, which are parts 10 and 11 of the Christ Our Refuge series and parts 31 and 32 of the What's Next for Planet Earth series. These messages are available in their entirety at http://www.dtbm.org.

59   I recommend writing "Psalm 56" beside 1 Samuel 21:10–12.

60   That was also where the tabernacle was in David's time.

61   McGee, *Thru the Bible*, at Psalm 56.

62   I recommend writing "1 Samuel 21:10–12" beside the title of Psalm 56 in your Bible.

63   G. Campbell Morgan was sort of a prototype of men like John MacArthur and W. A. Criswell. Morgan was a great Bible expositor known for reading a passage forty times before preaching on it!

64   Revelation 4:11.

65   1 Peter 5:7.

66   David had no army at this time because his soldiers did not start joining him until after he had escaped from Gath and hid out in the cave of Adullam (1 Samuel 22:1–2).

67   Emphasis added to verses in this chapter.

68   David may also have had the history of Joshua, Judges, Ruth, Job, and some of Samuel that was still being worked on.

69   Matthew 10:28.

70   I recommend writing "1 Samuel 21:13–15" by Psalm 34 in your Bible, and "Psalm 34" by 1 Samuel 21:13–15.

71   Abimelech, like Pharoah, was a dynastic designation not a proper name. MacArthur, *MacArthur Study Bible*, p. 771.

72   Revelation 3:17.

CHAPTER 9: *How to Overcome Feelings of Being Abandoned by God*

73   This chapter is drawn from a message presented the morning of 14 August 2005, which is from part 12 of the Christ Our Refuge series and part 33 of the What's Next for Planet Earth series. These messages are available in their entirety at http://www.dtbm.org.

74   D. Martyn Lloyd Jones, *Spiritual Depression: Its Causes and Cure* (Grand Rapids, MI: Eerdmans, 1965), p. 14.

75   James Montgomery Boice, *Psalms: An Expositional Commentary* (Grand Rapids, MI: Baker Books, 1998), p. 1:106.

76   Between 1 Samuel 21:15 and 22:1, write, "Psalm 13: David felt abandoned."

77   Emphasis added to verses in this chapter.

78   J. J. Stewart Perowne, *Commentary on the Psalms* (Grand Rapids, MI: Kregel, 1989), p. 181.

79   Lloyd Jones, *Spiritual Depression*, p. 14.

80   Adapted from Boice, *Psalms*, p. 109.

81   Lloyd Jones, *Spiritual Depression*, p. 19.

82   Boice, *Psalms*, p. 110.

83   Boice, *Psalms*, p. 111.

CHAPTER 10: *How to Get Out of the Pits of Life*

84   This chapter is drawn from messages presented the morning of 20 August 2005, the evening of 27 August 2005, plus the morning and evening of 4 September 2005, which are parts 14, 16, 17, and 18 of the Christ Our Refuge series and parts 38 and 39 of the What's Next for Planet Earth series. These messages are available in their entirety at http://www.dtbm.org.

85   Boice, *Psalms*, p. 347.

86   Bunyan's second imprisonment was probably for six months in the tiny one-room jail on the bridge over the River Ouse.

87   Slightly adapted from http://www.swordofthelord.com/biographies/bunyan.htm.

88   R. C. Sproul, *The Soul's Quest for God* (Wheaton, IL: Tyndale House, 1992), p. 207.

89   Emphasis added to verses in this chapter.

90   Charles R. Swindoll, *Shedding Light on Our Dark Side* (Dallas, TX: Word Books, 1993), pp. 100–101.

CHAPTER 11: *Living Life Successfully in a Cave of Troubles*

91   This chapter is drawn from messages presented the mornings of 18 September 2005, 2 October 2005, and 16 October 2005, which are parts 20, 21, and 23 of the Christ Our Refuge series and parts 41, 42, and 43 of the What's Next for Planet Earth series. These messages are available in their entirety at http://www.dtbm.org.

92   Charles R. Swindoll, *The Quest for Character* (Portland, OR: Multnomah Press, 1987), p. 84.

93   Emphasis added to verses in this chapter.

94   David had Moabite blood from his great-grandmother Ruth, so he sought help from the king of Moab, who probably had problems with King Saul as well.

95   J. Vernon McGee, *David: A Man After God's Own Heart* (Nashville, TN: Thomas Nelson, 2001), electronic edition at 1 Samuel 22–23.

96   McGee, *David*, electronic edition at Psalm 57.

CHAPTER 12: *The Certainty of God's Consequence Engine*

97   This chapter is drawn from a message presented the morning of 16 October 2005, which was from part 22 of the Christ Our Refuge series and part 43 of the What's Next for Planet Earth series. These messages are available in their entirety at http://www.dtbm.org.

98   Ray C. Stedman, "When Everyone Knows God," http://raystedman.org/romans1/0006.html (accessed 15 August 2008).

99   Thomas Chisholm, "Living for Jesus" (Rodeheaver Co., 1945).

CHAPTER 13: *Life in the Minor Key: Is Depression Sin?*

100 This chapter is drawn from messages presented the evening of 18 February 1990 and the morning of 30 October 2005, which was part of the Christ Our Refuge series.

101 A. J. Mason, "The Epistles of Paul the Apostle to the Thessalonians," in *Ellicott's Commentary on the Whole Bible* (Grand Rapids, MI: Zondervan, 1954), p. 8:145.

102 Emphasis added to verses in this chapter.

103 After much research, and forty years of reading Psalm 119, I am persuaded that Psalm 119 is Ezra's personal testimony as well as the probable content of his teaching and preaching to the exiles that came home to Jerusalem to seek the Lord.

104 Dwight L. Carlson, "Exposing the Myth That Christians Should Not Have Emotional Problems," *Christianity Today,* 9 February 1998.

105 Roland Herbert Bainton, *Here I Stand: A Life of Martin Luther* (Nashville, TN: Abingdon Press, 1990), p. 361.

CHAPTER 14: *There Are No Supersaints*

106 See 2 Timothy 4:6–8.

107 This was "a Jewish expression of horror and revulsion at blasphemy." MacArthur, *MacArthur Study Bible,* p. 1659.

108 Emphasis added to verses in this chapter.

109 As cited in *Hymns for the Family of God* (Nashville, TN: Paragon Associates, 1976), p. 47.

110 What was deepest within David was often reflected in psalms during different stages of his life: the growing years, the struggling years, the strong years, and the waning years. This chapter covers the last four big events of his struggling years.

111 MacArthur, *MacArthur Study Bible,* p. 416.

112 Read 1 Samuel 27 for full details.

113 Perowne, *Commentary on the Psalms,* p. 1:181.

114 For the full story of Saul's death, read 1 Samuel 31.

CHAPTER 15: *The Giant That Slew David Was Lust*

115 This chapter is drawn from messages presented the morning and evening of 23 April 2006, the evening of 14 May 2006, and the morning of 25 June 2006, which are parts 17, 18, 20, and 21 of the David's Spiritual Secret series and parts 46 and 47 of the Christ Our Refuge series. These messages are available in their entirety at http://www.dtbm.org.

116 Emphasis added to verses in this chapter.

117 Randy C. Alcorn, "The Radical Path to Purity," *American Family Association Journal,* September 2003, http://afajournal.org/2003/september/903purity.asp (accessed 15 August 2008).

118 For a biblical perspective of Bathsheba's part in this tragic downfall of David's, and how God beautifully restored her, see "Bathsheba and the God of the Second Chance" at Appendix 1.

119 This list was adapted from Alcorn, "Radical Path to Purity."

120 Warren W. Wiersbe, *The Bible Exposition Commentary* (Wheaton, IL: Victor Books, 1997), electronic edition, in loc.

121 R. Kent Hughes, *The Disciplines of a Godly Man* (Wheaton, IL: Crossway Books, 1991), p. 28, quoting Leon Morris.

CHAPTER 16: *How to Flee the Lusts of the Flesh*

122 This chapter is drawn from a message presented the evening of 20 November 2005, which is part 29 of the Christ Our Refuge series. This message is available in its entirety at http://www.dtbm.org.

123 Emphasis added to verses in this chapter.

124 Alcorn, "Radical Path to Purity."

125 See Ephesians 6:10–18.

126 See Judges 14:1–3, 7; 15:1–2; 16.1.

127 Judges 16:4.

128 "Some Philistine temples had roofs overlooking a courtyard, above wooden columns planted on stone foundations. The central pillars were set close to furnish extra support for the roof. Here the victory celebration and taunts flung at the prisoner below drew a big crowd. The full strength of Samson, renewed by God, enabled him to buckle the columns. As a result, the roof collapsed and the victory was Israel's, not Philistia's. He died for the cause of his country and his God. He was not committing suicide, but rather bringing God's judgment on His enemies and willing to leave his own life or death to God. He was the greatest champion of all Israel, yet a man of passion capable of severe sin. Still, he is in the list of the faithful (cf. Heb. 11:32)." MacArthur, *MacArthur Study Bible*, at Judges 16.

129 Wiersbe, *The Bible Exposition Commentary*, electronic edition, in loc.

130 R. Kent Hughes, *James: Faith That Works* (Wheaton, IL: Crossway Books, 1997), p. 190.

CHAPTER 17: *How to Sing the Song of a Soul Set Free*

131 This chapter is drawn from messages presented the morning and evening of 25 June 2006, which are parts 21 and 22 of the David's Spiritual Secret series. These messages are available in their entirety at http://www.dtbm.org.

132 Emphasis added to verses in this chapter.

133 For God's view on grieving or quenching the Holy Spirit, see Ephesians 4:30 and 1 Thessalonians 5:19.

134 *Hymns and Sacred Poems*, 1742.

135 See Romans 13:14.

CHAPTER 18: *The Miracle of Complete Forgiveness*

136 This chapter is drawn from messages presented the morning and evening of 1 July 2006 plus the morning of 16 July 2006, which are parts 23, 24, and 25 of the David's Spiritual Secret series. These messages are available in their entirety at http://www.dtbm.org.

137 R. Kent Hughes, *Ephesians: The Mystery of the Body of Christ* (Wheaton, IL: Crossway Books, 1997), electronic edition at Ephesians 4:32.

138 John F. MacArthur, *The MacArthur New Testament Commentary* (Chicago: Moody Press, 1983), electronic edition at 1 Corinthians 1:7.

139 Adapted from a statement attributed to Bishop Pollak by J. Vernon McGee, *Thru the Bible With J. Vernon McGee* (Nashville, TN: Thomas Nelson, 2000), electronic edition at 1 John 1:9.

140 These three paragraphs are quoted from John MacArthur, *The Murder of Jesus: A Study of How Jesus Died* (Nashville, TN: Word, 2000), p. 206.

141 R. Kent Hughes, *Hebrews: An Anchor for the Soul* (Westchester, IL: Crossway Books, 1998), electronic edition, in loc.

142 Dennis Jernigan, "All in All" (Shepherd's Heart Music, 1991).

143 Haldor Lillenas, "Wonderful Grace of Jesus" (Hope Publishing Company, 1946).

144 Adapted from Hughes, *Hebrews*, electronic edition, in loc.

CHAPTER 19: *David's Road Map: The Pathway Back to God*

145 This chapter is drawn from messages presented the mornings and evenings of 23 July 2006 and 13 August 2006 plus the morning of 20 August 2006, which are parts 26, 27, 28, 29, and 30 of the David's Spiritual Secret series. These messages are available in their entirety at http://www.dtbm.org.

146 Psalms 38, 32, and 51 are three of the seven penitential psalms; the others are Psalms 6, 102, 130, and 143.

147 Emphasis added to verses in this chapter.

148 Warren W. Wiersbe, *Be Holy* (Wheaton, IL: Victor Books, 1994), electronic edition, in loc.

149 George A. F. Knight, *Daily Study Bible Series: Psalms* (Louisville, KY: Westminster John Knox Press, 2001), electronic edition, in loc.

150 John F. Walvoord and Roy B. Zuck, *The Bible Knowledge Commentary* (Wheaton: Scripture Press, 1985), electronic edition at Psalm 51.

151 Adapted from two different stories of this hymn. The first was written by Kenneth W. Osbeck, *101 Hymn Stories* (Grand Rapids: Kregel Publications, 1997), p. 98.

152 Details of Charlotte Elliott's conversion recorded by J. Vernon McGee, *Thru the Bible With J. Vernon McGee* (Nashville, TN: Thomas Nelson Publishers, 2000), electronic edition, in loc.

153 In the world of the Bible, this meant beating the clothes in cold water against rocks and then bleaching them in the sun.

154 J. Vernon McGee, *David: A Man After God's Own Heart* (Nashville, TN: Thomas Nelson, 2001), electronic edition, in loc.

CHAPTER 20: *Overcoming Personal Attacks and Abuse*

155 This chapter is drawn from messages presented the evening of 20 August 2006, the morning and evening of 27 August 2008, plus the morning and evening of 12 November 2006, which are parts 31, 32, 33, 42, and 43 of the David's Spiritual Secret series. These messages are available in their entirety at http://www.dtbm.org.

156 John F. MacArthur Jr., *I Corinthians* (Chicago: Moody Press, 1983), electronic edition at 1 Corinthians 6:12.

157 C. J. Mahaney, *Humility: True Greatness* (Sisters, OR: Multnomah Publishers, 2005), p. 85.

158 Cited by C.H. Spurgeon, *The Treasury of David* (Grand Rapids: Zondervan, 1968), p. 2:65.

159 Lynn DeShazo, "More Precious Than Silver" (Integrity's Hosanna! Music, 1982).

160 This chapter is drawn from a message presented the morning of 10 September 2006, which is part 34 of the David's Spiritual Secret series. This message is available in its entirety at http://www.dtbm.org.

CHAPTER 21: *Living Deliberately for God—No Coasting Allowed*

161 Emphasis added to verses in this chapter.

162 Jeremiah, Jonah, and Jesus quoted directly from this psalm. Psalm 31:13's terror phrase (Hebrew – *magormisbib*) was used six times by Jeremiah (6:25; 20:3–4, 10; 46:5; 49:29; Lamentations 2:22). Jonah quoted 31:6 in Jonah 2:6. David opened Psalm 71 with the same words. But most significantly, in Luke 23:46 Jesus quoted Psalm 31:5 as His last words before His death on the cross!

163 This is also a word for *Masada*, that majestic refuge in today's Israel.

164 Stewart Perowne, *Psalms*, electronic edition, in loc.

165 Emphasis added to these four points.

166 Boice, *Psalms*, p. 271.

167 Alexander Maclaren, *Expositions of Holy Scriptures: Psalms* (New York: Hodder and Stoughton, 1908), accessed at http://www.ccel.org/ccel/maclaren/psalms.html.

CHAPTER 22: *Ending Well—Living Purposefully for God*

168 This chapter is drawn from messages presented the morning and evening of 8 October 2006, which are parts 35 and 36 of the David's Spiritual Secret series. These messages are available in their entirety at http://www.dtbm.org.

169 Emphasis added to verses in this chapter.

170 This poem then later appeared in the Christmas edition of *Beacon House News*, a magazine of the Northern Ireland Mental Health Association by Phyllis McCormack.

171 Kenneth W. Osbeck, *Amazing Grace: 366 Inspiring Hymn Stories for Daily Devotions* (Grand Rapids, MI: Kregel, 1997), p. 143.

172 Jan David Hettinga, *Follow Me: Experience the Loving Leadership of Jesus* (Colorado Springs, CO: NavPress, 1996), pp. 193–194, 218–219.

173 Adapted from Hettinga, *Follow Me*, pp. 191–192.

174 http://www.desiringgod.org/ResourceLibrary/Sermons/ByDate/1985/474 Ambushing Satan with Song/

175 http://www.desiringgod.org/ResourceLibrary/Sermons/ByDate/1985/474 Ambushing Satan with Song/

176 This section on David Livingstone was paraphrased from Henry Morton Stanley, *How I*

Found Livingstone, 1800s.

177   J. D. Douglas, Philip W. Comfort, and Donald Mitchell, eds., *Who's Who in Christian History* (Wheaton, IL: Tyndale House, 1992), electronic edition, in loc.

178   Thomas Obadiah Chisholm, "Great Is Thy Faithfulness" (Hope Publishing Company, 1923).

CHAPTER 23: *Gracefully Heading Toward Home*

179   This chapter is drawn from messages presented the morning of 15 October 2006, the morning of 22 October 2006, and the evening of 22 October 2006, which are parts 37, 38, and 39 of the David's Spiritual Secret series. These messages are available in their entirety at http://www.dtbm.org.

180   See Revelation 16 and 20.

181   Emphasis added to verses in this chapter.

182   G. Campbell Morgan, *The Gospel According to Matthew* (New York: Revell, 1929), pp. 64–65.

183   John O. Todd, *Never a Dull Day: An Autobiography of John O. Todd* (Lexington, KY: Lexington House, 1990).

184   W. A. Criswell and Paige Patterson, *Heaven* (Wheaton, IL: Tyndale House, 1994), p. 40.

185   Criswell and Patterson, *Heaven*, p. 52

186   Criswell and Patterson, *Heaven*, pp. 56–57.

187   Criswell and Patterson, *Heaven*, p. 91.

188   Criswell and Patterson, *Heaven*, p. 98.

189   David H. Stern, *Jewish New Testament Commentary: A Companion Volume to the Jewish New Testament* (Clarksville, MD: Jewish New Testament Publications, 1996).

CHAPTER 24: *Embracing God— A Long Obedience in Seeking the Lord*

190   This chapter is drawn from messages presented the morning and evening of 5 November 2006, which are parts 40 and 41 of the David's Spiritual Secret series. These messages are available in their entirety at http://www.dtbm.org.

191   Emphasis added to verses in this chapter.

192   http://www.ensignmessage.com/archives/rockof ages.html

193   See Deuteronomy 6:4–9.

194   The Pentateuch is the first five books of the Bible; a king of Israel was required to write a copy for himself and study it regularly (Deuteronomy 18–20).

195   Joni Eareckson Tada, et al., *When Morning Gilds the Skies* (Wheaton, IL: Crossway Books, 2002), p. 81.

196   Tada, *When Morning Gilds the Skies*, pp. 81–82.

APPENDIX A

197   Copyright 1941. Renewed 1969 by Lillenas Publishing Co.

BIBLIOGRAPHY

Alcorn, Randy C. *The Purity Principle*. Sisters, OR: Multnomah Publishers, 2003.

—————. "The Radical Path to Purity." American Family Association Journal, September 2003. Accessed at http://afajournal.org/2003/september/903purity.asp.

Bainton, Roland Herbert. *Here I Stand: A Life of Martin Luther*. Nashville, TN: Abingdon Press, 1990.

Barnett, John S. *Discipline Yourself for Godliness*. Tulsa, OK: Müllerhaus Publishing, 2007.

Bock, Fred. *Hymns for the Family of God*. Nashville, TN: Paragon Associates, 1976.

Boice, James Montgomery. Psalms: *An Expositional Commentary*. Vol. 1, Psalms 1–41. Grand Rapids, MI: Baker Books, 1998.

Carlson, Dwight L. "Exposing the Myth That Christians Should Not Have Emotional Problems." *Christianity Today*, 9 February 1998.

Criswell, W. A., and Paige Patterson. *Heaven*. Wheaton, IL: Tyndale House, 1994.

Douglas, J. D., Philip W. Comfort, and Donald Mitchell, eds. *Who's Who in Christian History*. Wheaton, IL: Tyndale House Publishers, 1992.

Ellicot, Charles John, ed. *Ellicot's Commentary on the Whole Bible: A Verse by Verse Explanation*. 8 vols. Grand Rapids, MI: Zondervan, 1954.

Elliot, Elisabeth. *Passion and Purity: Learning to Bring Your Love Life Under Christ's Control*. Old Tappan, NJ: Fleming Revell, 1984.

Hettinga, Jan David. *Follow Me: Experience the Loving Leadership of Jesus*. Colorado Springs, CO: NavPress, 1996.

Hughes, R. Kent. *The Disciplines of a Godly Man*. Wheaton, IL: Crossway Books, 1991.

—————. *Ephesians: The Mystery of the Body of Christ*. Wheaton, IL: Crossway Books, 1997.

—————. *Hebrews: An Anchor for the Soul*. Westchester, IL: Crossway Books, 1998.

—————. *James: Faith That Works*. Wheaton, IL: Crossway Books, 1997.

Kirby, Linden D. *Footprints in the Holy Land: A Devotional Guide*. Grand Rapids, MI: Discovery House Publishers, 1998.

Knight, George A. F. *Daily Study Bible Series: Psalms*. Louisville, KY: Westminster John Knox Press, 2001.

Lloyd Jones, D. Martyn. *Spiritual Depression: Its Causes and Cure*. Grand Rapids, MI: Eerdmans, 1965.

MacArthur, Jr., John F. *I Corinthians. The MacArthur New Testament Commentary*. Chicago: Moody Press, 1983.

—————. *The MacArthur Study Bible*. Nashville, TN: Thomas Nelson, 2006.

—————. *The Murder of Jesus: A Study of How Jesus Died*. Nashville, TN: Word Publishers, 2000.

—————. *The Vanishing Conscience: Drawing the Line in a No-Fault, Guilt-Free World*. Dallas, TX: Word Publishing, 1997.

Maclaren, Alexander. *Expositions of Holy Scriptures: Psalms*. New York: Hodder and Stoughton, 1908. Accessed at http://www.ccel.org/ccel/maclaren/psalms.html

Mahaney, C. J. *Humility: True Greatness*. Sisters, OR: Multnomah Publishers, 2005.

McGee, J. Vernon. *David: A Man After God's Own Heart*. Nashville, TN: Thomas Nelson, 2001.

—————. *Thru the Bible With J. Vernon McGee*. Nashville, TN: Thomas Nelson Publishers, 2000.

Morgan, G. Campbell. *The Gospel According to Matthew*. New York: Revell, 1929.

Osbeck, Kenneth W. *Amazing Grace: 366 Inspiring Hymn Stories for Daily Devotions*. Grand Rapids, MI: Kregel, 1997.

—————. *101 Hymn Stories*. Grand Rapids, MI: Kregel, 1997.

Perowne, J. J. Stewart. *Commentary on the Psalms*. Grand Rapids, MI: Kregel, 1989.

Sproul, R. C. *The Soul's Quest for God*. Wheaton, IL: Tyndale House, 1992.

Spurgeon, C. H. *The Treasury of David*. Vol. 2, Psalms 58–87. Grand Rapids, MI: Zondervan, 1968.

Stern, David H. *Jewish New Testament Commentary: A Companion Volume to the Jewish New Testament*. Clarksville, MD: Jewish New Testament Publications, 1996.

Swindoll, Charles R. *Growing Strong in the Seasons of Life*. Portland, OR: Multnomah Press, 1983.

——————. *The Quest for Character*. Portland, OR: Multnomah Press, 1987.

——————. *Shedding Light on Our Dark Side*. Dallas, TX: Word Books, 1993.

Tada, Joni Eareckson, et al. *When Morning Gilds the Skies*. Wheaton, IL: Crossway Books, 2002.

Todd, John O. *Never a Dull Day: An Autobiography of John O. Todd*. Lexington, KY: Lexington House, 1990.

Vander Laan, Ray, Stephen Sorenson, and Amanda Sorenson. *Faith Lessons on the Promised Land: Leader's Guide*. Grand Rapids, MI: Zondervan, 1999.

Walvoord, John F., and Roy B. Zuck. *The Bible Knowledge Commentary*. 2 vols. Wheaton, IL: Scripture Press, 1983–85.

Wiersbe, Warren W. *Be Holy*. Wheaton, IL: Victor Books, 1994.

——————. *The Bible Exposition Commentary*. Wheaton, IL: Victor Books, 1997.

Youngblood, Ronald F., ed. *Nelson's New Illustrated Bible Dictionary*. Nashville, TN: Thomas Nelson, 1997.

Biography of Author

JOHN BARNETT HAS TAUGHT GOD'S Word for over thirty years. Having served congregations in Michigan, Georgia, Rhode Island, California, and Oklahoma, he is now the senior pastor at Calvary Bible Church in Kalamazoo, Michigan. Since being called to the ministry as a young man, John's passions have been prayer and the ministry of God's Word. In 1998 he started Discover the Book Ministries, which provides audio, video, and text copies of his sermons free of charge online. Through DTBM, John also publishes devotional books and leads tours of the Holy Land. This ministry has grown to serve saints in all 50 states and over 180 countries. As a global Christian who has ministered the Word to believers in 40 nations, John's ministry is dedicated to outreach and evangelism. John shares his life with his beloved wife Bonnie and their eight children.

Discover the Book
Everyday
at DTBM.ORG

You are invited to visit the online home of Discover The Book Ministries. Learn more about Dr. John Barnett and the global mission of DTBM. Immerse yourself in a wealth of Biblical studies, ministry resources and practical daily direction for real life. From podcasts to videos, hundreds of Dr. Barnett's best sermons and teachings are offered in a variety of formats—one to fit every need.

Radio Broadcasts
Podcasts
Holy Land Video Tours
Audio, Print, and Video Sermons

Multi-Lingual PDF Library
MP3 and Book Library
Online Shopping
E-newsletter

Whether you choose to expand your spiritual horizons from home, while you're at work, or in quick moments spread throughout your busy day, our interactive website is here to serve you in your Christian walk.

Visit Us Today

Discover The Book Ministries
A Nonprofit 501(c)3 Bible Teaching Ministry